THE *DIARY* OF
JOHN MILWARD

SEPTEMBER 17TH, 1666
TO
MAY 8TH, 1668

The *DIARY* of
JOHN MILWARD, *ESQ*

Member of Parliament for
Derbyshire

SEPTEMBER, 1666

TO

MAY, 1668

Edited with some Notes

AND

An Introduction on his *Life*

BY

CAROLINE ROBBINS

CAMBRIDGE

AT THE UNIVERSITY PRESS

1938

CAMBRIDGE
UNIVERSITY PRESS

University Printing House, Cambridge CB2 8BS, United Kingdom

Cambridge University Press is part of the University of Cambridge.

It furthers the University's mission by disseminating knowledge in the pursuit of
education, learning and research at the highest international levels of excellence.

www.cambridge.org
Information on this title: www.cambridge.org/9781107536449

First published 1938
First paperback edition 2015

A catalogue record for this publication is available from the British Library

ISBN 978-1-107-53644-9 Paperback

CONTENTS

THE MILWARDS OF DERBYSHIRE

[Add. MSS, 6675 and 397 verso]

P.C.C. 1670, John Milward's Will

William = Alice Kniveton

Robert of Eaton = Anne Palmer of Broughton

Henry =

Felicia = John Fern of Snitterton

Robert = Margery Delhick of Newhall

William = Kathleen Fleetwood

Sir Thomas Milward of Eaton

Robert (M.P. Staff.)

Robert d. 1567

John of Bradlowtsh

Felicia = C. Adderley

John [I] = Mary Blount 1551–1633

Mary = Foster

Felicia = H. Agard

Anne

John [II] = Anne Whitehaugh 1599–1670

Robert = Mary Gresley = Wilmot 1597–1634 1644

Mary = John Bowyer d. 1648

Elizabeth = Robt. Constable

Dorothy = Wm. Copley

John

Felicia = Ch. Adderley of Thorpe

Frances = Sir Wm. Boothbye = Hill

Frances d. 1662

Mary Anne = H. Jennens

Henry d. 1681

Robert d. 1652

[III] John, Capt. d. 1669 = Sneyd (i) Sacheverall (ii)

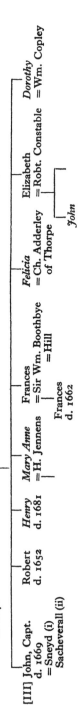

INTRODUCTION

I owe my first introduction to the Milward Diary to Mr E. S. de Beer. Had he undertaken the present edition all historians would have been grateful. As it is, however, he has no responsibility in the matter beyond his rather rash suggestion to me many years ago.

Miss Nancy Divine, of Hull, has helped me throughout in the transcription of the manuscript and in many vexatious and tiring tasks connected with the work. I owe her very much more than I can ever properly acknowledge.

My original intention in editing the Diary was to present it as nearly as possible in the form in which it has been preserved till now. The spelling, though full of inconsistencies, contains no difficulties, and the period is not without precedents for printed abbreviated forms. Such a transcript makes available for the reader the exact intentions of the author so far as we know them. On the advice of Mr Notestein, however, I abandoned this plan and myself decided that if I were to alter the manuscript forms at all I might as well attempt translation into modern nomenclature; and indeed, if anything at all is to be altered there seems to me little argument for retaining part of the original spelling. It is by no means easy to decide when Milward is abbreviating and when he is simply spelling eccentrically, and this I imagine to be true throughout the century. Here, then, I have attempted to impose consistency upon him, and have only preserved in the Index and Notes such variations as seem interesting. I thus hope to avoid offending those who are annoyed by any deviation from modern forms, and to placate those who like myself are interested in seventeenth-century pronunciation and spelling.

Post-Restoration English literature is as rich in domestic diaries as any period of our history. In Parliamentary diaries, however, it cannot compete with the years 1621–60. An interesting but at present inaccessible diary exists amongst the

Salway MSS. and probably covers the Convention Parliament of 1660. This was used by the editors of the *Old Parliamentary History*, and greatly enriches their last volumes. A few pages from the pen of Sir Edward Dering survive, a few scattered speeches by Holland, Temple and others may be discovered to throw light on the early years of the Cavalier Parliament, but until Milward started his account in 1666 there seems to have been a dearth of members willing to take notes. Before Milward's death his friend Anchitel Grey had started his magnificent collection which carries us through 1667 to 1699. It is possible that modern research will in time uncover further material for the neglected 'sixties. I think that Osbourne kept fuller notes of Parliamentary proceedings than any I have yet seen; I am sure that Robert Stockdale, of Knaresborough, took careful notes which were occasionally available for his friends' information. Should these ever be discovered they may prove immensely valuable. It is, however, difficult to believe that the scarcity of diaries now known to us to have survived is due altogether to faulty research or to wholesale destruction. It seems entirely likely that few members were bothering to keep careful records. They hoped the crisis was over and that times would prove more peaceful and less stirring. In addition, the increasingly good news services of journalists like Muddiman made knowledge of Parliamentary events less the exclusive preserve of members of either House.

I have not, then, been able to surround Milward with much complementary material. I have tried to correct his dates and notice his additions to or omissions from the *Journals* of the House. In one or two cases I have noted manuscript fragments which explain or expand the text. I have attempted to identify the people mentioned and to give in the case of members at least an indication of their party and their geographical alignment as an aid to the understanding of their recorded behaviour in debate. Sometimes a knowledge of a man's marriage or friendships will supply a key to the briefest speech, and besides throws a new light on the diarist himself. His selections are significant. Through them may be seen, less darkly than usual, Parliament and its interest to a seventeenth-century country gentleman.

The Diary, being a unique survival, illumines parties and politics during the years 1666–8. It records many debates on supply in 1666 which lead to the famous Proviso to the Poll Bill of that year. The Irish controversy and the struggle over the Act to exclude cattle is revealed here in its domestic as well as its imperial or political environment. The Diary adds perhaps little to our knowledge of Clarendon and his sins, but much to that of the personalities of those attacking or excusing him, in the debates of October and November 1667. Many manuscript accounts of the Skinner controversy exist, but even to these the Milward Diary forms a useful supplement, and contains hitherto unrecorded utterances.

Milward cannot be compared in interest, for the general reader at least, with Pepys or Reresby. He mentions few London scandals, and his character sketches consist for the most part of brief comments on speakers who spoke well, "impertinently" or not at all to the point. On the other hand he records, more carefully perhaps than any one else, the minutiae of Parliamentary business. Milward was new to Parliament, though not to public life. He had the habit of careful observation, and his Letter Book, also preserved in the British Museum, shows his interest in the details of administration. He records with a most impartial interest the greater and lesser controversies, debates on the Cattle Act, bills for the sale of land and sermons preached by command. Even at the height of the excitement about Clarendon, when Grey (or his eighteenth-century editors) omits practically all other business, Milward gives almost as much space to daily affairs—the dispute about the Forest of Dean, the woodmongers' and private bills—as he does to the more spectacular debates. A mass of information about London may be gleaned from his Diary, particularly during the rebuilding in 1666–7, but also during the trouble over coal prices in the following year. This kind of material could be illustrated indefinitely, but is best judged by a careful study of the Diary itself. It is this which reveals its chief charm and its real significance to the historian of the period. There must have been a hundred Milwards in Parliament, gentry trained in country business, but with many connections in London, whose interests and whose judgments were formed much as Milward's were. To this reader, at any rate, none could seem more kindly nor more sensible, more upright or more truly representative of those Parliamentary standards we admire. Milward may serve as an admirable reminder of the solidarity of English institutions in a period when their imperfections so often attract attention.

I do not think that Milward kept his Diary, as Marvell quite probably kept notes, for the purposes of party propaganda. He may have kept it for the information of the Cavendish family, whose heir, a young member of the Lower House in Milward's day, was to become the Duke of Devonshire of the post-revolution period. Had he lived, an increasing party bias might have become apparent. This bias is noticeable in nearly all surviving records of the crises of the 'seventies and 'eighties, and it is not without significance that the great debates of the last quarter of the seventeenth century are the work of Anchitel Grey, Milward's friend and fellow countryman. Milward consulted Grey on one occasion, afterwards comparing his information with that of Sir Thomas Osbourne. There is no evidence, however, that they did more than help each other verbally. Grey most certainly did not use Milward's record for 1667–8. Milward took trouble over his information, occasionally noting its source if other than his own hearing. Whilst there is some evidence that he wrote the Diary from day to day, there is also evidence of later revision which suggests the interest he took in it and in its exact information about debates he had heard. Whether he wrote for his family, his constituents or his patron, the Earl of Devonshire, he certainly also wrote for his own satisfaction and pleasure.

The manuscript of the Diary in the British Museum is, so far as I know, unique. It is obviously a copy from notes, made by more than one person, but I suspect all under the supervision of Milward himself. Some of the corrections are almost certainly in his handwriting. On the whole the Diary seems accurate and reliable. Occasionally a marginal date is misplaced or omitted. Names of people strange to Milward have very curious spellings. Much of the matter cannot be checked because no other record of the speeches summarised exists. On those occasions where

Milward can be checked he seems more trustworthy than Grey. He seldom notices a brilliant phrase in a speech, but often gives valuable insight into the order of a debate or the day's events. He works methodically through the business where the writer in Appendix II, for example, contents himself with a rather more orderly summary. The Diary occupies one hundred and ninety-four manuscript pages in the bound volume in the British Museum. This bears the arms of Sir William Boothbye, whose library is known to have survived until the last century. It was bought by the Museum from Thomas Simmons, of Leamington, and by him, I suspect, from the Boothbye library, but this cannot now be ascertained. But the family of Milward and Boothbye had more than one connection in Warwickshire, and there is no reason why a local antiquary should not have heard of the volume and made it his business to acquire it.

Three John Milwards at least lived in the hundred of Wirksworth in seventeenth-century Derbyshire. The eldest owned land in Thorpe, Bradley Ash, Darley and other villages, amongst them Snitterton, where his son, the second John Milward and author of this Diary, was to live. This land was also connected with the Knivetons, related to the Milwards of Eaton Dovedale, with the Sacheverolls, afterwards related to the youngest John Milward, and with the Cokaynes. Amongst the greater neighbours were the Manners, the Kendalls and the Cavendishes; amongst the lesser but still prosperous gentry were the Fitzherberts and the Boothbyes of Ashbourne. No county in England has a more complicated group of relationships within its borders, and nowhere, it seems, could more people claim cousins than in Derbyshire at this time.

The eldest John Milward was Sheriff of the county in 1620, and is commemorated at Thorpe by a monument which says that his wife was Mary Blount, and that he had two sons and two daughters. Mary, who died in 1651, is also commemorated in a monument in the chancel of Coleshill Hall, in Derbyshire, where she had lived during her widowhood with Lady Offaly. This testimony of stone and brass is confirmed by his will, proved on 30 May 1633, in which all his property was left as a trust for the education and upbringing of his children. After her death this was to go first to Robert and his heirs, failing which it was then to go to John.

Robert is supposed to have been a brave soldier and to have fought in Spain. He may also have been a member of one of the Inns of Court like his cousin and namesake, member for Stafford in the Cavalier Parliament. He died shortly after his father, and was survived by his widow. John, the author of this Diary, was born on St Simon's and St Jude's Day in 1599, married Anne Whitehaugh, and by her had many children.

John, the eldest child of the diarist, was the third of the Milwards mentioned above. He was educated at Repton and at Cambridge, and was admitted to Gray's Inn on 12 April 1651. He married first Frances Sneyd, of Staffordshire, and then Joyce, daughter of Henry Sacheverall of Morley, who erected a tablet to him at Darley, where he died in October 1669. This memorial still stands.

His brother Henry was born on 30 January 1649, and perhaps brightened this saddest of days for his Cavalier father. He went to Trinity College, Oxford, and to Lincoln's Inn in 1670, where he is entered as the son and heir of John Milward of Snitterton. He was his father's chief heir and the executor of his will, proved on 19 December in that same year. He became a magistrate and later Sheriff of his county. He died without issue, and was commemorated in bad verse by Leonard Wheatscroft, landlord of the "Hand and Shears" in Darley, who also lamented the death of his father before him. Wheatscroft apparently admired the family as good hunters and good neighbours. The profession of the elegist does not belie the tradition that Henry's death was the result of a drinking bout with Thomas, son of Nicholas Bowden, a lawyer.

A third brother, Robert, died in 1652 at the age of seventeen.

Of the daughters five may be traced. Mary Anne married Humphrey Jennens, of High Street, Birmingham, on 16 September 1657. Jennens lived in London during the months John Milward attended Parliament, and the Diary refers to him and to the illness in March 1667/8, of a daughter Anne. On the death of her father Anne inherited £2000. Jennens's son Charles is said to have helped Handel with the *Messiah*, and was Rector of Darley, where his father was buried.

Felicia married Charles Adderley and brought a moiety of Thorpe and Snitterton to him when the estate was divided.

Frances, born on 9 February 1634, married when she was eighteen Sir William Boothbye, and died leaving one daughter in September 1654. This daughter died in 1662. Sir William was the son and heir of a knight who suffered greatly during the Civil Wars and, perhaps because of this, as well as because of his relationship, seems to have been closely connected with his father-in-law. He was made deputy-lieutenant at Milward's express request in 1661, served as Sheriff of the county in 1662 and sat with Milward and others to hear the examination of Calton in 1664-5. Boothbye married a second wife, Mary Hill, and was buried beside her in the family chapel at Ashbourne. This monument still stands, although Ashbourne Hall where the Boothbyes lived so long is now destroyed and the land used as a building estate.

Milward mentions two other daughters in his will, one of whom had left an orphaned son without much provision for his upbringing. To him the diarist left some money, though he makes no mention of his sister. Little else is known about these daughters and their families. Both grandchildren died without issue before the end of the century.

The diarist himself, the second John Milward, had a long and active career. About this, in spite of some confusions arising from the existence not only of his father and his son, but also of a fourth John Milward contemporary with himself, it is possible to disentangle some reliable information. Venn's note in the *Alumnae Cantabrigienses* is almost certainly the result of the confusion between the father, a colonel during the Civil Wars, and the son, a captain of militia in the 'sixties. I do not think the diarist can be identified in the lists of Oxford and Cambridge. He does appear unmistakably as Sheriff of Derbyshire in 1635, and correspondence amongst the State Papers of that year shows him about his duties. In this and in succeeding years payments of fifteen shillings were made to him as Captain of Foot in the muster of the shire. In 1641 his name appears with those of many gentry of the county in a petition to the King concerning the dangers of the time. When the war broke out Milward bore arms for the King and was one of the six colonels who defended the losing cause in Derbyshire. Glover names five of them and gives the territory they were expected to defend: Milward at Bakewell, which is just north of Darley and Snitterton; Eyre, afterwards his fellow-deputy, at Chatsworth and the Peak; Fitzherbert at South Wingfield and Tissington; Frechville (Milward's predecessor as member for Derbyshire in the time of Charles II) in his own house and Scarsdale; and Harpur at Burton Bridge. Attempts to hold back Sir John Gell's troops were bravely made, especially during February 1644 by the Bakewell and Ashbourne groups, and were almost uniformly failures. After Tissington was taken the Royalists scattered to Chatsworth, Wingfield Manor and other houses.

In the account of Milward's case dated November 1645 in the records of the Committee for Compounding, he is said to have ceased fighting in July 1644. His fine of one thousand pounds was no greater because of his restraint of the soldiers from plundering the district during the wars. Pardon was granted him in December 1645. His relation, Sir Thomas Milward of Eaton, father of "Cousin Robert", compounded in August 1646 at the age of seventy-four, and was fined three hundred and fifty pounds. Many other friends suffered too. In a manuscript series of brief lives of Derbyshire sheriffs in the British Museum Milward's war record compares very favourably, in the biographer's eyes at least, with that of Gell. Mrs Hutchinson had no worse an opinion of that famous Parliamentary soldier. Milward and he had had dealings before, when Milward, as his successor in the Sheriff's office, had to hand over some moneys to him; they fought against each other during the war, met probably when Milward was fined, as Gell was one of the committee for Derbyshire, had some financial dealings in 1648, which are not clear, and may have been associated in the matter of a lead mine in Wirksworth in 1651.

Milward's son-in-law, Jennens, is said to have bought iron-works from a rival of the Sitwells. The diarist was amongst those petitioning for a "loyal ironmonger" at the Restoration, and

in his Diary refers to visits to Ironmongers' Hall. His record
of the Forest of Dean debates may also indicate a practical knowledge of its iron resources, but his precise interest in mines and
minerals is unknown. It is just possible that the fourth John
Milward, of London, whose family are buried at St Werburgh's
in Derby, was the Milward associated with the diarist's old
enemy in the debt of 1648, and the mines three years later, as
it is almost certain that it was this other John Milward that
acted as assessor for highways in St Werburgh's parish early
in the reign of Charles II. On the other hand, Gell's disgrace
during the Commonwealth may have brought the former enemies
together, and it seems clear from the references to London and
Londoners like Sheldon, Glanvill, Meynell and Glyn that
Milward had friends if not business in the city, who may well
have been connected with Gell and Derbyshire industries.

Milward's name, unlike those of many who fought on the
same side, does not appear in the Commonwealth list of Justices.
Except for the births, marriages and deaths of his family, his
life until the Restoration is unknown. At the Restoration, however, William Cavendish, eighth Earl of Devonshire, was once
again appointed Lord-Lieutenant of the County, and Milward's
name is among those appointed to help him as deputies. Milward's connection with the family almost certainly went back
to the wars. Its precise nature is uncertain, but he seems to
have been the earl's intermediary with the other deputy-
lieutenants, and, from the careful copies of his correspondence
on county business in the Letter Book, perhaps some kind of
a secretary. Possibly the Diary was kept for the earl's better
information, and in that case the diary kept by Grey, another
of the members for Derbyshire, may have had a similar origin.
The close connection between the Devonshires and the opposition party of the later years of Charles's reign, and the part
they played in the Revolution, may explain as already suggested
the zeal of two of their fellow Derbyshire men to keep careful
records of debates in the Lower House.

The Letter Book kept by Milward does not, however, have
any political significance, though it throws much light on county
affairs, and most admirably illustrates a deputy-lieutenant's work.

The letters start with a copy of the deputies' note to Devonshire dated 11 January 1660/61, and continue until November 1666. They are all in Milward's writing, though the last letter bearing his signature is dated 28 July 1665. The remaining letters are copies of letters from various members of the Government to the Earl. Milward's own interest appears to have been chiefly the militia. The Lord-Lieutenant writes to him that the improvement in the county is due to his care, and promises when opportunity offers to speak to Charles about Sir William Boothbye's deputyship, and will indeed, he says, be glad to do anything he can for Milward.

One episode, the Calton-Wylde affair, had for a moment a national rather than a local significance, but the zeal of the deputies and the inertia of the county, together with the treachery of one conspirator, soon brought it to a close.

Alarms after the "most happy Restoration" were not uncommon, and the Letter Book reveals such anxiety in Derbyshire. In 1664 the information given by Thomas Calton implicated a good many people of the county and the Midlands generally in a Presbyterian revolt against the King. A Captain Wright and a Thomas Wylde were chiefly talked of, but there were difficulties in discovering precise proofs. Milward wrote fully to Devonshire, and slightly less formally to his old comrade in arms, Frechville, member for the shire in the House of Commons. This letter is now among the State Papers, and as an example of Milward's epistolary style may be given here:

Ld Frechville.

Honoured Sr

I have received both your letters, but I have deferred to give you an account of them untill I could lykwyse give you an account of Caultons examination: who is now brought to Derbye, but ye assizes being begunn we could not in so short tyme bring in our proofes & witnesses against him. Thus farre we have proceeded. Mr Vernon ye high sheriff, Mr Gray, Sr Hen: Every, Sr Wm Boothbye & myselfe have had Caulton before us, his examinacon as it was sett downe by Mr Vernon I have transcribed & four you a true coppy of it here inclosed: we fynde Caulton very imperfect in his confession, inclyned more to discovere the presbyterians then ye Annabaptists: but yett very sufficyently ye realtye of the plott. We have left him in ye Gaolers handes, who I believe will carefully looke to him. We have asked him very fairly & doe percieve yt workes more with then a severer carriage. We have ffetcht in Capt: Wright: he standes altogether uppon his mistificacon, & plees his innocence is not in the least to be acquainted with this or any other plotte or to have so much as a thought of beating one souldyer. I am very much persuaded yt unlesse Mr Molinoux doe bringe in his proofes, & that they prove more positive & plaine against him, we shall not be able to prove him guiltye. We have taken too thousand poundes bayle of Wright & his sureties not to depart five miles from his house but wthout lycense, not to admitt any into his house but those as he shall give a good account off: and to be readye when soever my Lord Lieut: or any of his deput: lieuts or more of them shall send for him: and so we hav lett him goe to his owne house. I have wayted on my Lord of Devon: since his comīng to Chattesworth, and acquainted him wth my comīng to Darby in order to this business, wch he referred wholely to us. I was very importunate wth his Lsp to procure Mr Molinoux to appeare wth his proofes, as moste materiall. So this is all yt I can acquaint you wth at present: I heartily wish you now in ye county and hope to see you there before we proceede further against Wright Caulton & Wylde or in this business wthout any new discovery shall be made to be.

Wth my faythfull service I remaine Sr
Your most affectionate freind & servant

Jo: Milwarde.

Darby Aug: 10th 1664.

One of these prisoners was subsequently convicted for high treason.

Milward also acted as commissioner of taxes, as did nearly all the gentry of the county. His discretion was admired by his fellows, and it is not surprising to find a letter from George Sitwell to his son-in-law, Revell, in the March of 1663, which speaks warmly of Colonel Milward, seeks his good offices as arbitrator in a dispute not specified and declares himself and the rest satisfied to leave its settlement in his hands. He is a man who acts "*non nobis nati sed partem Patriae*, etc. . . ."

Beyond this indication of Milward's integrity and the evidence his activities afford of his public spirit, there is little about his character or private affairs in these records. Writing to the earl, he mentions a bad distemper, perhaps similar to that which interrupted his Parliamentary duties later; he mentions a cousin Cotton, who apparently had sought his help in obtaining command of a company of foot. Milward also writes with some indignation about his *sub poena* by the earl's steward in the midst of his public duties, though he professes himself as willing as any to fulfil all legal demands. Devonshire, however, at once replies that he knew nothing of the affair, and would certainly never have allowed it to happen if the steward had informed him of his intentions. Exactly what was the quarrel between the official and Milward the letters do not make clear.

In the November of 1665 a writ was issued for a new election in Derbyshire. Frechville had gone to the Lords, and Milward was elected to take his place, though he did not present his own writ of election until 17 September 1666, the day before Parliament was to meet. He doubled the fee of Mr John Agar, the Clerk of the Crown to whom it was given. The oaths were administered to him by Lord Ogle, a connection of the Cavendish family, and Laurence Hyde. From this day until 8 May 1668 Milward's doings are recorded in his Diary. Scattered references to him occur elsewhere. Those in the *Journals* are for the most part difficult to identify, as his cousin Robert Milward, son of Sir Thomas, of Eaton Dovebridge, and Recorder of Stafford, played a more prominent part in the same Parliament. Only when two Milwards are given in lists of committee men, or when one is called colonel, a title to which, I think, the lawyer Milward had no claim, or when the diarist himself mentions his appointment to a committee, is it possible to know which is intended.

Milward's own account of his activities seems to suggest that he was regular in his attendance, conscientious in his voting and careful to attend committees to which he was appointed, especially when they concerned county affairs or people. Such would be Mr Leigh's bill, Mr Kendall's, Lord Clare's and others. He saw Lord Rutland whilst he was in London, and naturally took much interest in Lord Roos's bill to illegitimise Lady Anne Roos's children. He performed an errand for a Mr Moore at Lambeth, where he frequently dined with the

Archbishop. Indeed, the fact that Milward celebrated his birthday at the palace with his son-in-law Jennens and his cousin
Milward points to some intimacy with Gilbert Sheldon, his
contemporary and neighbour. Milward dined with another
cousin, Joseph Glanvill, whose relationship is puzzling; with
Joseph Sheldon, nephew of the Archbishop and later Sheriff
of the city; with Fulk Lucy, with Seymour Shirley whose widow
was later to become Lord Roos's second wife, and all these but
Glanvill seem to be Derbyshire friends. Adrian Mays, keeper
of deer in St James's Park, may have come from the county
also, but this is uncertain, and there is no fuller information
about the connection with this official than Milward's laconic
entry for 1 November 1666. Milward dined too with Sir
George Carteret on 3 April 1668, and from time to time mentions
committee dinners.

His private affairs are barely mentioned. His son-in-law and
his cousins and his daughter Anne are referred to. He records
that he went home at Christmas in 1666 via Oxford. He records,
more frequently in the early months than later, sermons which
he heard. He refers late in the Diary to a bond which he took
out in the city, but gives no clue to the circumstances which
made it necessary. He reflects solemnly when he meets a corpse,
and occasionally refers to a visit. Throughout the Diary the
bitterest references are reserved for the Presbyterian "gang",
and his voting would show him a good churchman, even if his
record did not otherwise exist to prove it. He is interested in
county law and order, and most legal matters, perhaps because
his cousin Robert was so often concerned in these.

The Diary ends in May 1668, and we do not know if the
diarist attended the meetings which were only to prolong the
adjournment later in the year. His name appears in committee lists for the session of 1669, but no entry in the
Journals marks his death until the dispute that followed the
necessary election had to be settled. He died on 14 September
1670. Like his son Henry, he was commemorated by the landlord of the "Hand and Shears" in an elegy, and also in some
stanzas of a more general poem on the gentry of the district.
The village poet is inaccurate in his description of Milward as

a Lord-Lieutenant and in certain minor details, but his devotion
to him is obvious in every execrable line:

> He was a landlord to his tenants kind,
> But few like him about us now we find.
> He was a neighbour good of sweet behaviour,
> Loving the poor as soon as them that braver.
> He was a father to his children deare
> As by their learning breeding may appear.

I spare the reader more. He was buried in Darley church on
21 September 1670, and shortly afterwards was succeeded in
Parliament by William Sacheverall, whose election, which lasted
a week, according to Wheatscroft, was unsuccessfully disputed
by George Vernon, formerly Sheriff of the county.

Milward's political affiliations cannot be precisely designated.
The group to which he belonged were Cavaliers. Traces of his
feeling about the late wars are not uncommon, and Milward
speaks of the Cavaliers in the House in a proprietary way. On
the other hand, his patron's eldest son, William Cavendish,
a fellow member as yet, was to be the leader of the Whigs, and
the Sacheveralls at first and the Sitwells were to be prominent
in the same party. Can any signs of the early growth of such
a party feeling be found in Milward? I think so. For the real
origins of that party must be sought not in the republicans of
an earlier period but in that

> Gross of *English Gentry*, nobly born,
> Of clear Eastates, & to no faction sworn,

those "honest old cavaliers", who were to find increasing dis-
illusion in the restored monarchy, and to form the backbone of
the moderate opposition to its excesses.

These hated the Presbyterians as rebels and the Nonconformists as murderers and fanatics. They could blame on them
the land tax, but found the general excise favoured by the court
no better. Toleration was anathema to them, and the court
worked for it. Thus their fear of Popery was increased, and the
French alliance was to confirm it. A real nervousness about the
integrity of public officials overcame their dislike of seeming to

put too much distrust upon the King. Evil counsellors were blamed and some were ousted, but a strange reluctance on the part of Charles to be helped in this way more often did nothing to reassure the member for the loyalest of shires. Eventually common fear drew together very different opposition groups. Shaftesbury's attempted return to the demagogy of another age, and his unscrupulous use of religious fears resulted in his overthrow, and left the Government for the moment more respected than its critics. But the combination of moderate men, whether of Cavalier or of Roundhead origin, was a possibility which was realised in the groups formed at the crisis in 1688, and the strength of the former Cavalier element is shown in the extraordinarily small concessions gained then by the Nonconformist element.

Milward of course is a long way from the Whig alliance with the dissenter. He is a sound churchman of an uncompromising sort. He is nervous, however, about corruption, and thinks accounts should be carefully kept. He records his vote against the court where his cousin votes with them. He votes occasionally against his later judgment and notes it. He once mentions being solicited for votes, but then only on a private bill. He notices the thin attendance of one group or another. He shows a sturdy independence in his judgments, but that independence is always tempered by a profound loyalty to county friends and associates, which perhaps determined as much as anything else the cliques in the House.

NOTES

TO THE INTRODUCTION

The *Journal of the Derbyshire Archaeological and Natural History Society* is a rich mine of information on many county men and matters. The *Victoria County History* (2 vols. 1907), S. Glover's *History of Derbyshire* (2 vols. 1829 and also 1831–33), Lysons's *Derbyshire* (vol. v, *Magna Britannia*, 1818), the many works of J. C. Cox, *Familiae Minorum Gentium* (Harleian Society, vol. xxxviii, 1894) and the Manuscript Collections in Additional Manuscripts 6670–6686 and Harleian Manuscripts in the British Museum and in the Bateman collections at Derby, where the librarians are more than helpful, form a good introduction at least to the bewildering variety of Derbyshire families.

The Milward genealogy is rather difficult to trace. Dugdale (*Visitations*, 1662, printed 1879) is helpful but also confusing. Bassano, the eighteenth-century antiquary whose manuscripts are partly at Derby, is useful, and certain tables in the Add. MSS. (6675, f. 397 and f. d, and 5524, f. 146) show family relationships, but they are confused and inaccurate, and in the following notes I have confined myself to information gained from tombstones, state papers, parish registers, etc., which can reasonably be trusted. I think that the diarist was the nephew of Sir Thomas Milward of Eaton, father of Robert Milward, M.P. Cox's statement (*Churches of Derbyshire*, 1877, III, 124; I, 123) that the Milward family in all branches had died out by the eighteenth century cannot be proved. Distinct traces of Milwards in the county exist later, though I suggest they descend from a collateral branch of the family and are connected with the St Werburgh Milwards, later of London, whose tombstone was copied by Cox (*Churches*, IV, 27, 177), and who must also, I think, be identified with the long list of John Milwards given by Dugdale without other comment.

JOHN MILWARD I (i.e. in the diarist's immediate family), *c.* 1551–1633, aetat. 82: tombstone, now almost illegible, at Thorpe.

Lysons, p. 275.

Cox, II, 533, 441 and *passim*; *Old Halls of Derbyshire*, 1892, I, 117, etc.

I have not checked Cox's statement about the purchase of land by the Milwards, as it did not seem relevant here.

List and Indices, IX, 31, 6 November 1620. This may be another John Milward (see Dugdale, p. 1) but the fact that both the diarist and his son Henry were sheriffs later seems to point to this identification.

Will, P.C.C. 1633. Chancery Inquisitions post mortem (ser. 2), ccccxcvii, 175, Court of Wards 85/179.

ROBERT MILWARD, son of the above, 1597–1634.

Said by Bateman to have married a daughter of Sir George Gresley (afterwards connected with Sir John Gell in the wars).

Cox quotes Bassano as his authority for the story about the Spaniard (*Churches*, II, 533, where there is a reference to Harl. 5809 which I cannot trace). In Add. MSS. 6675, f. 221, is an epitaph on Robert. Also a Robert, of Bradley Ash, was admitted to the Inner Temple in 1617. This may be Robert, the "cousin" of the Diary, or might be this Robert, brother of the diarist (*Admission*, 1877, p. 218). A Robert Milward was admitted to Queen's College, Oxford, in January 1612, aged 16.

JOHN MILWARD II, the diarist, 1599–1670, Colonel, Add. MSS. 6675, f. (in red ink) 397 d and Bateman. Diary, 28 October 1666, for birthday.

Death in *Returns of Members of Parliament*, p. 521, by registers of Darley church (copy in Add. MSS. 6687, f. 296) and in *Derbyshire Archaeological and Natural History Society Journal* (*D.A.N.H.S.* hereafter), XVIII, 73, poem on J. M., d. 14 September 1670.

Cox (*Churches*, II, 165) gives a copy of the tombstone to Milward's wife which I have seen at Darley.

D.A.N.H.S. XVIII, 58, has a further poem which refers to the Milwards of Snitterton in verses 12 and 19. The editor has dated this 1670, but the reference to "Ould John Manners" (Earl of Rutland) and his recent death, as well as the otherwise puzzling references to the Milward family (p. 60), make it certain this should be some time after 1670, when Manners died, and probably after 1681, when Henry Milward died.

On p. 48 is a poem by the same author on the election following Milward's death. Add. MSS. 6705, f. 100, gives the number of votes polled in the election, 2875, Sacheverall winning by 643. This note (see f. 74) was written in 1774.

THE DIARIST'S CHILDREN

JOHN MILWARD III, Captain.

Venn, *Alumni Cant.* (1924, III, 194), confuses this John with his father; authority for attendance at Repton, which I cannot otherwise trace.

Marriage in Add. MSS. 6687, f. 295 d and in *D.A.N.H.S.* VI, 6, etc., and on monument at Darley discovered end of nineteenth century.

Death, *D.A.N.H.S.* VI, 9, 4 October 1669. Add. MSS. 6675, f. 397 d. See also *Register of Admissions to Gray's Inn*, 1521–1887, p. 256, 12 April 1651: John Milward, son and heir of John Milward of Snitterton.

Glover, I, 35, copy of an inscription at Ashbourne to Jane, late wife of Henry Sacheverall of Morley, written by her kinsman Thos. Milward; this would be the mother of John Milward III's widow.

HENRY MILWARD.

Add. MSS. 6687 as before.

D.A.N.H.S. VI, 4, born 30 January 1649.

Alumni Oxon. III, 592, Trinity College, 1667.

Lincoln's Inn Admissions, 1670, where he is described as the heir of John Milward of Snitterton (*Register*, 1420–1893, I, 306, January 1669/70).

Add. MSS. 6670, f. 223, paper dated 20 July 1679, signed by Henry Milward, Anchitel Grey, Every and Robert Coke (M.P. for Derby).

List and Indices, IX, 31, for sheriffs.

D.A.N.H.S. XXV, 164, Drinking bout.

D.A.N.H.S. XVIII, 74, Elegy upon Captain Henry Milward; p. 67, Upon Captain Milward's march at Chesterfield, which I should suppose to be part of militia drill or a hunting festival of some kind.

ROBERT MILWARD.

Son of John Milward of Snitterton, buried 12 April 1652, aged 17. Add. MSS. 6687, f. 296 d (red ink).

MARY ANNE, "my eldest daughter".

Marriage to Humphrey Jennens, of High Street, Birmingham, *D.A.N.H.S.* VI, 7, 16 September 1654.

On Jennens's purchase of iron works from Mr Clayton, the rival of George Sitwell, see *D.A.N.H.S.* X, 30.

Lysons, pp. ix, cxxxvii, 60–1.

Diary, pp. 33, 37, 211.

Coke Corr. Hist. MSS. Comm. 3rd Report, p. 165, death of Jennens's son, 31 July 1705.

FRANCES.

Born 9 February 1634, *D.A.N.H.S.* VI, 4.

Marriage to Boothbye, Dugdale, p. 21; Glover, I, 35, 44.

Death and burial, Add. MSS. 6687, f. 289, aged 21.

Sir William Boothbye, 2nd Bart. Monument in Ashbourne church says (in spite of Glover, I, 33 ff.) Boothbye was 78 when he died in 1708, four years after his second wife, Mary Hill. The monument also mentions his library at Ashbourne Hall (now a building estate).

Cox, *Churches*, II, 391; *Staffordshire Pedigrees*, p. 28; *Cal. of Com. for Compounding*, p. 1099; Add. MSS. 34306, f. 10 d, letter, 19 February 1660/1, from Milward to Devonshire about Boothbye; S.P.D., 29, CI, p. 34, Milward to Frechville about Calton and Wylde; Lists and Indices as before for shrievalty; Cox, *Three Centuries of Derbyshire History*, I, 37–8; Cowper MSS. (Hist. MSS. Comm.); Coke Papers; Boothbye's letter, 425 and much local gossip throughout.

The Boothbyes were associated with Bradley Ash as well as Ashbourne. Lysons, pp. 12–13.

FELICIA.
Married Charles Adderley of Thrope.
F.M.G. p. 577; Cox, *Churches*, II, 534; Lysons, pp. cxxxvii, 99, on Darley landowners.

ELIZABETH.
Married Robert Constable, of N. Cliffe, Yorkshire, and by him had one son John, remembered in his grandfather's will, and one daughter. All this branch of the Constables were dead by the beginning of the eighteenth century. Milward's will, P.C.C. 1670.

DOROTHY.
Married William Copley, of Claines, Worcestershire. Mentioned in her father's will with Anne and Felicia as alive when the will was made.

THE DIARIST'S PUBLIC CAREER

Lists and Indices, IX, 31; Harl. MSS. 2043, f. 145 (137). Notes on lives of Derbyshire sheriffs.

S.P.D. CCCIV, 20 December 1635, Council to John Milward.

Add. MSS. 6702, ff. 116–19, on payment as Captain of foot. Cf. Cox, *Annals*, I, 157.

D.A.N.H.S. XIX, 20–3, note by Sir George Sitwell on petition from Derbyshire.

Victoria County History, II, 126, on Civil War in Derbyshire.

Glover, I, Appendix, pp. 57 ff., long contemporary account of war and Milward and Fairfax.

Lysons, p. ix, on Milward and Civil War, from the above; H.M.C. 5th Report, pp. 134–5; *L.J.* VIII, 492; *ibid.* Hastings, II, 120.

Cal. of Com. for Compounding, p. 1025, 29 November, 15 December, 1645; Sir Thos., p. 1464; Sir Thos. died 1658 (Cox, *Churches*, III, 224).

Gell one of the commissioners, *D.A.N.H.S.* XIII, 135.

Gell's debt to Milward, *Cal. of Com. for Compounding*, p. 2750, Milward of Snitterton.

Petition about mines in Wirksworth, *ibid.* p. 1874.

Lists of Derbyshire justices in Cox, *Three Centuries*, I, 37 ff. Boothbye, who appears to have acted for the county, is not on this list.

Cox, *Three Centuries*, II, 32, Milward and another petition about a loyal ironmonger in 1660.

Ibid. I, 172 ff., lists of deputies.

C.S.P.D. 1660, p. 145, Lord-Lieutenant the Earl of Devonshire.

Cox, I, pp. 24–32.

Statutes of the Realm, V, 329 (13 C. II, stat. 2, c. iii), 381, 456, 429, for lists of tax officials.

Letter Book in Milward's handwriting, Add. MSS. 34306; bookplate of Thos. Bateman, Esq., Middleton Hall, Derbyshire; acquired at the Bateman sale by the Museum: the Calton entries begin f. 33. Cf. S.P.D. CI, nos. 28, 33, 34, etc.

Letters of the Sitwells and Sacheverall s, Sir George Sitwell, 1900, I, 46, letter to Revell dated 31 March 1663/4.

Connections of the Sacheveralls and Milwards and Cottons, Cox, *Churches*, II, 390.

Returns of Members of Parliament, p. 521.

S.P.D. cxxxiv, no. 58, a new election for Derby, 9 October 1665.

Diary, 17 September 1666.

C.J. viii *passim*, for committees; ix, 99, 19 October 1669. Colonel Milward given leave to go into the country, probably to attend the funeral of his son John. On 9 December 1669 and 5 April 1670, Colonel Milward is named on committees in the Journals.

MILWARD'S WILL

Milward's will, P.C.C., proved 19 December 1670. Milward left his eldest daughter, Anne, £2000, and to Felicia and Dorothy £1500 apiece. He left money for his grandson, John Constable, until he should be twenty-one years old, because of his late father's debts. The poor of Wensley, Darley, Thorpe and Ashbourne, etc., were remembered. His servant, John Sherwin, was given a life interest in his house at Thorpe, and John Clifton and Henry Else a like interest at Ballidon. His cousin Robert, who with Humphrey Jennens was named overseer to the will, was left a bequest with an affectionate message. Henry Milward, only surviving son, was left the residue and was chief executor of the will. Witnesses were Charles Hinton and Thomas Wardell.

JOHN MILWARD OF ST WERBURGH

Cox (*Churches*, IV, 24, 177); Lysons, p. 128; *D.A.N.H.S.* XL, 225, 228, mentions a John Milward there as assessor of highways, etc.

BIBLIOGRAPHY AND ABBREVIATIONS

The abbreviations which will be used hereafter are put first, and then the title.

Add. MSS. 33413.—The Milward Diary printed here.

Tanner 239 (Bodleian).—Appendix I. Speeches of Holland.

Add. MSS. 35865.—The Diary printed in Appendix II.

Add. MSS. 36916.—Ashley Papers. Newsletters from John Starkey, a London publisher. 17 October 1671 to 9 January 1671/2 (Starkey).

C.J.—*Journals of the House of Commons*, vols. VIII, IX.

A manuscript copy of this from the library of W. Bromley, of Baginton in Warwickshire, is in the British Museum. Add. MSS. 36837–36840, four volumes of this, cover this period. The last volume contains the erased portions of the *Journal* about the Skinner controversy.

L.J.—*Journals of the House of Lords*, vol. XII.

A manuscript copy of the *Journal* is in Rawl. A, 130, 16 March 1664 to 19 December 1667.

Add. MSS. 22263, ff. 10–23, contains a few copied entries from 12 November 1667 to 3 December 1667.

Eg. 2543, ff. 190–203, contains a few entries on the Clarendon impeachment, copies of the reasons why the Lords did not imprison Clarendon, the protest of Buckingham against this decision, etc. For this see Add. MSS. 28009, ff. 128, 159, etc.

H.M.C. 8th Report.—Historical Manuscript Commission, Eighth Report. House of Lords Manuscripts contain much additional matter on the activity of the Lords during the period.

Cobbett.—Cobbett's *Parliamentary History of England*. 12 vols. 1806–12. Vol. IV covers this period.

For Cobbett's material see *Bulletin of the Institute of Historical Research*, vol. X, no. 30, February 1933, pp. 171 ff. Very valuable.

Grey.—Anchitel Grey, *Debates of the House of Commons*, from 1667 to 1694. 10 vols. 1763. Reissue, 1769. Vol. I only used here.

Proceedings.—*The Proceedings in the House of Commons touching the Impeachment of Edward, late Earl of Clarendon, Lord High-Chancellor of England, Anno 1667. With many debates and speeches in the house.* 1 vol. 1700, two editions.

Davies in his *Bibliography of British History*, Oxford, 1928, no. 413, says this had a wide circulation in manuscript at the time of the trial (see note p. xxix). Its authorship is sometimes attributed to Littleton; my own copy has such an attribution in a contemporary hand written on it.

Carte.—Carte, Thomas, *The Life of James, Duke of Ormonde*, 2nd ed. 6 vols. Oxford, 1851.

State Trials.—Cobbett's collection (34 vols. London, 1809–28), vol. II. Adds nothing to the above of value.

Marvell, I and II.—Andrew Marvell, *Poems and Satires*, I; *Letters*, II. Edited by H. M. Margoliouth, Oxford, 1927.

The Letters frequently give accounts of Parliamentary affairs, though comment is generally absent. The Satires, however, give much comment, and a good deal of information besides.

Clarendon.—*The Continuation of the Life of Edward Earl of Clarendon.* I have used the edition published at Oxford, 1843.

Lister.—Lister, T. H., *Life and Administration of Edward, First Earl of Clarendon.* 3 vols. London, 1838.

D.N.B.—*Dictionary of National Biography*, with the valuable additions and corrections published occasionally by the Institute of Historical Research. There is no mention of the diarist here.

C.S.P.D.—*Calendar of State Papers Domestic.*

Returns.—*Returns of the names of every member returned to serve in each parliament.* 2 vols. folio, 1878. Index, 1891.

de Beer.—Members of the Court Party in the House of Commons, 1670–78, E. S. de Beer. In *Bulletin of the Institute of Historical Research*, vol. IX, no. 31, June 1933.

Most valuable. I have used it constantly in my notes on the members.

SOME ADDITIONAL BIBLIOGRAPHICAL NOTES, ARRANGED UNDER SUBJECTS CHRONOLOGICALLY

1666.   IRISH CATTLE ACT

Milward's remains the sole account of the debates in the Commons over this Act. His account may be supplemented by:

(1) Three speeches printed in the *Calendar of State Papers*, Ireland, 1667, pp. 533–42. The speaker has not been identified.

(2) Arguments about the Act, Harl. 4706, ff. 39–40.

(3) Letters about Irish affairs in volumes of the Historical Manuscripts Reports: Dartmouth, III; Ormonde, III, n.s.; Finch, I; Hastings.

(4) Carte, Ormonde, *passim*, but particularly vol. IV.

SUPPLY

Holland's three speeches in Appendix I.
Marvell, *Last Instructions.*

LORD MORDAUNT

Stowe, 425. 3, 10, 17, 21, 22 January 1666/7.

1667.   THE JULY PARLIAMENT

Chiefly remarkable for its brevity, the fact that, contrary to custom at this time, the King's speech was not printed, and for Tomkins's motion about the standing army.

Marvell, as above.

Add. MSS. 28092, f. 68, legal opinion on.

Historical Manuscripts Commission, *7th Report*, p. 486. Hastings MSS. ii, 154.

PROCEEDINGS AGAINST CLARENDON

Appendices I and II; Historical Manuscripts Commission, 5th Report, p. 326.

Manuscript versions of the *Proceedings* (Littleton) in Harl. 1218, 881, which includes Clarendon's petition, p. 24; Stowe, 368, 369 (the property of A. Capel, 1701), which includes the Bristol charges at the end; Rawl. A, 131. On the whole these seem more finished than the printed book. Names are in full throughout.

Clarendon's Petition appears in many manuscript copies, e.g. Harl. 1579, f. 128; 4888, no. 32; 7170; Add. MSS. 28009, f. 163.

Precedents for, Stowe, 425, f. 86. Legal opinion on, Add. MSS. 22263, f. 23.

Printed versions of the charges were current, e.g. *Articles of Treason exhibited in Parliament* [1668]; Manuscript in Add. MSS. 38175; Eg. 2543.

Reports which probably contain information about Clarendon are listed but not calendered in H.M.C. Fleming MSS. at weekly intervals throughout the sessions (e.g. 22 October, 5, 26 November, 3, 10, 17 December, 1667; 18, 25 February, 10, 17, 24 March 1667/8; 31 March, 7, 14, 21 April, 5 May, 1668). I suspect these of being copies of Muddiman news-sheets similar to those found in the *Calendars of State Papers*, etc.

Sir Thomas Osbourne's notes in Add. MSS. 28045, ff. 1–18, throw some interesting light on the methods of Clarendon's attackers.

THE ENQUIRY INTO MISCARRIAGES OF THE WAR

Copies of the Narratives of the War given by Albemarle and Prince Rupert to the House in 1667 are fairly common, and do not differ materially from those printed in the *Journals*, e.g. Harl. 7170, ff. 290 ff., and see also ff. 42–72 on enquiries in committee, etc., February to April 1667/8. An excellent account of the War is in D. Ogg, *England in the Reign of Charles II* (1934).

In Appendix II (Add. MSS. 35865) will be found some reports of the enquiry in the Commons.

Notes by Pepys, Rawl. A, 195a, 22 October 1667, which add little to the *Journals*.

Rawl. A, 191, 13, 21 February 1667/8. Preparations for defence of the naval authorities, etc. Proceedings against Brouncker (f. 237) and his defence.

S.P.D. 29, ccxxv, no. 42; five pages in Williamson's hand on the evidence in committee against Pett.

The Renewal of the Conventicle Act

See Appendix I for a speech (undated) by Sir John Holland.

The Controversy about Thomas Skinner

Add. MSS. 36840. *Journal of the House of Commons* noted above.
Add. MSS. 25116. October 1667 to December 1669.
Sloane, 3956. Mainly proceedings in the Lords.
Stowe, 303, ff. 1–66, as Sloane, 3956 above, ff. 67–71, House of Commons (belonged to Capel).
Maynard's speech printed in Grey, 1, 445, etc., is reproduced in many manuscript copies. These do not differ materially, except that in one the order of paragraphs is different, as though the scribe had omitted a section and then inserted his omission at the end.
Harl. 1579, f. 173; Add. MSS. 25116, ff. 147–175.
Stowe, 304, f. 89.
Hargrave, 47, f. 188 d.
Rawl. C, 436, f. 1.
Votes in the House of Commons, 7, 9 May.
Eg. 2543, ff. 207–8.
Printed: *The Grand Question concerning the Judicature of the House of Peers stated and argued*...1669 (attributed to D. Holles).
Historical Manuscripts Commission Report on House of Lords Manuscripts.

King's Speeches

These were usually printed soon after being given. Some originals exist in the State Paper Office. The Lords' *Journal* prints them also except in the case of the speech in July 1667, where a summary only is given. That this speech was not printed is commented on by Milward, by Marvell and others.

Other Speeches

Sir Edward Turner, the Speaker of the House of Commons, usually allowed his speeches to be printed at the same time as those of the King. Apart from these and the odd speeches listed above, I know of no separate copies of speeches in this period.

PARLIAMENTARY BUSINESS

I. SEPTEMBER TO FEBRUARY 1666–7

List of Acts passed in *Statutes of the Realm*, v, 584, 623, 624–47.

CHIEF BILLS

Finance.

Enquiry into expenditure and appointment of commissioners to report on it to the House.

Full effect not seen till 1669.

Supply: grant of £1,800,000.

The Poll Tax and the proviso about the above-mentioned commissioners.

Assessed land tax and excise debates. Milward says excise was generally disliked.

Irish Cattle Act.

Prohibiting importation of cattle into England. Milward's views are expressed in his account of his conversation with a Norfolk member, Sir William Doyley, where he says too much fuss is being made. The same problem has recently been receiving the attention of Parliament and of English farmers (*National Farmers' Union Year Book*, 1933, p. 393, par. 117, etc.).

Impeachment of Lord Mordaunt.

For alleged tyranny as Constable of Windsor.

Lord Roos's Bill.

John Manners (1638–1711), afterwards ninth Earl of Rutland and the first Duke, held much land in Derbyshire, where his family were connected by marriage in the sixteenth century with the Cavendishes. He married first Lady Anne Pierpont, from whom he obtained a divorce 22 March 1670, and then Lady Anne Bruce, daughter of the Earl of Ailsbury and widow of Sir Seymour Shirley, Bart. The bill which Milward reports on was to illegitimise the first Lady Roos's children, an act of obvious justice.

Responsibility for the Fire of London, and the rebuilding of the City.

Milward did not believe the origin of the fire could be discovered. He reports debates on the width of Lower Thames Street and so forth, which may interest students of London topography.

Sale of Land.

Many bills of this kind come up in all sessions of Parliament, particularly after the upheavals of the Civil Wars. A special Act of Parliament was necessary until the nineteenth century for the sale of land in many cases.

Election Petitions, Privilege, etc.

The reports of disputed elections often show party feeling at work, and this rather than strict justice often seems to decide the result.

The claims of privilege by members, particularly immunity for themselves and their servants from arrest, are often of the most trivial kind. The frequency of arrest for debt may be remarked.

Bill against Blasphemy.

Public morals were still the subject of Parliamentary attention, and a bill against blasphemy is debated.

Fishing and Agriculture.

Encouragement of the fishing industry and of the sowing of hemp and flax show the attention of the House to the commercial wealth of the nation.

A Bill to relieve the State of Poor Prisoners.

Supported by Milward's cousin Robert.

A Bill for reviewing all Statutes.

II. JULY 1667

The King wished for supply, but the House was so much disturbed by its fears of a standing army that a motion against that was the only business discussed before the King decided to prorogue the Houses till a more propitious moment.

III. OCTOBER 1667 TO MAY 1668

Parliament sat from 10 October to 19 December, and from 6 February to 18 March, and from 26 March to 9 May, and was then adjourned to successive dates (16 May, 11 August, 10 November, 1 March), and then prorogued until 19 October 1669, when it sat till 11 December. It was then prorogued till February and then till 24 October 1670, which was of course after Milward's death.

Chief business concerned the impeachment of Clarendon and the enquiry into the miscarriages of the war, which becomes very tedious. Milward adds one long speech to our knowledge of the activities of Pepys at this time.

Religion.

Religion and the question of toleration occupied several long debates, particularly in March and April of 1668.

The Irish Adventurers.

Occupied the attention of the House in the spring of 1668. The land question in Ireland had been the subject of much discontent and litigation since the Restoration settlement, so called, and the commissioners appointed to cope with it had failed to satisfy many.

Forest of Dean and Lindsey Levels.

The enclosure of the Forest of Dean and the matter of Lindsey Levels were debated in the main by persons connected with the districts and interests concerned.

Trade, Prices and Interest.

The price of coal, the matter of trade with Scotland and the lowering of interest charges together with very long debates on the allocation of the tax on wines, etc., occupy much space.

Tithe.

Tithe was discussed, a bill for its more speedy recovery being brought in.

Chief Justice Keeling.

The case of Chief Justice Keeling, who intimidated juries, was carefully discussed. The Judge got off lightly, perhaps because of his connection with the House, but the D.N.B. and Foster (Lives of the Judges) tell of his repeated offences.

Skinner's Case.

This case, which involved the Commons in a dispute with the Lords over their right to be a court of first instance in a matter involving a company, many of whose directors sat in the Lower House, begins in April 1668. Feeling ran high, and eventually records of the case were wiped out of the Journals of both Houses.

The Duke of Richmond's Bill on Allnage.

Two abortive bills are of interest, a Habeas Corpus bill and Temple's Triennial bill.

CALENDAR

FOR THE PERIOD COVERED BY THE DIARY

1666. SEPTEMBER:

17. Mon. Milward delivers his writ to Agar.
18. Tues. Parliament meets, debts of corporations. Election writs, adjourned to Friday.
(19. Wed.
20. Thur.)
21. Fri. The King's speech. Accounts asked for.
22. Sat. Bill *v.* Irish cattle. Scarcity of money. Recusancy.
(23. Sun.)
24. Mon. Prynne's Marriage bill. Peterborough and Northants elections. Revenue of Schools.
25. Tues. Debate on the Fire. Certiorates.
26. Wed. Second reading of Irish bill. Accounts.
27. Thur. Prynne's bill cast out. Rebuilding of London.
28. Fri. Ditto. Irish bill in committee. Milward at Lambeth. Accounts. Coining plate.
(29. Sat. St Michael the Archangel. Commons do not sit.
30. Sun.)

1666. OCTOBER:

1. Mon. Canary Co. patents. Hemp, flax, linen, etc.
2. Tues. Sale of gunpowder. Committee of Privilege.
(3. Wed. Monthly fast. Outram and Dalbin preach.)
4. Thur. Report on Mr Grey. Supply.
5. Fri. Great debate on the Irish bill. Freshwater fish.

1666. OCTOBER (*continued*):

6. Sat. Kendall's bill. Bristol election. Lady Arlington's bill.
(7. Sun.)
8. Mon. Downing on restraint of foreign goods. Irish bill. Countess of Essex.
9. Tues. Blasphemy bill. Wool. Canary Co. Hemp and flax.
(10. Wed. Two sermons, Stillingfleet and Frambton.)
11. Thur. Accounts. Bill for preserving fishing.
12. Fri. Lady Arlington's bill. Supply: Court move for excise.
13. Sat. Bristol election. Irish bill. Privacy of debate.
(14. Sun.)
15. Mon. Lord Cleveland's bill. Irish bill to Lords. Supply.
16. Tues. Blasphemy bill. Rupert thanked for his success. Supply. Cobbett ends till 3 January.
17. Wed. Milward absent till 11 a.m. Supply.
18. Thur. St Luke's Day. Supply.
(19. Fri. Milward absent.)
20. Sat. Sir Thomas Higgins's bill, and Countess of Essex.
(21. Sun.)
22. Mon. Tithe. French commodities. Privacy of debate again discussed.
23. Tues. Milward absent in morning.

1666. OCTOBER (*continued*):

23. Tues. Committee of Privilege debate.
Plympton election in afternoon.
24. Wed. Kendall's bill.
Lady Arlington's bill.
Thurland's bill against duelling.
A libel found in the House.
25. Thur. Kendall's bill.
Roberts and Winn.
Supply.
26. Fri. Noell's bill.
Recusants.
Discovery of daggers.
27. Sat. Plympton election.
Sale of chimney money.
(28. Sun. St Simon and St Jude.
Milward dines at Lambeth.)
29. Mon. Canary Co.
Supply.
30. Tues. Lord Campden's bill.
Debate on land tax and excise.
31. Wed. Petition from Mayor of Bristol.
Grand Committee.
Supply.
Twenty-four Commons attend the King.

1666. NOVEMBER:

(1. Thur. Holy Day.
Milward dines in St James's Park.)
2. Fri. Petition against Mordaunt.
Supply.
3. Sat. Mr Taylor's bill lost.
Supply.
(4. Sun. Milward goes to St Clement's. Dines with "Coz" Glanvill.)
(5. Mon. Milward dines with Sir Jos. Sheldon.)
6. Tues. Oaths administered.
(7. Wed. Monthly fast. Sancroft and Tillotson preach.)
8. Thur. Pest-house at Cambridge.
Supply.

1666. NOVEMBER (*continued*):

8. Thur. King refuses to part with chimney money.
9. Fri. Accounts called for.
Fire in Whitehall.
10. Sat. Milward absent till 11 a.m.
Coinage.
Supply.
Bill against duels.
(11. Sun.)
12. Mon. Mountague moves for Lord Roos's bill.
Duels.
Roberts and Winn case.
Whorwood on Supply.
Milward dines at Lambeth. Sees the Earl of Rutland.
13. Tues. Supply.
Proclamation against priests and Jesuits.
14. Wed. Supply.
15. Thur. Patents, Titles of honour to be paid for.
Berwick election.
16. Fri. Sale of Pride's land (son of "Pride the Traytor").
17. Sat. Poll bill.
Bill about escaped prisoners, etc.
Burial in woollen.
(18. Sun. Debates of 17th wrongly entered here by Milward.
Escape of prisoners.
Poll tax.)
19. Mon. Roberts and Winn case.
(20. Tues. Public thanksgiving for cessation of plague.)
21. Wed. Roberts and Winn case.
Milward at Lambeth.
22. Thur. Duels.
Roberts and Winn case.
Lambeth.
23. Fri. Leigh's bill.
Poor prisoners' bill.
Poll bill.
24. Sat. Prevention of plague bill.
Report on papist priest.
Poll bill.
Bill for making brick and tile.

1666. NOVEMBER (*continued*):

(25. Sun.)

26. Mon. Second reading of Poll bill.
          Lord Roos Committee.
27. Tues. Lords' amendments to Irish bill.
          Roberts and Winn case.
28. Wed. De Leure.
          Milward sees Archbishop.
          Poll bill.
29. Thur. Plays to be tolerated?
          Poll bill.
30. Fri. St Andrew's Day.
          Poll bill.
          Privilege.

1666. DECEMBER:

1. Sat.   Bill re suits caused by Fire.
          Poll bill.
          Milward at Lambeth.
(2. Sun.)
3. Mon.   Bill re suits, etc.
          St John and Henly.
          Collection of poll money.
4. Tues. News of Covenanters.
          Bill for rebuilding of London.
          Poll bill.
5. Wed.   Seymour on Lords' amendments to Irish bill.
          Mutiny against De Witt reported.
6. Thur. Bill re suits, etc.
          Poll bill.
7. Fri.   Roberts and Winn case.
          Poll bill.
(8. Sat. Houses adjourn to prepare for Sacrament.
9. Sun.   Houses take Sacrament at St Margaret's.)
10. Mon. No debate recorded.
(11. Tues. Milward leaves for Derbyshire via Oxford; stays until 8 January, when he is back in London in time to hear news of Leigh's bill. See notes to text for days he omits.)

1666/7. JANUARY:

8. Tues. Leigh's bill.
9. Wed.   Severe orders against absentees.
          Conference with Lords re appointment of commissioners of accounts.
          Irish bill.
          Wool bill.
10. Thur. Quakers' Petition.
          Bill for poor prisoners.
11. Fri. May and Austin election.
          Milward dines with Shirley.
          Hilton's bill.
          Higgins' bill.
12. Sat. Mosley's bill.
          Poll bill.
          Difference with Lords.
          Wine merchants.
(13. Sun.)
14. Mon. Petition re taxation of Bedford levels.
          Chune's privilege.
          Poll bill completed.
15. Tues. Shirley's bill for sale of land.
          Prynne on coal prices.
16. Wed. Stanley's bill.
          Land tax.
17. Thur. Lord Roos's bill.
          Scawen.
          Bedford levels.
          Attendance.
          Bill against Bribery.
          Burial of the dead.
18. Fri. House called over.
          King passes bills.
19. Sat. Lord Lindsey's bill.
          Land tax.
          Bill re attendance.
(20. Sun.)
21. Mon. Scawen's, Lord Roos's and Shirley's bills.
          Milward at Lambeth.
22. Tues. Russell's bill.
          Lord Mordaunt.
          French merchants.
          Fire of London enquiry committee.
23. Wed. Milward moves for Kendall's bill.
          Sandys's bill.

1666/7. JANUARY (*continued*):

23. Wed. Morice's bill for rebuilding of London.
Lord Roos's bill.
24. Thur. Milward again moves for
Kendall.
Chune's privilege.
Bedford Levels bill.
25. Fri. Southampton churches.
Fulk Grosvenor's bill.
Attendance.
26. Sat. Rebuilding of London
bill.
Lords ask for conference
re Mordaunt.
(27. Sun. Milward gives Monday's
debates under this date.)
28. Mon. Bedford Levels bill.
Lord Lindsey's bill.
Messages from Lords
re French commodities
and Mordaunt.
Rebuilding of London.
29. Tues. Stanley's bill.
Lord Roos's bill.
Mordaunt.
King's message.
(30. Wed. Public fast. Sermon at
Temple Church.)
31. Thur. Bill re disorders of seamen passed.
Blasphemy bill.
Grosvenor's bill.
Mordaunt's impeach-
ment.

1666/7. FEBRUARY:

1. Fri. Swaffham Prior bill.
2. Sat. Mordaunt's impeachment.
Prevention of Plague bill.
Rebuilding of London.
Coal imports.
(3. Sun.)
4. Mon. Hemp and flax bill.
Lords' message, etc.
5. Tues. R. Milward on bill for
poor prisoners.
Free conference with
Lords desired.
6. Wed. Chune's privilege.
Mordaunt's impeach-
ment.
7. Thur. Rigby's privilege.

1666/7. FEBRUARY (*continued*):

7. Thur. Pierpont's privilege.
Free conference.
Accounts bill.
8. Fri. Mordaunt's impeach-
ment.
Accounts.
Parliament prorogued till
10 October 1667.

1667. JULY:

25. Thur. St James's Day.
Tomkins' motion. Ad-
journed till Monday.
29. Mon. King's speech.
Milward writing on 7
August with one of
three copies before him.
Parliament prorogued till
10 October.

1667. OCTOBER:

10. Thur. Parliament met and
shortly adjourned till
Monday after debate
on King's speech and
dismissal of Clarendon.
14. Mon. Parliament meets.
Duels bill.
Address to the King.
15. Tues. Quakers' Petition.
Bill for poor prisoners.
Lending money to the
King.
Abuses in price of coals
reported.
Freedom of speech.
King's speech.
16. Wed. Bill re Lord's Day.
Bill against recusants.
Keeling complained of.
17. Thur. Townshend's Petition.
Encouragement of timber.
Miscarriages of the war.
(18. Fri. St Luke's Day.)
19. Sat. (misdated by Milward).
Highway robbery.
The dividing of the Fleet.
(20. Sun.)
21. Mon. Townshend's bill.
Tithe bill.
Miscarriages.
22. Tues. Levels.
Forest of Dean.

1667. OCTOBER (*continued*):
22. Tues. Dividing of the Fleet.
23. Wed. Prettyman's Petition.
   English prisoners abroad.
   Highway robbery.
   Excise.
   Miscarriages of the war.
   Tithes.
   Clarendon.
24. Thur. Petition re troops going
    to France.
   Coals and wood.
   Townshend.
   The Bedford Levels bill.
   Miscarriages of the war.
25. Fri. Discharge of suit against
    Sheriffs.
   Highway robbery.
   Coals.
   The war.
   Cambridge pest-houses.
26. Sat. Fees in law offices.
   Clarendon.
(27. Sun.
28. Mon.)
29. Tues. Certioraries.
   Clarendon, precedents
    for.
30. Wed. Highways.
   Money.
   Townshend.
   Exacting fees.
   Recusants.
31. Thur. Naturalisation bill.
   Irish lands.
   Durham bill.
   Prince Rupert's and Al-
    bemarle's narratives.
   Charges *v.* Pett.
   House adjourned to Mon-
    day because of All
    Saints' and All Souls'
    Days.

1667. NOVEMBER:
4. Mon. Escape of prisoners.
   Lighthouses.
   Bedford Levels.
   Weights and Measures.
   Book of Rates.
(5. Tues. Guy Fawkes's Day. Par-
    liament adjourns.)

1667. NOVEMBER (*continued*):
6. Wed. Complaints re hearth
    money.
   Wood and coals.
   Clarendon, articles against.
7. Thur. Clarendon.
   Sandys's bill.
   Downing.
   Highway robbery bill.
   Prynne on Pluralities.
8. Fri. Prynne's Marriage bill.
   Committee of Privilege.
   Clarendon.
9. Sat. Abuse of Post Office.
   Perkins's Petition.
   Wool.
   Miscarriages of the war.
   Clarendon debate con-
    tinued.
(10. Sun.)
11. Mon. Petition against Claren-
    don.
   Chamberlayne's patent.
   Clarendon.
12. Tues. Perkins's bill.
   Forest of Dean.
   Privileges.
   Clarendon's impeach-
    ment.
13. Wed. Message from the Lords.
   Trade between England
    and Scotland.
   Miscarriages of the war.
14. Thur. Petitions of persons in-
    jured by the Fire.
   Palmes's bill, Pett.
15. Fri. Lords debate Clarendon.
   Conference with Com-
    mons.
16. Sat. Clarendon.
(17. Sun.)
18. Mon. Wm. Palmes's bill.
   Bribery report.
   Clarendon.
19. Tues. Apsley's bill.
   Ashburnham and bribery.
20. Wed. Beckam's bill.
   Downing's bill.
   Privileges.
   Coals.
   Bribery.
21. Thur. Committee of accounts.
   Clarendon.

1667. NOVEMBER (*continued*):
21. Thur. Fretchville Holles's election case.
22. Fri. Milward late.
Ashburnham and bribery.
Privileges.
Holles elected.
23. Sat. Dawe's bill.
Petition against merchants.
Hobby on Jesuits' activity.
Conference with Lords.
Milward left early.
(24. Sun.)
25. Mon. Beckam's bill.
Heralds' demand.
Bribery.
26. Tues. Harbord's report.
Free conference desired.
Sandys's information.
Hyde's election.
27. Wed. Highway robbery.
Prize ships.
Trade with Scotland.
News the Lords desire a conference.
28. Thur. Pest-houses at Cambridge.
Lindsey Levels.
Free conference.
29. Fri. Highway robbery.
Sandys's information.
Report of conference.
(30. Sat. No debates.)

1667. DECEMBER:
2. Mon. Wood's bill.
Paston's bill for enclosing Hopton.
Bribery.
Message from Lords.
Protest by Commons.
3. Tues. Morton's Petition.
Printers.
Petition against Clarendon.
Naturalisation bill.
Clarendon's flight announced.
4. Wed. Palmes's bill.
King asked to stop ports.
Naturalisation bill.

1667. DECEMBER (*continued*):
4. Wed. Report about Clarendon.
Clarendon's defence.
5. Thur. Cambridge pest-houses.
Naturalising of ships.
Clarendon.
6. Fri. Yarmouth bill.
Trade.
Clarendon.
7. Sat. Enclosure near Wakefield.
Yarmouth bill.
Hearth money collection.
(8. Sun.)
9. Mon. Cambridge pest-houses.
Keeling's case.
10. Tues. Irish land.
Hearth money report.
Lords' message about Clarendon.
11. Wed. Knight's bill.
Indigent officers.
Keeling.
12. Thur. Surveyors to report on King's land.
Gerrard's bill.
Clarendon.
Harbord's report at Committee of Accounts.
13. Fri. Naturalisation bill.
Smuggling of cattle.
Banishment of Clarendon.
Keeling.
14. Sat. Naturalisation bill.
Clarendon.
Prize ships.
London.
Message from Lords.
(15. Sun.)
16. Mon. Higgins's report of coals and wood.
Carr's Petition.
Debate on Lords' message.
Milward absent in afternoon.
17. Tues. Carr's Petition.
Trade.
Bill of accounts.
18. Wed. Trade with Scotland.
Accounts.
Prize ships.
Clarendon.
19. Thur. Indigent officers.

1667. DECEMBER (*continued*):

19. Thur. Charges *v*. Pett.
Bills signed.
House adjourns from 19
December to 6 February 1667/8.

1667/8. FEBRUARY:

6. Thur. House to be called before a vote taken.
Adjourns.
10. Mon. Privileges.
King to be petitioned re dissenters.
King's speech.
11. Tues. Forest of Dean.
Report of men going to France.
Trevor Williams and Committee of Privilege.
Complaint against Clarendon.
12. Wed. Sandys and car-men.
Acts against export of wool.
Sheriffs and suits from Fire.
Forest of Dean.
Libels.
13. Thur. Abuses of hearth money.
Enfranchisement of Durham bill.
Houses called.
14. Fri. Juxon's bill.
Brooke on miscarriages.
15. Sat. Petition against sale of timber.
Lindsey Levels.
Miscarriages.
(16. Sun.)
17. Mon. Order of House.
Forest of Dean.
Miscarriages.
18. Tues. Sandys and Irish cattle smuggling.
Temple's Triennial bill.
19. Wed. Keeling.
King on toleration.
Supply.
League with Dutch.
Committee of grievances.
Vernon and Irish adventurers.

1667/8. FEBRUARY (*continued*):

20. Thur. Regulation of price of wine.
Miscarriages of the war.
21. Fri. Juxon's bill.
Letter from Duke of York.
Coleman's report on Gerrard.
Supply.
22. Sat. Coleman's further report.
Miscarriages.
(23. Sun.)
24. Mon. Jones on abuses of Irish Cattle Act.
Sale of offices. (Coventry?)
25. Tues. No debate recorded.
26. Wed. Cleveland's bill.
Birch on silk throwsters.
Felton's case.
Supply.
27. Thur. Forest of Dean.
King's money.
Abuses of chimney money.
Supply.
28. Fri. Heblethwaite's bill.
Forest of Dean.
Seamen's tickets.
Sectaries.
29. Sat. Regulation of collection of chimney money.
Constantine and Poole.
Supply.

1667/8. MARCH:

(1. Sun.)
2. Mon. Irish cattle.
Lenthall *v*. Cornbury.
3. Tues. Heblethwaite's bill.
Sheriffs' bill.
Fitton and Gerrard.
Libel against Gerrard.
4. Wed. Lincolnshire Fens.
Cleveland's bill.
Writs of error.
Conventicles.
5. Thur. Bedford Levels.
Pepys's defence of Commissioners of Navy.
House attends the King.
6. Fri. Southampton churches.
Naturalisation.
Dowdeswell.
Sheriffs' bill.

1667/8. MARCH (*continued*):
6. Fri.   Six clerks in Chancery.
          Supply asked by King.
          Debate on it.
7. Sat.   Highway robbery bill.
          Supply.
          Milward's daughter ill.
(8. Sun.)
9. Mon.   Silk throwsters.
          Supply.
10. Tues. Ailsbury's bill re Fens.
          Highway robbery.
          Supply.
11. Wed. Sheriffs' bill.
          Dr Wharton's and Mr
          Brooke's bills.
          Debate on King's speech
          and the Church.
          Vote on supply.
12. Thur. Bedford Levels.
          Supply.
13. Fri. Felton's bill.
          Two-hour debate on
          Conventicles.
          Supply.
14. Sat. Abuses of Chimney
          money.
          Report on Accounts.
          Meers on wine imports.
(15. Sun.)
16. Mon. Heblethwaite's bill.
          Irish adventurers' Peti-
          tion.
          Notice of adjournment.
17. Tues. Arrears of poll money.
          Debate on tobacco excise.
18. Wed. Debate on taxation.
          Duke of Buckingham.
          Bishops' subsidy.
          House adjourns for Holy
          Week.
26. Thur. Writ of election in place of
          Sir Edmund Walpole.
          Chamberlayne's bill.
          Durham bill.
          Permission for Churchill,
          etc., to go to Ireland.
          Miscarriage.
          Supply.
27. Fri. Wanklin's Petition.
          Chimney money.
28. Sat. Wanklin's Petition.
          Sir Peter Pindar.
          Downing.
          Supply.

1668. MARCH (*continued*):
(29. Sun.)
30. Mon. Conventicles.
          Milward speaks re Jus-
          tices of Peace.
          Irish bill.
          Wool house at Romney.
          House attends King.
          Poll bill.
          Miscarriages.
31. Tues. Decay of churches.
          Highway robbery.
          Supply.

1668. APRIL:
1. Wed.   Wakefield bill.
          Chimney money abuses.
          Supply.
2. Thur. Forest of Dean.
          Supply.
          Lenthall *v.* Cornbury.
3. Fri.   Hollingshead's bill.
          Indigent officers.
          Bedford Levels bill.
          Judge Tyrrell.
          Ecclesiastical Courts.
4. Sat.   Sir Trevor Williams's
          Petition.
          Supply.
(5. Sun.)
6. Mon.   Lenthall.
          Forest of Dean.
          Privileges.
7. Tues. Lenthall and Stonehouse.
          Lindsey Levels.
8. Wed.   Lucien Fowler.
          Bill for trial of peers.
          Customs.
          Lighthouses.
          Toleration.
9. Thur. Bill re Mr Taylor's estate.
          Sandys on grants of office.
          Birch on silk throwsters.
          Supply.
          Message from Duke of
          York.
10. Fri. Thanks to Duke of York.
          Fees in Chancery.
          Conventicles.
          Supply.
          Lords send down bills.
11. Sat. Hollingshead's bill.
          Vaughan's election.
          Lowering of interest.
          News of Harman.

*d*2

1668. APRIL (*continued*):
(12. Sun.)
13. Mon. Lindsey Levels.
         Debate on business to be
         settled before adjourn-
         ment.
14. Tues. Morton's complaint against
         Constantine.
         Rebuilding of London.
         Accounts.
         Penn and the war.
15. Wed. Whorwood's private bill.
         Silk throwsters.
         Highway robbery.
         Ashdown Forest.
         Vintners.
         Conventicles.
16. Thur. Whorwood.
         Forest of Dean.
         Miscarriages and Penn.
17. Fri. Taylor's bill.
         East India Co. against
         Skinner.
         Supply.
         Harman.
18. Sat. Fowler's bill.
         Richmond's allnage.
         London.
(19. Sun.)
20. Mon. Complaint against Heralds.
         Bennet's privilege.
         Richmond's allnage.
         Irish Adventurers heard.
21. Tues. Indigent officers.
         Howard on Penn.
         Harman.
22. Wed. Falling interest rates.
         Supply.
         Hollingshead's bill.
         Gerrard.
23. Thur. Habeas Corpus bill.
         Apsley's bill.
         Intestacy bill.
         Indigent officers.
         Cloth.
         Chamberlayne's patent.
         Irish Adventurers.
24. Fri. Crouch on Conventicles.
         Message from King.
         Habeas Corpus bill.
         Penn.
         East India Co. v. Skinner.
25. Sat. St Mark's Day.
         Supply.
         Amendments to bill.

1668. APRIL (*continued*):
(26. Sun.)
27. Mon. Lady Howard's Petition.
         Indigent officers.
         Supply.
28. Tues. Wool.
         Whorwood.
         Lucie's bill.
         King's money.
         Conventicles.
         Lady Howard.
29. Wed. Lucie's bill.
         Ashdown Forest.
         Supply.
(30. Thur. Omitted.)

1668. MAY:
1. Fri. Fowler's bill.
        Supply.
        Vaughan reads East India
        Co. Petition.
2. Sat. Lindsey Levels.
        Naturalisation bill.
        London.
        East India Co.
(3. Sun.)
4. Mon. Message from King.
        Privileges.
        Jurisdiction of Lords.
        Penn.
        London bill adjourned.
5. Tues. Bill re Earl of Sussex.
        Stanley's bill.
        London bill.
        Conference with Lords.
6. Wed. Juxon's bill.
        Gerrard's case.
        Whorwood's alimony.
        City bill.
7. Thur. Brouncker.
        Carr's bill.
        Debate on adjournment.
        Debate on conference
        with Lords.
8. Fri. Last Milward entry.
        Probert's case.
        Oakley.
        Trial of peers.
        Brouncker.
        Forest of Dean.
        Conference with Lords.
        Debate in Commons till
        4 a.m.
9. Sat. C.J. gives brief notice of
        adjournment.

ALPHABETICAL CHECK-LIST
OF PERSONS

Members of the House of Commons in capital letters, with the name
of their constituency next to their name.

Abbot, George.
  Archbishop of Canterbury, 1611–33.
  Mentioned 11 March 1667/8.

Agar, John or Thomas.
  Clerk of the Crown at Middle Temple.
  Milward delivered his election writ to him 17 September 1666.

Ailsbury, Robert Bruce, 1st Earl of.
  Lord-Lieutenant for Bedfordshire, etc.
  Bill for draining the Fens mentioned, 10 March 1667/8.
  His daughter, Lady Diana, whose husband, Sir Seymour Shirley (q.v.),
    is mentioned 11 January 1666/7. She later married Lord Roos (q.v.).

Albemarle, George Monk, 1st Duke of.
  Mentioned very frequently in debates on the war: 16, 21 October,
    16 November 1666, 28 January 1666/7, 19, 23, 24, 25, 31 October,
    7, 13, 21, 27 November, 19 December 1667. [His Duchess,
    2 March 1667/8.]
  Relation to Pride noted, 16 November 1666.

Allen, William.
  Adjutant-General of Horse and Commissioner for the settlement of
    Ulster during the Interregnum. An account of his career is given
    by C. H. Firth, *Clarke Papers*, I, 432–3, but this reference to Allen
    is not noticed by him.
  Mentioned 20, 23 April 1668.

Allsop, probably Thomas or Robert.
  Both of Middle Temple and Chesterfield.
  A Derbyshire name; indeed, Robert Milward's mother was an Allsop.
  Mentioned in connection with the Roos case, 21 January 1666/7.

ANCRAM, Charles Carr (Ker), Earl of. Wigan.
  Court party.
  24 November 1666. On de Leure, the Papist.
  29 January 1666/7. Takes Stanley's bill to the Lords.
  23 October 1667. Sent with others to thank Rupert.
  30 October 1667. On recusants.
  31 October 1667. Brings in Rupert's narrative.
  7 November 1667. Takes Sandys's bill to the Lords.

Andrews, John.
  Of the Bailiff's Office. "A mariner of Barking" (Pepys).
  Mentioned 23 November 1667.

Andrews, Bishop Lancelot. See Bishops, Winchester.

Anglesey, Arthur Annesley, 1st Earl of.
Vice-Treasurer, Receiver-General for Ireland, etc. (*D.N.B.*).
29 November 1667. Report of speech against impeachment of Clarendon.

Anselm, Saint.
Archbishop of Canterbury, 1093–1109 (*D.N.B.*).
Mentioned 29 October 1667.

Antrim, Randall Macdonnell, 2nd Earl and 1st Marquis of.
A great profiteer in Irish lands; a Catholic, and much disliked both by Ormonde and the Adventurers. He was, however, confirmed in his possessions, 1663. A full account of Ormonde's views on his case is in Carte, IV, 154 ff.
Mentioned during the debates on the Adventurers' Petition, 20, 23 April 1668.

APSLEY, Sir Allen. Thetford.
A Cavalier. Related by marriage to Colonel John Hutchinson (*D.N.B.*).
21 October 1667. Affirms Captain Cock's statement.
19 November 1667, 23 April 1668. On money he lent Charles I.

Archbishop of Canterbury. See Abbot; Anselm; Arundel; Cranmer; Juxon; Laud; Sheldon, Gilbert, who is, of course, the Archbishop referred to by Milward himself as his host at Lambeth, etc.

Archer, Judge John.
Chief Justice of Common Pleas, 1663.
Mentioned 2 December 1667.

Arlington, Henry Bennet, 1st Earl of.
Mentioned 25, 31 October 1667, 14, 15 February 1667/8.

Arlington, Lady Isabella.
Of Nassau. Daughter of M. Beverwaert (said by Clarendon, *Cont.* p. 1220, to be a natural son of Prince Maurice).
Naturalisation of, mentioned 4, 6, 12, 24 October 1666.

ARNLEY (ERNLEY), Sir John. Cricklade. Court Party.
27 February, 12 March 1667/8. To lay a tax on wine.
11 March 1667/8. On Government and religion.

Arundel, Thomas.
Archbishop of Canterbury, 1396–1414, and Lord Chancellor (*D.N.B.*).
Mentioned 29 October 1667, 29 November 1667.

Ash, James.
Son of Jo. Ash of Goldsmiths' Hall (see Beaven's *Aldermen*).
27, 28 March 1668. Petition against by Wanklin.

ASHBURNHAM, Sir John. Sussex.
  A Cavalier and official (*D.N.B.*) dismissed for bribery.
  19 November 1667. Accused of taking £500 from the wine
    merchants.
  22 November 1667. Dismissed the House.
  2 December 1667.
Ashley, Anthony Ashley Cooper, Lord.
  Later 1st Earl of Shaftesbury. Country party (*D.N.B.*).
  29 November 1667. Speech in House of Lords reported on im-
    peachment.
Ashton, Robert.
  High Sheriff of Derbyshire, 1664–5.
  Mentioned 17 September 1666.
ATKINS, Sir Robert. East Looe.
  Later a judge. Court party.
  13, 15 October 1666. On Bristol election and Cleveland.
  11 January 1666/7. On Austin and May, and for Higgins.
  22 January 1666/7. Impeachment of Mordaunt.
  24 January 1666/7. On Chune's case.
  28 January 1666/7. Reports from Lords on Mordaunt.
  31 January 1666/7. Again on Mordaunt.
  14 October 1667. For Clarendon.
  29 October 1667. Certioraries to the Lords.
  8 November 1667. For Clarendon.
  6 December 1667. In the Chair.
  10 December 1667. On the Irish Adventurers.
  29 February 1667/8. To lay a tax on the vintners.
  3 March 1667/8. Against Heblethwaite's bill.
  11 March 1667/8. For indulgence, "to little purpose".
  16 April 1668. Against Penn.
  24 April, 2, 7, 8 May 1668. Concerned in the Skinner case.
Attorney-General. See Palmer.
Aubrey, Captain Hopkins.
  Mentioned 6 May 1668. See *C.J.* 6 May 1668.
AUSTIN, Robert. Winchelsea.
  See also May. The Winchelsea election dispute. See *C.J.* under same
    dates. Country party.
  9, 11 January 1666/7.
Austin, Thomas ("the late").
  Trustee for lands granted by Charles II to repay Apsley.
  Mentioned by Apsley, 23 April 1668. Cf. *C.J.* VIII, 612, etc.
Backwell, Alderman Edward. See Blackwell.
Bacon, Francis, Lord St Albans (*D.N.B.*).
  Impeached 1621.
  Mentioned 6 February 1666/7, 29 October 1667.

Banckert, Captain Adriaen van.
The Dutch commander mentioned 31 October 1667.

Barclay, Sir William (and many spellings, *D.N.B.* Berkeley).
Mentioned in connection with attacks on Penn, 14, 21, 24 April, 4 May 1668.

Barker, Alderman William.
"A proud, cross, unmannerly but artful and indefatigable man" (Carte, IV, 314).
Concerned in a matter of lands in Ireland with Vernon (q.v.), 31 October 1667, 19 February 1667/8.

Barrett. See Bradshaw.

BATTEN, Sir William.   Rochester.
Admiral; regarded as a knave by Pepys. Died 1667 (*D.N.B.*).
Mentioned 29 November 1667.

Beckham (Bircham), John.
Of Norfolk. See also H.M.C. 8th Report, p. 121 b.
Bill mentioned 20, 25 November 1667, 18 March 1667/8.

Belknap, Judge.
Sir Robert Belknappe, Chief Justice of Common Pleas, 1375 ff. See Arundel. Trial, 1389.
Mentioned 29 November 1667.

Bellingham.
Milward may have confused Sir Daniel, formerly Lord Mayor of Dublin, and Deputy to Anglesey (q.v.), with R. Bellings (Carte, IV, 208). Both were concerned in Irish affairs. Mentioned 23 April 1668.

Bennet, one "Mr" (probably a Member of the House).
23 November 1667. Evidence about a Jesuit.

Bennet, John.
Collector of hearth money in the city of London.
A witness in the bribery case, 22 November 1667, and compare *C.S.P.D.* 1667/8, p. 58.

BENNET, Sir John.   Wallingford.
Later Baron Ossulston. Court party.
11 December 1667, 21 April 1668. On indigent officers.
12 February 1667/8. A foolish libel discovered in a packet of letters seized at the door by Cooper.
20 April 1668. On privilege.

Berkeley, Lord.
George, Earl of Berkeley, whose daughter's marriage to King-mill Lucy is mentioned 28 April 1668.

Berkley, Mr.
A witness in the Roos case, 26 November 1666.

Bertie, Montague.
Earl of Lindsey, great Lord Chamberlain. See Lindsey. Father of
10th Baron and 17th Earl of Crawford and Lindsey.

Beverley, Sir Thomas.
One of the Irish Commissioners.
Accused of denying the King's interest in Ireland, 20, 23 April 1668.

Bierly (Byerley), Colonel Anthony.
Of Michridge Grange, Durham. See Cosins, II, 155, 237.
Concerned with Dr Wharton's and Perkins's case, 9, 12 November
1667.

Bigland, the brothers Edward and Henry.
Sons of the Rector of Leake, Nottinghamshire. Well-known lawyers
of Gray's Inn.
7 May 1668. Milward goes to them about a bond for £500.

Birch, Colonel John. Penryn.
Country party. Burnet says Birch was concerned in the excise and
was very rough and bold (*D.N.B.*).
With the exceptions noted below he speaks in this period on finance.
22 September, 24, 31 October, 2, 30 November 1666.
14 October, 9 November 1667. For Clarendon.
29 November, 14, 17 December 1667, 26, 27 February 1667/8.
11 March 1667/8. For the dissenters.
12 (twice), 17, 28, 30 March 1667/8.
4, 8 April 1668. ("Impertinent") for indulgence.
9 April 1668 (twice). For the silk throwsters and for a tax on strong
waters.
11 April, 1 May 1668.
2 May 1668. Against naturalising of Jews.
4 May 1668. Sent to the Lords.

Birkenhead (Berkenhead), Sir John. Wilton.
Court party (*D.N.B.*).
24 January 1666/7. On Chune.
23 November 1667. Defends the Water Bailiffs.
22 February 1667/8. Quotes Batten on payment by ticket.
11 March 1667/8. For reading the reasons for the Declaration of
Breda, and again on standing armies and toleration.
12 March 1667/8. No member to be a collector of taxes.
21 April 1668. Against attack on Sandwich.
5 May 1668. For Stanley.

Bishops:
Of Durham: John Cosin, 1660–72.
Favoured the Roos divorce.
Mentioned 31 October, 21 November, 19 December 1667,
13 February 1667/8, 26 March 1668.
Much information about the Durham affairs mentioned here may
be found in Cosin's *Correspondence*.

Bishops (*continued*):
  Of Exeter: Seth Ward, 1662–7.
    Mentioned 2 October 1666.
  Of Hereford: Herbert Croft, 1661–91.
    Mentioned 21 November 1667.
  Of Llandaff (llandaste): Theophilus Field, 1619–27.
    Mentioned in connection with Francis Bacon, Lord St Albans (q.v.).
  Of London: Humphrey Henchman, 1663–75.
    Mentioned 24 October 1666.
  Of Norwich: Edward Reynolds, 1661–76.
    Mentioned 17 October 1667.
    (H. le Spencer, 1370–1406, q.v.)
  Of Peterborough: Joseph Henshaw, 1663–79.
    Mentioned 24 September 1666.
  Of Rochester: John Dolben (Dalbin), 1666–83.
    Preached before elevation to Bishopric: see Dalbin.
    Mentioned as Bishop, 29 November 1667.
  Of St Asaph: Henry Glenham, 1667–70.
    Mentioned 21 November 1667.
  Of St David's: William Lucas, 1660–78.
    Mentioned 21 November 1667.
  Of Salisbury: Seth Ward, promoted from Exeter, 1667–89.
    May be meant in disputed election of October 1666 (see under
    Exeter above).
  Of Winchester: Lancelot Andrews, 1618–1626.
    Quoted 18 March 1667/8.
  Of Winchester: Brian Duppa, 1660–2.
    Mentioned 3 December 1667, 11, 15 February 1667/8, 2 March
    1667/8, 2 April 1668.
  Of Winchester: George Morley, promoted from Worcester, 1662–84.
    In disgrace after fall of Clarendon.
    Mentioned 21 November 1666.

Black Rod. Sir John Eyton.
  Mentioned 21 September 1666, 8 February 1666/7, 29 July 1667,
  10 February 1667/8, etc.

Blackwell (Backwell), Edward.
  The Alderman and financier (*D.N.B.*).
  Mention is made of land mortgaged to Blackwell in Hackney and
  Stepney by Lord Cleveland (q.v.).
  15 October 1666. Much about Lord Cleveland's debts may be found
  in the *Cal. of Com. for Compounding*, p. 2156, etc.
  2 December 1667. Mentioned in the bribery case.

Blewet, Mary. See Stonehouse.

BLUDWORTH, Sir Thomas.   Southwark.
  Vintner, Alderman (1658), late Lord Mayor.

BLUDWORTH, Sir Thomas. Southwark (*continued*).
26, 29 November 1667. Mentioned in connection with Colonel Sandys's (q.v.) information about a "cheat upon the king".

Bodville, John.
Son of the Earl of Radnor. Married Anne Russell.
Estate of, mentioned frequently. Often referred to as the case of Roberts and Winn, contending parties in the dispute. See also *C.J.* and H.M.C. 8th Report, *passim* 25 October, 12, 19, 21, 22, 27, 28 November, 7 December 1666.

BOSCAWEN, Edward. Truro.
Country party (?) (*D.N.B.*).
31 October 1667. For Pett.
11 March 1667/8. For the dissenters.
11 April 1668. On the lowering of interest rates.

Bradshaw, Godfrey; and Barrett.
Mentioned 9 November 1667, as traitors who destroyed dykes and enclosures, and see also p. 121, n. 1.

BRANDON, Lord. See Gerrard.

BRERETON, William, Lord. Chester City.
Baron of Laughlin in Ireland.
Irish peerage referred to, 14 March 1667/8.

Brice (Bryce, Boyse), Mr.
A long account of the case about the Manor of Witney, Oxfordshire, which Clarendon had leased from the Bishop of Winchester, may be found in *C.J.* IX, 74. Lister (III, 484) quotes Clarendon who had sub-let the Manor to Mr Granger.
Mentioned 3 December 1667.

Bridgeman, Sir Orlando.
Lord Keeper, 1667–72 (*D.N.B.*).
Mentioned 10, 15, 30 October, 19 December 1667, 14 February 1667/8, 30 March 1668.

Bristol, Mayor of, Thomas Sangton, Esq.
Mentioned in disputed election case, 31 October 1666.

Bristoll (Bristow), Thomas. See Pierpont.

BRODERICK (Branderick, etc.), Sir Allen. Orford.
Commissioner for Ireland, and said to be a profiteer in Irish lands. Court Party. Later Lord Midleton (*D.N.B.*).
26 October 1667. Excuses Clarendon.
26 March 1668. His liberty to go to Ireland debated.
20 April 1668. Mentioned by Howard of Escrick (q.v.).

Brooke, Laurence.
Almost certainly Laurence Rooke, of *C.J.* 10 and 11 March 1667/8. Bill to sell land.

BROOKE, Sir Robert.   Aldeburgh, Suffolk.
   Country party.
   22 January 1666/7. Chairman of committee of enquiry on Fire.
   23, 31 October, 9, 13 November 1667. Chairman of enquiry into
      miscarriage of the war.
   10 December 1667. Brings in the Irish Adventurers' Petition.
   14, 17 February 1667/8. On miscarriages of the war again.
   18 February 1667/8. "And gang" for Temple's Triennial bill.
   20, 21 February 1667/8. To go to the Duke about Harman.
   24 February 1667/8. On selling offices.
   30 March 1668. To obstruct vote on supply.
   17 April 1668. Brings in Petition against Skinner.
   22 April 1668. With Williams opposes falling interest.
   28 April 1668. To make the Conventicle Act apply to Papists.
   7, 8 May 1668. Brouncker's impeachment.

BROUNCKER, Henry.   New Romney.
   Expelled the House, 21 April 1668. "A hard, vicious man" (Evelyn).
   Attacked for his share in miscarriages of the war, 19, 21 October,
      4, 14 November 1667, 17, 21 April, 7, 8 May 1668.

Brouncker, William, Viscount.
   Commissioner for the Navy, and Admiral, friend of Pepys (D.N.B.).
   Mentioned 22 February, 5 March 1667/8; defended by Pepys.

BROWN, Sir Adam.   Surrey.
   Court party.
   10, 24 April 1668. On penalties of dissenters.
   5 May 1668. On Sussex's bill.

BROWN, Sir Richard.   Ludgershall.
   An Alderman (D.N.B.).
   26 October 1666. On London Fire enquiry.
   23 November 1667. Defends the Water Bailiffs against Sir William
      Ryder's petition.

Brown, Judge Samuel.
   Justice of Common Pleas.
   Mentioned 3 December 1667.

Bruce, Lady Diana. See Ailsbury.

Bryce. See Brice.

BUCKHURST, Charles Sackville, Baron.   East Grinstead.
   Later Earl of Dorset. Court Party.
   23 October 1667. On committee of enquiry into the miscarriages of
      the war.

Buckingham, George Villiers, Duke of.
   The 1st Duke (D.N.B.).
   Mentioned 8 November 1667, in connection with impeachment
      precedents.

Buckingham, George Villiers, Duke of:
The 2nd Duke (*D.N.B.*).
Mentioned 13 October 1666, as listening at the back door to a debate of the Commons.
26 November 1666, 21 January 1666/7, as opposing Lord Roos.
19 December 1667, as one of the Commissioners to pass bills.
14 February 1667/8, as attacked by a libeller.
18 March 1667/8, duel of.

Bulckeley, W. and William Barker.
31 October 1667. In case of Irish Adventurers.

BULLER, Francis. Saltash, Cornwall.
7 May 1668. On a longer adjournment.

BURWELL (BURELL), Dr Thomas. Ripon.
Court party. Married stepdaughter of the Dean of Durham, Chancellor of the diocese of Durham.
9 November 1667. Perkins's petition.
26 March 1668. On Durham bill.

Butler, Mr.
9 December 1667. Obstructs the bill for erection of pest-houses at Cambridge.

Cambridge, Mayor of, John Herring, 1666/7.
Mentioned in connection with the erection of pest-houses, 8, 24 November 1666.

Cambridge, University and Vice-Chancellor (D. Wilford).
Mentioned in connection with the pest-houses, 8 November 1666.

Campden, Lord.
Baptist Noell, 2nd Baron, etc. His fourth wife was daughter of the Earl of Lindsey. A trustee of the Lindsey estate. See also Noell.
Mentioned 26, 30 October 1666, 28 January 1666/7.

Caron, Margaret (Zenooks).
See Lister, II, 538; one of Clarendon's acquisitions since 1660 had been Caron House, formerly the property of Sir Noel Caron.
11 November 1667.

Carpenter, William.
With Andrews in the Bailiff's Office, and a farmer of excise.
23 November 1667.

CARR, Sir Robert. Lincolnshire.
Brother-in-law of Arlington. Court party, but acting with Brooke and his group at the time.
8 November 1667. Against Clarendon.
14, 28 November 1667. Against Lindsey Levels bill.
16 November 1667. On Clarendon's impeachment.
18 December 1667. Teller for Noes on banishment of Clarendon.
15 February 1667/8. On Lindsey Levels.

CARR, Sir Robert, (*continued*):
 18 February 1667/8. For Temple's Triennial bill.
 20 February 1667/8. To Duke about Harman.
 2, 4, March 1667/8. On bill about Irish cattle.
 6 March 1667/8. Sent to the Commissioners of Accounts. Dines with
  Milward.
 11 March 1667/8. Says that dissenters should define their wants.
 12 March 1667/8. On excise.
 13 March 1667/8. Against Conventicle Act.
 26 March 1668. On miscarriages of the war.
 30 March 1668. To allow wool houses on Romney Marsh.
 3 April 1668. Complaint against the judges.
 7, 13 April 1668. On Lindsey Levels bill.
 5 May 1668. To desire the Lords to have a conference.
 7 May 1668. On a church in St Martin's parish.

Carr, Stephen and William.
 In Gerrard's case (q.v.) (*C.J.* 17 December 1667).
 Stephen was one of Pepys's clerks mentioned 17 December 1667,
  21, 24 February 1667/8.
 William, clerk to the Life Guards (H.M.C. 8th Report, p. 115).
 12, 22 April, 6 May 1668.

Carter, Sir John.
 Of Worcester.
 Mentioned 18 February 1667/8, as petitioning against Milward and
  Theswell, offenders against the Irish Cattle Act.

CARTERET, Sir George.   Portsmouth.
 Treasurer of the Navy, 1669. Court party.
 26 September 1666. Brings in naval accounts.
 31 October 1667. Mentioned.
 22 February 1667/8. Against Carr, and on payment by ticket.
 3 April 1668. Dines with Milward.
 23 April 1668. Ordered to bring in accounts.

CARY (CAREW), Sir Nicholas.   Gatton.
 18 December 1667. Against banishment of Clarendon.
 12 March 1667/8. On discovery of those who had cheated the King.

Cary, Sir William.
 21 January 1666/7. Gives evidence in Roos case.
 21 February 1667/8. Presents Carr's petition.

CASTLETON, Lord.   Lincolnshire.
 Sir George Sanderson, an Irish Viscount.
 10 March 1667/8. Against Lord Ailsbury's bill for draining the Fens.

CAVENDISH, Henry. See Ogle, Lord.

Cavendish, John.
 A fishmonger in the reign of Richard II.
 Mentioned 3 March 1667/8. See de la Pole, Michael.

CAVENDISH, Lord William. Derbyshire.
Son of the 3rd Earl of Devonshire and Elizabeth Cecil. Married to
a daughter of the Duke of Ormond. Afterwards 1st Duke of
Devonshire.
13, 14 December 1667. Against Clarendon.

Chamberlain, the Lord. Edward Montagu, 2nd Earl of Manchester.
Mentioned 30 October, 28 November 1666.

Chamberlayne, Dr Peter.
30 October, 11 November 1667, 26, 28 March, 23 April 1668. Patent
applied for, etc.

Chapman, Sir Christopher. See Clifton.
7 December 1667. Land sold to Gervas Clifton.
See Waters, *Wakefield in the Seventeenth Century*, p. 121.

Charles I.
Mentioned 30 January 1666/7, 26 October 1667, 23 April 1668.

Charles II.
Mentioned constantly.
Speeches: 21 September 1666, 29 July, 10, 15 October 1667, 10, 17
February 1667/8, 23 April 1668.

CHARLTON, Sir Job. Ludlow.
Court party: see 23 October 1666. He was a lawyer.
All speeches except those specified are on election disputes or
privilege.
4 October 1666.
18 October 1666. On committee about chimney money.
23 October.
24 January, 7 February 1666/7.
8, 20, 22 November 1667.
18 December 1667. On committee for bill of banishment.
17 March 1667/8. Against taxing retailers.
7, 8 May 1668.

CHETWIND, Walter or William. Stafford Borough.
Court party. An iron-master. (Wedgwood, *Stafford M.P.s.*)
8 April 1668. Fowler's bill.

CHEYNEY, Charles. Great Marlow.
Connected by marriage with the Cavendishes. Marvell calls him a
courtier (*Letters*, p. 321).
18 December 1667. Teller for Ayes, but see *C.J.*, where Trevor is
given in seats.

Cholmondeleigh.
8 April 1668. Guardian to Richard Fowler (q.v.).

CHUNE (CHOWNE), Henry. Horsham, Sussex.
Court party (?).
14 January 1666/7. Privilege against Thomas White, a former
Parliament man.

CHUNE (*continued*):
24 January 1666/7. The same.
6 February 1666/7.
11 March 1667/8. Against the dissenters.

CHURCHILL, Sir Winston (Vincent). Weymouth.
Father of the Duke of Marlborough. Court party (*D.N.B.*).
26 March 1668. One of the Commissioners for the Irish settlement.

Clare, Gilbert Holles, 3rd Earl of.
Owned land in Derbyshire (Add. MSS. 34306, f. 24d); married a
Pierpont.
10, 11, 19 December 1667, 15 February 1667/8, Bill to sell land.

Clarendon, Edward Hyde, Earl of.
Chancellor until August 1667. Mentioned very frequently.
8, 15 October, 22, 28, 30 November 1666, 29 July 1667.
Throughout October, November and December 1667. Proceedings
against.
11 February 1667/8.
2 April 1668. Case against (see Stonehouse).
7 May 1668. Case cited.

Clarkton, Mr.
1 April 1668. Bill with Sir Gervas Clifton for Wakefield enclosure.

Clement, Thomas (?).
20 April 1668. Mentioned by Doleman (q.v.), but I think the copyist
has muddled a reference, possibly to a house near St Clement's.
C.J. 20 April, mentions Doleman as making a complaint.

CLERGES (CLARGES), Sir Thomas. Southwark.
Brother-in-law of Monk (*D.N.B.*).
7 March 1667/8. On bill to prevent highway robbery.
23 April 1668. On indigent officers.

Cleveland, Thomas Wentworth, Earl of.
1591–1667. A Cavalier (*D.N.B.*). *Cal. of Com. for Compounding*,
p. 2156, etc.
15 October 1666. Mortgages in Stepney and Hackney.
26 February, 4 March 1667/8. Bill to sell land to pay debts.

CLIFFORD, Sir Thomas. Totnes.
Court party. Comptroller (q.v.). Afterwards Lord High Treasurer
(*D.N.B.*).
31 October 1666. Moved for a general excise.
27 November 1667. Against Downing's proposals for trade with
Scotland.
11, 13 December 1667. In Keeling's case.
17 March 1667/8. Against taxing goods at the Customs house.
7 May 1668. On the inconveniences of adjournment.

CLIFTON, Clifford.   East Retford.
3 March 1667/8. On bill for indemnifying Sheriffs.

Clifton, Sir Gervas.
7 December 1667, 1 April 1668. With Mr Clarkton in the matter of enclosures at Wakefield.

Cock, Captain George.
(*D.N.B.*).
Mentioned in debates on division of the Fleet, 19, 21 October, 20 February 1667/8, 17 April 1668.

Coke (Cooke), Sir Edward.
1552–1634. (*D.N.B.*)
Cases referred to 29 November 1667, 3 March 1667/8.

COKE (COOK), Robert.   King's Lynn.
Son-in-law of Danby. Court party.
28 February 1667/8, 8 April, 7 May 1668. Against the dissenters.

Colchester, Captain John. See Winter.
12 November 1667. Petition about Forest of Dean.

COLEMAN, Richard.   Salisbury.
Recorder of Salisbury. Died before 1673.
11 January 1666/7. Excellent speech on Austin and May dispute.
21, 22 February 1667/8. In Gerrard-Carr dispute.

COLLINGWOOD, Daniel.   Berwick-on-Tweed.
Election dispute, 4 October, 15 November 1666.

Comptroller. See Clifford.
Mentioned 3 December 1667.

Conningham, Thomas, and Dick (Dyck Lewis).
Irish Adventurers; affairs described in Carte, IV, 315 ff.
Mentioned 19 February 1667/8. Irish State Papers, etc.

Constantine, William.
A lawyer who sat for Poole, but had election voided 1661. Accused of sedition by Morton (q.v.), 29 February 1667/8.
14 April 1668.

Cooke, Colonel Edward.
One of the Irish Commissioners.
A trustee of the Lindsey estate in Ireland.
Mentioned 19, 28 January 1666/7.

Cooper, John.
Receiver for indigent officers.
Mentioned 11 December 1667, 21 April 1668.

Cooper (another).
Mentioned as Keeper of the Door, 12 February 1667/8.

COPE, Sir Anthony.   Oxford County.
22 October 1666. On publication of Commons' debates.

CORNBURY, Henry Hyde, Lord.   Wiltshire.
Eldest son of Clarendon and successor in title (*D.N.B.*).
Mentioned in connection with the attacks by the Commons and others upon his father, 3 December 1667, 11, 12, 15 February, 2 March 1667/8, 2 April 1668.

Cosin, John.   See Bishop of Durham.

Cotton, "My Coz".   See Introduction p. xviii, and Milward, Robert.

COTTON, Sir John.   Huntingdon Borough.   Court Party.
27 February 1667/8.   For a luxury tax.
11 March 1667/8.   The seditiousness of toleration.

COVENTRY, Henry.   Droitwich.
Court party.   Later Secretary of State (*D.N.B.*).
11 January 1666/7.   Against the Mayor of Winchelsea.
6, 7 February 1666/7.   On Mordaunt.   On supply.
23, 26 October 1667.   Defends Clarendon.
31 October 1667.   Coventry-Seymour incident referred to.
7, 11, 17 November 1667.   Defends Clarendon.
14 December 1667.   For relaxing navigation laws to help rebuilding of city.
17 February 1667/8.   Quotes Rawleigh (q.v.).
2 March 1667/8.   To receive evidence in Lenthall case (q.v.).
11 March 1667/8.   For a moderate comprehension.
16 March 1667/8.   Against the Irish Adventurers.
10 April 1668.   On fees in Chancery.
20 April 1668.   On privilege.
23 April 1668.   Reproves Howard for attack on Irish Commissioners, of whom he had been one.
24 April 1668.   Against expelling Penn.

COVENTRY, Sir John.   Weymouth and Melcombe Regis.
Grandson of Lord Thomas Coventry (*D.N.B.*).
Election reported, 20 November 1667.

Coventry, Lord Thomas.
Lord Keeper (*D.N.B.*).
Mentioned 4 December 1667.

COVENTRY, Sir William.   Great Yarmouth.
Son of the Lord Keeper and brother of Henry. A country party leader.
11 January 1666/7.   Against Mayor of Winchelsea.
25 July 1667.   Against Tomkins's motion.
14 October 1667.   Against Clarendon.
19 October 1667.   Division of the Fleet not a miscarriage.
22 October 1667.   We are not sufficiently supplied with seamen.
25 October 1667.   The King has stopped horses and men going to France.
31 October 1667.   Mentioned as Treasurer of the Navy in debate on miscarriages.

COVENTRY, Sir William (*continued*):
4 November 1667. Mentioned.
14 December 1667. Opposes his brother over timber imports.
17 February 1667/8. On division of the Fleet.
24 February 1667/8. Mentioned.
27 February 1667/8. On treasurers.
17 March 1667/8. Against laying a tax at the Customs house.
7 May 1668. On adjournment.

CRANBOURN, James Cecil, Viscount. Hertfordshire.
Country Party.
Mentioned 6 May 1668.

Cranmer, Thomas.
Archbishop of Canterbury 1533–56.
Mentioned 11 March 1667/8.

Cresset, John.
Of Temple.
Mentioned as a witness (*C.J.* IX, 22, 24), 22 November 1667, in connection with Hartlib-Bourchier case.

Cromwell, Oliver.
Lord Protector.
Mentioned 19, 21 January 1666/7.
26 October 1667, 7 November. Clarendon said to have helped.
22 February, 4, 11, 12, 16 March 1667/8, 23 April 1668.

Crooke, Sir George.
Judge and law reporter. 1560–1642 (*D.N.B.*).
Mentioned 15 October 1667.

CROUCH, Thomas.   Cambridge University.
Court party.
11 January 1666/7. Chairman of committee and reporter of Shirley's bill.
15 January 1666/7. Shirley's bill.
7 December 1667. On hearth money.
11 December 1667. On Keeling.
12 March 1667/8. On Bedford Levels bill and Sir John Cutts.
14 March 1667/8. On hearth money.
27 March 1668. Reports from committee of a bill for the better regulation of hearth money.
24 April 1668. On Conventicles bill.

Crowder (or Croucher, Crowther, etc.), Dr.
Chaplain to the Duke of York and at the Restoration made parson of Treddington, Worcestershire. See Clarendon, *Cont.* p. 1269.
Case mentioned, fourteenth article against Clarendon, 7 November 1667.

Cutts, Sir John.
Of Childersley, Cambridge.

Cutts, Sir John (*continued*):
12 March 1667/8. Sandys moves he may be heard on the matter of the Bedford Levels.
(Compare *C.S.P.D.* 27 November 1667.)

Dalbin (Dolben), Dr John.
Dean of Westminster and then Bishop of Rochester (q.v.) and Archbishop, etc. "Of heavenly eloquence" (*D.N.B.*). Married Sheldon's niece.
Mentioned in connection with sermons to Parliament, 24 September, 3, 4, 11 October 1666.
See also Rochester, Bishop of.

DALTON, John. Derby.
18 January 1666/7. Reported as a defaulter; defended by Grey as being old and lame of gout.

Dawe, Captain Henry.
Of the "Princess."
Bill mentioned 23 November 1667.

Dawes, Sir Thomas.
His executors mentioned, 8 April 1668.
Compare *C.S.P.D.* 1 April 1668, for a letter from Jane Dawes to Arlington.

de la Pole, Michael.
1st Earl of Suffolk, 1330–89.
Complained of to the House of Commons by John Cavendish and impeached, 1386.
Mentioned 29 October 1667, with William de la Pole; 12, 29 November 1667, 3 March, 1667/8.
See also Cavendish.

de la Pole, William.
4th Earl and 1st Duke of Suffolk, 1396–1450 (*D.N.B.*).
Impeached on very similar grounds to those used against Clarendon.
Mentioned 29 October, 15 November 1667.
See also de la Pole, Michael.

de Leure (many spellings).
A Romanist.
Mentioned 24, 28 November 1666.

DENHAM, Sir John.   Old Sarum.
The poet (*D.N.B.*).
30 October 1667. Tells a story and speaks against Recusancy bill.
7 November 1667. Defends Clarendon.
15 November 1667. Speaks on Lords' refusal to commit Clarendon.
11 March 1667/8. Toleration means a standing army.
13 March 1667/8. For Conventicle Act.
17 April 1668. The evidence against Brouncker false.

De Witt, John.
The Stadholder.
Report of mutiny against, 5 December 1666.

Dick. See Conningham.

DOLEMAN, Sir Thomas. Reading.
Court party.
20 April 1668. Complains of the Heralds' Office.

DOWDESWELL, Richard. Tewkesbury.
Country party.
14 October 1667. With Maynard. Atkins and Marvell speak against
thanking the King for dismissing Clarendon.
6 March 1667/8. Bill about his son (see Wimbleton).
See p. 113, n. for speech about Clarendon.

DOWNING, Sir George. Morpeth.
Diplomat and writer. A frequent speaker on trade.
Court party (D.N.B.).
28 September 1666. Against coining plate.
8 October 1666. On restraint of French and Dutch commodities.
9 October 1666. Carried message to Lords.
24 October 1666. Against excise on tobacco.
10 November 1666. To be sent to Lords with bill about coining
money.
17 November 1666. On burying corpses.
5 December 1666. On Irish Cattle Act "excellently."
10 January 1666/7. On coining plate.
2 February 1666/7. On enlarging Thames Street.
15 October 1667. To encourage loans of money to the Exchequer.
Bill read 20 November 1667.
7 November 1667. On money lent to the King.
26 November 1667. On hides and leather.
27 November 1667. On trade with Scotland.
12 December 1667. On hides and leather.
20 February 1667/8. On wine taxes.
29 February 1667/8. On wine taxes.
28 March 1668. On exports.

DOYLEY, Sir William. Great Yarmouth.
Court party.
22 September 1666. Opposes Irish Cattle bill.
28 September 1666. Talks to Milward about Irish Cattle bill.
23 October 1667. Reports on conversation with Dutch Ambassador
(q.v.) on release of prisoners.

Drummond, Major-General.
4 December 1666. Letter to Ruthe about Scottish Covenanters
mentioned.

DUNCOMBE, Sir John. Bury St Edmund's.
> Court party. Chancellor of the Exchequer. Treasurer to the Ordinance.
> 26 September 1666. Brings in accounts of ordinance.
> 2 October 1666. Bill to allow sale of gunpowder by licence only causes strong debate.
> 11 October 1666. Presents accounts.
> 22 October 1667. On division of the Fleet.
> 14 February 1667/8. Reports about a libel.
> 17 February 1667/8. On miscarriages at Sheerness.
> 17 April 1668. The House to name the commission for £300,000.

Duppa, Brian. See Bishop of Winchester.

Durham, Bishop of. See Bishop of Durham.

Durham, Mayor of.
> 1666. Thomas Mascell.
> 1667. Henry Wanless.
> Mentioned 11 January 1666/7.

Dutch Ambassador.
> Conrad Van Beuningen, almost immediately replaced by Jan Meerman.
> Mentioned 23 October 1667.

Edward III.
> Mentioned 9 November 1667.

Edward VI. See Cranmer.

EGERTON (EDGERTON), Randell or Randolph. Staffordshire.
> A soldier. Court party.
> 26 November 1666. On Roos bill.
> 28 February 1667/8. Warns the House against sectaries.
> 27 April 1668. For Lady Howard.

Elizabeth, Queen.
> Mentioned 30 October 1667; with Burleigh in debate on Conventicle Act, 11 March 1667/8.

Eliot, Sir John.
> Died 1632 (*D.N.B.*).
> Mentioned, with Valentine, 15 October, 12 November 1667.

Elliott, Captain Thomas.
> Of the "Saphire", "Revenge", etc.
> A witness, 20 February 1667/8, 17 April 1668.

Elsmore (Ellesmere), Lord Chancellor.
> Sir Thomas Egerton, 1540–1617.
> Mentioned 4 December 1667.

Emperiall (Imperiali), Jo.
> "The Genoese ambassador." Killed in the time of Richard II, and the cause of a famous precedent (3 Rich. II, no. 18).
> Case mentioned 9 November 1667 (cf. Grey, 1, 11, 30).

Emperors Theodosius and Honorius.
Mentioned 11 March 1667/8.

ERLY. See Irby.

ERNLEY. See Arnley.

Essex, Countess of.
Widow of the Parliamentary general, and wife of Sir Thomas
Higgins. After her death he attempted to get Parliamentary
decision in his favour in some disputed property left by her. See
Higgins.
8 October 1666.

Exchequer, Christopher Turner, Chief Baron of.
Mentioned 11 February 1667/8.

Exeter, Bishop of. See Bishop of Exeter.

Exeter, R. Cecil, Earl of.
2 October 1666. Mentioned in election dispute.

FAGG, Sir John.   New Steyning.
(D.N.B.)
29 April 1668. Ashdown Forest bill.

(Fance, Bonham.
Estate mentioned 12 October 1666, though Milward had forgotten
the name; cf. C.J. same date.)

FANSHAWE, Thomas, 2nd Viscount.   Hertfordshire.
Court party.
25 November 1667. About bribery.
11 March 1667/8. Against toleration.

Farmer, Samuel.
Mentioned 7 November 1667 (cf. Lister II 460–2).

Faucis, Simon. A Jew.
Mentioned 2 May 1668.

Fauconberg, Thomas Belasyse, Earl.
Son-in-law of Cromwell (D.N.B.).
8 October 1666. Duel with Sir Thomas Osbourne mentioned.

FELTON, Sir (Thomas) or Henry (cf. C.J. same date).   Suffolk.
Son of Sir Francis Felton. Court party.
26 February 1667/8. Breach of privilege.
13 March 1667/8.

FINCH, Sir Heneage.   Oxford University.
Court party. "Mr Sollicitor." Lord Keeper, 1673. Afterwards 1st
Earl of Nottingham. Milward much admired Finch.
25 September 1666. Against appointing committee to examine
causes of London Fire. Against Robert Milward on Certioraries.
5 October 1666. "Excellent" on Irish Cattle bill.
18 October 1666. Chimney money committee.
31 October 1666. "Excellent" on excise and against land tax.

FINCH, Sir Heneage (*continued*):
  12 November 1666. To be of Roos's counsel.
  11 January 1666/7. "Excellent" against Higgins's bill.
  12 January 1666/7. "Excellent" on conference with Lords.
  28 January 1666/7. "Excellent" against denying counsel to Mordaunt.
  14 October, 11 November 1667. Against Clarendon.
  15 November 1667. The Lords not obliged to impeach.
  16 November 1667. Differs with Vaughan about power of King's Bench.
  4 December 1667. "Good" on Naturalisation bill.
  10 December 1667. Against petition of Irish Adventurers.
  29 February 1667/8. On retailers.
  6 March 1667/8. Against tunnage tax.
  18 March 1667/8. For Bishops.
  26 March 1668. For Churchill, and for retailers of wine.
  28 March 1668. Bill about retailers.
  2 May 1668. "Excellent" on Skinner affair, and against London bill.
  8 May 1668. One of the managers of conference about Skinner.

Finch, John, Lord Chief Justice.
  (*D.N.B.*). 1584–1660. Impeached 1640.
  Mentioned 29 October, 18, 29 November 1667.

Fitton, Alexander.
  For his famous case with Lord Gerrard see *D.N.B.* The case had a tragic end in 1712, when representatives of both contesting families were killed in a duel.
  Mentioned 11, 12 December 1667, 21, 22 February, 3, 13 March 1667/8.
  See also Gerrard, Lord Charles.

FITZHARDING, Sir Maurice Berkeley, afterwards Viscount. Wells.
  Court party. Keeper of the Privy Purse.
  Always mentioned in connection with the King's messages to the House, or the messages of the House to the King.
  3, 4 December 1667, 5 March 1667/8, 13 April 1668.

Fitzherbert, Captain.
  One of the Derbyshire family who had fought on the King's side with Milward during 1643/4.
  21, 28 November 1666. In connection with Moore's letter to the Archbishop.

FITZJAMES, John. Poole.
  14 April 1668. On Constantine (q.v.).

FITZWILLIAM, William, Lord. Peterborough.
  24 September, 2 October 1666. Election dispute with Palmer. Dispute decided "very clear for him" 8 November 1667; and cf. *C.J.* IX, 17.

Fleet, Warden of.
  Sir Jeremy Whichcott.
  (23 October 1667), 4 November 1667, 6 March 1667/8.
FORD, Sir Richard.   Southampton.
  A Londoner.   Court party.   Adversary of dissenters.
  6 March 1667/8.   Approves tunnage tax.
  7 May 1668.   Takes Mr Hampden down.
FORTESCUE, Francis or Edmund.   Plympton.
  23, 27 October 1666.   Plympton election dispute.
Fountain, Serjeant John.
  (*D.N.B.*)
  24 January 1666/7.   Concerned with the Bedford Levels bill.
Fowler, Lucien and Richard.
  8, 18 April, 1 May 1668.   Bill about guardianship (Temple and
    Gore, q.v.).
Frampton, Robert, Dr.
  Later Bishop of Gloucester, 1681–1690.   A tolerant man (*D.N.B.*).
  Mentioned in connection with his sermons to the Houses, 24 Sep-
    tember, 10 October, 11 October 1666.
France, King of.
  Louis XIV.
  Mentioned 22 September, 5 December 1666, 14, 24, 25, 26 October,
    4, 11 November 1667.
Frechville, Lord.
  Milward's predecessor as M.P. for Derbyshire.
  24 January 1666/7.   Concerned in the Bedford Levels bill.
  24 October 1667.   His troops, now disbanded, said to be going into
    service of King of France.
FROGMORTON.   See Throckmorton.
GARROWAY, William.   Chichester.
  An old Cavalier.   Generally acted in this reign as a member of the
    Country party (but see Marvell's *Letters*).
  24 September 1666.   Carries thanks of House to the King.
  29 October 1666.   On sale of chimney money.
  8 November 1666.   Proposes an eleven months' tax and a poll tax.
  7 December 1666.   Famous proviso to Poll bill.
  25 July 1667.   Seconds Tomkins.
  15 November 1667.   Against a special charge for Clarendon.
GEORGE, Lord.   Cirencester.
  See also Richard Gorges, as the copyist may not always have distin-
    guished between them.
  24 October 1667.   Against Colonel Sandys's Fen bill.
  12 March 1667/8.   Against an excise (as Mr George).
  17 April 1668.   Moves that the King should name the Commis-
    sioners.

Gerrard, Lord Charles.
  1st Baron Gerard of Brandon. Afterwards Earl of Macclesfield. An
  old Cavalier (*D.N.B.*).
  Dispute over Tamworth property with Alexander Fitton (q.v.) and
  Carr (q.v.) mentioned 12, 15 December 1667, 21, 22 February,
  3 March 1667/8, 22, 27 April, 6 May 1668.
  11 November 1667. Mentioned as telling King of France how
  valuable Dunkirk was.
Gerrard, Sir Gilbert.   Northallerton.
  Courtier and official. Married Bishop of Durham's daughter;
  manages bill for Durham elections.
  31 October 1667, 26 March, 6 May 1668.
Giles, Sir [Mompesson].
  "A member in Edward III's time."
  Milward has here confused Sir Giles Mompesson, whose monopoly
  of ale-houses was attacked by Parliament in 1621, and Richard
  Lyons, vintner, an associate of Lord Latimer, who was impeached
  by Parliament in 1376. Cf. Grey, I, 142, report of this debate.
  Vaughan mentions Mompesson.
  Mentioned 21 April 1668.
Glanvill, probably John.
  A lawyer and the son of the famous Sir John Glanvill (see *D.N.B.*),
  lawyer and Parliamentarian during the preceding reign and Civil
  Wars.
  Mentioned by Milward as "My Coz" 4 November 1666, and related
  to him through the Bourchiers.
Glyn (Glynne), Sir John.
  Serjeant-at-law. Died 15 November 1666 (see *C.S.P.D.* 1666/7 on
  that date).
  28 November 1666. Milward meets his corpse.
Godwin, Earl.
  (*D.N.B.*) Died 1053.
  Mentioned 29 October, 16 November 1667.
Goldsboro or Goldsborough, Sir William.
  Senior Clerk.
  25 November 1667. Mentioned in bribery case.
Goodrick, Sir Francis.   Aldboro (Yorkshire).
  Died 1673.
  14 October 1667. "The two Goodricks" for Clarendon.
  9 November 1667. For Clarendon.
Goodrick, Sir John.   Yorkshire.
  Died 1670. Elder brother of above.
  14 October 1667. As Sir Francis above.
  9 November 1667. On nature of treason.
  7 March 1667/8. On supply.
  11 March 1667/8. To refer toleration to a convocation.

GORGES, Lord Richard. Newton.

See under George above. Court party.

29 February 1667/8. On retailers.

11 March 1667/8. Against toleration.

12 March 1667/8. On the Fen bill.

GORING, Percy. Bramber.

6 April 1668. On privilege.

GOWER (GORE), Sir Thomas. Malton.

Father-in-law of Temple (q.v.).

24 January 1666/7. Against Chune.

3 March 1667/8. For Heblethwaite's bill.

16 March 1667/8. Takes Heblethwaite's bill to the Lords.

26 March 1668. Brings in a proviso about the manor of Creak in the North Riding to the Durham bill.

3 April 1668. To make a bill about a complaint against Tyrrell.

8 April 1668. Opposes Fowler's bill, which he says threatens his son-in-law's interests.

16 April 1668. On the expulsion of deer from the Forest of Dean.

18 April 1668. Fowler's bill again.

6 May 1668. Vindicates Gerrard (q.v.).

Granger. See Fitton.

GREY, Anchitel. Derby.

The diarist (*D.N.B.*).

18 January 1666/7. About old Mr Dalton.

24 January 1666/7. Takes Kendall's bill to Lords.

16 December 1667. Gives Milward information about a debate in the House afterwards contradicted by Sir Thomas Osbourne.

10 February 1667/8. Complains of arrest of his servant, at Mr Payton's suit, but cf. *C.J.* of same date, where Hull, Husband and Chandler are mentioned.

Grey, Thomas or Edward.

Concerned in the dispute with Collingwood over Berwick election. Convicted of bribery. Collingwood returned. In the *Returns* however, P. Osbourne is said to have taken the place of Ed. Grey deceased, 2 March 1676/7, where Grey's name appears in the list for Berwick with Widdrington's.

4 October, 15 November 1666.

Grosvenor (Grawenor), Fulk or Leicester.

25, 31 January 1666/7. Bill to sell land.

Halifax, Sir George Savile, Marquis of.

(*D.N.B.*)

14 March 1667/8. Mentioned as not present.

Hall, Henry.

Petition about the Forest of Dean, 12 November 1667. Cf. *C.J.* same date. See Winter.

HAMPDEN, Richard.   Wendover Borough.
Probably Country party (*D.N.B.*).
7 May 1668. No inconvenience could be suffered in dissolving the present Parliament.

Hanson (Hampson), Sir Thomas.
28 February 1667/8. Complained of (see Lund, John).

HARBORD, Sir Charles.   Launceston.
See under Herbert, which Milward uses for him throughout, though comparison with the *Journals* make identification quite clear. Surveyor-General. Court party.
22 September 1666. Opposes Irish Cattle bill.
25 September 1666. For a committee of enquiry into the Fire.
31 October 1666. Moves for a general excise.
26 October 1667. On the bill of accounts.
6 November 1667. On price of coals.
15 November 1667. Against Clarendon.
21 November 1667. Reports on accounts.
26 November 1667. Reports again.
12 December 1667. Names of twenty commissioners of accounts.
11, 12 February 1667/8. Forest of Dean.
18 March 1667/8. Against wine tax.
2 April 1668. Forest of Dean.
28 April, 4 May 1668. On recall of monies due to the King.

Harding, Dr.
Dean of Rochester until 1667, then parson at St Martin's.
Preaches 30 January 1666/7.
7 May 1668. Concerned in matter of new church in parish of St Martin's.

Hardye (Hervey).
Mentioned as a Jesuit by Milward 24 October 1666, and a Popish priest. *C.J.* 20 October 1666.

HARLEY (HARLOW), Sir Edward.   Radnor.
Governor of Dunkirk. Father of Robert Harley. A dissenter (*D.N.B.*).
11 November 1667. In connection with the charges against Clarendon about Dunkirk.

Harlib, Hartley, correctly Hartlib, Samuel.
Son of the friend of Milton, sometime legal agent for Newcastle-on-Tyne, employed in the customs and excise and by no means a good character. See Turnbull, G., *Sam Hartlib*, London, 1920, pp. 45–7.
Mentioned as a witness in the bribery case, 22 November 1667.

Harman, Sir John.
   A sea captain (*D.N.B.*). "A very gallant and deserving man."
   Mentioned and called to account for the miscarriages very frequently:
      21 October 1667, 20, 21 February 1667/8, 26 March, 9, 10, 11, 17,
      21 April, 7 May 1668.
Haselrigg, Sir Arthur.
   (*D.N.B.*)
   Mentioned 6 February 1666/7. See Stamford, Lord.
Heblethwaite, Sir Thomas.
   Of Norton.
   Bill, 28 February, 3, 16 March 1667/8, 10 April 1668, and see *C.J.*
      16 April 1668.
Henchman, H. See Bishop of London.
Henly, Sir Andrew.
   3 December 1666. Reported struck by Lord St John in Westminster
      Hall.
Henry II.
   Mentioned 9 November 1667.
Henry VI.
   Mentioned 15 November 1667.
Henry VIII.
   Mentioned 12 November 1667.
HERBERT, Sir Charles. Hindon.
   A Herbert sat for Hindon, but when Sir Charles is referred to here
      Sir Charles Harbord is certainly meant.
HERBERT, James. Pembroke County.
   11 February 1667/8. Election mentioned.
HERBERT, William, Lord. Glamorgan.
   Mentioned 11 February 1667/8.
Heron. See Horn.
HICKMAN (HINKMAN), Sir William. East Retford.
   11 March 1667/8. Against the abuses in Chancery.
   18 March 1667/8. On taxation.
HIGGINS, Sir Thomas. New Windsor.
   A courtier. Later an ambassador. Married the Countess of Essex,
      who died in 1656; her property and its settlement was the subject
      of his famous bill.
   20 October 1666. Debate about his case against the "Putches of
      Somerset".
   11 January 1666/7. His bill read and rejected.
   20 November 1667. On the price of coals.
   11 December 1667. "Excellent" in defence of Keeling.
   16 December 1667. On the price of coals.
   12 February 1667/8. For Winter in matter of Forest of Dean.

Hilton, Henry, Esq.
　Of the bishopric of Durham.
　Mentioned 11 January 1666/7.
　His gift referred to, 23 October 1667.

Hoare (Hore), Philip.
　"A rebel, or the grandson of a rebel."
　Philip Hoare, grandson of Philip Hore of Kilsachlan deceased, case
　　in *Cal. S.P. Ireland*, 1663 *passim*.
　23 April 1668. Case mentioned.

Hobbes, Thomas.
　1588–1679. His *Leviathan* ordered to be burnt as an "atheistical
　　book", 17 October 1666.

HOBBY, Peregrine.　Great Marlow.
　23 November 1667. Complained about the Jesuits.

HOLLAND, Sir John.　Aldeburgh, Suffolk.
　22 September 1666. Opposes Irish Cattle bill.
　17 October 1667. Presents Townshend's petition.
　24, 30 October 1667. On Townshend's petition.
　See Appendix I.

Holles, Denzil, Lord.
　1599–1680. Country party (*D.N.B.*).
　12 November 1667. Case mentioned.

Holles, Lady.
　Esther de Lou, wife of Denzil, Lord Holles (*D.N.B.*).
　2 November 1666. Naturalisation mentioned.

HOLLES, Sir Fretchville.　Great Grimsby.
　Court party (*D.N.B.*).
　21, 22 November 1667. Election debated.
　22 February 1667/8. In defence of Brouncker.
　27 February 1667/8. On tax by subsidy.
　8 April 1668. On Milford Haven lighthouse. "Impertinently" on
　　toleration.
　10 April 1668. On privilege.
　17 April 1668. On Harman.
　4 May 1668. Defends Barclay.

Holles, Gilbert.
　3rd Earl of Clare (q.v.). Country party (*D.N.B.*).
　29 November 1667.

Hollingshead, Francis.
　8 January 1666/7. Solicits for Leigh, Francis (q.v.).
　3, 11, 22 April 1668. Leigh's bill mentioned.

HOLMES, Sir Robert.　(Winchester, 1669.)
　Court party.
　Mentioned 21 October 1667.

HOLT, Sir Robert.   Warwickshire.
Court party.
5 February 1666/7. Sent to the Lords about Mordaunt.
15 November 1667. To adjourn.
21 November 1667. For a conference with the Lords.
5 December 1667. Against the bill for Cambridge pest-houses.
13 December 1667. Reflects on the Lords for escape of Clarendon.
11 March 1667/8. Dissenters should say what they want.
12 March 1667/8. Against laying a tax on retailers of wine.
13 March 1667/8. Against toleration.
1 April 1668. For exempting forges from chimney tax.
HOOKE, Sir Humphrey.   Bristol.
Court party. "A loyal man."
6, 13, 31 October 1666. Election debated.
Horn (Heron), Sir Henry.
Son of Sir Edward Heron, named with Killigrew in connection with
the Lincoln Levels bill. *C.J.* 21 January 1664/5.
28 November 1667. Lindsey Levels bill.
Howard.
Of Escrick. Probably William Howard, practising law in Ireland,
1665. *Cal. S.P. Ireland*, p. 611.
20, 23 April 1668. On the Irish Adventurers.
Howard, Henry.
A London investor in Ireland.
20 April 1668. Mentioned in connection with the Irish Adventurers.
Howard, Lady Honor. See Sir Robert Howard.
HOWARD, Sir Philip.   Carlisle.
Court party.
24, 28 November 1666. On his religion and the information about
de Leure.
HOWARD, Sir Robert.   Stockbridge.
Court party (*D.N.B.*). Very prominent in the proceedings against
Clarendon.
26 October 1667. On examination of witness against Clarendon.
6 November 1667. First article against Clarendon.
7 November 1667. On the division of the Fleet.
8 November 1667. For impeachment.
11 November 1667 (twice). Against Clarendon.
18 November 1667. Information of bribery.
21, 23 November 1667. Conference with the Lords.
27 November 1667. Warns the House to adjourn because the Lords
will desire a free conference.
29 November 1667. Reports to the House.
2 December 1667. Conference with the Lords.
5 December 1667. For sending vote to the Lords.
6 December 1667. Sent to the Lords.

HOWARD, Sir Robert (*continued*):
12 December 1667. Moves to take Simmons, the boatman who helped Clarendon, into custody.
17 December 1667. A proviso about payment of seamen by ticket.
15 February 1667/8. Division of the Fleet due to evil counsel.
18 February 1667/8. For Temple's Triennial bill.
29 February 1667/8. On the wine tax.
2 March 1667/8, 8 May 1668. Mentioned.
13 April 1668. With Lee, moves that redress of grievances and supply go together.
21, 24 April 1668. Concerned in impeachment of Penn.
27, 28 April 1668. Lady Howard against him.
2, 4 May 1668. On the East India Company and Skinner.
7 May 1668. Mentions many bills as still incomplete.

Humphreys, Toby.
Farmer of hearth money in the North Riding.
Mentioned 14 March 1667/8.

HUNGERFORD, Sir Edward.   Chippenham.
Court party (*D.N.B.*).
26 October 1666. To Lords with petition for enforcement of recusancy laws.
24 November 1666. On de Leure.
11 April 1668. Sir Charles Hungerford moves to reduce interest money.

HYDE, Sir Frederick.   Haverfordwest.
Court party. Serjeant-at-law.
26 November 1667. Election voided in committee voted good by the House.

HYDE, Laurence.   Oxford University.
"My Lord Chancellor's younger son." Created Earl of Rochester, 1681.
18 September 1666. Introduces Milward.

IRBY (ERLY), Sir Anthony.   Boston.
9 March 1667/8. On wine tax.
12 March 1667/8. Moves for committee on supply.
26 March 1668. Against Churchill and Broderick going to Ireland until Adventurers have been heard.

Jambey (Jambi), King of.
Mentioned 2 May 1668.

James I.
Mentioned 6 December 1667, 11 March 1667/8.

Jennens, Humphrey.
An iron-master. "My son"; married to Milward's daughter Anne.
28 October 1666. Dines at Lambeth to celebrate Milward's birthday.
5 November 1666. Dines at Sheldon's.
7 March 1667/8. Tells Milward of the illness of his daughter, from which she recovered, as we find her mentioned in Milward's will of 1669.

Jerret, Sir Philip (or Tirwhit, see *Returns*, p. 524, n. 5).
21, 22 November 1667. Contested Great Grimsby against Sir F. Holles, who was returned.

Jervas, the Attorney (of Staffordshire?).
11 April 1668. Mentioned.

JOLLY (JOLIFFE), John. Heytesbury, Wiltshire.
Connected by marriage with the Fittons.
12 December 1667. Brings Fitton's petition in.

JONES, Thomas. Shrewsbury.
Later Chief Justice and Knight (*D.N.B.*).
20 February 1667/8. Against the bill on the adulteration of wine.
24 February 1667/8. On amendments to the Irish Cattle bill.
6 March 1667/8. Against laying a tax on tunnage.
13 March 1667/8. Against the Conventicle Act.
26 March 1668. Against Broderick's going to Ireland.

Jordan, Sir Joseph.
Vice-Admiral with long record of service (*D.N.B.*).
24 April 1668. Mentioned in debate on miscarriages of war.

Juxon, Sir William.
Nephew of Juxon (Abp. of Canterbury 1660–63) and his executor (H.M.C. 8th Report, p. 113).
14, 21 February 1667/8. Bill of relief against J. Pory.
6 May 1668.

Keeling, John.
Formerly M.P. for Bedford. Lord Chief Justice.
Proceedings against, 16 October 1667, 9, 11, 13 December 1667.
3 April 1668. Mentioned.

Keeper, Lord. See Bridgeman.
Mentioned as official in debate on Temple's Triennial bill, 18 February 1667/8. Mentioned 30 March 1668.

Kendall, Henry.
Held land at Darley, etc.
Bill for sale of land, 6, 24, 25 October 1666, 23, 24 January 1666/7.

KILLIGREW, Sir William. Richmond, Yorkshire.
Court party. Dramatist, etc. (*D.N.B.*).
Speaks always on the Lindsey Levels bill, 14, 28 November 1667, 28 March, 7, 11 April, 2 May 1668.

King, Colonel Edward.
12 December 1667. Mentioned derogatorily as being nominated amongst the Commissioners.
Not mentioned in the *C.J.* list.

King of France. See France.

KIRBY, Colonel Richard. Lancaster.
Court party.
27 November 1666. Leigh's bill.

KIRBY, Colonel Richard (*continued*):
   12 January 1666/7. Presents wine merchants' petition.
   23 October 1667. To thank Prince Rupert and Albemarle for their narratives.
   25 October 1667. Sent to get a letter of intelligence from Albemarle.
   22 November 1667. Named (falsely in Milward's opinion) as a recipient of bribes.
   6 March 1667/8. On fees in Chancery.
   11 March 1667/8. Takes Wharton's bill to Lords. Asks for the Declaration of Breda to be read.
   11 April 1668. To attend the Duke of York.
   5 May 1668. For Stanley.

KNIGHT, Sir John. Bristol.
   Court party. "A talkative wine merchant of Bristol" (Marvell, *Letters*, p. 305): the record below justifies the stricture. A great persecutor of Quakers (*D.N.B.*).
   24 October 1666. Against excise on tobacco.
   4 November 1667. On lighthouses.
   13 November 1667. On trade with Scotland.
   27 November, 5, 11, 17 December 1667. For the naturalisation of prize ships.
   20 February 1667/8. Against bill on adulteration of wine.
   27 February 1667/8. On Poll bill.
   12 March 1667/8. On Privy Seals.
   17 March 1667/8. Against excise on tobacco.
   18 March 1667/8. "Impertinent" speech against the tax on retailers of wine.
   28 March, 4 April 1668. On the same.
   9 April 1668. Against 1s. tax on strong waters.

LAKE, Sir Launcelot. Middlesex.
   Court party.
   18 February 1667/8. Against Temple's Triennial bill.
   12 March 1667/8. On the loan for the City of London.
   2 May 1668. Against the London bill.

Latimer, William, 4th Baron.
   1329–81. Impeached 1376 (*D.N.B.*).

Laud, Archbishop.
   Mentioned 29 October, 18, 29 November 1667.

Lawes, Captain. Certainly Captain Henry Dawe (q.v.).
   23 November 1667. Bill to sell land (not mentioned in *C.J.*).

LEE, Sir Thomas. Aylesbury.
   Country party. Said to take bribes (*D.N.B.*).
   5 December 1667. Against declaring the Lords responsible for Clarendon's escape.
   9 March 1667/8. On subsidies.

LEE, Sir Thomas (*continued*):
   11 March 1667/8. Against Brooke's bill to sell land.
   12 March 1667/8. Against the tax on wine.
   17 March 1667/8. Against taxing retailers.
   8 April 1668. No new oaths to be imposed (in debate on sectaries).
   11 April 1668. Seconds motion to reduce interest. Thanks the Duke of York.
   13 April 1668. Grievances and supply go together.
   17 April 1668. The House should postpone appointment of Commissioners until their power in regard to poll money known.
   1 May 1668. Reports on Fowler.
Leigh (Legh, etc.), Francis.
   Of Newton (see Lysons, p. cxxxiv).
   Bill to sell land round "Ninckle Grange" (Newton Grange in Derbyshire) managed by Francis Hollingshead and pressed by the Milward cousins in the House, 29 October, 23, 27, 28 November 1666, 8 January 1666/7, 3, 11, 22 April 1668.
Leigh, Humphrey.
   Sergeant-at-Mace.
   Mentioned 26 October 1667, 2 May 1668.
Lenthall, Sir John.
   1625–81 (knighted, 1677).
   Son of William Lenthall, the Speaker (*D.N.B.*; *C.J.* pp. 68, 74, etc.), and nephew of the Master of the King's Bench (q.v.).
   Concerned with Mrs Stonehouse (q.v.) and others in a case brought against Clarendon, who was defended in the House by his son, Lord Cornbury, 3 December 1667, 11, 15 February, 2 March 1667/8, 2, 3, 6, 7, 8 April 1668.
Lenthall, Sir John.
   Master of the King's Bench (q.v.).
Lewen, John.
   A Papist turned out of Charles II's guard.
   Mentioned 21, 24 February 1667/8.
LEWIS, Sir William. Lymington.
   26 October 1667. Moves that Clarendon's trial be legally conducted.
   8, 9, 15 November 1667. On Clarendon.
   11 March 1667/8. Against Brooke's bill. Against reading the reasons for the Declaration of Breda.
Lindsey, John Bertie, Earl of.
   10th Baron and 17th Earl of Crawford and Lindsey.
   A Presbyterian Royalist (*D.N.B.*).
   19, 28 January 1666/7. Mentioned.
   13 April 1668. Named chief undertaker and trustee.
LITTLETON, Sir Edward. Staffordshire.
   7 November 1667. Affirms nineteenth article against Clarendon, i.e. his responsibility for the division of the Fleet.

LITTLETON, Sir Thomas. Much Wenlock, Salop.
Held minor office later under Buckingham. A leading figure in
Parliament. Marvell calls him "great Littleton". Country party
(*D.N.B.*).
22 October 1666. On a bill for preventing miscarriages.
11 January 1666/7. To prove Austin's election valid.
24 January 1666/7. Did not make report on attendance of members.
25 January 1666/7. Makes his report.
25 July 1667. Supports Tomkins.
14, 23, 26 October, 6, 7, 18, 21, 26, 29 November, 5 December 1667.
Against Clarendon always. See also Appendix II.
18 February 1667/8. Supports Temple's Triennial bill.
19 February 1667/8. Would know the King's debts.
11 March 1667/8. Would have Declaration of Breda read. Would not
have dissenters forced to define wants.
12 March 1667/8. Against excise.
13 March 1667/8. Against Conventicle Act.
17 March 1667/8. For a tax on tunnage.
18 March 1667/8. Excuses Buckingham's duel.
3 April 1668. On the militia.

Llandaste (Llandaff). See Bishop of Llandaff.

London, Bishop of. See Bishop of London.

London, Lord Mayor of.
Sir Thomas Bludworth, 1665–6 (q.v.).
Sir William Bolton, 1666–7.
Sir W. Peake, 1667–8.
Sir William Turner, 1668–9 (q.v.).
Mentioned 11 January 1666/7, 24 October, 6 November 1667.

LONG, Sir Robert. Boroughbridge.
Court party. Auditor of Exchequer. Married a daughter of John
Thynne (*D.N.B.*).
21 February 1667/8. Reports on expenditure of last poll money.

LOVE, Alderman W. London.
A Presbyterian. Country party. See Beaven's *Aldermen*.
26, 29 November 1667. To get a report about a cheat upon the King.
22 April 1668. Against reduction of interest.

LOWTHER, Sir William. Pontefract.
Court party.
17 October 1666. Chairman of committee for naval monies. Reports
from it.
10 October 1667. On committee to draw up thanks to the King for
his speech.
14 October 1667. The committee reports.
8 November 1667. Argues by precedent that the Commons may
impeach a peer.

LUCIE, Sir Richard.
  Formerly M.P. for Hertfordshire. Died 1667. His son Kingsmill
    (died 1678) married Theophila, second daughter of George, Lord
    Berkeley (q.v.).
  28, 29 April 1668. Bill to sell lands.

LUCY, Sir Fulk.   Chester County.
  29 October 1666. Leigh's bill.
  28 November 1666. Dines with Milward in connection with Leigh's
    bill.
  8 January 1666/7. Did not speak for Leigh's bill.

Lund, John (Jo. Tunne).
  28 February 1667/8. Petition against Hanson.

Lyons, Richard.
  See Giles, Sir. Impeached 1376 (50 Edward III).
  Mentioned 29 October 1667 (21 April 1668).

MALLETT, John.   Minehead.
  (A Michael Mallet sat for Milbourne Port.)
  7 February 1666/7. Reports on a lease made to a bishop.

Manton, Richard.
  A noted dissenting divine (D.N.B.).
  Mentioned 11 March 1667/8.

March, Earl of.
  Edward Mortimer, 1287–1330, 1st Earl of March.
  Mentioned 29 October 1667.

Marlboro', the Lady.
  Wife of Colonel Wanklin.
  27 March 1668.

Marsh, Thomas.
  "The under-clerk", and also in the Customs house.
  22 November 1667. Said to have been bribed.

MARVELL (MARVIN), Andrew.   Kingston-upon-Hull.
  The poet. Country party. Said to be silent in the House, but has a
    number of speeches recorded here (D.N.B.).
  14 October 1667. For Clarendon. See also p. 328.
  31 October 1667. For Pett.
  7 November 1667. Accuses Seymour of saying the King was not fit
    to govern.
  15 February 1667/8. "Most sharp" against Arlington.
  22 February 1667/8. On payment of seamen by tickets.
  13 March 1667/8. Against Conventicle Act.
  26 March 1668. Against Churchill and Broderick going to Ireland
    until the Adventurers have been heard.
  30 March 1668. Against Conventicle Act.

MASSEY, Sir Edward. Gloucester.
Court party. A Presbyterian (*D.N.B.*).
10 December 1667. Against the Irish Adventurers.
17 February 1667/8. On the miscarriages of the war and fortifications of Sheerness.
11 March 1667/8. Disagrees with Birkenhead on a standing army being necessary for toleration.
28 March 1668. Against Sir Peter Pindar.

Master of the Black Rod. See Black Rod (Eyton).

Master of the King's Bench.
Sir John Lenthall, Warden of the Prison.
17 November 1666. Bill against him for escape of prisoners.

May, Baptist.
See Austin and Winchelsea. May sat later for Midhurst (1670). Court party.
9, 11 January 1666/7.

MAYNARD (MAINARD), Sir John. Beeralston.
Serjeant-at-law. A Parliamentarian. Formerly a friend of Clarendon. Married a daughter of Henly (q.v.).
18 September 1666. On election writs.
25 September 1666. For a committee on the Fire.
6 October 1666. With "old Parliament gang" opposes election of the loyal Hooke.
24 October 1666. Libel addressed to.
8 January 1666/7. Against Leigh.
10 January 1666/7. Report on poor prisoners.
12 January 1666/7. On Mosley's estate.
22 January 1666/7. Impeachment against Mordaunt, of which he was manager.
14 October 1667. For Clarendon. See also p. 328.
15 October 1667. On word "utensil" in bill for relief of debtors.
11 November 1667. On Clarendon.
28 February 1667/8. Severe speech against payment by ticket.
27 March 1668. On question of privilege.
2, 8 May 1668. On Skinner affair.

Mays, Adrian.
In the King's service from 1661 at least, as guardian of gardens. Keeper of fowl and deer in St James's Park.
1 November 1666. Milward dines with him.

MEERS, Sir Thomas. Lincoln City.
18 December 1667. On trade with Scotland.
22 February 1667/8. Against payment of seamen by ticket.
27 February 1667/8. For a tax at the Custom house.
28 February 1667/8. Informs against sectaries.
6 March 1667/8. Report on foreign commodities.

MEERS, Sir Thomas (*continued*):
    11 March 1667/8. For reading reasons for the Declaration of Breda.
    13 March 1667/8. For the Conventicle Act.
    14 March 1667/8. Reports on Commissioners of accounts.
    28 March 1668. Against the Wine bill.
    8 April 1668. No comprehension to extend to a toleration.
    2 May 1668. On the Skinner affair.

Meynell (Menel), Alderman Francis.
    (Beaven.) A goldsmith who had bought land in Bradley, Derbyshire, in 1655 (Glover, p. 158, l. 2).
    23 October 1666. Milward goes to attend his corpse at Ironmongers' Hall on its way to be buried at Bradley.

MILWARD, John. Derbyshire.
    17 September 1666. Delivers his writ.
    18 September 1666. Takes the oath, administered by Ogle and Hyde.
    21 September 1666. Committee of Privilege.
    28 September 1666. Dines at Lambeth. Talks with Doyley (q.v.) about the Irish Cattle bill.
    1 October 1666. Committees on receiving and paying money; Fire of London.
    2 October 1666. Votes against the Powder bill.
    15 October 1666. Goes with Seymour and the Irish bill to the Lords.
    17 October 1666. Ill.
    18 October 1666. Favours the sale of chimney money.
    19 October 1666. Ill.
    20 October 1666. Dines at Lambeth. Ill.
    21 October 1666. Takes a smart purge.
    23 October 1666. Goes to Ironmongers' Hall to attend corpse of Francis Meynell. Votes against the court on the Plympton election.
    25 October 1666. Dines at "New Tavern" with Kendall's committee.
    28 October 1666. At Lambeth.
    31 October 1666. Attends a deputation to the King though not appointed to it.
    1 November 1666. Dines with his cousin Milward at Mays's.
    4 November 1666. To St Clement's with Jennens. Dines with "Coz" Glanvill.
    5 November 1666. To St Clement's with Jennens. Dines with Jos. Sheldon.
    7 November 1666. Votes for Cambridge Vice-Chancellor in matter of erection of pest-houses.
    8 November 1666. Votes on eleven months' tax, against a land tax, for an excise of foreign goods to be imposed at the customs.
    10 November 1666. Watches fire at Wallingford House.
    12 November 1666. At Lambeth with Rutland.
    15 November 1666. Votes for Ayes to rate titles in Poll tax.

MILWARD, John (*continued*):

21 November 1666. Presents Moore's letter, which Captain Fitzherbert sent up, to the Archbishop. Sees Bishop of Winchester.

22 November 1666. At Lambeth. Rutland there.

27 November 1666. Votes against altering the word "nuisance".

28 November 1666. Sees Scarsdale about Moore's letter. Dines
with Fulk Lucy. Goes to Leigh's committee. Meets Glynne's corpse.

30 November 1666. Votes against polling Doctors of Divinity at £5.

1 December 1666. Dines at Lambeth.

3 December 1666. Stays late at Mordaunt's committee.

5 December 1666. Near the King, but could not hear his speech.

7 December 1666. Against Garroway's proviso to the Poll bill.

11 December 1666. Home via Oxford.

8 January 1666/7. Returns to London.

9 January 1666/7. Takes place without disturbance. Votes against
bill for burying in woollens.

11 January 1666/7. Does not vote in Austin-May case. Dines at the
"Dog" with Seymour Shirley. Votes against Higgins.

12 January 1666/7. Votes for the wine merchants.

18 January 1666/7. Votes for old Mr Dalton.

21 January 1666/7. Goes to the Lords to hear Buckingham and
Rutland (Roos case).

22 January 1666/7. Votes for French merchants' licences.

23 January 1666/7. On Roos committee. Dines with them.

24 January 1666/7. Moves for Kendall.

25 January 1666/7. Votes on attendance of members.

27 January 1666/7. Votes against proviso in London bill.

30 January 1666/7. Goes to the Temple to hear Dr Harding preach.

7 February 1666/7. Opinion on revenue.

7 August 1667. Writes up recollection of King's speech in July
session.

29 October 1667. Attends Atkins to the Lords about Certioraries.

6 November 1667. Against committing heads of charges against
Clarendon.

8 November 1667. On committee of privilege discussing Fitzwilliam's election.

9 November 1667. Votes against impeaching Clarendon on the first
article.

11 November 1667. Votes for impeachment.

13 November 1667. The sectaries favour Pett.

21 November 1667. Reports the Lords' debate.

22 November 1667. Comes late.

23 November 1667. Would agree with the Lords.

25 November 1667. Thinks Heralds fee-grabbers.

4 December 1667. Speaks on Naturalisation.

5 December 1667. Goes out of the House disgusted over argument
about the Lords.

MILWARD, John (*continued*):

6 December 1667. Does not stay out debate on trade with Scotland.

11 December 1667. Goes out of debate early.

13 December 1667. Listens carefully to Keeling case.

14 December 1667. Goes out of the House at six. House sits till nine.

16 December 1667. Given information by Grey.

17 December 1667. Against committing Carr's petition.

11 February 1667/8. At committee discussing election of Trevor Williams and James Herbert.

14 February 1667/8. Does not think the House can decide on responsibility for miscarriages.

15 February 1667/8. Votes against blaming miscarriages on the Council.

18 February 1667/8. Strongly dislikes Temple's Triennial bill.

19 February 1667/8. On committee of grievances about Colonel Vernon's case.

22 February 1667/8. Is persuaded Fitton cannot do much.

29 February 1667/8. Votes for sending Constantine into custody.

6 March 1667/8. Unable to record all goods to be taxed in bill. Dines with Sir Robert Carr.

7 March 1667/8. Summoned by Jennens to daughter Anne.

10 March 1667/8. Votes for eighty days in Highways bill on Committee.

11 March 1667/8. Votes for Brooke's bill.

13 March 1667/8. To Lambeth. Votes for Conventicle Act.

17 March 1667/8. Late at afternoon session.

26 March 1668. Votes against enfranchisement of Durham bill.

30 March 1668. Speaks to the House; will not inform against bad magistrates, but would point out decimators and committee men if they will be thrown out.

31 March 1668. Thinks vintners and prohibition party join to prevent the King's getting supply.

1 April 1668. Votes for Wakefield Enclosure bill.

2 April 1668. Will not vote in Lenthall-Cornbury case though thinks Cornbury probably right.

3 April 1668. (*C.J.*) Committee on Tyrrell.

8 April 1668. Is against sending to the King to decide about toleration.

9 April 1668. Votes for taxing strong waters.

10 April 1668. Votes for taxing retailers.

15 April 1668. At the committee for the Conventicle bill.

16 April 1668. Votes for deer in the Forest of Dean.

17 April 1668. Votes against the commitment of Harman.

20 April 1668. Votes for Richmond's allnage. Votes against Poole.

21 April 1668. Anne's illness prevents his hearing Harman's defence, but he is for that "modest man".

22 April 1668. On committee for Leigh's bill.

Milward, John (*continued*):
28 April 1668. Against Williams' proviso to Conventicle bill about recusants, as it only clogs the bill.
1 May 1668. Votes against proviso in Revenue bill although it might be good.
5 May 1668. Thinks London poor will suffer by London bill.
7 May 1668. Goes to Gray's Inn and takes out a bond for £500 at the two brothers' Bigland (q.v.). Goes to Lambeth.

Milward, Robert. Stafford Borough.
Second son of Sir Thomas Milward of Eaton, Recorder of Stafford, who died, after suffering financially in the Civil Wars, at the age of fifty-seven, in 1653.
Robert Milward, and therefore his cousin John, was related to both Charles Cotton, through the Cokaynes, and Izaak Walton, through the marriage of Margaret Milward to Henry Walton in the mid-sixteenth century. A story of Robert's gallantry during the Civil Wars is related in Harris Nicholas's *Life of Walton*.
Robert, who was remembered affectionately in Milward's will, was quite a prominent member of the House. He was frequently in the Chair during the session 1666/7, but his name appears less often during the next winter, both in the *Journals* and in his cousin's Diary. Court party. J. C. Wedgwood gives a brief life in his *Stafford M.P.s.* Two letters of his are reported in H.M.C. 5th Report, pp. 145, 207.
25 September 1666. Against Certioraries.
2 October 1666. For putting the question whether bill for preventing embezzlement of powder should be cast out.
6 October 1666. Moves for Kendall.
12 October 1666. In Chair on supply.
23 October 1666. For Richard Slanning and court interest in the Plympton election, but Fortescue won. John Milward had voted for him.
24, 31 October 1666. In the Chair.
25 October 1666. In the Chair for Kendall committee in the Exchequer Chamber, and at dinner of same at the New Taverne in Dawell Row.
28 October 1666. Dines with cousin at Lambeth.
1 November 1666. Dines with cousin in St James's Park.
3 November 1666. In Chair for land tax committee.
12 November 1666. Proposed for Roos committee.
17 November 1666. On legal matters. On supply.
[19 November 1666. (See *C.J.*) Permission to go out of town.]
27 November 1666. Goes out of town.
8 January 1666/7. Does not speak for Leigh.
4 February 1666/7. Could not report on poor prisoners.
5 February 1666/7. Makes his report.
18 February 1667/8. Against Temple's Triennial bill.

MILWARD, Robert (*continued*):
13 March 1667/8. For the Conventicle Act.
17 March 1667/8. Votes against tax on retailers.
3 April 1668. To bring in a bill about indigent persons.
8 April 1668. Fowler's bill.

Milward, William.
His wife was sister to John, Earl of Thanet.
18 February 1667/8. Case mentioned.

(Mompesson, Sir Giles. See Giles, Sir.
Mentioned 21 April 1668.)

Mordaunt (Mordant), Charles, Viscount.
Afterwards Earl of Peterborough. Constable of Windsor.
Attacked by the House for alleged tyranny in this office, and saved
from its attacks by the King.
2 November, 3 December 1666, 17, 22, 25, 26, 28, 29, 31 January, 2,
4, 5, 6, 7, 8 February 1666/7, 25, 26 October and 2 December 1667.

MORICE (MAURICE, MORRIS), Sir William.   Plymouth.
"Mr Secretary" until 1668 (*D.N.B.*). Court party.
18 September 1666. Message from the King about adjournment.
29 October 1666. Message from the King to hurry supply.
8 November 1666. The King will not part with chimney money.
24 November 1666. Bill for getting brick and tile for London.
23 January 1666/7. Bill for taxing coals to raise money for rebuilding
London.
7 February 1666/7. Messages about prorogation.
23 October 1667. For Clarendon.
24 October 1667. On the division of the Fleet.
25 October 1667. Mentioned.
30 October 1667. Against new oaths in Recusancy bill.
4 November 1667. On the division of the Fleet.
3 December 1667. Sent to the King.
9, 17, 19 December 1667. On adjournment.
6 March 1667/8. To hasten supply.
11 March 1667/8. To adjourn debate on toleration.
16, 30 March 1668. On adjournment.
24 April 1668. To hasten supply.
4 May 1668. Message from the King.

Mortimer. See March.

MORTON, Sir John.   Poole.
3 December 1667. Against export of hides and leather.
29 February 1667/8. Complaint against Constantine, a former candi-
date for Parliament at Poole.
7 March 1667/8. Money should be raised by taxing rich men.

MORTON, Sir John (*continued*):
14 April 1668. Complaint against Constantine again.

Mosley, Sir Edward.
Formerly member for Michael. Dead before 1665.
12 January 1666/7. Estate of. Maynard (q.v.) defended his son's interest against Mosley.

MOUNTAGUE (MONTAGUE), Sir William.   Stamford.
Married a Cotton. Lawyer and later a judge (*D.N.B.*).
6 October 1666. Opposes Kendall's bill.
24 October 1666. Moves to stop suits between landlord and tenant arising out of the Fire.
12 November 1666. Moves for "Mr Sollicitor" and Robert Milward to be on Roos committee.
21 January 1666/7. Mentioned.
29 January 1666/7. Carries Roos bill to Lords.

MUSGRAVE, Sir Philip.   Westmorland.
Governor of Carlisle. Court party (*D.N.B.*).
10 February 1667/8. Against dissenters.
11 March 1667/8. Indulgence will not purge the Shires.
26 March 1668. For leaving the Durham bill to the Lords.
1 April 1668. For Wakefield bill.

Neville, Richard.
Earl of Salisbury. 1400–60.
Mentioned 29 October, 29 November 1667.

NEWBURGH (NEWBOROUGH), James Livingstone, Earl of.   Cirencester.
Died before 1671.
8 May 1668. Mentioned by Probert in his plea of privilege.

Nicholas, Edward.
Former Secretary of State (*D.N.B.*).
Mentioned 4 December 1667.

NOELL, Edward.   Rutland.
Afterwards Earl of Gainsborough. Married Elizabeth, daughter of Southampton. Court party. Son of Baptist Noell, Viscount Campden (q.v.).
26, 30 October 1666. Bill to sell land.

Norfolk, James.
Serjeant-at-arms. Appointed 25 April 1660, and said by rivals for the office to have been on the Parliamentary side in the Civil War.
See also Serjeant-at-arms.

Norrice (Norris), Lord and Lady.
Of Rycote. (See *L.J.* xII, 93, 108; H.M.C. 8th Report, p. 109.)
Mentioned 19, 28 January 1666/7.

NORTH, Henry.   Suffolk.
8 November 1667. "Very good" speech against impeaching Clarendon.

Northampton, James Compton, 3rd Earl of.
His daughter is said by Milward to have married Noell (q.v.), but see above. Compton himself married Mary Noell, daughter of the 3rd Viscount Campden.
26 October 1666.

NORTHCOTE (NORTHGATE), Sir John.   Barnstaple.
Cousin of Sir Hugh Pollard. Court party (*D.N.B.*).
22 February 1667/8. Against Brouncker.
1 April 1668. Against Wakefield enclosures.
8 April 1668. Against Lighthouse bill.
5 May 1668. Against Stanley's bill.

Nycholls (Nichols), Andrew.
Mentioned 8 May 1668 in Probert's case.

OAKLEY, Sir Richard.   Salop.
Studied at Gray's Inn. Court party.
8 May 1668. On a matter of privilege.

OGLE, Henry Cavendish, Earl of.   Northumberland.
Viscount Mansfield, afterwards Duke of Newcastle. Married a Pierpont (*D.N.B.*).
18 September 1666. Administered oath to Milward.

Opdam, Jacob van Wasenald.
The Dutch admiral killed at Lowestoft, 3 June 1665.
Mentioned 21 October 1667.

ORME, Humphrey.   Peterborough.
15 October 1666. To sell chimney money.

Ormond, James Butler, Duke of.
(*D.N.B.*)
5 December 1666. Mentioned.
16 March 1667/8, 20 April 1668.

OSBOURNE, Sir Thomas.   York.
Afterwards Earl of Danby. Court party (*D.N.B.*).
8 October 1666. Report of duel with Fauconberg.
26 October 1667. Against Clarendon's alleged statement that Charles was a Catholic.
7 November 1667. Affirms the tenth and thirteenth articles against Clarendon.
16 December 1667. Tells Milward about a debate.

OSSORY, Roger Boyle, Earl of.   Arundel.
His wife was a sister of Lady Arlington (q.v.).
Mentioned in the Bristol debate, 6, 13, 31 October 1666.

Outram (Owtram), Dr.
> Parson at St Margaret's, Westminster. A Derbyshire man (*D.N.B.*).
> Mentioned in connection with sermons, 24 September, 3, 4, 11 October, 9 December 1666.

Oxford, A. de Vere, Earl of.
> (*D.N.B.*)
> 15 November 1667. Message from the Lords.

Page (Pearse), James.
> Surgeon-General to Navy. Not to be confused with Robert Pierce, 1622–1710 (*D.N.B.*), often mentioned by Pepys. The Duke of York's surgeon.
> Mentioned 21 October 1667.

Palmer (possibly Geoffrey). Peterborough.
> Son of the Attorney-General (*D.N.B.*).
> 24 September 1666. Election called in question by Lord Fitzwilliam (q.v.); cf. *C.J.*
> 2 October 1666. Election debated. Milward on committee. Palmer lost his case.

PALMES, William. Maldon.
> Receiver-General for Rutland.
> 14, 18 November 1667, 4, 19 December 1667. Bill to sell land in Derbyshire.

PASTON, William. Norwich.
> (See *C.J.* 2 December 1667 and *C.S.P.D.* 1667, p. 473.)
> 2 December 1667. Bill to sell land in Gloucestershire.

Payton, Mr.
> 10 February 1667/8. Complained of by Colonel Grey (see under Grey).

PENN, Sir William. Melcombe Regis and Weymouth.
> Admiral and father of the Quaker and colonist.
> 19, 21 October 1667. Attacked for share in naval disasters.
> 22 February 1667/8, 14, 16, 21, 24 April 1668, 4 May 1668. The same.

PEPYS (PEPPES), Samuel. Castle Rising.
> The diarist. Court party. Naval administrator (*D.N.B.*).
> 24 November 1666. On Cambridge pest-houses.
> 24 October 1667. Against Sandys's Lindsey Levels bill.
> 5 March 1667/8. A long speech defending payment of seamen by tickets. (This has been printed by Mr E. S. de Beer, *Mariner's Mirror*, January 1928, p. 55.)

Perkins, Jane and Henry.
> 9, 12 November 1667. Petition about land bought by Dr Wharton of "another Perkins" brought into the House by Dr Burrell.

Peterborough, Bishop of. See Bishop of Peterborough.

Peters of Kent.
> Mentioned 22 January 1666/7.

Pett, Commissioner Peter.
(*D.N.B.*)
Mentioned in debates on miscarriages of the war and much "befriended by the old gang" and by the "Secretaries" (sectaries?).
22, 31 October, 13, 14 November, 19 December 1667, 7 May 1668.

PIERPONT, R.   Northampton Borough.
(*D.N.B.*)
A case of privilege. 30 November 1666.
7 February 1666/7. Privilege violated by Bristoll.

Pindar, Sir Peter.
Of the Custom house at Chester. (See H.M.C. 8th Report, p. 289.)
Mentioned 28 March 1668, as exacting undue fees.

Plympton, Mayor of.
Nicholas Horseman.
23 October 1666.

POOLE, Sir Courtney.   Honiton.
Alleged inventor of hearth money. Court party.
28 February 1667/8. Against payment of seamen by ticket.
3 March 1667/8. Against Heblethwaite's bill.
11 March 1667/8. Against Laurence Brooke's bill.

Poole, Periard.
One of the officers of '49.
Mentioned 20 April 1668.

Pory (Perry), John.
Treasurer to Archbishop Juxon.
Mentioned 14, 21 February 1667/8, 6 May 1668.

PRETTYMAN, Sir John.   Leicester.
23 October 1667. Petition about privilege.

Pride, Thomas.
Died 1658. Colonel Pride, "the traitor", was married to Elizabeth, niece of George Monk, illegitimate daughter of Thomas Monk.
16 November 1666. Bill to sell land. Milward confuses the Colonel and his son, Thomas, whose bill this is.

Privy Seal, Lord.
John Robartes.
Mentioned 19 December 1667.

PROBERT (PROLETT), Sir George.   Monmouth Borough.
Married a sister of Trevor Williams (q.v.). Court party.
8 May 1668. Petition about his privilege.

PRYNNE (PRIN, etc.), William. Bath.

The famous Parliamentarian (*D.N.B.*).

18 September 1666. On special writs.

22 September 1666. For Popish recusants to leave the City. Presents a Marriage bill which was thrown out.

25 September 1666. On Certioraries.

24, 27 September 1666. Bill against episcopal power of granting marriage licences.

12 October 1666. To bring in a bill for regulating attorneys.

13 October 1666. Wishes to fine M.P.s for absence from prayers.

15 October 1666. Opposes Lord Cleveland's bill.

15 January 1666/7. On price of coals.

24 January 1666/7. Against Chune's claim of privilege.

29 January 1666/7. Opposes Roos.

6 February 1666/7. Against Chune.

24 October 1667. On woodmongers.

26 October 1667. Moves to examine witnesses before impeaching Clarendon.

29 October 1667. Mentioned in debate on precedent for impeachment.

7 November 1667. Against pluralities.

8 November 1667. Against clandestine marriages. On Clarendon.

11 November 1667. Justifies the sale of Dunkirk.

16 November 1667. Bare impeachment not sufficient for imprisonment.

26 November 1667. Against a conference with the Lords.

17 February 1667/8. On miscarriages.

27 February 1667/8. To levy a tax on French commodities.

11 March 1667/8. For taking away causes of religious separation.

18 March 1667/8. On duels.

2 May 1668. "Poorly" for Lords in Skinner case.

4 May 1668. Suspected of reporting debates outside the House.

(Pydor.) See Brown, Sir Richard.

Mentioned in account of petition in *C.J.* 23 November 1667.

Pyne, Valentine.

Master gunner (*D.N.B.*).

Mentioned 17 February 1667/8.

Queen Consort.

Katherine of Braganza.

Mentioned 22 September, 26 October 1666.

Queen Elizabeth. See Elizabeth.

Queen Mother.

Henrietta Maria. Mentioned 22 September, 26 October 1666.

Rainolds, John.

Dean of Lincoln. Died 1607.

Disputant on Puritan side 1604, Hampton Court.

Mentioned 11 March 1667/8.

Rainsford (Raynsford), Sir Richard.
    Exchequer Judge. Presided over the Commissioners on the Act of
    Settlement. Formerly member for Northampton (*D.N.B.*).
    Mentioned 28 November 1667, 20, 23 April 1668.

Ratcliff, Sir George.
    Secretary to Strafford.
    Precedent mentioned 18, 29 November 1667.

RATCLIFF, John.   Chester.
    8 January 1666/7. "An ill reporter of Mr Leigh's bill."
    11 March 1667/8. Wants severer penalties for dissenters.

Rawleigh (Raleigh), Sir Walter.
    1552–1618.
    Quoted on forts by Prynne or Coventry, 17 February 1667/8.

Read, Mr.
    Mentioned by Sandys, 28 April 1668.

REEVES, Sir George.   Eye, Suffolk.
    Court party.
    16 November 1667. For sending reasons to Lords.
    (23 November 1667. A "Mr Reeve" mentioned.)

Reynolds.
    Servant to Newborough.
    Mentioned 8 May 1668.

Richard II.
    Mentioned 3 March 1667/8.

RICHARDSON, Thomas, Baron Cramond.   Norfolk.
    Court party.
    14 December 1667. Bill for naturalisation.
    3 March 1667/8. Justifies Heblethwaite's bill.
    1 April 1668. On Wakefield enclosures.
    8 April 1668. Against bill for trial of peers.

Richmond, Charles Stuart, 3rd Duke of. (*D.N.B.*)
    Bill on Allnage mentioned 18, 20 April 1668.

RIGBY, Edward.   Preston.
    Country party.
    7 December 1666. Officers to get no fee for tax collection.
    7 February 1666/7. Plea of privilege for tenants.

Roberts.
    And Winn: the case of the Bodville estate. See under Winn, also
    Bodville.
    25 October, 12, 19, 21, 22, 28, 29 November, 7 December 1666.

ROBINSON, Sir John.   Rye.
    Court party. Afterwards Governor of the Tower.
    31 October 1667. Mentioned in debate on the miscarriages of the war.

Rochester, Bishop. See Bishop of Rochester.

Rochester, Dean of. See Harding.

Rook, see Brooke.

Roos, John Manners, Lord.   Leicester County.
(*D.N.B.*)
Brought in a bill to bastardise Lady Anne Roos's children. This was
passed, and some years later a bill of divorce was also passed, and
he then married Ann, daughter of Lord Ailsbury, and widow by
then of Sir Seymour Shirley (q.v.).
12, 26 November 1666, 12, 17, 21, 23, 29 January 1666/7.

Rothe, John Leslie, 7th Earl of.
4 December 1666. Mentioned in connection with affairs in Scotland.

Rupert, Prince.
Mentioned in connection with enquiries into naval miscarriages,
thanked for share in victory, etc., 16 October 1666.
21, 22, 23, 24, 31 October, 21 November, 1667, 22 February 1667/8.

Rushworth, John.
(*D.N.B.*)
His account of proceedings in 1626 mentioned 8 November 1667 by
Lowther.

Russell, Edward.
22 January 1666/7. Bill for sale of land in Chiswick by executors.

Rutland, Earl of.
Father of Lord Roos above, and evidently known personally to
Milward.
12, 26 November 1666, 21, 29 January 1666/7.

Ruyter, M. van.
Mentioned.

St Asaph, Bishop. See Bishop of St Asaph.

St David's, Bishop of. See Bishop of St David's.

St John, Charles, Lord.   Southampton County.
Afterwards Country party. Later Marquis of Winchester.
3, 4, 5 December 1666. His affair with Sir Andrew Henly.
6 November 1667. Against Clarendon (second article).
14 December 1667. To report on conference.
16 December 1667. Reports.
15 February 1667/8. Against waste of timber in the New Forest.
10 April 1668. On Habeas Corpus bill.

Sancroft, Dr.
Dean of St Paul's. Later Archbishop, and non-juror (*D.N.B.*).
2, 7 November 1666. Preaching mentioned.

Sandwich, Edward Montague, Earl of.
Commander of the *Blue Squadron*, mentioned 26 October 1667, 20
February 1667/8, 11, 14, 16, 21 April, 4 May 1668.

SANDYS (SANDS, SANDIS, SAUNDERS, etc.), Colonel Samuel. Worcester.
Court party. His family owned land in the Fen country which was
the subject of much litigation.
18 October 1666. Seconded by Williams, suggests officers lend
money to the King, and all rich men.
22 October 1666. On debates becoming public.
17, 23, 24, 28 January 1666/7. On the matter of the Bedford Levels.
22, 24 October 1667. On the same.
30 October 1667. Against the bill against recusants.
4, 7 November 1667. Bedford Levels bill.
26, 29 November 1667. Information of a sick man with something
to disclose about a cheat upon the King.
2 December 1667. On bribery.
5 December 1667. Opposes enclosure for Cambridge pest-houses.
12 February 1667/8. On abuse of car-men outside the House.
18 February 1667/8. Petition about William Milward and Theswell.
27 February 1667/8. To raise the price of wine one-third.
5 March 1667/8. Levels bill.
11 March 1667/8. Toleration and a standing army go together.
12 March 1667/8. Levels bill, and for the tax on wine.
13 March 1667/8. For the Conventicle Act.
26 March 1668. Against Churchill and Broderick going to Ireland.
On Harman.
3 April 1668. Mention of faults in his Levels bill.
9 April 1668. To recall grants made to the King.
24 April 1668. Against Penn.
28 April 1668. On Richard Lucie's bill.
2 May 1668. Against the London bill.
4 May 1668. The House must make good the charges against Penn

Sawtin, Mr (Sawyer, Sir Robert, 1633–1692, D.N.B.?). Mentioned 22
November 1667.

Scarsdale, Robert Leake, Earl of.
Chaplain to Archbishop Sheldon.
Mentioned 28 November 1666.

SCAWEN, Robert. Cockermouth.
Chiefly concerned here with a bill to restore his son Francis, falsely
outlawed for stealing a mare, to his full rights in blood.
12, 17, 21 January 1666/7.
13 December 1667. Complaint against Keeling on this matter.
9 April 1668. Opposes repair of Corrie Bridge.
24 April 1668. Against impeachment of Penn.

Scrogg(s), Sir William.
Later Chief Justice, 1678. A friend of Buckingham (D.N.B.).
9 December 1667. Opens case for defendants against Cambridge
pest-houses.

Scrogg(s), Sir William (*continued*):
>20 April 1668. Accuses three parts of the House, including the Speaker, of being Adventurers (in Ireland).
>23 April 1668. On the Adventurers' case again.

Secretary, Mr. See Morice.

Serjeant-at-arms. See Norfolk, James.
>Mentioned 2, 24, 31 October 1666, 6 February 1666/7, 12, 22, 25 November 1667, 13 February 1667/8, 21 April 1668.

SEYMOUR, Edward. Hindon.
>Became Speaker 1673, Treasurer of the Navy 1676. Court party. His father Sir Edward was member for Totnes. (*D.N.B.*)
>5 October 1666. Reports as Chairman on Irish bill.
>13, 15 October 1666. Carries above to Lords.
>29 October 1666. Reports on Canary Company.
>1 December 1666. Affronts Speaker.
>5 December 1666. Amendments to Irish Cattle bill.
>11 January 1666/7. Opposes Higgins's bill.
>29 January 1666/7. Long "impertinent" speech against Roos.
>4 February 1666/7. Conference about Mordaunt.
>26 October 1667. Opens case against Clarendon.
>31 October 1667. Affronted by Coventry.
>6 November 1667. Third article against Clarendon.
>7 November 1667. Accused by Marvell of saying the King was unfit to govern.
>8 November 1667. Moves for impeachment of Clarendon.
>12 November 1667. Takes impeachment to the Lords.
>13 November 1667. Reports on same.
>27 November 1667. In the Chair in committee on trade.
>29 November 1667. One of the managers of a conference.
>6 December 1667. Being absent, his place is taken by Atkins.
>19 February 1667/8. Wants agreement with Dutch to be read.
>21 February 1667/8. In the Chair.
>11 March 1667/8. Against comprehension, but for less severe penalties.
>7 April 1668. Opposes Lenthall's bill.
>8 April, 1 May 1668. Opposes Fowler's bill.
>5 May 1668. Opposes Stanley's bill.

SHAW, Sir John. Lyme Regis.
>Collector of customs. Recorder and one time Mayor of Colchester. Court party.
>11 November 1667. Against Clarendon's custom policy.

Sheldon, Gilbert.
>Archbishop of Canterbury. Of a Derbyshire and Staffordshire family, with friends in those counties with whom he lived in retirement during the Civil Wars (*D.N.B.*).

Sheldon, Gilbert (*continued*):
   Milward dines with him fairly often, and was on terms of some
      intimacy, as it was at Lambeth he apparently celebrated his first
      birthday in London with his cousin and his son-in-law.
   28 September, 28 October, 12, 21, 22, 28 November 1666.
   25 March 1668.

Sheldon, Sir Joseph.
   Nephew and biographer of the above. A Sheriff of London and
      afterwards Lord Mayor. His daughter married Sir John Cotton.
   Mentioned 5 November 1666, when Milward dines with him;
      25 October 1667.

Shirley, Sir Seymour.
   See also Ailsbury and Roos.
   Bill, 11, 15, 21 January 1666/7.

Shirley. See Stanley.

Simmons (Symonds).
   A boatman belonging to one of the Custom-house ketches.
   Mentioned as having conveyed Clarendon away, 12 December 1667.

Skinner, Thomas.
   An East India Merchant.
   The Lords gave judgment for him against the East India Company,
      and the Company's petition against this judgment was brought
      into the house by Sir Robert Brooke, 17 April 1668, and debated
      24 April, 1, 2, 4, 7, 8 May 1668.
   The matter caused such disputes between the Houses that all records
      were later expunged from the *Journals*, but see H.M.C. 8th Report,
      pp. 107 ff., 165 ff., etc.

SLANNING, Sir Nicholas.   Plympton (Plimton).
   Later cup-bearer to the Queen (*D.N.B.*; *C.J.* VIII, 642). Court party.
   23, 27 October 1666. Election debated.
   3 April 1668. Against Tyrrell.

SMITH, Sir Thomas.   Chester City.
   28 March 1668. Defends Sir Peter Pindar.

SMITH, Sir William.   Buckingham Borough.
   Mentioned 4 May 1668.

"Sollicitor, Mr." See Finch, Sir Heneage.

Southampton, Thomas Wriothesley, Earl of.
   Mentioned 26, 28 September 1666, 26 October 1667.

"Speaker, Mr." See Turner, Sir Edward.

Speaker of Irish Commons attacked 20 April 1668.

Spencer, Henry le.
   Bishop (q.v.). of Norwich.
   Case mentioned (14 Edward III), 9, 29 November 1667.

SPRAG, Sir Edward. Dover.
  Concerned with the war, 1665–67 (*D.N.B.*).
  19, 22 October 1667. Defends the division of the Fleet.
  7 November 1667. Against Clarendon.
  27 February 1667/8. For a tax on wine to prevent excesses.

SPRY, Arthur. St Mawes.
  Court party.
  7 March 1667/8. On tunning.

Stamford, Lord.
  And Haselrigg (*D.N.B.*).
  Mentioned 6 February 1666/7, 29 November 1667.

Stanley (Shirley), Sir Charles.
  See H.M.C. 8th Report, p. 110*a*.
  Bill to sell land.
  16, 29 January 1666/7, 5 May 1668.

Stanley, Thomas. Brother of William Stanley.
  2nd Baron Stanley. Bill of impeachment rejected by Henry VI,
    1459. See *Rot. Parl.* v, 349, ff. 369–70.
  Mentioned 29 November 1667.

STEWARD, Robert. Castle Rising.
  26 November 1666. In the Chair.
  9 November 1667. Long speech on nature of treason.
  8 April 1668. Speaks well against toleration.
  25 April 1668. On supply.
  4 May 1668. On London bill.

Stillingfleet, Dr.
  Noted divine and later Bishop of Worcester 1689–99 (*D.N.B.*).
  Mentioned in connection with sermons to House, 24 September,
    10, 11, 24 October 1668.

Stonehouse.
  Petition of John, Mary and Dorothy Stonehouse against Clarendon.
    See Noble, *House of Cromwell*, II, 537, where relationships of
    Lenthalls and Stonehouses, etc., are given. For this case see
    C.J. IX, 74, etc.
  Mentioned 3 December 1667, 15 February 1667/8, 7 April 1668.

Story, Dr John.
  Convicted of treason and executed 1571 (*D.N.B.*; Holdsworth, IV,
    232, etc.).
  Mentioned 9 November 1667.

Stradling, Dr George.
  Chaplain to the Archbishop. A Royalist (*D.N.B.*).
  28 October 1666. Preached at Lambeth.

Strafford, Thomas Wentworth, Earl of.
  Mentioned in Mordaunt case and in Clarendon's, 26 January,
    5 February 1666/7, 29 October, 8, 15, 18, 29 November 1667.

STRANGWAYS, Colonel Giles.   Dorset.
See bitter reference to him by Marvell on his death in 1675 (*Letters*, p. 320).
13 March 1667/8.   "Excellent" on toleration.

STREETE, Thomas.   Worcester.
Court party.   Later a judge (*D.N.B.*).
11 December 1667.   Moves to hear Keeling before condemning him.

STRICKLAND, Sir Thomas.   Westmorland.
Court party.   Roman Catholic, 1676/7.
8 November 1667.   A good speech on precedents of impeachment.
11 March 1667/8.   Against sending the matter of toleration to the King.
26 March 1668.   For the Durham bill.

Stroude, Richard.
Case (4 Henry VIII) mentioned 12 November 1667.

Surveyor-General.   See Harbord, Sir Charles.

Sussex, Thomas Savile, Earl of.
5 May 1668.   Bill for securing £500 to Lord Thomas Savile.

SWALE, Sir Solomon.   Aldborough, Yorkshire.
Court party.   Roman Catholic.   Derbyshire family (Harl. MS. 5509, f. 16).
30 October 1667.   Against the bill against recusants.

SWINSEN, John.   Tamworth.
Country party.
13 October 1666.   "Excellent" for Irish cattle bill.
15 October 1666.   "And that party" against the sale of chimney money.   For land tax.
11 January 1666/7.   Against Higgins.
31 October 1667.   With Marvell and Boscawen for Pett.
29 November 1667.   Reports on conference with the Lords.
5 December 1667.   Against sending vote to Lords.
6 March 1667/8.   Against tax on tunnage.
11, 13 March 1667/8.   Against Conventicle Act.
8 April 1668.   To refer toleration to the King.
2 May 1668.   On committee in Skinner affair.

TALBOT, Sir John.   Knaresborough.
Court party.
18 December 1667.   Teller for Ayes on Clarendon bill.

Taylor, Richard.
Formerly member for King's Lynn.
Bill on his estate, 9, 10, 17 April 1668.

Taylor, William.
An officer of Windsor (*C.J.* VIII, 645).
Petition against Mordaunt, 2, 3, 6 November, 3 December 1666, 25 October 1667.

TEMPLE, Sir Richard. Buckingham.
Politician with somewhat stormy record in early Parliament of
Charles II. Country party at this time. (*D.N.B.*)
5 October 1666. Corrects "Mr Sollicitor" on the word "nuisance".
11 October 1666. Moves to give the King £1,600,000 with which to
carry on the war.
6, 9, 16, 21 November 1667. Against Clarendon.
29 November 1667. On accounts.
5 December 1667. Against the vote against the Lords.
17 February 1667/8. On Sheerness.
18 February 1667/8. Brings in his Triennial Bill. (Temple had
strongly opposed the repeal of the earlier Triennial Act in 1664.
H.M.C. 7th Report, p. 485.)
19 February 1667/8. On Dutch League.
29 February 1667/8. To lay a tax on wine at Customs.
8, 18 April, 1 May 1668. Mentioned in connection with Thomas
Gower's (Gore's) bill and against Fowler.

Thelfe. Probably copyist's error for William Tibbes.
A clerk to the Irish Commissioners.
Witness against Antrim, 20 April 1668.

Theswell, Robert. See Milward, William.
18 February 1667/8. Offenders against Irish Cattle Act.

THOMAS, Robert. Cardiff (probably in 1665).
See W. R. Williams, *Parl. Hist. of Principality of Wales*, p. 107.
Disputed election with Bassett. Became 2nd Baronet, 1673. Married
Mary Button. Later Gentleman of Privy Chamber. His one
speech in this session is recorded by Cobbett (p. 384) and by the
author of the *Proceedings* (p. 26) and by Milward below.
7 November 1667. Fourteenth and nineteenth articles against
Clarendon.

THOMPSON, Sir William. Walbrook.
Possibly Country party.
11 March 1667/8. Toleration economically sound.
12 March 1667/8. Against excise in London on wine and brandy.
11 April 1668. Against falling interest rate.
24 April 1668. Mentioned in debate on Skinner case as a member of
the East India Company.

Thomson. Probably Robert Thomson, a London investor in Irish
lands.
A witness in the Irish case.
19 February 1667/8.

THROCKMORTON (FROGMORTON), Sir Benham. Gloucestershire.
Court party.
11 February 1667/8. Gives case for commoners of Forest of Dean.
16 April 1668. Against the forbidding of deer in the Forest of Dean.

THURLAND (THURLOW), Sir Edward.   Reigate.
Court party (*D.N.B.*).
24 October 1666. Against duels.
2 May 1668. Not proper for Lords to try what Westminster Hall
cannot.

THYNNE (THIN), Sir James.   Wiltshire.
"The first of his line", says Clarendon (*Cont.* p. 915).
Uncle of Thomas Thynne, member for Wiltshire, 1670 (*D.N.B.*).
28 February 1667/8. Against insolence of sectaries.

Tiddman (Tyddiman, Teddeman), Sir Thomas.
Shipowner of Dover. Vice-Admiral (*D.N.B.*).
14 April 1668. Concerned against Penn.

Tillotson, Dr.
Broad Church (*D.N.B.*).
2, 7 November 1666. Asked to preach and preached.

Tirwhit. See Jerret, Sir Philip.

TOMKINS, Sir Thomas.   Weobley.
Country party. Tribute in Marvell's *Last Instructions*.
25 July 1667. Famous motion against a standing army.
17 December 1667. Presents Carr's petition.

TORRINGTON, Christopher Monk, Earl.   Devonshire.
Son of Duke of Albemarle.
2 December 1667. Moves not to depart from any just privilege of the
House.

Townshend, Horatio.
1st Viscount (*D.N.B.*).
Bill about land in Norfolk near East Rainham, 21, 24, 30 October,
19 December 1667.

Treasurer.
Thomas Wriothesley, 4th Earl of Southampton.
See Southampton.

TRELAWNEY, Sir Jonathan.   Cornwall.
Court party.
12 March 1667/8. To borrow from the City.
26 March 1668. On Durham bill.
8 April 1668. On lighthouses.

TREVOR, Sir John.   Great Bedwin.
Court party. Secretary of State. A follower of Buckingham. Died
1672 (*D.N.B.*).
14 October 1667. To thank the King for dismissing Clarendon.
23 October 1667. Sent to Rupert and Monk about the division of the
Fleet.
15 November 1667. On adjournment.

Trump, Robert.
  Servant to Sir John Harman.
  Mentioned 17 April 1668.

TURNER, Sir Edward.   Hertford.
  "Mr Speaker", succeeded later by Charlton and Seymour. A lawyer, but could not practise while the House adjourned. During a prorogation the mace was not carried before him, and he could therefore act as a private person. Hence his question to the House below, 7 May 1668.
  18 September 1666. Mentioned twice. Chaplain mentioned.
  21 September 1666. Reads the King's speech.
  12 October, 3 November 1666. Leaves the Chair.
  8 November 1666. Keeps the Chair.
  30 November 1666. For the dissenters.
  1 December 1666. Affronted by Seymour.
  3, 4 December 1666. Leaves Chair.
  5 December 1666. Speaks.
  25, 29 July 1667. Mentioned.
  10 October, 12, 21, 27 November, 6, 13, 19 December 1667.
  (17 March 1667/8, but see Sir William Turner below.)
  26 March 1668. Writ for election caused by Walpole's death. On Commons' power to tax Lords.
  31 March 1668. On ecclesiastical courts.
  23 April 1668. Rebukes Howard for attacking Coventry.
  24 April 1668. Against the impeachment of Penn.
  1 May 1668.
  7 May 1668. Asks if he may practise his calling during adjournment and is told he may not.
  8 May 1668. On privilege.

TURNER, Sir William.   Harwich.
  "Prict for next Lord Mayor" (1668/9).
  14 March 1667/8. On finance.
  17 March 1667/8. On tax on wine.

Tunne, Jo. See Lund.

Twisden, Judge Thomas.
  King's Bench (D.N.B.).
  3, 4 December 1667.

Tyrrell, Judge Thomas.
  Formerly member of Parliament for Maldon.
  Mentioned 4 December 1667, 3 April 1668.

Valentine, Benjamin.
  Mentioned 15 October 1667.

Vane, Sir Henry.
  (D.N.B.)
  Mentioned 29 October 1667.

VAUGHAN, Francis, Lord.   Carmarthen County.
Court party. Married a daughter of the Earl of Southampton (q.v.).
Milward identifies him as with one eye.
14 October, 6, 11 November 1667. Against Clarendon.
VAUGHAN, Sir Henry.   Carmarthen County, in place of Lord Vaughan
(q.v.).
11 April 1668. Election debated.
VAUGHAN, John.   Carmarthen Borough until 1679.
Married a daughter of Halifax. Later Earl of Carbery, etc. (*D.N.B.*).
Not to be confused with Vaughan below, though Milward does
not distinguish between them, and all references to John Vaughan
are listed below.
VAUGHAN, John.   Cardigan County.
Knight and Chief Justice, May 1668. Country party. A chief mover
against Clarendon whose bitter remarks on him may be read in the
Life (pp. 923–4).
14, 26, 29 October, 6, 9, 11, 15, 16, 21, 29 November, 2, 5 December
1667. Concerned in proceedings against Clarendon.
25 October 1667, 12 February, 6, 11 March 1667/8. A bill to discharge Sheriffs from suits arising from the Fire.
12 February, 16 April 1668. Forest of Dean.
19 February 1667/8. Against bill on jurors.
27 February 1667/8. On abuses of vintners.
9 March 1667/8. On Subsidies.
17 March 1667/8. On finance.
26 March 1668. Durham bill. On taxing nobles.
8 April 1668. On trial of peers. Against toleration.
21 April 1668. Defends Sandwich.
24 April 1668. Against Penn.
28 April 1668. For the Conventicle Act.
1 May 1668. On supply.
1, 2, 4, 5, 8 May 1668. On Skinner case.
8 May 1668. On Probert's privilege.
Vernon, Colonel Edward.
Discovered a conspiracy to the Lord-Lieutenant, 1663 (Carte, IV,
124).
Mentioned in the Irish case, 19 February 1667/8, 20 April 1668.
Vernon, Colonel George.
Probably the High Sheriff of Derbyshire during the Carlton-Wylde
affair, 1664/5, and the opponent of Sacheverall in the election
following Milward's death, and later M.P. for the county in 1678/9.
Mentioned in Introduction.
Viner, Sir Robert.
Afterwards Lord Mayor. Married a Fulwood of Middleton Hall,
Derbyshire.
Mentioned 25 October 1667.

Walker, Sir Edward.
  Garter King-at-Arms.
WALKER, Sir Walter (? Robert or Thomas). Exeter.
  3 April 1668. Ecclesiastical Courts.
WALLER, Sir Edmund. Hastings.
  The poet, old but active. Country party.
  9 November 1666. Carries a message to the Lords about seamen.
  11 January 1666/7. For Higgins's bill.
  14 October 1667. For thanking the King for dismissing Clarendon.
  23 October 1667. Sent to Rupert and Monk.
  30 October 1667. Against the Recusancy bill.
  29 November 1667. One of the conference with the Lords.
  2 December 1667. On Clarendon.
  12 March 1667/8. Tax to be on unlicensed vintners.
  17 March 1667/8. For laying tax on retailers.
  8 April 1668. On lighthouses. For the dissenters.
  22 April 1668. Against falling interest.
  24 April 1668. Against the expulsion of Penn.
  7 May 1668. On adjournment and the Speaker's mace.
  8 May 1668. On the Skinner case, etc.
Wallis (Wallace), James.
  The Scottish general and Covenanter (D.N.B.).
  4 December 1666.
WALPOLE, Sir Edward. Norfolk.
  Grandfather of Robert Walpole. A Royalist.
  16 January 1666/7. Message to the Lords about Mordaunt.
  26 October 1667. On deliberating a just case justly (that is, the
    Clarendon impeachment).
  11 November 1667. In favour of parting with Dunkirk.
  19 November 1667. For acquitting Ashburnham.
  10 December 1667. To put off the Adventurers' petition.
  26 March 1668. Notice of death.
WANKLIN (WANKLEY), Colonel Thomas. Westbury.
  Court party. Expelled, 1677/8.
  27 March 1668. Petition against Mr Ash, son of Jo. Ash of Gold-
    smiths' Hall.
  28 March 1668. The same.
Warden of the Fleet. See Fleet.
Warren, Sir William.
  Shipbuilder and Alderman of the City.
  Mentioned 29 November 1667.
WARWICK, Sir Philip. Westminster.
  Vice-Treasurer to Southampton. Court party (D.N.B.). Friend of
    Juxon, of whose will he was overseer.
  26 September 1666. Gives accounts of office.
  26 October 1667. Defends Clarendon.

WARWICK, Sir Philip (*continued*):
11 November 1667. Against Clarendon.
11 March 1667/8. On toleration.

Water Bailiffs.
Petition against, 23 November 1667.

WELD (WILD), George.   Much Wenlock.
Court party.
17 February 1667/8. On Sheerness bill.
26 February 1667/8. On Cleveland's bill.
11 March 1667/8. Against Brooke's bill.
17 March 1667/8. Against excise on retailers of tobacco.
1 April 1668. Opposes Clarkton's bill.
4 May 1668. Carries bill for Penn's impeachment to the Lords.

WERDEN (WORDEN), Colonel Robert.   Chester City.
Mentioned in Penn's case, 4 May 1668.

Westminster, Dean of. See Dalbin, Dr.

Westminster and Southwark Bailiffs.
Ordered, 24 October 1667, to search woodmongers' sheds.

Weymondsold, Davies.
Manors in Wimbledon mentioned 6 March 1667/8.

Wharton, Humphrey.
Mentioned 31 October, 19 December 1667, in connection with some
lead mines leased to Bishop of Durham (see Cosin's *Correspondence* II, *passim*). Married a sister of Colonel Bierly (Byerley) (q.v.).

WHARTON, Dr Thomas.   Beverley.
The bill for settling disputed mortgage in which he and Perkins and
Bierly concerned mentioned 9, 12 November 1667, 11 March
1667/8.

Wharton (Wooten), Dr.
Parliamentary Chaplain. Preached 9 December 1666, 29 July 1667.

WHEELER, Sir Charles.   Cambridge.
26 October 1667. Clarendon the only obstruction to settlement of
realm.
7, 11 November 1667. Against Clarendon.
19 February 1667/8. On the abuses of Church government.
11 March 1667/8. For indulgence.

White, Thomas.
The Attorney. Of Dorset, an old Parliamentarian.
Mentioned in the matter of Chune's privilege, 6 February 1666/7.

WHORWOOD, Brome.   Oxford.
Country party. "Great Whorwood", according to Marvell.
12 November 1666. Bitter speech about supply, and going home
"like fools as we came".

WHORWOOD, Brome (*continued*):
   14, 15, 16, 28 April, 6 May 1668. A bill about alimony demanded by
     his wife.

Whorwood, Jane. See above.

WILD, Sir William. London.
   King's Serjeant (1661) and Recorder (1659–68).
   King's Bench. Turned off Bench, 1679.
   Mentioned 2, 9 December 1667.

Wildman, Major John.
   An Alderman and Parliamentarian. Said to be Buckingham's friend
     at this time (Carte, IV, 222).
   12 December 1666. Mentioned as a villain.

WILLIAMS, Colonel Henry (alias Cromwell). Huntingdon.
   "Surly Williams, the accomptants' bane", of Marvell.
   18 October 1666. On loan for the King.
   22 April 1668. Fastened upon bill for falling interest. Opposed by
     Waller.

WILLIAMS, Sir Trevor. Monmouth County in the *Returns*, but Milward says Pembroke.
   11 February 1667/8. Election debated.
   4 April 1668. Petition from vintners.
   28 April 1668. Proviso to Recusancy bill.

WILLIAMSON, Sir Joseph. (Thetford, 1669.)
   Secretary of State 1674–9. Court party (*D.N.B.*).
   31 October 1667. Brings letter from Arlington.

Wimbleton, Davies.
   (See *C.J.* 6 March, etc. Davies Weymondsold, whose estates were
     in Wimbledon, Surrey. His sister married Mr Dowdeswell (q.v.).)
   6 March 1667/8. Mentioned.

WINCH, Sir Humphrey. Bedfordshire.
   Court party. A legal family.
   11 March 1667/8. For comprehension. Against toleration.
   2 May 1668. Tells a story.

Winchelsea, Mayor of. See Austin, Robert; and May.

Winchester, Bishop of. See Bishop of Winchester.

WINDHAM, Sir Edward. Bridgwater.
   King's Marshal.
   8 November 1667. Against Clarendon.
   11 November 1667. Petition against Clarendon by Margaret Caron
     (Zenookes).
   16 November 1667. Against Clarendon.
   22 November 1667. Mentioned in bribery information.
   16 March 1667/8. Takes Coventry down irregularly.
   17 April 1668. To name commissioners for £300,000.

WINDHAM, Sir Hugh.   Minehead.
  16 October 1667. Complains of Keeling.
  11, 13 December 1667. In connection with Keeling's case.
  4 March 1667/8. Informs the House of Cromwellian Conventicles.
  11 March 1667/8. Against toleration.
  12 March 1667/8. To lay tax on wine.
  28 March 1668. On fees at the Customs house.

Windham, Judge Wadham.
  Brother of Sir Hugh, also a Judge.
  28 November 1667.

Winn, Griffith and Thomas and Roberts.
  Bodville's estate. See Bodville, Roberts.
  25 October, 19, 21, 22, 27 November, 7 December 1666.

WINNINGTON, Sir Francis.   New Windsor.
  Later Country party (*D.N.B.*).
  9 December 1667. Counsel for plaintiff in matter of pest-houses at
    Cambridge.

Winter, Sir John.
  An iron-master (*D.N.B.*). His case mentioned as early as 1640
    (Notestein, *D'Ewes*, p. 119).
  Petitions, etc., in connection with the Forest of Dean.
  22 October, 12 November 1667, 11, 12, 17 February 1667/8.
  Cf. *C.J.* 12 February 1667/8, a very full account.

WISEMAN (WYSEMAN), Sir Richard.   Maldon.
  Court party.
  3 April 1668. "Most learnedly" on ecclesiastical courts.

Wood, Thomas.
  2 December 1667. Bill to sell land read a second time. Not noticed
    in *Journals.*

Wooten. See Wharton, Dr.

Worden. See Werden.

WREN, Mathew.   St Michael.
  Court party. Secretary (1667–72) to the Duke of York (*D.N.B.*).
  20 February, 26 March 1667/8.

York, James Stuart, Duke of.
  Afterwards James II.
  Mentioned very frequently in connection with debates on naval
    affairs and the division of the Fleet: 19, 21, 22, 26, 31 October,
    4, 7, 13 November, 10, 19 December 1667, 14, 15, 17, 20, 21, 22
    February, 5, 12, 16 March 1667/8, 26, 31 March, 9, 10, 11, 17, 20,
    21 April 1668.

YOUNG, Sir Walker.   Clifton, Dartmouth, Hardness.
  (Vice Thomas Kendall, deceased January 1666/7.)
  11 March 1667/8. "Impertinently" for indulgence.

PARLIAMENT OBSERVATIONS

of the

DAILY PROCEEDINGS *in this* SESSION

BEGINNING *SEPTEMBER*

THE 18TH, 1666.

SEPTEMBER 17TH. This day I delivered in the Parliament's writ[1] with the indentures returned by Mr. Ashton, the High Sheriff, concerning my election to Mr. John Agar, the Clerk of the Crown, at his office in Middle Temple, from whom I received my certificate. He said his fee was two shillings or half-a-crown. I gave him five shillings.

SEPTEMBER 18TH. This day the Parliament met; the number of members that then were present was about an hundred and fifty. The Earl Ogle and Mr. Laurence Hyde, my Lord Chancellor's younger son, were the Commissioners that gave me the oaths of allegiance and supremacy, which when I had taken I went into the House and took my place as a member of it.

At the Speaker's coming into the House he made three congies to his Chair, and so went to the table.

Then came in his chaplain, who read common prayers, and after that the Speaker took his Chair.

Then a bill was brought in and read concerning corporations that owed money to any man, and the remedy prescribed how to recover a due debt from the same corporation. The bill was ordered to be read a second time on Friday following.

[1] A writ for the Derbyshire election was issued on 9 October 1665 (*C.J.* VIII, 613, S.P.D. 29, CXXXIV, no. 58). There was no session of Parliament between the adjournment of the Oxford Meeting on 31 October 1665 and that beginning 18 September 1666.

Several motions were made to the Speaker for the granting new writs for the election of members in the places of those that were dead or called up to the House of Peers.

It was moved by Serjeant Maynard that before a writ was granted out or sent to any place for a new election the person dead or removed should be nominated in the House.

It was also moved by Mr. Prynne that every person that is or shall be called to the House of Lords shall have his special writ before the Speaker shall grant out any writ for the electing another member in his place; and his reason was, because a member that is to be called up to the House of Peers remains still a member of the House of Commons until he hath received his writ by which the King calls him up to sit in the House of Lords.

Mr. Secretary told the Speaker that the King did conceive that by reason of the late terrible fire in London many of the members of the House of Commons might be surprised with such a consternation that it might put a present stop to their coming up, and the House at the first day's meeting might not be so full as His Majesty desired. Therefore His Majesty desired that the House should be adjourned until Friday next, at what time he would speak to them of the great affairs of the kingdom.

Accordingly the House did adjourn till Friday next.

SEPTEMBER 21ST. This day the King in his robes and crown made a speech to the Parliament in the Lords' House.[1]

The speech was sent to [the] Speaker of the House of Commons, who read it to the House. It was voted to send the thanks of the House to His Majesty for his gracious speech and to assure him that they would take some speedy course for raising money for the carrying on the war against the Dutch.

And they sent to the Lords to desire their concurrence to the same, and several Grand Committees were nominated for several businesses.[2] And divers persons were added to those

[1] Cobbett, IV, 332, begins with the King's speech.

[2] C.J. VIII, 625, gives Milward's name in the list of the Committee of Privileges. A complete list of the committees on which Milward served is not given here. The *Journals* do not always distinguish between the diarist and his cousin Robert, as, for example, on 16 October. See p. 24, n. 1 below.

committees. I was added to the committee of privileges. It was debated whether it was not against the privileges of the House to desire the Lords' concurrence as aforesaid. It was voted generally that it was not any breach of their privilege.

It was also determined that if there be more than one that stand for a place and one of them be unduly returned, yet he ought to sit as a member in the House until the opponent come and bring it to a trial, and then if his return be proved to be illegal he is to withdraw from sitting in the House.

But if two stand for one place, and both of them be returned, and one only can serve, in this case neither of them is to sit as a member of the House until the election be determined.

It was this day ordered that the House shall be called on Monday, the first of October, and what member soever shall be then absent and cannot give a satisfactory answer for his absence, he shall be fined and shall pay twenty pounds.

It was also ordered this day that the officers of receipts shall bring in their accounts on Monday, the 24th of September of all the moneys that they have received of the taxes, prizes and militia money, and how it is and hath been disbursed, to a committee or to some select members to be appointed to examine their accounts and to report them to the House.

When the King was sat in the House of Peers he sent down the Master of the Black Rod to the House of Commons. When the Speaker had acquainted the House that the Master of the Black Rod was at the door and had asked the House whether he should be sent for in, he was then called in, and after that he had made three obeisances to the Speaker he came hastily to the Speaker's Chair, and then told Mr. Speaker that the King commanded the House of Commons to attend him in the House of Peers. Which done, he returned, the Speaker not moving his hat to him.

The House then attended the Speaker to the House of Lords.

SEPTEMBER 22ND. This day was the bill brought in against the importation of Irish cattle into England. At the debate it was opposed by Sir Charles Harbord and a Norfolk knight,

Sir William Doyley, Sir John Holland and others. It was
ordered to be reassumed into debate.[1]

It was moved to the Speaker that in regard of the scarcity of
lodgings and habitations for them whose houses and dwellings
have been burned, all Popish recusants (except the Queen's
and Queen Mother's attendants) that would not come to the
church nor had been at the church for six months last past, and
that would not take the oaths of supremacy and allegiance, and
all sectaries that had not come to the church for the last six
months and all foreigners that were not denizated or tolerated
by the King should depart the city and not remain within ten
miles of it upon the penalty of ten pounds a month.

This bill was brought in by Mr. Prynne, but it was laid
aside.

It was very earnestly moved that all plate should be brought
into the Mint and coined for the increase of coin, in regard that
the very specie of money is supposed to be wanting.

There were these objections against this motion: 1st Objection:
First, that at this time it would be a dishonour to the nation and
that foreign nations nations which are not our friends, and
those that were our professed enemies would be encouraged by
it and induced to believe that we were reduced to that hardship
and want of treasure that we were forced to coin our plate into
money to maintain the war.

2nd Objection: Secondly, that the plate so coined would suffer
a very great loss, the fashion of much of it being very costly
and of great value, worth 8s. an ounce, yet at the Mint would
not be valued at above 5s. the ounce.

Another bill was brought in against the importation of French
commodities. It was backed with these arguments: 1st Argument: First that the linen cloth brought in did yearly stand us
in seven or eight hundred thousand pounds, and that we did
not export for it of our English commodities above fourscore
thousand pounds in one year; the rest then of necessity must

[1] See bibliographical note above on the Irish cattle Act, p. xxviii.
Norfolk opposition to this and similar Acts at all periods is due to the
fact that the county has always devoted much attention to fattening
cattle, imported from less fertile, or less expensive, districts.

be supplied with our money, by which means our coin was exhausted.

2nd Argument: Secondly that the King of France did prohibit all our English commodities, and that if any of our commodities were found in his dominion they were assuredly burned. Colonel Birch.

It was also resolved that the general grievances of our nation should be taken into consideration.

The House took up the debate of the present great scarcity of coin, the way how to make it more plentiful, and whence the cause of the scarcity thereof did proceed.

Some said that the London bankers were the principal causers of it, for the treasure[1] of [the] kingdom from all places [there]of being brought into their hands, it had no circulation of returning into the country again, for the making more plentifully and for men's present supply of money.

It was proposed that a book of register should be had, that if men's estates were entered there, and the clearness of their estates were well understood, men might be supplied upon all occasions; that is, if men's estates were well known they might have credit enough for money. Colonel Birch.

It was truly and well said that if the importation of foreign goods did not exceed the exportation of our own commodities it would be a certain way to enrich us and to increase our treasure.

SEPTEMBER 24TH. It was this day moved that for the preventing of ravishing infants, and for the avoiding unlawful and clandestine marriages, that no persons should be married but they should first be asked three times in the church, and in case the man should dwell in one parish and the woman in another, the minister of that parish where the man dwells and where the banns were published should send a certificate to the incumbent of that parish where the woman dwells, that so the banns may be published there also. And that neither the bishop nor Chancellor nor any other officer should grant a licence to marry but it should incur a *praemunire*.[1]

---

[1] A correction of the MS. here seems to be in Milward's own handwriting.

And if any minister do marry any persons without they be asked 3 times in the churches as above said, he shall, for his first offence, forfeit the value of his benefice for two years, and for his second offence in that kind, shall be suspended and made uncapable of any future benefice.

And if the woman so married shall be of the full age of five and twenty years, that she shall not be capable of any dower.

Mr. Prynne brought in this bill, which was generally disliked and said to be full of dirty language.

The election of Sir Geoffrey Palmer's son who was chosen a burgess of Peterborough was this day called in question. There was two things in debate concerning his election.

First, whether he or his competitor, which was the Lord Fitzwilliam of Northamptonshire, had the greater number of votes.

Secondly, whether the return was legally made: for there are two which pretend to have power to make returns: viz: the Bishop of Peterborough and my Lord of Exeter.

This day there was a motion for the repealling that statute against the exportation of raw hides: and that there might be free exportation of horses, corn, and all other commodities.

The ministers that were named to preach at the monthly fast were Dr. Dalbin, the Dean of Westminster, and Dr. Outram, the parson of St. Margaret's, Westminster.

The ministers named to preach at the general fast the tenth of October were Mr. Stillingfleet and Mr. Frambton.

This day a message was sent to the House of Lords to desire their concurrence for the giving His Majesty thanks for his gracious speech, and to offer their assistance in raising a supply for carrying on the war.

Mr. Garroway was ordered to carry the message to the Lords. The Lords readily agreed to the message, and said they would send it to the King, and desire him to appoint a time when he would be attended by both the Houses.

There was a long debate about the revenues of free schools, hospitals etc.

Some moved to have new commissioners added to the ancient founders, which I think was justly opposed, because it [is] evident that new ones have stripped the old ones and their founders of all their intents.

But it is very just and reasonable to provide that the revenues be not unjustly converted to other uses, than was by the donors first intended.

SEPTEMBER 25TH. The House this day entered upon a long and serious debate concerning the fire of London, whether it was by the hand of God, or by design, and whether a committee should be named for the examination of it. Sir Charles Harbord, Sir John Maynard and others for it, Mr. Solicitor and many others were against it, whereupon it was put to the question, and it was carried in the affirmative for a committee to examine it. I was in my judgment against it.

This day the House of Lords sent to us to let us know that the King would have both Houses attend him that afternoon in the Banqueting House.

And after both Houses had presented their desires, His Majesty told them that the money that had been formerly given him had been very successful this year, and that he would as freely lay out whatsoever they should give him for the safety and good of the nation as formerly he had done.

This day the Committee of Privileges should have sat, but it is a rule that when the King sends for the Houses to attend him, all committees for that time are superseded.

A bill was brought in against Certioraries[1] at sessions by Mr. Prynne, to prohibit them unless good cause was showed to the Court or Sessions: Mr. Solicitor was for the continuance of Certioraries, my cousin Milward was against them and carried it.

SEPTEMBER 26TH. This day the bill against Irish cattle was read the second time; very many excellent speeches were made against the committing of the bill especially by the Solicitor, who certainly said as much as the cause would bear. Others

---

[1] Certiorari—an original writ issued out of King's Bench to command judges in inferior courts to return records of the case in question; or a writ to remove a case into Chancery. For this bill see also, H.M.C. 8th Report, p. 113 a.

spoke for the committing the bill and carried it. And so a committee was nominated for the business.

Sir Philip Warwick as Vice-Treasurer to the Earl of Southampton gave an account of his office, and Sir George Carteret brought in his accounts as Treasurer to the Navy; and Sir John Duncombe brought in his accounts as Treasurer to the Ordnance: all these delivered up their accounts to the House, upon which there were many speeches made and long debates upon the manner of examining them; in conclusion there was a committee nominated to examine them.

These two debates held the House till one of the clock.

SEPTEMBER 27TH. This day Mr. Prynne's bill against the episcopal power of granting licences for marriages was cast out, after that he had made a long speech to justify it.

The bill for free schools and hospitals etc. was cast out.[1]

The rest of the day was spent in debate concerning the rebuilding the City of London, the debate [held] till two of the clock.

Three things were offered the House in order to it.

First a model or models: many spoke for them but more spoke against them.

Secondly it was moved that every man might have leave to build upon his own area and propriety, the place where he dwelt, but that also was rejected.

Thirdly it was moved that two large streets, the one from Temple Bar to Leaden Hall, the other from the Bishop's Gate to the Thames, should be first built and then all other streets should be orderly fallen upon and where of necessity they must be enlarged, every man's propriety should be considered: and the right owners should build upon his own ground.

Though this was something controverted and [not] fully satisfactory in all particulars yet it was much assented to and with my consent.

This bill was formerly referred to a committee, but upon the debate the committee desired the House to resume it, whereupon it was moved in the House to present the whole business of the City to the King and to refer it to him to determine it, but upon

---

[1] *C.J.* VIII, 628. This bill is not mentioned.

a full debate it was judged improper to trouble the King with it unless the House also could send some proposals to His Majesty that might tend to the convenience of the speedy rebuilding of it.

It was the general opinion of the whole House that if some speedy way of rebuilding the City was not agreed upon that the City would be in danger never to be built, for if the citizens found a difficulty in it, and that things were not speedily provided for, the merchants and wealthiest of the citizens would alter their course of their life and trade and remove themselves and estates into other countries and so the City would remain miserable for ever.

In the afternoon the accounts were debated at the committee and many speeches were made which I think might well have been spared and the accounts with less ado have been rightly stated and perfected.

SEPTEMBER 28TH.   This day it was first moved and assented to that certain persons should have liberty upon special business to go into the country for ten days.

In the next place it was moved to resume the debate for the rebuilding the City of London: and so long as I stayed it was stoutly moved to refer it to the King, and the City: but in the end it was left unresolved.

In the afternoon the committee met to consider the bill to prohibit importation of Irish cattle. I told my sense against the bringing in of Irish cattle to a Norfolk gent Sir William Doyley who was mainly against the bill: I asked him whether they did breed any beasts in Norfolk; he said they did.

I then asked him whether they could not feed these beasts in their own country; he said they could: I then asked him what need had they then of Irish cattle? He said that if they might be supplied for one year with cattle out of Ireland, they being at present in want of stock, they would desire no more.

The committee could not agree about the penalty to be imposed upon the cattle to be brought in and so it was left at that time.

I went this day to Lambeth, and dined with His Grace who received me with extraordinary favour.

The debate of the accounts was this day resumed and it was moved that the Lord Treasurer should be sent to, to give order that every man that passed any accounts should bring them in with his hand put to them.

It was reported by Sir George Downing from the committee nominated for the increase of coin, that the sense of the committee was against the enjoining the coining of plate but that it should be left to the will and pleasure freely of the owners. And that there should be a remedy provided for the loss and charge that shall fall upon those that shall coin their plate and bullion.

And that they may have the same weight in coin that they have in plate with such abatement as the plate must of necessity suffer in the melting and coining and that the allowance and salary of the Mint and workmen should be raised out of some other commodities not much raising the price of those commodities and abating the King's customs.

This was proposed to be done after this manner: viz: it is supposed that the whole charge of the Mint will be defrayed for one year with the sum of two thousand pounds.

That the tax should be laid upon wines at 10s. a tun, which is two shillings sixpence an hogshead which will be one half farthing a pint, which is an insensible way of raising wine.

The House this day adjourned until Monday because Saturday was the feast of St. Michael the Archangel.

OCTOBER 1ST. This day there was very little done in the House; two things were principally debated. First the patent of the Canary Company.

Secondly the bill for sowing hemp and flax, in which was debated the allowances for the tithe in the behalf of the vicars.

They that undertake the plantation, do offer to pay the vicars for their tithes 2s. 6d. for every acre that is now broken up: but it was moved they should allow them more, or else the tithe in kind.

The House should have been called to-day, and the fine of £20 imposed upon all that were absent, but it was deferred until Monday next.

In the afternoon I went first to the committee for the accounts of the receivers and payers out of the money that was raised for the royal aid; but the debate at the committee was so confused in the way how to proceed in it that I left the committee.

Thence I went to the committee nominated to enquire into the firing of London: that if it were possible to find out the plot if there were any.

The committee examined one man who was then a prisoner whose house was burned and he suspected to have fired his own house but they did make nothing of it.

OCTOBER 2ND. There was this day a very strong debate of a bill brought in by Sir John Duncombe for the calling in the trade of selling gunpowder, that every man that had any gunpowder to sell should bring it in to the officers of the King's Ordnance and Arms, and that no man should sell any but by a licence first had from them.

The ground or pretext of this bill was that the King's powder was embezzled and transported beyond the seas, which was the reason that there was a want and scarcity in the land. And this restraint was not proposed to be general or perpetual, but only when there was a war either at land or sea.

This bill was generally disliked by the House, and had been cast out if it had not been put to the vote, but at the last it was resolved that the bill should be laid aside (but not cast out) until there was some better expedient found out to prevent the embezzling and purloining the powder, it being urged that if this bill was cast out there would not any other bill be brought in this session, and so no provision would be made to prevent an abuse of so great and dangerous a consequence.

But yet the House being not satisfied about the continuing this bill in the House, though laid aside for the present, it was put to the question whether the question should be put whether the bill should be cast out or not.

Upon which the House was divided, and the ayes that were for the putting the question went out, and the noes that were against stayed in;[1] the ayes that went out were 102, of which

[1] *C.J.* VIII, 630, 102–92, Strickland and Goodrick, Littleton and Garroway.

my cousin Milward was one; the noes that stayed in were 92, of which I was one, and so the ayes carried it.

There was this day a bill brought in against divers persons in several counties, that had collected money for the indigent officers, and had never accounted for it, but had great sums of it in their hands, and would neither pay it into the indigent commission officers nor could be got to give any account of it.

It was ordered that the Sergeant-at-Arms should be sent for divers of them to answer their contempt, and that their estates should be seized to satisfy for the money unpaid.

In the afternoon I went to the Committee of Privileges. I am one of that committee where the election of Mr. Palmer the Attorney-general his son and the Lord Fitzwilliam of Northamptonshire for a burgess place of Peterborough was debated.

The Lord Fitzwilliam petitioned the House against Mr. Palmer who was returned and sat in the House; he suggested two things against the legality of his election.

First that the return was not just because the Sheriff had sent the precept to Bailiff of the Dean and Chapter of Peterborough, who made the return of Mr. Palmer, and should have sent it to the Bailiff of the Hundred, who was Bailiff to the Earl of Exeter, who also offered his return of the Lord Fitzwilliam to the Sheriff.

Secondly the Lord Fitzwilliam alleged that he had an hundred voices more than Mr. Palmer had.

The decision of this election was put off because that the witnesses and electors could not with safety be brought up by reason that the town is sorely infested with the plague.

The House adjourned until Thursday in regard that the monthly fast was to be observed to-morrow.

OCTOBER 3RD. This day the House of Commons observed the monthly fast at St. Margaret's, Westminster, where we had two excellent sermons: the first was preached by Mr. Outram, the parson and constant preacher of the church. His text was Eccles: the 7th chap: v: 14th. "In the day of adversity consider."

His proposition or particulars were four.

1. First that God doth send adversity upon a people.
2. What adversity and judgments are.
3. The grounds or reasons why judgments are sent.
4. Fourthly the means to prevent or remove them.

The application to ourselves. That God hath sent his judgments upon us: civil wars: foreign war: scarcity or poverty, a destroying plague, pestilence, a dreadful consuming fire.

The grounds or causes of these judgments are our sins. The means to remove them is true repentance and amendment of our lives, for fasting and prayer without amendment will not do it.

The second sermon was preached by Dr. Dalbin, Dean of Westminster; his text was Luke the 13th chapter: v: 9th. "And if it bear fruit, well: if not, then after that thou shalt cut it down." The scope of his sermon was to show the main drift of the parable of the fruitless fig-tree.

When God starts a nation or Kingdom he expects fruit from it, yes, even from those kingdoms that are not (and have not been) acquainted with his word and gospel, and that they should bring forth fruits of moral virtues infused into them by nature and civil reason as of temperance, justice, and that reigning sins even in those nations have been the destruction of them.

But the Jews, they were God's chosen people after a more peculiar manner and by divers such prerogatives: yet they continually provoked him by their sins and rebellions; he had digged them with his spade and corrections, and many a time with his severe judgments, to see if they would be brought to bring forth fruits: but when they continued fruitless then came the axe to cut them down as a fruitless fig-tree.

The application was to ourselves; we have been and still are guilty of many gross and abominable sins; God hath digged and dunged us and sent many judgments among us: a civil war, a fearful plague, a consuming fire, a general poverty and a foreign war. If after all this we bring not forth fruits meet for repentance, and for the time to come amend our lives, who can tell but that the next judgment (nay, we may justly fear it) may be, cut it down, why cumbreth it the ground? may be an utter excision: from which the good Lord deliver us.

OCTOBER 4TH. This [day] Sir Job Charlton reported to the House the result of the Committee of Privileges concerning the election of Mr. Grey of Nerbe;[1] he petitioned against Mr. Collingwood, who was returned and sat in the House as a member of it, chosen a burgess of Berwick. It was voted that Mr. Grey's petition should be received and Mr. Collingwood, the present sitting member, was ordered to make good his election, and he was allowed six weeks' time to bring up his witnesses.

The House sent their thanks to the Dean of Westminster and to Mr. Outram for their pains in preaching yesterday.

This day the Lords sent down to the House for the naturalising the Lady Arlington, a Dutch lady.

The bill was received and laid by to be passed at leisure.

Then was taken up the great debate for raising money for the King's carrying on the war.

It was the desire of all men to raise the King money according to a due proportion: but there was a long debate that held the House till one of the clock, both when to consider of it, how much was necessary, and the manner of raising it. It was at last concluded that a committee should be nominated to examine the charge of the Navy, and how much was necessary to carry on the war for the future: that they should inspect into the former charge of the ten last years, and so make report of it on Friday or Saturday next or as soon as possibly they could; and that on Thursday next, the 11th of October, the House should go into a grand committee to consider how much was necessary to be raised to maintain the war for this next summer.

This day it was voted that a committee should be nominated to bring in a bill for the suppressing atheism, swearing, cursing, lying, profaneness and luxury and to be speedily reported to the House.

OCTOBER 5TH. This day was the great debate about the Irish bill, and Mr. Seymour made the report of it from the committee, who was the Chairman: upon which report there was a strong debate about the amendment of the amendments returned to the committee.

[1] The MS. reads *Nerbe* here: Derby or Newark?

The two things insisted on were these: first whether the word "a nuisance" was proper to be used in the bill.

To this Mr. Solicitor made an excellent speech, and said that the word was never used in any former act, to which Sir Richard Temple immediately replied and made it appear to him that the very word "a nuisance" was used in a late act that was made for prohibiting the exportation of leather.

Mr. Solicitor did acknowledge it in the House and that it was his mistake.

The second thing was concerning the seizure of Irish cattle, which was to be made by the constable, headborough, churchwarden or other officers who should have power after the 2nd of February next to seize of any Irish cattle brought in contrary to this act, and to sell them, and the seizers to have one half of them and the other half should be for the poor of the parish where they were seized.

This was very much opposed, and amendment of the bill moved and that it should be recommitted. This was put to the question; and the ayes for recommitting it were 106 and the noes were 102, of which number I was one, against my mind.[1] It is much feared that recommitting this bill may be of ill consequence. And I fear the success of this bill; God grant I be mistaken.

The Solicitor in his speech reflected upon the House as though some members of it should entrench upon the King's prerogative by insisting upon the word "a nuisance", which was (justly) ill taken, for they did it not.

To-morrow the House will fall upon the amendment of the bill.[2]

This day was a bill brought in for the preservation of fish in fresh waters. It was chiefly against nets that were above twenty yards in length, and that were not two inches and an half in mesh, and that this should be considered of by the judges and justices of peace at the assizes and sessions. Tweed and Ouse are excepted.

---

[1] *C.J.* VIII, 631, 106–102, Birch and Massey, Chetwind and Weld.
[2] Milward was writing the Diary on this day evidently.

Another bill was brought in for the reviewing of all the statutes and to bring them to one head. A committee was nominated for it.

OCTOBER 6TH.   The first that was this day moved was that Wales should have the same privileges as England has.

Mr. Kendall's bill to enable him to sell land for the payment of his debts was read by my cousin Milward's opening his case and the great equity and reason of it whereon it was grounded; although it was opposed by Mr. William Mountague and others, it was ordered a second reading.

The House then fell upon a very great debate concerning the election of a burgess of Bristol, which took up all that morning.

The debate was whether Sir Humphrey Hooke should be admitted, who was chosen five years ago, but then gave his voice for my Lord Ossory and subscribed his election and resigned his interest to him, notwithstanding which by two indentures two returns were made, one for Sir Humphrey, the other for my Lord Ossory; but my Lord Ossory was admitted to sit as a member in the House, and so continued till he was called this year by the King's writ to the House of Lords.

It now was the debate whether Sir Humphrey Hooke should be admitted upon his former election, or that a writ should be sent down for a new election. The House was divided about it: Serjeant Maynard and all the old Parliament gang were for a new election, and the Royal party were for admitting Sir Humphrey: it appears that Sir Humphrey Hooke is a loyal person, and out of his respects to Lord Ossory suspended his voice for that time to him, and now that the Lord Ossory is called to the Lords' House he lays claim to his former election, which the other party now opposeth and stands for a new election in hopes to bring in one of their own judgment. It was put to the question and it was carried for Sir Humphrey Hooke but [by] four votes of which I was one.[1]

The bill for naturalising the Lady Arlington sent down from the Lords was this day read and passed.

---

[1] *C.J.* VIII, 631, 6 October. That it be referred to the Committee of Privileges. 83–94, Goodrick and Sandys, Knight and Strangways; apparently a further vote followed, not recorded in the *Journals*.

OCTOBER 8TH. This day report was made by Sir George Downing (from a committee) concerning the restraint of importation of French and Dutch commodities. And it was resolved that after such a time no French or Dutch commodities should be brought in or used in England, and that the King should be humbly moved for the present to send out his proclamation for to prohibit the same until an act may be passed to confirm it.

The report was made of the amendment of the Irish cattle bill[1] and now it was thus, that no Irish cattle nor pork nor beef should be imported after the 2nd of February next, and if any be brought in after that day it shall be lawful for any constable, headborough, churchwarden or tithing man to seize such cattle and to keep them safe in some public or convenient place the space of 48 hours and to repair to some justice of the peace within the county; and if the party whose beasts are so seized do not come in within that time, and make it truly appear by two witnesses upon oath (to whom the justices are empowered to give such oath) that they are not Irish cattle, that then it shall be lawful to sell the cattle by those that did so seize them, and they that seized them are to have one half of them and the other half are to go to the poor of the parish where such cattle were seized.

This bill is now committeed to be engrossed.

This day it was reported that Lord Fauconberg and Sir Thomas Osbourne fought a duel on Saturday last at Islington, and that the Lord Fauconberg received a wound in his thigh.

It was moved the House would take into consideration the case of the Countess of Essex, deceased, upon whom was settled £1,300 per annum for her maintenance and in lieu of her jointure, which said allowance of £1,300 per annum was in arrear and unpaid £4,500.[2] It was answered by those that should pay it that it was disposed by Parliament in Oliver's time to officers of the Lord of Essex and to the army, and so pardoned by the Act of Oblivion.

This as was alleged came to an hearing in the Court of Chancery and the Lord Chancellor not being satisfied in the point

---

[1] *C.J.* VIII, 632, 8 October. Seymour on the Irish bill.
[2] *C.J.* VIII, 632, £4550 here, instead of £4500 as in Milward.

required the opinion of two of the Judges: who upon the debate differed in their opinions, or at least did not determine it, whereupon it was brought into the House for the determination of it, whether it was within the compass of the Act of Oblivion or not. It was stiffly debated in the House both that it was within the Act and by others that it was not, and also it was debated whether the House would take it upon them to determine it or not. In the conclusion it was carried in the affirmative that the House should hear and determine it.

OCTOBER 9TH. The bill against blasphemy and profaneness was read again the second time. It was thoroughly debated whether the House should pass the bill or whether it should be first sent to the Convocation.

At last it was voted that the bill should be committed, and that the committee should consider of it, and the punishments for the several degrees of men.

It was voted that a bill should be brought in to prevent duels and of the punishments also to be inflicted upon duellers, and to provide for reparation of those that shall be provoked by deeds or words which do tend to dishonour.

A bill was brought in for setting poor on work, and to increase the trade of making woollen cloth, which is greatly decayed in Gloucestershire and divers other counties.

It was taken into debate, the inspection into the patent and charter of the Canary Company and inconveniences by it that comes to the kingdom, and likewise of all other charters patent and grants to companies, all which was to be referred to a committee.

The bill for sowing hemp and flax and the increase of the manufacture of linen cloth was read the second time, but it was also taken into consideration the inconvenience and damage it will be to poor vicars to have their tithe in kind of hemp and flax out of which the allowance of half-a-crown for every acre is sowed; some said half-a-crown an acre was enough, others moved that they should have their tithe in kind, but this was likewise referred to a committee.

In regard that the account of the Navy and war with the Dutch were not in readiness, it was moved in the House that

the committee should sit to-morrow after morning prayer to
prepare a report for it to the House against Thursday or Friday.

Sir George Downing carried a message to the Lords to desire
their concurrence to petition the King to grant out his proclamation to prohibit the importation of foreign commodities till an
act be prepared.

In regard of the fast the House adjourned until Thursday.

OCTOBER 10TH. This day two sermons were preached to the
House of Commons at St. Margaret's, Westminster, the one by
Dr. Stillingfleet, the other by Mr. Frambton.

Dr. Stillingfleet's text was Amos the 4th, verse 11th. "I
have overthrown some of you as God overthrew Sodom and
Gomorrah; and you were as firebrands plucked out of the fire
yet have you not returned to me, saith the Lord."

1. It consisted of God's judgments.
2. His mercy mixed with it.
3. And their incorrigibleness.

In his judgments four things to be considered.

1. First the judgment itself.
2. The suddenness of it.
3. Thirdly the effect of it.
4. Fourthly the person that sent it. J. etc.

Mr. Frambton's text was Jeremiah 3rd, verse 21 and 22.
"A voice was heard upon the high places weeping and supplications of the Children of Israel for they have perverted their
way and they have forgotten the Lord their God. Return ye
backsliding people and I will heal your backslidings.

"Behold we come unto thee for thou art the Lord our God."

His sermon was an excellent paraphrase upon this text. "A
voice was heard in the high places:" that is a public lamentation
was heard. "They have perverted their ways:" that is they
have committed idolatry.

"They have forgotten the Lord their God:" that is they have
committed sin and served strange gods.

"Return ye backsliding children:" weeping, supplication and
tears are available, but not without turning to God by true
repentance and amendment of life.

"I will heal your backslidings:" words of comfort to the greatest sinners that turn to God with tears, supplications and true repentance.

OCTOBER 11TH. It was ordered this day first that the thanks of the House should be sent to Dr. Stillingfleet and Mr. Frambton for their pains the day before at the general fast and that they and Dr. Outram and Dr. Dalbin, the Dean of Westminster, should be entreated to print their sermons if it was not against their pleasures and resolutions.

The bill for preserving the breed of fish was read the second time.

The report was made to the House of the account of Naval charge for the last two years, which did amount to £3,000,252. The accounts seemed to be taken and allowed with favour by them that were appointed to take them, for neither the militia money that is the King's supply of one month's tax for three years, which came to above £200,000 nor the prize goods which are acknowledged to be £500,000 were in their charge nor accounted in this estimate and yet this was not taken notice of: but Sir John Duncombe brought in a new and larger account of expense and other layings out which the House would not allow, for it was put to the question and carried that his addition should not be allowed.

The House entered upon the debate of raising the King's supply for the war. It was proposed by Sir Richard Temple that £1,600,000 should be given the King for the maintaining and carrying on the war till next year. The Court party thought it would be too little unless an addition was added to it for the land forces.

This caused a long and hot debate[1] till two of the clock or after; in the end it was put to the question, and the House was dividing, and candles called for by some, but then it was voted to adjourn the ascertaining the sum and the manner of raising it until to-morrow morning.

[1] *C.J.* VIII, 634, 149-125. H. Coventry and Brouncker, Whorwood and Phillips.

OCTOBER 12TH. The bill for naturalising the Lady Arlington was read the second time.

A petition was read in the behalf of a gentleman (whose name I have forgot)[1] who had been abused by an attorney in suffering a fine and recovery for the selling of lands; the petition was received. Upon this petition it was voted that Mr. Prynne should bring in a bill for the regulating attorneys, both as to their number and their abuses.

The bill concerning Certioraries was read the second time, that they should not be granted but upon very good cause shown.

The House resumed the debate about the King's supply.

The Speaker left the Chair and the House went into a Grand Committee. My cousin Milward was voted Chairman and accordingly took the Chair.

The House immediately fell into a great distemper for that part that had voted a supply of £1,600,000 but the day before would have that debate now resumed, and to have it laid aside and that the House should proceed to a land tax for raising the money.

If this had been put to the question and carried then all other ways of raising money had been excluded.

Another party which is the Court party moved for a general excise of all things, which was no way pleasing.

They that were for the land tax said that the Speaker had left the Chair against the orders of the House, and so questioned the legality of the committee and moved that the Speaker should resume the Chair; the rest of the House opposed it.

This debate was prosecuted with many excellent speeches on both sides, and held until two of the clock in the afternoon, but at last the House grew more calm, and it was concluded that the Speaker should take his Chair again and that my cousin Milward should quit his Chair. When the Speaker had taken his Chair again it was moved that the King should have £1,800,000; the £200,000 should pay interest and get credit

[1] *C.J.* VIII, 634, 12 October. Bonham Fance is the gentleman whose name Milward forgot. From this date Milward's notes on the debates on supply may be compared with Marvell's *Last Instructions*, ll. 151–306, and may be enlarged by the addition of Holland's three speeches in Appendix I.

for ready money; and that to-morrow at ten of the clock the House should resolve again into a Grand Committee and that the Speaker should give directions to the committee for the manner of their proceedings; and that a due consultation should be had of the best way to raise the £1,800,000.

OCTOBER 13TH. It was this day moved by Sir Robert Atkins that the Mayor of Bristol (who was not then Mayor, but one of the Sheriffs, when the double return was made for the Lord Ossory and Sir Humphrey Hooke) might be excused from his appearance at the committee to answer the double return, but it was resolved upon the question that he should come up.

The bill engrossed for the Irish cattle was read, and very much opposed with very impertinent arguments as I think. Mr. Swinsen made an excellent speech for the bill: which none that opposed it did answer but yet said something on the by though nothing to the purpose. In the end it was put to the question whether the bill engrossed should pass or not: the House thereupon was divided; we that were the ayes for it were 161 and the noes that opposed it were 101.[1]

The bill was to be sent up to the Lords on Monday next by Mr. Seymour.

It was moved that the House would be more careful to maintain their honour and privileges and not to suffer the members to talk one with another, and to be in discourse when the House are in any debate, nor to suffer any person to go from place to place with his hat on, and that the private door that goes into the Speaker's chamber be nailed up, or at least that the key of that door be brought every morning to the board and there to remain during the sitting of the House.

It is said that the Duke of Buckingham came at that back door and heard the debates of the House.

And it is said that many others that are not members came in at the back door and heard the debates of the House, and carried them abroad.

[1] *C.J.* VIII, 635, 165–104. Lord St John and Strangways, Broderick and Massey. For Swinsen's name above the MS., which includes many curious variants of this name, has here Scrovifen.

It was moved also by Mr. Prynne that everyone that was not at prayers in the House should for every time's failing pay one shilling to the poor.

It was resolved that upon Monday the House should go into a Grand Committee and at ten of the clock to proceed to the manner of raising the £1,800,000 for the King's supply; and so the House adjourned till Monday eight of the clock.

OCTOBER 15TH. This day the bill of Lord Cleveland was brought in, who upon good reasons desires three years more time to be allowed him for the redemption of his lands at Hackney and Stepney that was mortgaged to Mr. Backwell.

It was complained of Sir Robert Atkins and Mr. Prynne that at the committee it was made to appear that Sir Robert Atkins was in print in the paper that set out [the] Earl of Cleveland's case, contrary to the rule of Parliament.

It is supposed that Sir Robert Atkins and Mr. Prynne do not favour Lord Cleveland his case.

This day the Irish bill was carried up to the House of Lords by Mr. Seymour; I went along with it.

The Lord Chancellor and several other Lords met him at the bar and there the Lord Chancellor received the bill.

The House went into a Grand Committee and there took up the debate of raising the King's supply.

After many speeches made to no great purpose and not all to the promoting or forwarding the business Mr. Orme, one of the burgesses for Peterborough proposed the selling of the chimney money at eight years' value: the yearly value of the chimney money being rated at £200,000 per annum. This would come to £1,600,000 at eight years' value, and in all probability might be raised in six months.

If this may be consented to by the King and the same made practicable it would free the King from paying interest for taking up ready money, and would do the King's business, and might be of more advantage to the King and kingdom for carrying on the war than £2,000,000 would be that require a longer time to be raised in.

This seemed to take with many (and I confess with me also)

and I am of the same opinion to this day, and that it was the best way and the speediest to raise so great a sum, that hath as yet been proposed, and for these reasons.

First, because it will raise a speedy supply without interest, and that a land tax can never do.

Secondly, it would give great satisfaction to the people generally for taking away of the tax of paying for their chimneys, it being a tax so extremely hateful to the people.

Thirdly, it takes away one continued tax, although we pay for it, and it may be a leading also to the taking away the tax of the excise and so reduce all payments to the old way of subsidies.

It was proposed what compensation the King should have in lieu of this if he should give way to sell it, it being one part of His Majesty's settled and constant revenue.

It was resolved that before the King should part with it, that some way should be found out to satisfy the King in full measure.

The excise of tobacco, sugar and pepper were propounded.

It was objected against this sale of the chimney money by divers members.

First, that it was uncertain whether the chimney money being sold would raise £1,600,000.

Secondly, that so great a part of the City of London being burnt, it is very probable that the sum to be raised would fall short of it very much.

Thirdly, that the people in general are not able to pay eight years' value ready money for their chimneys, and so the £1,600,000 would not be so speedily raised as was expected it would be.

Fourthly, that there would be great difference between landlord and tenant about purchasing the chimneys.

But these objections were well answered and may be more fully at any time.

Mr. Swinsen and that party were much against it.

OCTOBER 16TH. This day[1] a bill was read the second

---

[1] *C.J.* VIII, 636, 16 October. MS. omits date. A "Mr Milward" on the committee for the bill about blasphemy, no indication of which Milward being given.

time against atheism, blasphemy, swearing, cursing and profaneness.

The bill was generally assented to, and voted to be committed; but withal first it was moved that first it should be asserted and defined what atheism is, what blasphemy is and what an oath is and what is swearing: and that the Convocation now sitting should be consulted with or some divines sent for to the committee.

I am of this committee.

It was moved that thanks should be sent to Prince Rupert and the General by the House in behalf of themselves and the kingdom for their good service this summer, but at last it was resolved that it should be left to the King both to give them thanks and to reward them.

The debate about the King's supply was resumed and the sale of chimney money again debated; it was prosecuted by some and mainly opposed by others and those especially that would have the £1,800,000 raised by a land tax. It will be the great contest whether the land tax (which is the opinion of the Presbyterian party) or a general excise (which the Court party proposeth) should be resolved on as the best way to raise the £1,800,000. I wish a medium between both may be found out.

The Lords sent down to have a conference with the House of Commons in the Painted Chamber concerning their petitioning the King to send out his proclamation for the prohibition of the importation of French wines and commodities until an act may be passed to prohibit them. But the House being in debate about the raising the King's supply, and the mace being broken and not then in readiness, the messengers sent from the Lords, waiting almost two hours, returned, and so the conference was appointed to be to-morrow about ten of the clock.

OCTOBER 17TH. I came not to the House this day till almost eleven of the clock, having been very ill all night, being taken with an extreme pain and griping in my belly, which caused a vomiting and extreme looseness which continued five days. I was informed that it was moved in the House that certain atheistical books should be burned, among which Mr. Hobbes's *Leviathan* was one.

After I came to the House again the debate for selling the chimney money was resumed, which being rated at £200,000 per annum, and valued at eight years' purchase, would raise the King £1,600,000, and it was affirmed that it would be the speediest way to bring in the King's supply.

And so it will be if three things can be made good.

First if it be really true that the chimney money will raise the full sum £1,600,000.

Secondly that the compensation that is to be given to the King in lieu of it be not a greater grievance than the chimney money.

Thirdly, that every man shall be able and willing to purchase his own and tenants' chimney money.

Before the House rose this day it was put to the question whether the House should sit to-morrow, it being St. Luke's Day; it caused a division in the House, and we that were the noes and sat in the House were 94, but through the carelessness of the tellers one was lost of our number and so was given in but 93. And the ayes that went out were said to be the same number, so it was put to the Speaker, who gave his voice with the ayes, and so it was carried against us to sit on the holiday.

The whole charge of the Navy for 27 naval months, viz: from the first of September, 1664, to the last of September, 1666, was reported from the Committee to the House by Sir William Lowther, who was Chairman to that committee.

	£	s	d
First for 28,410 men at 4s per head............	306,828	0	0
which is for one month................[sic]	113,640	0	0
Officers of the ordnance for 27 months........	290,137	2	6
which is for one month....................	10,745	0	0
which is for 26 months....................	279,392	0	0
For building new ships....................	80,834	0	0
which is for one month....................	2,993	0	0
Which is for 26 months....................	77,840	0	0
For widows and orphans....................	12,076	0	0
which is for one month....................	447	0	0
which is for 26 months....................	11,628	0	0
For sick and wounded with prisoners........	40,000	0	0
which is for one month....................	1,482	0	0

	£ s d
which is for 26 months................	38,518.0.0
Merchants' ships lost in 27 months.......	11,606.0.0
which is for one month................	429.0.0
which is for 26 months.................	11,176.0.0
To be abated for wear and tear for the two winters that the ships were in harbour..	150,000. 0.0
So as the whole estimate of the charge of the war at the sea for those two last years, being 26 months by naval account is....	3,223,194.17.5
The whole charge for one year[1]..........	1,611,597. 8.8

OCTOBER 18TH. This day the House resumed the debate for raising the £1,800,000.

Colonel Sandys moved that an Act of Parliament should be passed to empower the King to send out Privy Seals to all rich and moneyed men to lend this tax upon good security, and that all great officers should be called upon to lend to this tax. It was seconded by Mr. Williams (alias Cromwell) and by divers others also.

It was resolved that a bill should be brought in to-morrow for the same, but it was afterwards moved by Colonel Sandys to suspend that resolution for that day and promised to renew that motion.

The rest of the day was spent till almost three of the clock about the debate of chimney money.

It was resolved at the last that a committee should be appointed to sit and to have an inspection into the rolls, books and papers, and to use all other good means that may be to find out the true yearly value of the chimney money and to bring in the report to the House.

It was resolved that the same committee, with the addition of the Gentlemen of the Long Robe, and especially that Sir Heneage Finch and Sir Job Charlton, should consider of the way and means to give the King a compensation for the chimney money and to bring in a report also of it with the other.

There is a great contest and debate about raising the £1,800,000; some would have it laid by the land tax as it is

---

[1] *C.J.* VIII, 637–8. These figures are not given.

now and the same to begin at the end of the next fifteen months, but this will raise no present money.

Others are rather for a general excise, which will never be endured.

Others are for the sale of chimney money, which I like best, so that if a just and good recompense be made to the King and that it do not prove to be a means of bringing in the general excise.

Others are to raise the money by Privy Seals, which I like not amiss, but some are jealous that this will entrench on the Act of Oblivion, and that it would be chiefly laid on those that best may bear (and indeed deserve) it, viz: on all those that have got vast estates in these times of rebellion.

OCTOBER 19TH.   I was not well this day and was not at the House.

OCTOBER 20TH.   This day was wholly spent in debating the business between the Countess of Essex[1] and Sir Thomas Higgins.

I went this day to dinner to Lambeth and came home very ill and fell into a violent fit of vomiting and purging.

OCTOBER 21ST.   I took a smart purge, which wrought very effectually.

OCTOBER 22ND.   After a private bill or two the bill for hemp and flax was read again with the amendments. It was moved that the vicar in lieu of his tithe in kind should have for every acre of ground new broken up (and that never was broken up before) the rate of 2s. 6d.; this was thought too little by some, and therefore voted the vicar 5s. per acre, but being put to the question it was carried for 2s. 6d. per acre.

The rest of the morning was taken up in preparing the reasons of the House to answer the Lords' objection at the conference concerning the proclamation against the French commodities, which the committee immediately dispatched and reported to the House, and forthwith sent to the Lords to desire a further

---

[1] *C.J.* VIII, 638. MS. reads Putches of Somerset, an obvious error for Countess of Essex. See Diary under 8 October.

conference; the Lords appointed to meet them in the Painted Chamber to-morrow at eleven of the clock.

In the meantime that this committee withdrew in order to this conference, Colonel Sandys moved the House to take into consideration the miscarriage of the House in that their votes and debates were published abroad, yea and into Holland also, as appears by the Dutch Gazettes, and by our own also, and that reports have been unduly and untruly made to the King of some members, and that things most false have been laid to their charge. It was therefore moved by Colonel Sandys and seconded by Sir Anthony Cope, Sir Thomas Littleton and divers others, that a bill should be brought in for the reforming and preventing such miscarriages for the future, and for inflicting severe and condign punishment upon all such detractors as shall be discovered.

OCTOBER 23RD. This day I went to Ironmongers' Hall in Fenchurch Street to attend the corpse of Alderman Meynell which that day was carried toward Bradley to be interred there.

In the afternoon I came to the Committee of Privilege, where the election of Sir Francis Fortescue and Sir Nicholas Slanning was debated; Fortescue was returned by the Mayor and Corporation a burgess for Plympton and Sir Nicholas Slanning was returned by the same for the same place. The dispute was whether the Sheriff had made two returns or but one, there being two indentures returned to the Clerk of the Crown with the writ for the election. It was pleaded by Fortescue's counsel that there was but one return. First because the indenture returned for Slanning was not the original that was sealed by the Mayor and Aldermen, but only a counterpart of it. Secondly, because these words, "If the Parliament and Committee of Privileges shall think fit to admit him," were contained in the indenture, which are words never used in any return. It was at last put to the vote whether there was two returns or but one. My cousin Millward, Sir Job Charlton and the Court party voted that there was two returns, but myself and others carried it in the negative.

OCTOBER 24TH. This morning Mr. Kendall's bill was read and committed.

The Lady Arlington's bill was read again and so made a perfect act for her naturalising; testimony being given that one month before the second time [of] reading the bill she had taken the oath of allegiance and supremacy and had received the sacrament of the Lord's body at the hands (as I take it) of the Bishop of London.

A severe bill was brought in by Mr. Thurland against duels, that if any man do send or carry a challenge the party that sends it shall be imprisoned during life, and shall forfeit all his goods and personal estate, one half to the King and the other half to him that shall sue for it, and half his freehold lands for ever to the King. If they fight and one be killed it is death without clergy and the King shall not pardon it. He that is killed shall be hanged on a gallows two days with his head downwards. If a man receive a challenge and do not discover it to the Lord lieutenant or to a deputy Lieutenant or to a Justice of the Peace within eight and forty hours after he receives it he shall be imprisoned for ten years and shall forfeit his personal estate. This doth extend likewise to all those that shall go out of the land to fight a duel. If a duel be fought upon the instant and sudden meeting and that any former malice be proved the parties shall incur the same punishment.

The Serjeant at Arms of the House of Commons was sent to apprehend Hardy the Jesuit, but could not meet with him.

Mr. Mountague brought in a bill to stop all present suits that may arise between landlord and tenant that may arise about the houses burnt in the City.

The Speaker left his Chair and my cousin Milward took the Chair and the House fell into a debate of the way and means how to raise the King a full recompense for the chimney money, if it please His Majesty to part with it.

The excise of tobacco, sealed paper and sugar and some other commodities was proposed by Colonel Birch, who made a very long speech upon it, but it was opposed by Sir George Downing and Sir John Knight, and in the end nothing was concluded, but the debate was adjourned until to-morrow.

A libel against several members was found in the House in the form of a letter directed to Sir John Maynard.

OCTOBER 25TH. Mr. Kendall's bill was read again this day[1]
and committed, and divers of the committee dined at the New
Tavern in Dawell Row and then went to the House and sat in
the Exchequer Chamber, at which committee my cousin Milward
was Chairman; after several debates and perusing the deeds
we voted it to be reported to the House.

The great cause of Mr. Roberts and Winn came before the
House and after much said concerning it the House ordered
that when both parties are prepared with their counsel and
have their witnesses in readiness they shall be heard at the Bar
of the House of Commons.

The rest of the day was spent in the debate of raising the
King's supply by the sale of chimney money.

After some time spent in that debate it was ordered that
to-morrow the House should begin to consider what sum shall
be judged convenient to be raised out of the sale of chimney[s].

OCTOBER 26TH. This day was read a bill from the House of
Lords to enable Mr. Noell (who has married the Earl of
Southampton's daughter) to sell some lands settled upon her
for her jointure, which lie far off, and to bestow it on lands that
lie nearer and more convenient for her.

The rest of the day was spent upon a report from the committee concerning recusants; it was at last resolved to petition
His Majesty that all papist priests and Jesuits (except such as
are allowed the Queen Consort and the Queen Mother) (except
such of them as are born Englishmen) shall be banished the
kingdom after thirty days, and are so to depart the realm upon
pain of death if they shall be taken in England after the thirty
days; and that all recusants or such as are justly to be suspected
such are to be disarmed.

That the oaths of allegiance and supremacy are to be tendered
to all the members of the House and that they are to receive the
sacraments of the Lord's body at St. Margaret's, Westminster,
or to bring a certificate from some known minister that they

[1] *C.J.* VIII, 641, 25 October. MS. omits date. The Bodville or
Roberts and Winn case recurs throughout the session, e.g. 26 October,
C.J. VIII, 642, etc.

have received it in some other church. That the said oaths are to be tendered to His Majesty's servants and to all officers and soldiers of the army. And to all persons known or suspected to be recusants and that they also receive the sacrament.

That all judges and barons of the Exchequer and all justices of the peace at assizes and sessions are to give a strict charge that the penal statutes against recusants be put in execution.

This petition was sent up to the House of Lords by Mr. Hungerford, who was Chairman at the committee.

There was two desperate kinds of knives or daggers found in an house that was burnt, two of which was brought into the House.

Indeed they were as desperate instruments or weapons as ever I saw. Upon examination they were said to be the weapons or instruments of two Frenchmen that lay at that house before it was burnt; the Frenchmen deny them, but do acknowledge themselves to be Roman Catholics.

Sir Richard Brown had the man in examination which owned the house, and the Frenchmen also, and they do say that there were an hundred or more of these daggers.

It was afterwards affirmed that these desperate instruments were purposely made every year and sent into Greenland in great numbers, as most useful and very commodious for the trade of fishing for whales.

OCTOBER 27TH. This morning the election of Sir Francis Fortescue and Sir Nicholas Slanning for burgess of Plympton was reported, and it was resolved to be but one return and that Sir Francis Fortescue was duly elected.

The rest of the day was spent in the debate about the sale of the chimneys; it was long debated whether the House should not first send to the King, to know his pleasure whether he will be pleased to part with the chimney money if we can recompense it with another revenue of equal value.

This after a long debate was left unresolved.[1]

---

[1] Marvell writing to Hull on the 27th speaks of the slow progress of supply "which is not for want of any ardour...but out of our houses' sense also of the burden to be laid upon the subject". Cf. letter of 7 November (*Letters*, p. 41 f.).

OCTOBER 28TH. This day, being Sunday and my birthday (Simon and Jude), my Lord Archbishop commanded me to keep the day at Lambeth. My cousin Milward and my son Jennens went with me thither to dinner. Dr. Stradling, my Lord's Chaplain, preached; his text was, "Ye have said, it is vain to serve the Lord: and what profit is it that we have kept his ordinance and we have walked mournfully before the Lord of hosts" (Malachi 3rd chapter, 14th verse).

My Lord used us most courteously.

OCTOBER 29TH. This day Mr. Leigh's bill for the sale of Newton Grange[1] and four tenements to enable him to pay his debts was brought in by Sir Fulk Lucy, and was read and received and voted a second reading.

Mr. Seymour reported from the committee their sense of the Canary Company, which report was very near an hour long. The committee agreed that the Corporation of the Canary Company was a monopoly and destructive to trade, and therefore illegal.

It was long debated whether an impeachment should not be drawn up against the patentees, but at last it was resolved to send up to the Lords to desire their concurrence in petitioning the King to call in that patent.

Secretary Morice brought His Majesty's letter to the House to show the necessity of speedy raising money to carry on the war, and to quicken the House for his supply; and it also told them that in case an honourable peace should be concluded on (of which as yet he assured them he heard not one word) yet he hoped the House would go on and make good their engagement of raising the £1,800,000.

This put the House (although then it was one of the clock) upon the debate, and it was moved by Mr. Garroway and that party that the bill for the sale of the chimney money should be brought in to-morrow and to be taken into debate, and if it was found to be practicable then to resolve on that way to raise the money, but if it could not be made practicable then to lay it aside, and so fall upon a new expedient. The laying it wholly aside was not liked, but opposed by some, but rather to suspend

[1] *C.J.* VIII, 643, 29 October. MS. omits date. Newton Grange, misspelled in MS. Ninckle Grange, is in Derbyshire.

the debate of it for a time and to fall upon the other two ways of raising the sum by a land tax or a general excise, and to debate them together; and which of them appeared to be the better way to raise the sum of money, that to take it into debate with the chimney money, and then which of those two should prove more effectual for raising the £1,800,000 to fall upon that.

The House voted that this debate should be resumed to-morrow morning and so adjourned.

OCTOBER 30TH. This morning the Lord Campden's bill for selling some lands in order to settle other lands upon his son Mr. Noell's wife for her jointure was read the second time and so was committed.

The Lords sent a message to the House to desire a conference, at which they declared their concurrence with the House of Commons in their vote against French commodities. They sent a second message to desire another conference, at which they declared that the Lord Chamberlain shall be desired to carry this concurrence of the two Houses to the King, and to desire His Majesty to appoint a time when certain members of both Houses may attend His Majesty for his condescension to the bill.

In order to this twelve Lords and twenty-four Commons are appointed to attend His Majesty.

The rest of this day was spent in the debate whether the excise or the land tax should be first taken into the House's considera-tion in order to the raising the £1,800,000. It was at last resolved that the general excise to-morrow morning should be first fallen upon, but not to be voted either for or against it, until the land tax be likewise taken into debate, and then to resolve which of the three, the chimney money, the land tax or the general excise shall be made use of as most practicable for the speedy raising money for the King's supply.

OCTOBER 31ST. This day a petition was presented to the House in the behalf of the present Mayor of Bristol who was in the Serjeant's custody. The House sent for him up for making a double return, between Lord Ossory and Sir Humphrey Hooke when he was Junior Sheriff of Bristol; upon his submission and acknowledging his offence he was set at liberty.

The Speaker then left his Chair and my cousin Milward took his Chair, the House going into a Grand Committee.

The debate was about the excise of certain foreign commodities, which endured four hours' debate.

Mr. Solicitor made an excellent speech for the excise of foreign commodities in order to the easing of the land tax, which I very well approved of.

Others, as Sir Thomas Clifford and Sir Charles Harbord, moved for a general excise of all inland goods, which was much disliked.

In conclusion it was resolved to refer it to five or six members to consider and to bring in a report of such commodities as was thought fit to be excised, and also the impost and custom and the value of it, as it is already laid on those commodities, and what they may well bear more and how the same may be best collected; and that Colonel Birch should be the principal agent in the business (for he first moved it), and this report to be brought into the House on Friday next.

This day we had a message from the Lords that they concurred with us in the vote concerning Papists.

They sent a second message to us that they had sent to the King for his consent to it, and that His Majesty had commanded both Houses to attend him at Whitehall at five of the clock.

Accordingly twelve Lords and twenty-four Commons did attend His Majesty (I went in with them but was not of the number), where was read and presented to him the votes of both Houses against the importation of French commodities and their votes against Papists; the King was pleased to consent to send out his proclamation against both.

NOVEMBER 1ST. This day the House sat not, but observed it as an holiday.

I dined this day with my cousin Milward at Mr. Adrian Mays's in St. James's Park, he being keeper of the fowl and deer etc. in that park.

NOVEMBER 2ND. This day the bill for naturalising the Lady Holles was read.

A petition was brought in by Mr. Taylor, an officer of Windsor, against the Lord Mordaunt, the Governor thereof: Taylor was sent for into the House, who justified his petition, and thereupon it was ordered to be read and to be taken into consideration.

The House then resumed the debate about raising the £1,800,000.

Colonel Birch reported to the House the sense of the committee concerning the excise of certain foreign commodities: which report upon debate did not give any satisfaction to the House either as to the value or the income, or as to the manner of imposing and collecting of it.

It was moved that it should be put to the question whether it should be voted against and so be wholly laid aside; but that motion was over-ruled: and that it should be only suspended for the present, and if necessity required it should be taken again into consideration.

It was lastly ordered this day that Dr. Tillotson and Dr. Sancroft, Dean of St. Paul's, should be sent to and desired to preach at St. Margaret's on Wednesday, being the public fast.

NOVEMBER 3RD. This day[1] the committee appointed to hear and consider Mr. Taylor's bill made this report, that when they were met and called for the petition to be produced it was missing and could not be found; it was supposed to be stolen off the table where it was laid. The House took this as an high abuse and therefore resolved on Tuesday, when the House is to be called and the oaths of supremacy and allegiance are to be tendered and taken by all the members, every member is to purge him from embezzling the petition by protesting his own innocency.

Taylor hath presented the petition again in the very same words.

The Speaker left the Chair and my cousin Milward took the Chair, and the House spent the rest of the day until three of the clock in the debate about the land tax; after a long debate and many long speeches for and against it the House adjourned without a question.[2]

[1] MS. dates this and following as 23 and 24 November.
[2] Cf. Marvell to Hull, 6 November (*Letters*, p. 43).

NOVEMBER 4TH. I went forenoon and afternoon to St. Clement's church, where was preached two sermons and I dined that day with my cousin Glanvill.

NOVEMBER 5TH. My son Jennens and I went to St. Clement's church and afterwards to dinner to Sir Joseph Sheldon's.

NOVEMBER 6TH. This day was wholly spent in calling the House and taking the oaths of supremacy and allegiance.

At the same time every member purged himself both from the two libels that was found in the House and also from taking away the petition of Mr. Taylor's from off the table.

NOVEMBER 7TH. This day being the monthly fast there preached at St. Margaret's Dr. Sancroft, Dean of Paul's, and Dr. Tillotson. Dr. Sancroft preached first; his text was I Samuel, 3rd Chapter, 18th verse: "It is the Lord, let him do what seemeth him good." The parts were these two: the first part of Eli's faith, "It is the Lord." Secondly, Eli's patience, "Let him do what seemeth him good."

He only preached on the first part, Eli's faith, which was manifested in his acknowledging God to be the author of his judgments.

So God may be said to be the author of judgments five manner of ways.

First, by permitting such a thing to be done.

Secondly, by limiting the acting of such things.

Thirdly, by pre-ordaining and foreseeing the order of them.

Fourthly, by approving the doing of them.

Fifthly, by executing of them.

It was a very honest plain sermon.

The second sermon was preached by Dr. Tillotson; his text was Leviticus, chapter 26, verse 18: "And if you will not for all this hearken unto me, then will I punish you seven times more for your sins."

The parts were two: first a supposition, "If you will not for all this hearken unto me."

Secondly the effect, "Then will I etc." It was a very ordinary sermon.

NOVEMBER 8TH. This day the bill had a second reading concerning giving directions to the country for the preventing the spreading of the plague.

Also there was a great debate concerning the pesthouse at Cambridge and the enclosing some acres of the common next to it with a wall. In that bill the Mayor of Cambridge was put before the Vice-Chancellor, which being excepted against by some and justified by others, caused it to be put to the question, and upon it the House was divided; I went out for the Vice-Chancellor and we carried it.

The whole bill was said to be defective in many particulars and therefore it was moved that it should be amended.

The rest of the day the Speaker kept his Chair and the debate was about the raising the King's supply.

Secretary Morice declared to the House that the King would not part with the chimney money.

Assurance being given in the House that the same excise would not be any farther prosecuted, Mr. Garroway made this proposition to the House, that thirteen hundred and twenty thousand pounds of the £1,800,000 should be raised by eleven months' tax at the rate of £120,000 per mensem and that the other four hundred and fourscore thousand pounds should be raised by the poll bill, sealed paper and excise of certain foreign commodities.

This debate went on fairly for a while, but presently we fell into cross debate.

First against the settling of thirteen hundred and twenty thousand pounds per mensem before it was known what the other ways proposed would raise.

It was put to the question whether part of the £1,800,000 should be raised by a land tax and it was carried in the affirmative.

Secondly, whether by a land tax of eleven months; this also though opposed was carried in the affirmative, of which I was one.

Thirdly, whether this £120,000 per mensem should be laid upon a land tax; it was carried in the negative, of which I was one.

Fourthly, whether poll money should be added, which was carried in the affirmative.

Fifthly, whether the excise of foreign commodities should be likewise added, which was fifthly debated; the debate held till after seven of the clock and the candles half burned, and the House was twice divided: first, whether part of the £1,800,000 should be raised by the excise of foreign commodities, which was carried in the affirmative; I gave myself for it. Secondly, whether these words, "To be settled by the custom house and there gathered" should be added: the noes carried it seven[1] voices; I was for the ayes.

NOVEMBER 9TH. This day the House fell into the debate of the expenses of the money raised for the carrying on the present war, and to call the officers to a just account how they had laid it out, and to discharge the sums they had received, in regard there were so many and great complaints that the seamen were yet unpaid. It was said that the money was all spent, and many grievous complaints made against them for want of pay. But in regard the House of Commons had not power to administer an oath, the House sent to the Lords to desire their concurrence to join in a committee, that so they might examine witnesses upon oath. Mr. Waller carried up the message, and the Lords returned this answer, that they would send an answer by messengers of their own.

Whereas the Parliament had made an order before that we should all receive the sacrament to-morrow, it was this day resolved to put it off until the second Sunday in December.

About four or five of the clock in the afternoon a fire broke out in the guard stable over against Whitehall, which gave a great alarm to the town.

Wallingford House was in great danger but yet had no harm. By the King's great care and painful endeavour and by blowing up some part of the stables it pleased God the fire was mastered and only a part of the stables was burnt.

NOVEMBER 10TH. In regard of the fire, which kept me up until almost two of the clock, I came not to the House this day until almost eleven of the clock.

---

[1] *C.J.* VIII, 647, 115–122. Osbourne and Meers, Talbot and Phillipps, and other votes not recorded in Diary.

The first thing that was taken into debate after I came into the House was about the sending up a bill to the House of Lords by Sir George Downing concerning coining of plate.

Then the House took into consideration at what to begin in order to the raising £1,800,000.

It was resolved to begin with sealed paper and so on to the foreign excise, then to the poll bill and last to the land tax, and that it be referred to a committee to consider what may be raised by the sealed paper and to make a report thereof to the House.

NOVEMBER 12TH.   This day Mr. Mountague moved that Mr. Solicitor and my cousin Milward might be admitted to be of counsel for my Lord Roos[1] and to open and plead his cause in the Lords' House.   But it was denied him, for it appears to be against the rules of the House to permit any members of the House to be of any counsel in any cause which afterwards shall be debated in the House where those of their counsel shall be judge of the cause when it comes before them.

The next thing moved was the bill concerning the preventing of duels that it should have a second reading, but in regard the House was not full it was voted that the bill should not then be read but deferred until there were a full House, because there was some clauses in it which might be of ill consequence, as that all estates, real and personal, should be forfeited to the King, which would be the undoing of whole families.

The next thing taken into debate was the business of Roberts and Winn, which being like to prove a business of long debate in regard that counsel on both sides, and fourscore witnesses (as it was said) were to be examined, it was put to the question whether it should not be put off for some time, because of the proper business of the day, viz: the raising the King's supply, which would be retarded if the other cause was then heard; this question endured a long debate but in the end it was resolved that Roberts and Winn's business should for some time be laid aside.

Then there fell to be a long dispute about some words that were spoken by Mr. Whorwood in the House; the words were

[1] *C.J.* VIII, 649, 12 November. Lord Roos not mentioned.

these, "When we have raised the King's supply we may go home like fools, as we came."

It was moved by some that he might explain himself; others said that he ought not to do it, upon a motion only, unless it was first put to the question and then voted by the House. Others moved that it might be passed over in silence; others said it was fit he should be reprehended (for so inconsiderate a speech) in the seat where he then sat; others moved that he should be called to the Bar and there answer for them. At last it was resolved that the words should be passed over without any further prosecution of them.

I dined at Lambeth House and went to my Lord of Rutland at night, who came to London this day.

NOVEMBER 13TH. The King's supply was resumed this day, and it was resolved that all stock and household goods should be excepted out of the poll bill and not assessed.

It was also resolved that one pound for every hundred pounds in good debt and ready money should be paid by the poll bill, that any man was possessed of over and above his own just debts.

This day the King's proclamation came forth for the banishing of Papist priests and Jesuits.

NOVEMBER 14TH. This day the House went into a Grand Committee and resumed the debate for the raising the £1,800,000 for the King's supply.

The first thing in debate was that the commissioners that were appointed to raise this money should not be charged by oath.

Secondly, that the assessed should not be sworn to present upon oath.

Thirdly, that the bankers and scriveners should not be required to discover other men's money that was in their hands.

Lastly, that all money that was lent to the King upon the late Act at Oxford, which gave the King £1,200,000 and yet not repaid, and all other money lent to the King in order to the raising the £1,800,000 granted to His Majesty this present sitting should not be taxed by this poll bill.

It was moved that the Chairman should make his report of

this day's resolves, but that motion was over-ruled, in regard the bill was not as yet perfected, offices and many other things not being as yet brought into debate, out of which there is expectation that good sums of money will be raised for the ease of the land tax.

It was ordered that the humble thanks of the House should be presented to His Majesty's gracious condescension to send out his royal proclamation against Popish priests and Jesuits, and to prevent the growth of Popery, and in so ample and fit expressions, and that the Lords shall be sent to to desire their concurrence with them in these their humble desires.

NOVEMBER 15TH. This day the House resumed the debate about raising the King's supply. It was moved in the House that those Baronets that had not paid their full fine and sum for their patents, that were at the first valued, which was £1,100 a patent, for maintaining forces in Ireland, should now pay the same, but it was not resolved.

But it was put to the vote whether Baronets and all other titles of honour should be rated in the poll tax; the House was divided upon it. It was carried in the negative; and [by] but one vote, for the ayes were 115, of which I was one, and the noes were 116.

The election of Grey and Collingwood for a burgess of Berwick was tried and Collingwood carried it; both bribery and subornation was proved against Grey. The House adjourned.

NOVEMBER 16TH. This day a bill was brought in for the sale of some lands that were Thomas Pride's, the son of Colonel Pride the traitor.

This young Pride married General Monk's niece; she had £4,000 to her portion. It was agreed at the marriage that Pride should purchase £400 per annum, which then being presented to General Monk, who was at that time in Scotland, and his advice and consent being required to it, he gave his consent with this caution, that £400 per annum that was to be purchased should be none of the King's nor Bishops' lands, nor the lands of any sequestered Cavalier or then delinquent.

One thousand pounds of the four is paid; the other £3,000

is stopped until this land be sold, and now the House is petitioned that an act may pass to enable them to sell this land to purchase the £400 per annum.

NOVEMBER 17TH.   This day[1] a vote passed for the assessing of offices at 3s. by the pound, and lawyers and physicians at 2s. per pound, and to-morrow [*sic*] the whole report of the poll bill is to be made.

Sir George Downing made a report from the committee that the linen that dead corpses were buried in stood the kingdom yearly in the full sum of £150,000, and therefore moved a bill might be brought in against it, and that all corpses for the future should be buried in woollen.

This day a bill was brought in against the Master of the King's Bench for escape of prisoners, and his giving them liberty to go at large, which some say is an escape.

It was moved that the creditors might proceed against him with law, as well in the vacation as in the term time, and that he might be prosecuted in other courts as well as in its own court (which I suppose is the King's Bench). This was readily consented to by some, but opposed by others, who said it was the taking away his inheritance, for the place is granted to him and so it is his inheritance, and then by consequence the privileges of his place is part of his inheritance, and this was my cousin Milward's opinion.

We had after this a long debate whether military officers should be polled by their pay at 3s. per pound and whether judges and other officers likewise.

My cousin Milward this day made his report to the House from the Grand Committee of the great debate of the poll bill, and upon his report of particulars the former debate of the judges, lawyers and military officers and their profits were taken into consideration; in the conclusion we agreed with the committee in the affirmative, and a bill is to be brought in accordingly.

NOVEMBER 19TH.   This day was wholly spent in hearing the cause between Roberts and Winn; the issue will be whether of the two wills shall take place.

[1] *C.J.* VIII, 650–1. Very much fuller than the Diary.

Roberts produceth the first will for the settling of Bodville's estate upon his son Charles Bodville Roberts, whom he had by Bodville's daughter.

Winn he produceth the second will, who, it seems, is a kinsman to Bodville; by this will Winn saith that Bodville gave the land to his son.

Roberts's case and witnesses took up this whole day, and Wednesday next was appointed to hear Winn's counsel case and witnesses also.

NOVEMBER 20TH.   This day was set apart for a public thanksgiving for the cessation of the plague.

NOVEMBER 21ST.   This day was spent in the further hearing of the cause between Roberts and Winn.

The Lords sent a message to the House that it pleased the King to receive their thanks to him for setting forth his proclamations, and that the members of both Houses did attend His Majesty at Whitehall at three of clock.

This day I went to the Whitehall to the Archbishop, with whom I found the Bishop of Winchester; I presented Moore's letter which Captain Fitzherbert sent me up to His Grace. Both the Bishops read it; the Archbishop put it into his pocket, and said that he would give me an account of it, and made me promise to dine with him to-morrow.

NOVEMBER 22ND.   This day the bill against duels was read the second time and committed.

The rest of the day was spent in the debate of the business between Roberts and Winn; at the last it was voted that Roberts his bill should be committed.

I went to Lambeth to dinner and asked my Lord what he thought of Moore's letter; he told me he delivered it to my Lord Chancellor, but had not received his sense of it.

NOVEMBER 23RD.   This day Mr. Leigh his bill was read the second time and committed.

The bill for poor prisoners' relief that were in prison for execution for debt and that were not worth five pounds besides their wearing apparel and working tools was read the second time and committed.

The rest of the day was spent about the poll bill, and it was voted and carried in the affirmative that honours and dignities should be taxed to the half of that they were taxed in the last poll bill.

NOVEMBER 24TH. This day the bill was read the second time for preventing the spreading of the plague and infection, and for restraining and keeping in people in order that are sick and may be suspected; the bill was committed.

The bill for enclosing common for the pesthouses in Cambridge was read the second time, in which bill it was observed that in the commission to be granted to the commissioners for the same the Mayor of Cambridge was put before the Vice-Chancellor; this being taken notice of, the Speaker was desired to amend the bill, and to place the Vice-Chancellor first; which being spoken against by some, as Mr. Pepys, and others, it was put to the question and the House was divided upon it; they that were for the bill as it was first brought and were the ayes were 31; the noes that were against it and went out were 51, of which I was one, and carried it.[1]

Mr. Hungerford reported that a Frenchman, de Leure, did charge Sir Philip Howard for dissuading him from coming to the Church of England.

This de Leure, having formerly been a Papist priest or friar mendicant, and now pretends himself an English proselyte, upon examination he proves to be an impostor, and sometimes he is known to be a preacher at conventicles and sometimes he is found to be at mass. The Lord Ancram acquainted the House that he knew him beyond seas, where he was in orders, and that he and another like him were put in trust with a good sum of money laid up in the monastery where they lived; these two compacted together to carry away the treasure by parcels in their wallets, which in the end they did, and so went their way. His partner was afterwards taken and hanged at the gates of the monastery, and this de Leure fled over into England, and here

[1] *C.J.* VIII, 653, 22–51, Pepys and Lewis, Tomkins and Crouch.

hath counterfeited a proselyte, whereupon the House hath given order to apprehend him.

The rest of the day was spent in the debate whether the dignified clergy should be comprised in the poll bill; upon the question it was carried in the affirmative.

Before the House did rise the Lords sent down the Irish bill with some amendments, which was received and appointed to be read on Monday next.

This day the poll bill had its first reading, and ordered to be read again on Monday next.

This day Mr. Secretary Morice brought in a bill, which he said had the King's approbation, for the making of brick and tile, and for providing other necessaries for the rebuilding of London.

The House sent up a message to the House of Lords to desire an account of their assents to a bill sent them up some days since concerning the Canary patent.

NOVEMBER 26TH. The poll bill was this day[1] read the second time and the Speaker left the Chair and the House was resolved into a Grand Committee, and the House chose Mr. Steward to be Chairman.

In the afternoon I went to the committee of the Lords' House to hear my Lord Roos his business; it seems the Duke of Buckingham had objected against his bill, because in it he was styled the Lord Roos, the Duke affirming that that title did belong to him, being descended of the heir general to the house of Rutland.

The bill thereupon was amended, and it ran thus, "John Manners, commonly called Lord Roos."

Mr. Berkley was examined before the Lords and he affirmed that he had been offered five hundred pounds to say that he had lain with the Lady Roos, and being asked who offered him that money he said, "Randall Egerton." To which Major-General Egerton answered that he never offered him any money to say so, neither had he any reason to do it, in regard he was altogether a stranger and unknown to my Lord Roos, but he

---

[1] *C.J.* VIII, 653, 26 November. MS. omits date.

acknowledged that he said to Mr. Berkley, that it was believed that he had lain with her, and that then he might do well to confess it, and so to do right to so honourable a family as my Lord of Rutland's, and he did believe my lord would be thankful to him. To which he replied that if he should say so of the Lady Roos, no lady would let him lie with her after for ever.

NOVEMBER 27TH. This day the Irish bill was read with the Lords' amendments; the Lords had put out the word "a nuisance" and in its place had put in other words, as "inconvenience", "damages" or the like. After a long debate it was put to the question whether the word "a nuisance" should be altered and put out or not; it was carried in the negative: 70 voices were for the affirmative and 86 for the negative, of which I was one, which I did afterwards repent, because upon a due consideration I did perceive that it put a causeless distrust upon the King.[1]

The next amendment in the bill did concern the 20,000 Irish cattle that was offered to be given to the poor people of London who had suffered by the fire.

The Lords had declared in their amendments that those 20,000 beasts should not be sent in alive, but should be killed in four ports of Ireland and barrelled up and sent into England.

This displeased the Londoners and courtiers, who said that a gift in this nature would be no benefit to them, and therefore they desired that the beasts might be sent alive into England.

This was looked upon by the greater part of the House as a device and project to cross the whole bill, and under the colour of 20,000 to bring in many 20,000's.

Some moved that the 20,000 beasts should be sent in alive and to restrain their coming in to certain time, with some other circumstances; nothing was resolved, but it was referred to a committee to consider of it.

My cousin Milward[2] went out of the town and left Mr. Leigh's business to be reported by Colonel Kirby, who reported it this day; in the afternoon we met at a committee about it where

---

[1] *C.J.* VIII, 654, 70–86, Crouch and Rigby, Carr and Lee.
[2] *C.J.* VIII, 654. Robert Milward had been given leave (*ibid.* p. 651) on 19 November.

Mr. Kirby was Chairman, and upon the difference between him and Colonel Kirby we adjourned the committee until tomorrow.

The report of Roberts's and Winn's business was made to the House, and two preambles were presented.

The first was a very long one, and was penned by the counsel, and there was in it a deal of ugly and filthy language.

The shorter preamble was presented, but was unsatisfactory to many, whereupon the bill was not committed to be engrossed.

Several men spoke in the behalf of Winn as justifying his title; others moved that a composition might be made between them, and so the business was put off for a week.

NOVEMBER 28TH. It was moved this day that the business between Roberts and Winn should be heard again this day, but in regard of the business of the day it was put off until Monday next.

De Leure, who was in the custody of the Serjeant-at-Arms, petitioned that in regard he had been a Romanist and now was converted and brought into the true light of the gospel, and acknowledging that he never said anything that might call in question Sir Philip Howard's sincerity in religion, and denied that he ever said any of those words concerning Sir Philip as was charged upon him, and in regard he was branded an impostor and counterfeit, that he might be admitted to an hearing to make his own defence.

It was resolved that de Leure should be set at liberty, but that he do engage to appear at the committee to clear himself, and that the committee do make report thereof to the House.

The Lords sent to have a conference about a message sent them from the House, in which they desired the Lords to join with them in a committee to examine the accounts of officers upon oath. At the conference the Lords told them they wanted a precedent that the committee of Lords and Commons had power to administer an oath.

I desired the Lord Scarsdale to desire the Archbishop that I might speak with him; His Grace immediately came to me. I humbly prayed an account of Moore's letter, and his directions with the letter that I might be able to give some instructions to

Captain Fitzherbert how to demean himself in farther prosecution of the business in the country; His Grace told me that my Lord Chancellor had the letter still in his keeping. I prayed him that he would speak to my Lord for the letter, and that day being a council day that he would ask him for the letter and for his sense likewise of it. His Grace told me that my Lord Chancellor was ill and kept his chamber, and did believe that he would not come that day to the council table, and therefore at present he told me he could give me no farther account of it, but desired that Captain Fitzherbert would diligently observe their meetings if any more.

The House proceeded to the business of the day and resumed the poll bill; and took into consideration that paragraph that concerned the lawyers, civilians and canonists and all their inferior officers and practisers, and all doctors of physic and professors thereof should be brought within the poll, and that all the amendments should be consented unto.

I went with Sir Fulk Lucy to dinner, and afterwards returned to the chamber where we met in a committee about Mr. Leigh's bill, where we prepared it for a report.

At my return to my lodgings at six of the clock at night I met Glyn's corpse going to be buried; the solemnity was very great.

NOVEMBER 29TH. This day at my coming to the House it moved that plays[1] might be tolerated and acted in the common theatres, and whether any members of the House of Commons should be admitted to go to acts of the playhouses, but it was not resolved.

Then the House fell upon the business of the day, and first thing taken into debate was servants' wages, whether servant should be polled 1s. for his head and also 1s. in the pound for his wages; it was resolved that all servants should be polled for their heads 2s. and 1s. in the pound for his wages, and that all men that did not [sic] receive alms of the parish or by reason of their poverty did not pay to church and poor should not pay for their children if they were under sixteen years of age.

The paragraph in the poll bill that said that all Popish recusants, aliens and all that did not come to divine service should

---

[1] *C.J.* VIII, 655, does not mention Plays.

pay double poll was much debated, some in favour of aliens, some in favour of Papists and some in favour of sectaries and that all of them should be favoured and the whole paragraph left out.

Some moved that sectaries only should be favoured and that a proviso for them should be annexed to the paragraph; others moved to spare all or none. It was at last concluded that the whole paragraph should stand and be added to the bill.

It was moved whether the House should sit to-morrow, being St. Andrew's Day; many were against it and so was I; others were for it, and urged the necessity of expediting the King's business; others moved that the House should sit this whole afternoon, that so we might not sit to-morrow; but it was resolved at last that we should sit to-morrow, and every day both forenoon and afternoon until the King's business was perfected.

NOVEMBER 30TH. This day the House went through the poll bill; the last paragraph that was debated was concerning the poll of dignified clergy, viz: Archbishops, Bishops, Deans, Archdeacons, Canons and Prebendaries, Residentiaries and Doctors of Divinity.

Concerning Doctors of Divinity there was a long debate; some would not have them to be polled at all, some to poll them at 5s. and some to poll them at £5.

It was put to the question whether they should be polled at £5; the House was divided upon it; the ayes that were for it were 67, the noes were 65, of which I was one, and do confess I was in the wrong; and so the ayes carried it.

It was moved that whosoever kept a Nonconformist minister in his house should be polled at such a rate: this was in relation to Colonel Birch.

But the Speaker coming out of his Chair put an end to the business, and said that if the nonconformist had any personal estate of money or good debts the act would reach him, but for his poll he was to pay as other men, only 1s. for his head.

That, that now was unresolved in the House and was entered upon, was who should name commissioners for the executing this act for poll money. Some said the Chancellor should name them with four more of the peers, others said the King should appoint them; others said the House of Commons should name them; but it was laid aside for this day and ordered to be resumed to-morrow.

The House was moved this day in behalf of Mr. Pierpont of Nottingham (a member of the House), whose servant was arrested during the sitting of the House (which was a breach of privileges), that the person that kept him in prison should be sent for and committed to the Serjeant-at-Arms, if he did not show lawful cause for arresting and imprisoning him, and that in the meantime Mr. Pierpont's bailiff should be set at liberty.

It was a question started by some, whether the privilege extended to servant[s] that were not menial, and served within the house, or whether the privilege did belong to menial servants only.

It was resolved that a bailiff that was trusted with gathering his master's rents and management of his master's estate, and received wages from him, although he lived not constantly in the house of his master, the privilege of the Parliament extended to him as well as to a menial servant.

DECEMBER IST. This morning a bill was brought in to prevent suits that might arise between relations concerning rents and houses that were consumed in the late fire in London: all which are to be referred to be decided by the twelve judges.

Mr. Seymour affronted the Speaker most peremptorily about putting a question; he did the Speaker manifest wrong.[1]

The House then resumed the business of the day, about nominating commissioners for the poll bill, whether the King or the House of Commons should name them.

It was at last resolved that those commissioners that were named in the act for the royal aid should serve for the poll bill.[2]

[1] *C.J.* VIII, 656, does not report this.

[2] Marvell, writing to Hull on 1 December, says: "We have been constantly taken up with perfecting the Poll Bill." To this Act (*Statutes of the Realm*, V, 624 ff.) was attached the famous proviso for an examination of accounts. After many wrangles about the personalia of the commission (e.g. *C.J.* IX, 36) it was at last appointed (see below, p. 164, n. 2) and presented a report in 1669.

I went to dinner to Lambeth and coming back to the House it was in debate whether there should be any head collectors; some did press it very much that there should be none but subcollectors only (to save fees) and they to pay it in to the Receiver-General whom the King should name; but at last it was resolved that there should be head collectors.

DECEMBER 3RD. This morning the bill was read the second time for stopping suits between parties in London concerning houses that were burnt and rents unpaid, but the debate lasted not, for the Speaker said it would fall of itself, but what he meant I know not.

Then came in the report [of] St. John's striking Sir Andrew Henly in Westminster Hall on Thursday last, the judge then sitting there: for which offence as they report the law is that he should lose his hand that he struck with, forfeit his goods, and the King also shall have his lands *annum, diem et vastum*, and in that time may cut down and sell all his wood. The report of it being made to the House, the Lord St. John acknowledged his fault, that it was a very heinous offence both against the King and his laws, and the honour of the House, and besought the pardon of the House, and submitted himself to whatever punishment the House should inflict, and also petitioned the House that they would intercede the King for his pardon. Many in the House spoke for him; others moved that before his address was made to the King that he should ask forgiveness of all the judges, because his offence was committed in Westminster Hall when the judges were sitting in the Courts of Justice there. Others that he should bring in his petition to the King to-morrow morning and that the Speaker and many of the members should present it to the King for his pardon; and this was so resolved.

The Speaker then left his Chair and the poll bill was taken in hand and gone through; only some few small amendments were referred to a subcommittee, to be considered of and ordered to [be] brought into the House to-morrow.

It is resolved that the commissioners shall meet in their several counties the 15th of January and then disperse themselves into their several hundreds, and then to nominate assessors and to appoint subcollectors for the gathering of the money in every township, according to the several taxes and polls directed in their warrants.

When the assessors have brought in their assessments which they are to do by the first of February, then the subcollectors are to be appointed to collect and bring in the money to the head collectors by or before the 8th of March, and they are to have 2d. in the pound for collecting it and bringing it in. Then the head collector is to pay it in to Receiver General appointed by the King at or before the 15th of March, and he is to have 1d. in the pound for his salary. And the Receiver General is to pay it into Exchequer by the last of March.

In the afternoon I was at the committee appointed to hear the Lord Mordaunt's case and Taylor's; I stayed very late at the committee and until it was voted there that Lord Mordaunt's imprisoning Taylor was illegal and arbitrary.

DECEMBER 4TH. This day the King sent to the House Major-General Drummond's letter[1] to the Lord Rothe of the defeat of the Scottish Covenanting rebels, who were 1,500 horse and foot; that they had furnished themselves with arms by seizing on divers magazines, and of the horses of some gentlemen which they found in readiness, which caused the owners of those horses to be very much suspected.

Had not those rebels been thus timely prevented they had in a short time been a very great body. They fought with courage a good while and killed many of our men, but in the end they were routed and all or most of their foot were taken and slain, and many of their horses, but the number is uncertain, because the fight was in the beginning of the night when it began to wax dark; there is known to be taken one hundred prisoners and twenty; their commander is called Wallis; they swore to defend the Covenant and to live and die in defence of it.

This morning the bill for making brick and tile was read the second time for the rebuilding London. It was moved that the commission should extend to twenty miles from London, and

[1] *C.J.* VIII, 657–8, does not mention this letter about the battle of Rullion Green fought on 28 November.

that the city should appoint an officer to inspect the making and goodness of the brick and tile, and that that was not well burnt should be broken and cast away; and that for his salary he should have 1d. per thousand. This bill was voted by some to be committed and by others to be cast out as a project.

The Speaker left his Chair and the committee proceeded to examine the amendments of the poll bill; and in the forenoon and afternoon (for we sat until eight of the clock at night) we perfected the bill and made it ready to be reported to the House in the next morning.

The House made an order that we should sit from nine of the clock in the morn until twelve, and from two till six until the King's supply be completed.

The Lord St. John's petition to the King for his pardon was read and voted that the Speaker and members should attend the King with it when His Majesty is pleased to give them leave.

DECEMBER 5TH. This day Mr. Seymour made his report of the proviso in the Lords' amendment of the Irish bill concerning the charitable gift of the Duke of Ormond and other persons of honour, who gave 20,000 head of cattle for the relief of the poor distressed people of London whose houses were burnt; this motion of gift came to the House of Lords first, and before the House of Commons were acquainted with it.

The Lords providing that this free gift should not prove destructive to the bill sent down the bill to the House of Commons with this proviso, that the 20,000 cattle so given should not be sent alive, but killed and salted up in barrels, and that the Lord Mayor and Aldermen should be at charge of salting and barrelling and transporting the beef.

This the House of Commons at the first disliked not, but upon the motion of divers members who served for the City, who affirmed that this would be no advantage to the City and poor people, and therefore moved that the beasts might be sent in alive and sold, and then the money that was taken for them would be serviceable for the poor people. Whereupon the House refers it to a committee of which Mr. Seymour was Chairman; he makes his report from the committee, that they judged it best that the cattle should come in alive, as most advantageous to the poor people; but yet notwithstanding they did suspect that it would be prejudicial to the Irish bill that did restrain the importation of Irish cattle, especially for this next year. The House fell into a debate about it which held three hours, whether the cattle should be sent in alive or dead.

In the end after many long and excellent speeches both for and against it (in which the justness of the Irish bill was brought in, which Sir George Downing excellently made good) it was resolved not to agree with the committee, but rather with the amendment and proviso of the Lords, that the beef should be brought in salted in barrels; whereupon the House was divided and it was put to the question, and the noes carried it, of which I was one.

It was verily believed by most that this gift was in order to destroy the Irish bill, and under the pretence of sending in the 20,000 alive they would send in many 20,000's, and therefore it was moved that rather than to send in the 20,000 alive, that the English should advance as great a supply to the city as this would be, whensoever it should be moved to it.

After dinner we met in the House and attended the Speaker to the Whitehall to attend His Majesty with the Lord St. John's petition; the Speaker made a speech to the King and presented the petition to him, which the King received as I am informed, for although I was present and very near, yet could not hear what the King said. The King said, "I will read it and do according to law and justice."

The Speaker then returned to the House and adjourned until to-morrow at eight of the clock.

It was this day reported that there was a mutiny in Holland against de Witt: and also of the Spaniards surprising Casale, a very strong place in Italy, in the possession of the King of France: I wish these reports may prove true.

It is reported that we have good store of good masts and other necessary provision for the Navy safely come home. E.V.[1]

DECEMBER 6TH. This day the bill for composing differences and suits betwixt landlord and tenants and parties concerned in

---

[1] MS. gives E.V. clearly here, an abbreviation I cannot trace.

their interest, for and concerning the houses lately burnt in the City was read the second time and committed.

The rest of the day was spent in debate of the poll bill, how to meet with those that had not families and those that sojourned and were resident sometimes in one place, sometimes in another, and for servants that did leave their masters and go to other services at the time of their polling. It was resolved that in both they shall be polled in that place where they shall be at the time when the bill shall be executed.

DECEMBER 7TH. This morning it was earnestly moved that the bill that concerned Roberts and Winn should be brought in and reported, but it was put off till Monday.

The House took the poll bill into hand, which was perfectly gone through. Mr. Rigby brought in a proviso concerning assignments of the money, that officers for such money should have no fees, but it was accounted unreasonable and cast out.[1]

Mr. Garroway brought in another proviso that concerned the accounts which held a long debate of some hours and very excellent speeches made both for and against it: not in regard of the subject of it, for all seemed to desire that officers should be called to account for the money received by them, but it was not proper to do it by a proviso, and that the same should be annexed and made a branch of the poll bill; upon which the House was divided and it was put to the question whether the proviso should be committed. It was carried in the affirmative but I was for the negative: because I am confident the proviso was improper to be annexed to the bill, though with all my heart I desire to have a strict account from the officers how the money was laid out.

It was moved in the House that the receiving of the sacrament on Sunday next was contrary to an order made this morning.

After a long debate it was put to the question whether that order should be debated, upon which the House was divided and it was carried in the negative, and so I voted.

Then it was put to the question whether the House should

---

[1] *C.J.* VIII, 659, gives no figures for this vote.

adjourn until Monday in order to a due preparation for the receiving the sacrament; it was carried in the affirmative, and so I gave my vote.[1]

DECEMBER 9TH. This day the House received the sacrament at St. Margaret's, Westminster, where Dr. Outram preached in the morning; his text was Hebrews, 13th chapter, 10th, 11th, 12th verses.

The points or parts were three. First a position, "We have an altar whereof they have no right to eat that serve tabernacles."

Secondly the reason: "For the bodies of those beasts whose blood the high priest brought into the sanctuary for sin are burnt without the camp," verse 11.

Thirdly an inference, "Wherefore Jesus also that he might sanctify the people with his own blood suffered without the gate," verse the 12th.

He most excellently explained the sense of the words, and showed the excellency of Christ above the type set out in Moses, law which in those bloody sacrifice[s] prefigured Christ, who offered up himself and shed his blood to wash away the guilt and to cleanse from sin itself. And to instruct us that since God was so displeased with sin that no less would satisfy but the blood of his beloved son, that we should not crucify the Lord again, by making his death and suffering ineffectual by continuing in sin. But as God hath renewed his covenant with us, and we ours with him in this blessed sacrament, so we should be careful to keep it, and not to break the same by committing and continuing in any of our former sins.

In the afternoon preached Mr. Wharton, our Parliament chaplain; his text was, "To them that by patient welldoing seek for glory and honour and immortality, eternal life." Romans, chapter 2, verse 7.

He made a good honest moral commonplace sermon.

---

[1] *C.J.* VIII, 659, 119–83, Seymour and Garroway, Lord Hawley and Talbot. On debating the order about receiving the sacrament, *ibid.* pp. 54–98, Lee and How, Dolman and Meers; on adjournment till Monday, 102–47, J. Mallett and Holt, M. Mallett and Wm. Herbert.

58   MILWARD'S DIARY

DECEMBER 11TH. This day I went out of London and went by Oxford and so home.[1]

JANUARY 8TH. This day I came into London to the Parliament.

The day before I came Mr. Leigh's bill that was solicited by Francis Hollingshead was cast out of the House, Serjeant Maynard speaking against it as an ill precedent for the future.

It was ill reported by Mr. Ratcliff (as I am informed) who was the Chair at that committee, but besides neither Sir Fulk Lucy nor my cousin Milward spoke in the business (my cousin Milward indeed not well understanding it) or else I believe it might well have passed the House.

JANUARY 9TH. I went this day to the House; notwithstanding the severe orders of sending for those that were absent the second day of January, I took my place without any disturbance.

The cause depending between May and Austin for the due election of a burgess for the town of Winchelsea should have been heard this day, but it was put off until to-morrow.

There was this day a conference between the Lords and Commons at which two things were debated.

One was that the Commons thought themselves wronged that the Lords without them had petitioned the King to grant his commission to a select number of commissioners of Lords and Commons to take the accounts: this the Commons say is illegal and unparliamentary, but of this no report was made to the House.

The other was about the word "a nuisance" in the Irish bill, which the Lords would have amended, but the Commons' not assenting to it obstructs the passing the bill at present.

There was this day read the bill engrossed for the burying corpses in woollen, that whosoever shall bury any corpse in linen after the 25th of March, 1667, shall pay £5 for every corpse so buried.

[1] Milward thus missed debates 10–15, 17–22, 29 December; 2–5, 7 January, 1666/7. Articles of impeachment against Mordaunt, *C.J.* VIII, 666–7, and daily business, *passim*; Marvell's *Letters*, 15, 22, 29 December and 5 January, etc. Cobbett resumes his narrative 3 January.

The end aimed at in this bill is to prevent the burying French and Dutch linen cloth, to set up a manufacture of our own linen and to advance the price of wool.

This bill was very much spoken against; at last it was put to the question: the ayes that were for it and went out were 133; the noes that were against the bill stayed in and were but 51, of which I was one; and so the ayes carried it.

JANUARY 10TH. The Quakers this day sent in their printed book in way of petition, by a woman; the House received it and immediately sent to the Serjeant to apprehend the woman, but she was gone. She gave me one of them as I was going into the House.

Serjeant Maynard made his report of the committee's sense of the bill for prisoners and particularly for the county of Devon, where there was a stock of £2,000 and an house to set people on work within a mile or less of Exeter, out of which there was to be raised an allowance for the keeper of the house, and an allowance for a minister to read divine office, and every Lord's day to instruct those that were set on work there and belonged to the house, and the prisoners that were in the gaol at Exeter that were not without the compass of the clergy for their offences, should upon order from the justices of the peace be brought to the workhouse and be there set on work, until the next sessions or gaol delivery, at what time they were to be remanded to prison at Exeter in order to their trial.

The Lords sent two bills to the House for the passing two estates of land, and to desire a conference concerning the Mint and coining of money.

The Commons attended them; Sir George Downing made his report of that conference both of the Lords' amendments and how far [they] agreed to the bill.

One amendment was that they added one thousand pounds per annum (if there were cause) to the salary for the officers of the Mint.

Another amendment was that whereas it was said, "The King's Mint", in the singular number, "or Mints" should be added in the plural number.

JANUARY 11TH. This day was resumed the great debate about the election of May and Austin.[1] Austin is the member now sitting; May endeavours to prove the election invalid and void upon these grounds:

First, because the persons that voted for Austin, which were nine, six of them were Quakers, or such as had not received the sacrament within 22 months before the election, nor had taken oaths according to the act.

To this it was replied that May had [votes] by seven persons, and four of them never came to the church, for indeed it seems the allowance is so small that they have seldom a minister there.

And also that one of May's votes, which was the Town Clerk, was indicted of felony.

Secondly (which was more insisted on) it was urged that the Mayor which made the return had not received the sacrament of 12 months before the election, or before he was chosen Mayor. And so by the Act of Regulating Corporations he was not a legal Mayor, and so could not make a legal return. There was excellent speeches made on both sides, both by Sir Robert Atkins, Sir Thomas Littleton and Mr. Coleman, a young lawyer, to prove Austin's election good and lawful, in case the Mayor should not prove to be a legal Mayor at the time of the election and when he made the return, and they gave this reason for it, that being elected Mayor and acting as Mayor, his ministerial acts in reference to other men were lawful and good.

On the other side Sir William Coventry and his brother, Mr. Henry Coventry, and some others, spoke exceeding well and truly quoted the words of the act, which are positive and plain against the Mayor's power of making a return in this.

After a long debate it was put to the question whether the House should agree with the committee, who had voted the election void; the House thereupon was divided and the noes carried it almost by a double number. I went out of the House before the question and did not give my vote for either, for the election was clearly against the words of the act: and yet Austin had very much reason on his side.

[1] *C.J.* VIII, 674, does not mention this, as it was probably debated in committee.

I was invited to a committee dinner by Sir Seymour Shirley to the Dog Tavern, and after went to the committee, where the bill to enable him, being under the age of one and twenty, to settle a jointure on the Lady Diana Bruce, the Lord Ailsbury's daughter (whom Sir Seymour was then to marry), was debated. The bill was examined and some amendments made, and the bill prepared to be reported, Mr. Crouch being Chairman at the committee.

Mr. Henry Hilton, Esq., of the Bishopric of Durham, left at his decease his lands charged with these gifts and charitable uses, viz: £24 per annum to 16 or 18 parishes in several counties for 99 years, to be distributed to the poor of those parishes yearly, and also several annuities as rent charges to several parishes in London and Surrey. And left the Lord Mayor of London and four of the chief Aldermen (as a corporation) and the Mayor of Durham trustees to see the said performed and made good.

It so proved that the divisor had not power to dispose of his land to make good this charitable gift because the land that should raise this yearly money was held *in capite*, or some part of it, and so a third part of it belonged to the heir, nor could the donors or trustees discharge their trust, they not having power to do it, because the Mayor and Aldermen were not a legal corporation.

Upon these mistakes and insufficiencies the heir at law claims the lands, and great suits were waged and commenced between the trustees and the heir. After a long suit and great expense they came to an agreement, viz: that the heir should have one third part of the land, and the several parishes should have two parts, that is of £24 the parishes should have £16 and the heir £8, and both parties desired that this agreement should be confirmed by an act of Parliament. The bill was brought in, twice read and committed.

Sir Thomas Higgins his bill was this day read the third time, being engrossed; it was learnedly debated and argued both for and against him. The issue was whether it was within the compass of the Act of Oblivion or not.

Many spoke for him, as Mr. Waller and others; against him

spoke Mr. Seymour, Mr. Swinsen and Sir Robert Atkins and Mr. Solicitor, who spake most admirably and made it appear most evidently that it was within the compass of the Act of Oblivion.

It was put to the question whether the bill should pass or not, whereupon the House was divided: the ayes that went out were 60 odd; the noes that stayed in were 80 odd, of which I was one, and so Sir Thomas Higgins his bill was cast out.

JANUARY 12TH. This day Mr. Maynard's bill concerning Sir Edward Mosley's estate was brought into the House, which after Serjeant Maynard had opened in his son's behalf against one Mosley it was ordered to be heard upon Monday next.

Then was reported the reasons that were prepared to satisfy the Lords in those particulars wherein they dissented from the House of Commons concerning the poll bill, which were in these three:

First, the Lords did not agree in the taxing of aliens double.

Secondly, they did not agree that the House of Commons should nominate their commissioners for taxing their estates.

Thirdly, they did not agree that the House of Commons should tax them for their titles.

When the reasons were prepared they sent a message to the House of Lords to desire a conference about them, which the Lords consented to.

At the conference the Solicitor justified reasons with a most excellent speech.

The Lords sent down two bills to the House, my Lord Roos his bill and Mr. Scawen his bill.

The wine merchants' petition was brought in by Colonel Kirby. It was that the House of Commons would intercede for them to the King that he would be pleased to give them leave to bring in their ships laden with French wines and goods, paying him his due customs.

There was a great debate about the petition, much said in their behalf and very much against them.

It was at the last put to the question and their petition was cast out; I gave my vote for them.[1]

---

[1] *C.J.* VIII, 675, 43–64, Kirby and Garroway, Hide and Downing.

JANUARY 14TH. This day a petition was brought in that the taxes of Bedford levels might be laid by the pound rate and not by the acres, as now they were, because of the inequality of the value of the acres. A bill was brought in and read the first time.

A petition of Mr. Chune, a member of the House, was brought in, who prayed relief against an attorney, who had arrested him at the church on a Sunday (for ten thousand thousand [sic] pounds) for words pretended to be spoken by Mr. Chune, within the time of his privilege of Parliament. The petition was referred to a committee, who ordered that the attorney should be sent for and the business be heard on Saturday next.

The House was called and everyone that was absent was voted a defaulter, and every member that was a Knight of the Shire gave ten shillings to the officers, and every burgess for a corporation gave five shillings.

The Lords sent to desire a conference, at which they consented to the reasons given by the Commons on Saturday last for the passing of the poll bill as it was sent up to them.

They only made this one amendment, that the commissioners should not be nominated by the Commons, that should tax them for their estates, but they were contented that the Commons should tax them for their titles of honour.

The report of this amendment and their enlargement of the time for one month longer than the Commons had proposed for levying the poll money was made to the House and assented to, and so the poll bill was perfected.

The Lords also this day passed the Irish bill with the word "a nuisance", and so that bill was likewise perfected and passed both Houses.

JANUARY 15TH. This day Sir Seymour Shirley's bill was reported by Mr. Crouch for the enabling him to settle a jointure on his lady. The House agreed with the committee and ordered it to be engrossed.

Mr. Prynne this day made his report from the committee for the bringing down the price of coals.

The report did consist of three heads, that might concern the cause of making coals so dear and scarce.

First, the want of a convoy to secure them in the passage to London.

Secondly, the pressing men of the coal ships for the service of the Navy.

Thirdly, the engrossing and monopolising and exacting of the wharfingers and the car-men.

To return the first and second it was moved humbly to petition the King to grant a convenient convoy and guard for the ships and a protection also to the seamen, that none should be pressed out of the coal-ships, above the number of four out of a ship of an hundred tons, nor above six out of a ship of two hundred ton nor above eight out of a ship of three hundred tons, and those to be pressed between the first of September and the first of April and at no other time.

This was very long in debate, for it took up the House this whole day and being put to the question whether the committee should be agreed with in this report, it was carried in the affirmative, and so I gave my vote.

The abuse of the wharfingers will be taken into consideration and of the carmen.

JANUARY 16TH. This day Sir Charles Stanley's bill for the sale of land was read and ordered a second reading.

The House fell into a long debate about its going into a Grand Committee to proceed upon the bill for the land tax.

It was debated in the House first to put the Lords in mind of passing the bill concerning Canary wines and the Lord Mordaunt's impeachment; this was consented to and Sir Edward Walpole was ordered to carry up the message.

The Lords sent down two bills to be passed by the Commons.

JANUARY 17TH. This day[1] Lord Roos his bill was brought from the Lords and read the first time and ordered to be read again the second time on Saturday next.

Colonel Sandys his bill for Bedford levels was read and though much opposed was ordered to be read again on Monday next.

Mr. Scawen's bill was also brought in from the Lords and read. It concerned the restoring of his son, to make him capable

---

[1] Cf. *C.J.* VIII, 675, 12 January, *ibid.* p. 677, 17 January.

of inheriting, being formerly convicted and condemned for stealing a mare (though falsely). It was ordered to be read again the second time on Saturday next.

The three bills concerning the members of the House were read.

First, concerning the attendance of the members: that every man elected a member shall have at the time of his election two sufficient men to be sureties for him, that he shall attend the House within 12 days after his election, unless he be sick or have some just or lawful excuse.

Secondly, that none shall be elected but he shall bring a sufficient certificate that he hath received the sacrament according to the rites of the Church of England within such a certain number of months, nor shall the vote of any man for his election be allowed but from him that hath received the sacrament within so many months last past.

Thirdly, that none shall be admitted to be present at the election but such as have lawful votes except necessary servants to attend their masters, nor shall any soldiers or commanders, but such as have voices to elect, and they no otherwise armed than with their ordinary riding arms.

That no man that is to be elected shall invite or give any meat or drink or any entertainment to any for their votes. Nor shall any man settle his land to several persons in such a manner as to gain by plurality of votes.

There are other paragraphs of this bill, and several penalties to be inflicted, as will appear in the act if this bill pass.

This day the Lords sent down to the House to acquaint them that they did agree with them in their bill for burying of the dead in woollen.

The French merchants brought in the second petition, which after a long debate was read and received.

The Lords sent down a second message that the King would come to Parliament to-morrow at eleven of the clock, and pass such bills as were prepared, and that he commanded the Houses' attendance.

JANUARY 18TH. This day the defaulters were called and when it came to the county of Derby Mr. Dalton was called; Mr. Grey made a fair excuse for him, as that he was an old man and lame of the gout, but the House not being satisfied with it, it was put to the question whether he should be spared or no: the House divided upon it, but it was carried in the affirmative that he should be spared; I gave my vote for him.

We went to attend the King in the House of Lords, where the Speaker made a good speech and presented to [him] the poll bill, the Irish bill and divers others; the King passed them all and made a very good speech with some reflection on the Irish bill, in reference to the word "a nuisance", which had been so much insisted upon (yet not naming it).[1] He said he never as yet broke his word with us, nor did ever give us just cause to suspect him or to distrust him, nor had he done any act of oppression since he was restored to us; and that he would determine this session on Monday seven night.

When we returned to the House we had a long debate whether we should proceed in calling over the members; it was put to the question; the House was divided upon it and the noes went out and carried it; I was one of them.

In this debate it was stood upon whether the House was not adjourned as to that debate by the Black Rod's coming to the House and summoning the House to attend the King, and besides after our return before we resumed that debate of calling defaulters: we ordered a new business but this although the debate held long could not be determined until it was put to the question and so decided by a negative.

JANUARY 19TH. This day the Lord Lindsey's bill was read, who desired that more trustees may be added to Colonel Cooke, who is in Ireland, and was chosen a trustee in Oliver's time to preserve the Lord Norrice his estate; this bill was opposed by Cooke's party and endured a long debate, and they that were for the bill alleged that the infant to whom the estate belongs, not being able to take the estate into his own hands, if Colonel Cooke should die, being the only trustee remaining, Cooke's

---

[1] Marvell writing to Hull on 19 January (*Letters*, p. 51) remarks on the bills passed and gives a list (*ibid.* p. 54) in his letter of the 9th. Cf. *Statutes of the Realm*, v.

wife would claim the third and so do a prejudice to the infant; and therefore it [was] thought very just to make an addition of some trustees.

The House proceeded to the bill for the land tax to perfect it. It was resolved that the money raised by it should be paid in eleven months, viz: the 1st of May, 1668, the 1st of August, the 1st of November, the 1st of February, 1668.

There was a long debate about a proviso that was brought in, viz: that a certain sum, £1,200,000 should be appointed to pay the seamen only at their return from their service.

This endured a long debate but in the end was referred to a committee.

Then was read one of the three bills to oblige the attendance of the members.

JANUARY 21ST. This day Mr. Scawen's bill was read for restoring his son from the attainder (he having been in Oliver's time indicted and convicted for stealing a mare); it was twice read and engrossed and sent up to the Lords, it being plainly proved that he was falsely accused by two perjured witnesses, the one of them being proved perjured in this case and the other being fled to avoid his punishment.

The Lord Roos's bill was read and committed.[1]

Then Sir Seymour Shirley's bill was read the third time and sent up to the House of Lords.

I went to the House of Peers to hear the debate between the Duke of Buckingham and the Earl of Rutland about the barony of Roos, but it was put off until to-morrow.

The House then went into a Grand Committee.

I went to Lambeth to dinner.

In the afternoon I went to the Lord Roos his committee. His business was weakly begun by Mr. Alsopp; Sir William Cary his evidence was not to the advantage but rather did hurt. Mr. William Mountague was Chairman.

It was ordered to be heard again by the said committee on

[1] C.J. VIII, 679–90. Both Milwards were named on the committee for the bill about Lady Roos's children. Milward again appears to be writing up his Diary on the same day as the events it records.

Wednesday next, and in the meantime bills are to be set up to give notice to the Lady Roos or her agents to make her defence.

JANUARY 22ND. This day Mr. Russell's bill was read for the sale of Chiswick.

The bill for the confirmation of the King's proclamation for prohibiting the importation of French goods was brought in.

The Lords sent down a message to the House that they did consent that some members of the House of Commons should be examined before the Lords as witnesses for the Lord Mordaunt.

The House returned this answer, that such members as was desired should be at the hearing and likewise examined, but not as members but in nature of witnesses only.

The House also ordered that Sir John Maynard, Sir Robert Atkins and divers others should manage the impeachment against the Lord Mordaunt.

The House read the petition of the French merchants for the obtaining the King's licence for the wines etc. And also to include all other merchants through all the ports of this kingdom that were in the same condition; and that this clause should be added to the bill; this was much opposed, and the House was divided upon it. It was carried in the affirmative and so I gave my vote, though I doubted afterwards I gave it the worse way.

Sir Robert Brooke being Chairman at that committee brought in the report of the firings of London.

The examinations of divers persons were read, and there appeared to be many wicked and desperate expressions in them, but yet there are none of them that can be laid hold on to extend to the punishment of death of them that uttered them or to prove it to be a general design of wicked agents, Papists or Frenchmen, to burn the city.

The most material that was reported was that one Peters of Kent (whom some say is brother to the Lord Peters) should say that our King should be King of England but a few days.

I cannot conceive that the House can make anything of the report from the committee.

JANUARY 23RD. This day I moved for Mr. Kendall's bill and got it ordered to be the first reported to-morrow morning.

Mr. Secretary Morice brought in a bill for imposing a charge upon coals, for the rebuilding the several places of London; it was voted by all to be a good bill, but because the petition for it was not first brought in before the bill, to obtain leave to bring it in, it being a bill of that nature for the imposing a charge upon the subject and raising money which ought not to pass without the leave of the House (it being affirmed to be against the rules of Parliament), it was ordered that a petition should be preferred first to the House and then that the bill should be read the next day.

Colonel Sandys his bill for the regulating the taxes of Bedford levels was debated and ordered to be read, and also to be heard at the Bar with counsel on both sides to-morrow at two of the clock.

In the afternoon the committee sat about my Lord Roos's bill. It was there debated until almost eight of the clock at night. I[t] found there a great deal of impertinent but resolute opposition, but in the conclusion it was carried clear for the Lord Roos; and the bill that was sent down by the Lords engrossed was read and examined by paragraphs and passed without any one amendment or any negative.

Lord Roos made a committee dinner at the Dog for some gentlemen; I was one.

JANUARY 24TH. This day I moved for Mr. Kendall's bill, and got it first read and passed, and Mr. Grey carried it up to the Lords.

Mr. Chune's case was reported by Sir Job Charlton for the breach of privilege. It was spoken against by Mr. Prynne, who would have his arrest to be no breach of privilege, he not allowing any time to members to be freed from arrest but only (as he said) *eundo, morando, redeundo*; and Sir Robert Atkins would have no breach of privilege if the arrest was made above 20 days before or after the session.

But Sir John Birkenhead spoke very well to the contrary and so did Sir Thomas Gower, and gave precedents of a longer time and reasons also for it, and also alleged that the Lords had forty days allowed them for their privilege, and they also affirmed that the time of privilege was never limited.

The House voted Mr. Chune's arrest to be a breach of privilege, and ordered that the person that caused him to be arrested should be sent for by the Serjeant.

The Lords sent to desire a conference about the accounts and consented to the House of Commons bill with some amendments which was not this day read.

The most of the forenoon was spent in a confused debate whether Sir John Birkenhead, who had a report from the committee for the printers, or Sir Thomas Littleton, who had a report from the committee for the attendance of the members, should be heard first.

The debate took up all the morning, and in the end neither of them made his report.

In the afternoon the bill for the levels was heard; Serjeant Fountain, being concerned in the bill, pleaded his own cause, and counsel was heard on both sides, and in conclusion it was carried for Colonel Sandys that the levels should pay taxes by the pound rate and not by the acres.

It was expected that the committee for the repair of London should make their report, but it was put off for this time.

JANUARY 25TH. This day the bill for Southampton was read, in which town there are five parish churches unto which the allowance is very small; the bill did move that those five parish churches might be reduced to two, and the allowances to be so divided between them, and what was wanting of a sufficient maintenance might be supplied by the town.

This was opposed upon the account of raising and imposing a charge upon the town without a legal proceeding, and so the bill was not passed.

The Lords sent three bills down to the House, two of their own; the third was a bill sent up from the House of Commons.

Mr. Fulk Grosvenor's[1] bill to enable him to sell land was passed.

Sir Thomas Littleton made his report from the committee of the bill concerning the attendance of the members. The bill was adjourned first by vote, and secondly it was put to the question whether it should be reported before to-morrow in the afternoon; I was in affirmative for the first and in the negative in the second.

Then was read and examined the bill for the monthly tax, which was passed.

Then it was debated whether the bill should be sent up to the Lords presently or not; it was much opposed in regard the Lord Mordaunt's impeachment was not over, nor the Canary patent determined. For it was said that if the King shall determine this session on Monday according to his resolution, and as he delivered himself in his speech, these two bills and the bill for accounts will not be passed, but in all probability will be left; but in conclusion the bill for monthly tax was ordered immediately to be carried to the Lords.

The bill for rebuilding of London was moved to be reported, but in regard of the great weight and consequence of the business, the day being far spent (it being then almost three of the clock) it was adjourned until to-morrow in the afternoon.

JANUARY 26TH.   This day[2] the bill for rebuilding the city of London was reported to the House with its amendments; before it was thoroughly reported it was adjourned until the afternoon in order to the House's attendance of the Lords in the Lord Mordaunt's impeachment.

When we came to the Lords the House insisted on these two things, first whether the Lord Mordaunt (who kept his seat in the Lords' House) should not appear at the Bar at time of his trial, and for this the House affirmed that they had a precedent.

Secondly whether the Lord Mordaunt should have counsel allowed him to plead his cause, for it is said he may have counsel

---

[1] *C.J.* VIII, 683. Leicester given for Grosvenor's first name instead of Fulk.

[2] MS. misplaces the marginal date by one paragraph here against the first mention of the London bill above.

allowed him in point of law to consult with, but not to plead for him, as my Lord Strafford's case, but for matter of fact it is said he can have no counsel.

Upon this the Commons withdrew and the business was adjourned till Monday.

The House met in the afternoon, and the report from the city's committee was resumed and the amendments assented to.

They had in debate the largeness of the streets, the height and wideness of the buildings and the measure of the brick and timber, the time to begin and to consider of men's proprieties.

JANUARY 28TH. This day[1] the bill of Colonel Sandys in settling the taxes of Bedford level, being engrossed, was read the last time and so sent up to the Lords.

The Lord Lindsey's bill was read concerning the estate he had by the Lady Norrice, which was left in trust with Colonel Cooke. It was moved that the Duke of Albemarle and the Lord Campden should be added as trustees; this was mainly opposed by Colonel Cooke's agents and by his wife, by way of petition, and by the Court party, but it was carried against them, the two Lords were added to the trust, and so the bill passed.

The Lords sent down two messages to the House this day.

First to acquaint the House that they had agreed with them in the act for the monthly tax; and that they also had agreed with them to wait on the King with the petition of the French merchants concerning their wines and French commodities, and to pray the King to appoint a day when he would please they should attend His Majesty.

The second message was to acquaint them that they had considered of the two questions that were put to them on Saturday last: first whether Lord Mordaunt should sit in his place at his trial or stand at the bar.

Secondly whether he should be allowed counsel to plead for him.

The members of the House went immediately to the Lords

---

[1] *C.J.* VIII, 684. MS. misdates this entry the 27th, a Sunday.

and received this answer. First that the Lord Mordaunt should not keep his seat during his trial, but should sit within the House on a stool, barehead.

Secondly that they find by an order of the House, and by a former precedent, that he may have counsel to plead for him.

This answer being reported by Sir Robert Atkins did not satisfy the House. For first they say that he being indicted stands guilty until upon trial he be acquitted, and therefore during his trial he ought to stand at the Bar, the most proper place for him.

Secondly for allowing him counsel although Mr. Solicitor spoke excellently, that it might be of dangerous consequence to deny a commoner of England counsel in a matter only criminal and not capital, yet Sir Robert Atkins was of opinion that it was custom, and therefore lawful, to deny counsel to persons in matters criminal. But he said that they might be allowed counsel to be near at hand to them, to advise and consult and to assist them in point of law, but not to plead for them.

Many precedents were read to this purpose or effect. Whereupon it was resolved the journal and records should be consulted against the next morning, and so to attend the Lords in order to his trial.

The rest of the day was spent until four of the clock in examining the amendments in the bill for rebuilding the city of London, in which two things are yet unresolved. First what breadth those streets (which now are but ten or eleven yards wide and appointed to be first built) shall be established; and for in widening them, how they shall be paid for the ground that shall be taken from them that are the owners of it, for the enlarging those streets.

Secondly, that there shall be 39 new churches built, and to be built with the materials and sale of the grounds where those churches stood that are demolished by the fire and are not to be rebuilt, and with the sale of those churchyards.

And that those churchyards that are so to be sold shall be added to the streets to enlarge them, where of necessity the streets must enter into them. And for the rest of those churchyards that are not taken into the streets, they shall be put to common uses for buildings and cellars.

This although it was much pressed yet it found much opposition in regard that the ground whereon the churchyards and the churches had been built had been dedicated to a pious use and therefore ought not to be profaned by converting them to a common use, nor men's bones to be disturbed, but rather they should be still left for burying places.

For it cannot be imagined that when the city is rebuilt and fully peopled that the churchyards of the 39 now built churches will be sufficient for burying places for all the city.

It was put to the question whether the proviso for the sale of the yards of the churches to be demolished should be added to the bill or no; the House was divided upon it; the ayes went out and were 42, the noes that stayed in were 36, of which I was one.

JANUARY 29TH. This day Sir Charles Stanley's bill was read the last time; it appeared that he was tenant but for term of life without impeachment of waste, but had not power to raise any part of the estate, which was £1,300 per annum. The bill did pray that he might be enabled to lease £400 per annum, to raise a sum of money to pay debts, and to raise money for his daughters' portions, and also to have power to settle an £100 per annum annuity on his younger son for his life.

The bill was passed and sent up to the Lords by the Lord Ancram.

My Lord Roos's bill was read and opposed by Mr. Prynne, because it moved to bastardise Ignotus etc. as to my Lord Rutland's estate and yet to make him etc. capable to inherit the land that came by his mother.

It was also mainly opposed by Mr. Seymour, by a long impertinent speech, but in the end it was passed by the vote of the House, and the bill sent up by Mr. Attorney Mountague.

The debate was resumed concerning the Lord Mordaunt, whether he should be permitted to sit within the rails of the Lords' House at the time of his trial, and whether he should be allowed counsel to plead for him.

Many speeches were made for and against him; some moved that a conference might be desired with the Lords to determine these two questions, especially since there were precedents on both sides.

It was at last resolved that he should have counsel allowed him, but the House would not consent that he should sit within the rail at his trial, but that he should stand at the Bar.

The Lords sent to the House to let them know that the King would have both the Houses to attend him at Whitehall at three of the clock that afternoon with the French merchants' petition.

The Houses accordingly attended the King and His Majesty granted the petition.

JANUARY 30TH. This day being the day that our late ever blessed King was barbarously murthered was kept with fasting and abstinence.

I went to the Temple to sermon, where Dr. Harding, the Dean of Rochester, preached. His text was Matthew 10th, 39th verse: "He that will save his life shall lose it and he that will lose his life for my sake shall save it." He made a very good sermon and moved many to tears in applying it to our late King's sufferings.

JANUARY 31ST. This day was read the bill for preventing fightings and disorders of seamen at their pay day; power was given to the officers of the Naval forces to punish any such disorders, by fining such as should fight and be disorderly, the fine not exceeding one pound, or to imprison them not exceeding one month; but if their offence should be of an higher nature, that then they should send them to the next gaol.

This bill was passed.

The next bill that was read was against blasphemy, swearing and execrations, which after some amendments was sent up to the Lords.

Mr. Fulk Grosvenor's bill was read and sent up to the Lords.

A committee from the House went up this day to the Lords in order to the management of the impeachment against the Lord Mordaunt.

They acquainted the Lords that they had agreed with them in allowing him counsel, but hoped that they would not without precedent insist upon his sitting within the Bar at his trial.

The Lords gave them their sense in writing, which was this, that they had the right of judging in what manner the Lord Mordaunt should be tried, and therefore they would not admit that he should stand at the Bar; whereupon the committee returned to the House, and Sir Robert Atkins reported it. Upon this report there was a long debate and many very good speeches made both for and against it.

It was resolved that the House would not depart from their privilege nor agree that the Lord Mordaunt should sit within the Bar at his trial.

The bill for rebuilding London was brought in and passed.

FEBRUARY 1ST. This day a bill was read for the town of Swaffham Prior,[1] where there are two parishes of the same name and two churches, the lands belonging to both being held by one tenant, so that at this day the lands cannot be well distinguished: the scope of the bill was to keep the parishes still separated and to put both churches into one and to distinguish the lands properly belonging to both.

FEBRUARY 2ND.[2] The House ordered that the members that were instructed to manage the impeachment against the Lord Mordaunt should withdraw to consult of reasons to give satisfaction to the Lord[s] why they could not agree with them that the Lord Mordaunt should not be permitted to sit within the Bar at his trial, and then to desire a conference with the Lords.

The House had a conference with the Lords about the plague bill.

Then was read the bill that was engrossed for the rebuilding the city of London.

A proviso was brought in [by] Sir George Downing for the enlarging the streets that goeth along to the Thames called Thames Street, which is 100 yards from the Thames. The members that were chosen for London moved to have it according to the proviso, 30 foot broad, but others think it necessary

---

[1] *C.J.* VIII, 687, supplies the name Swaffham Prior, etc., which is omitted in the MS.

[2] *C.J.* VIII, 688. Although the motion to sit Saturday is given, there is no entry under that date, 2 February.

to be 40 foot, which being put to the question it was carried for the forty foot.

It was likewise resolved that the building that street by the Thames (dye-houses excepted) should not be built till a Lady Day, viz: March 25th, 1669. And they give this reason for it, because say they that street will be sure to be built at any time, and if it should be now begun to be built it would take up all the workmen and obstruct the building of the whole city.

The amendment of the bill for the imposition of twelve pence upon every chauldron of coals was read; this imposition is to continue ten years. And the money raised out of it is to be bestowed towards the rebuilding of the city, and to be entered into a book of parchment or vellum, which book is to be kept in the Chamber of London, that any man without any fee given may have access to it, and free liberty to look into it; and that an account of all money brought in and disbursed shall be brought into the Exchequer by some officer (entrusted by the Mayor and Aldermen) upon oath.

FEBRUARY 4TH. This day the reports of the bills for hemp and flax, and that of the prisoners who are in for debt, which is to be reported by my cousin Milward, were presented to the House, and the reporters did contest whose report should be first made; it was put to the vote and the report for hemp and flax carried it, though I gave my vote against it.

The tithe of hemp and flax that was due to the vicars endured a long debate; it was moved at the first that the vicar should be allowed for the tithe twelve pence an acre, but that was rejected as too little; then eighteenpence an acre was proposed and that was likewise rejected, and then two shillings sixpence was offered, and with that sum the bill was sent up to the Lords, who sent the bill down again with the amendment of five shillings an acre, which being put to the question it was carried for 2s. 6d. an acre; I gave my vote for five shillings.

My cousin Milward could not get on his report this day.

The Lords sent a message that they were ready for a conference to hear the House's reasons why they did not agree with the Lords to try the Lord Mordaunt, he sitting within the Bar.

Mr. Seymour gave the reasons, which the Lords presented to the whole House of Peers, and their answer we are to expect.

Then was brought in the city bill, which was read and sent up to the Lords.

After the bill for 12d. a chauldron or ton of coals had been a while debated it was ordered to be engrossed.

Then was taken up the debate about churches that were to be built and what should be done with those churches that will stand void; this will be referred until the next session of Parliament.

FEBRUARY 5TH. This day my cousin Milward made his report of the bill for the prisoners that were in for debt, and making it appear upon oath that they are not worth £5 besides their wearing apparel and necessary tools to work with in their profession, shall be set at liberty by three justices of the peace, one of them being of the quorum, unless they that sued them can make it appear by good and sufficient proof that they are worth above five pounds.

The London bill was brought in and read and after a long debate about the provisos it was passed and sent up to the Lords.

The House sent a message to the Lords by Sir Robert Holt to desire a free conference, to debate their reasons why the Lord Mordaunt should not be permitted to sit within the Bar at his trial; after a long attendance the Lords gave them this answer, that they would adhere to their former sense, which was that they had the power to try the Lord Mordaunt as they pleased, and that they would not agree with the House of Commons that he should stand at the Bar to be tried.

Among other reasons they gave them several precedents, as of my Lord Strafford's and others that were tried standing at the Bar.

FEBRUARY 6TH. This day the House took into debate the case of Mr. Chune, whether White, the attorney that arrested Mr. Chune at the church on Sunday for words (calling him a traitor) should be fined or not. It was put to the question, and carried in the affirmative. Then it was put to the question how much the fine should be; some voted £500, others £1,000, and it was carried that his fine should be £1,000.

It was certified and made appear to the House that he had

been a mischievous rascal, one that had bought the King's lands and had been a rebel.

It was then debated in the House, if the House did fine a thousand pounds, what course should be taken to levy it. This at present put the House to a stand, and although the fine should stand, he having arrested Mr. Chune against the privilege of Parliament, yet it was not resolved how the fine should be levied.

Several opinions were delivered in the case. Mr. Prynne said that the arrest of a member was limited to a time *eundo, morando et redeundo*, but it was voted and carried against him. Others were for a *terme certaine* of 40 days before the Parliament and 40 days after the session, and that if any man was elected a member 40 days before the sitting of the Parliament and was arrested within any of those 40 days it was a breach of the privilege.

This debate held long, but not determined;[1] but the opinion and sense of the House was that as the Lords had 40 days allowed them, so the members of the House of Commons ought to have their 40 days allowed them. But no certain time was allowed, but it is left still to the Parliament to judge of the time of privilege.

But concerning White's fine, it was respited as to the levying of it, in regard the Parliament was to sit so short a time, and besides it was not proper to fine him unless he had been first in the custody of the Serjeant.

Then the House took into debate the Lord Mordaunt's case, and of the Lords' denying a free conference about it, since the Commons had sent them their reasons why he should not be tried sitting within the Bar.

It was very well debated and most excellently that it was the privilege and right of the Commons of England, when they impeached any man in the names of the Commons of England, that the party impeached should stand at the Bar at the time of his trial. After a serious debate Mr. Henry Coventry moved that they should send up to the Lords to desire a conference, in reference to their former denial of a free conference. This was resolved and a message was sent up accordingly.

The Lords proposed a precedent of the Bishop of Llandaff,

---

[1] *C.J.* VIII, 691, 26–26, Trelawney and Mallett, Lee and Holt. The Speaker decided for the Yeas.

who they said was a scrivener or a projector for Sir Francis Bacon, Lord Chancellor; the Bishop they say was impeached, but not tried at the Bar. To this it was answered that his trial was prevented, because he was not impeached by the Commons of England, and therefore it was let fall.

The Lords also alleged my Lord Stamford's case, that he was impeached for striking Sir Arthur Haselrigg; but it was answered this was an act done in time of rebellion, and the quarrel was composed, and so it was no precedent in my Lord Mordaunt's case.

But on the contrary it was proved that persons have been impeached both by Lords and Commons, and been tried at the Bar, and that the Journal of the Peers do make good the same.

FEBRUARY 7TH. This day it was moved that Mr. Rigby's tenant that was sued and the trial to be brought down the next assizes should be stopped, it being voted to be a breach of privilege.

Sir Job Charlton reported from the committee of privileges that Mr. Pierpont's his bailiff being imprisoned and ordered to be discharged upon his privilege was still detained by one Bristow, the new Under-sheriff; it was therefore ordered that the Sheriff should be sent for up to answer it.

Mr. Mallett made his report concerning a lease made by a bishop to a certain man for his life; this man being absent and beyond sea for some certain years, and so reported to be dead, the bishop leaseth the same thing to another man, and received a fine. Afterwards the first lessee proves to be alive and comes over into England and enters upon his farm. The question is how the second lessee shall be relieved for his fine paid. The question was left uncertain and not determined, but in my judgment the bishop should make repayment of the fine received.

The Lords sent down a message that they would admit of conference at eleven of the clock, and accordingly the House of Commons met them and showed them their reasons that they denying them a free conference (to debate their right and to show their reasons that the Lord Mordaunt ought to be tried at the Bar) was against the rules of Parliament and destructive to the privileges of it.

The Lords after this sent down a message that they would admit of a free conference, at which conference it was debated and stood upon by them that the Commons should examine their precedents, whether it was against the rules and privileges of the Commons to be denied a free conference in this case by the Lords.

Secretary Morice delivered a message from the King that to-morrow the King would be in the House of Lords and would determine this session and prorogue the Parliament.

The Lords sent down the bill for the rebuilding of the city with some amendments, but it was for the present laid aside; the bill for accounts resumed which the Lords had sent down with some amendments.

In the preamble they made this alteration, viz: whereas it was said in the bill, "the public money" they altered to these words, "the money granted"; and whereas this word, "accounted" was in the bill they put in this word, "examined".

These alterations the House did not agree to, and the whole scope of the debate (which held long) was that the House intended that there should be an account given of the [twenty] five hundred thousand pounds, and of twelve hundred and fifty thousand pounds, and of the prize goods, and of the militia money, and how the same hath been disbursed, whether for the war only as it was intended.

They that spake against the sense of the House, as Mr. Harry Coventry and others, said that the twelve hundred and fifty thousand pounds was so to be accounted for, but not the five and twenty hundred thousand pounds, because that money was not given with that resolution, and therefore if the officers did produce the King's warrant for the disposing any of that money to any other use it was a sufficient discharge to the officer that paid it.

My opinion of this debate was this, that if the King had laid out any money of his own proper revenue to the raising or maintaining the forces of this war, it is great reason he should be reimbursed out of the £2,500,000, but as the Lords had amended the bill there was no power left, either strictly to charge those that disbursed the money, or to punish them if they had embezzled and mis-spent the same.

The Lords sent down the city bill with some amendments, which were read and assented to, and so the bill was passed.

The petition of the extractors of spirits and strong waters was read; they desired a reformation of their grievances, by reason of the excise imposed upon them. The matter of the question was whether they should pay excise for the liquor at the first extraction, or afterwards when it was contracted into a less quantity. It was debated but not resolved, and so the bill was left.

FEBRUARY 8TH. This day two or three private bills were read and passed and sent up to the Lords.

The House was preparing their reasons for the further satisfaction of the Lords, that it was against the privilege of the House to be denied a free conference about the Lord Mordaunt's trial.

Also the House was in debate of the bill of accounts, and whether they should adhere to their own preamble or to that that the Lords had made as an amendment, but whilst these things were in debate the Black Rod came to let the House understand that the King was come to the House of Lords and commanded their attendance, whereupon the House attended the Speaker to the King, who after he had passed such bills as were presented to him, made a short speech,[1] and so put an end to this present session, and prorogued the Parliament until the 10th October next.

This session of Parliament by the King's proclamation met on St. James's Day, July the 25th, 1667.[2]

JULY 25TH. This day the Parliament met, and there was a very good appearance, it being the first day. The Speaker told us that the King had sent for him the night before and had commanded him to acquaint the House that he had intended

---

[1] Charles II's speech was printed, as was also Sir Edward Turner's.

[2] Cf. C.J. VIII, 692; L.J. XII, 111–114; Cobbett, IV, 363. The report of Charles's speech in the Lords' *Journals* is "to this effect" (114); it was not printed. Hastings MSS. II, 154, mentions a rumour to this effect and describes the Speaker "rubbing his eyes with his handkerchief all the way to his coach, and looked between anger and pity". The Commons' bold vote is noticed in an account of the Lords' debates in Rawl. A, 130, and in H.M.C. 7th Report, p. 486. See also Marvell to Hull, 27 June,

to have come to the House that day and to have spoken to them, but in regard he did believe that the House would not be so full the first day as he desired, it was his pleasure that the House should be adjourned until Monday, and then he would come and speak to them.

Sir Thomas Tomkins told the Speaker that the country for which he served had a fear of a standing army, and therefore in this behalf he moved that His Majesty might be humbly petitioned to dissolve those new raised forces. This motion was seconded by Mr. Garroway, but withal he thought it not convenient to move His Majesty to disband them before the peace should be concluded.

Sir William Coventry said the motion for disbanding the army was a good motion, if the peace were certainly concluded, but in regard that was not certainly known he moved that the vote might not pass, but be laid aside until the peace was certainly known.

Sir Thomas Littleton was against the deferring the vote, but that it might be then put to the question, whether the vote should pass for sending to the King for his gracious assent to

25, 30 July (*Letters*, pp. 55–6) and *Last Instructions* (*Poems and Satires*, p. 161) written between August and November 1667, and confirming Milward's account even in such things as the Commons' haste and lack of prayers on Monday (*ibid.* l. 858). The following lines are illustrative:

"up ambles *Country Justice* on his Pad,
And Vest bespeaks, to be more seemly clad.
Plain *gentlemen* are in Stage-Coach o'er thrown,
And *Deputy-Lieutenants* in their own.
The portly *Burgess*, through the weather hot,
Does for his Corporation sweat and trot.
And all with Sun and Choler come adust;
And threaten *Hyde* to raise a greater dust.
But, fresh as from the *Mint*, the Courtiers fine
Salute them, smiling at their vain designe.
And *Turner* gay up to his Pearch does march,
With Face new bleacht, smoother'd and stiff with starch.
Tell them he at *Whitehall* had took a turn,
And for three days, thence moves them to adjourne.
Not so, quoth *Tomkins*; and straight drew his tongue,
Trusty as Steel, that always ready hung;
And so proceeding in his motion warm,
Th' Army rais'd, he doth as soon disarm...."

the disbanding the new raised forces, for, said he, if we put it off until Monday, it may be it may please the King then to prorogue the House and then the vote will be lost.

Whereupon it was put to the [question whether the] vote for sending to the King should pass or not; it was carried in the affirmative, without any one voice in the negative, and it was ordered that the members that were Privy Councillors should carry the vote to the King, and so the House adjourned until Monday.

JULY 29TH. On Monday[1] the Speaker came not until almost an hour after the King was come to the House of Lords; we had not time to have prayers nor did I see the Chaplain. The Black Rod came and commanded our attendance, and after a very short speech the King prorogued the House until the 10th of October, which was not pleasing and satisfactory to all men.

This speech of the King's was not printed at this day, August 7th, and it is said it will not be printed. There are three copies of the speech and in several hands, of which three this is one here transcribed.

"My Lords and gentlemen.

"I summoned you by proclamation when we were in a great strait, but that being over, I cannot tell how to oblige you better than to send you home again at such a time as this. I wonder what any one thing I have done since I came into England should give you a jealousy that I intend to govern by a standing army. I am more an Englishman than so; and if others do but observe the law as well as I shall, there will be no need of any such thing. And for the forces lately raised, I did not give out any one commission until the enemy was landed, and I am sure the officers themselves desire to be disbanded. I raised some forces last year, but soon as the danger was over I disbanded them. There is now a peace concluded which will speedily be published, and which will give great satisfaction to all Christendom. I hope we shall meet the 10th of October next to restore our nation to its former splendour. I hope I shall do my part. And now, my Lord Chancellor, do your duty."

[1] *C.J.* VIII, 692. MS. omits date.

My Lord Chancellor:
"His Majesty hath commanded to prorogue this Parliament,
and it is prorogued till the tenth of October next."

OCTOBER 10TH, 1667. This day the Parliament met; the House
was reasonably full for the first day: it is supposed there were
between two and three hundred members.

The King came to the House of Lords and made a very short
but a most gracious and good speech indeed upon the matter,
wholly committing all business to the care of the Parliament.

At the return of the Speaker from the House of Lords the
heads of the King's and Lord Keeper's speeches were reported
to the House by the Speaker.

That forenoon's business afterwards was to appoint a committee[1] to draw up an address to give His Majesty the thanks of
the House for his gracious speech and good acts of grace done
by him since the last prorogation. Sir William Lowther was
Chairman of that committee, and so the House adjourned until
Monday next.

OCTOBER 14TH. This day the bill for preventing duels was
read and ordered to be read again upon Saturday.[2]

Then the House took up the debate of the address of thanks
to be presented to His Majesty.

Sir William Lowther, from the committee, made his report
and enumerated the several acts of grace for which we were to
present our humble thanks.

---

[1] *C.J.* IX, 1. The committee for the address is interesting. Clarendon
(*Cont.* p. 1238) says Tomkins made an insolent speech and Cobbett
(IV, 369) quotes from him. Marvell (*Letters*, p. 56) says: "There never
appeared a fairer season for men to obtain what their own hearts could
wish either as to redresse of any former grievances or the constituting
of good order and justice for the future." From this date cf. Appendix I
for some of Holland's speeches on Clarendon, and Appendix II for a
fragmentary diary of proceedings on Clarendon and on the miscarriages
of the war.

[2] Grey's *Debates* begin on 16 October, after a brief note on the
opening of the session, omit debates 14, 15, 17, 21, 22 October, briefly
note the meeting on the 23rd and 25th, omitting the 24th. Milward on
the whole reports more fully the happenings of this first year covered
by the *Debates*.

    1. First for disbanding so speedily the new raised forces.

    2. Secondly for putting all Popish recusants out of his guards and military employments.

    3. Thirdly for providing a remedy against the abuse of the act that did prohibit the importation of Irish cattle.

    4. Fourthly for calling in the Canary patent.

    5. Fifthly for taking away the seal and laying aside the Lord Chancellor.

This morning was wholly spent in speeches concerning the Lord Chancellor, whether the King's laying him aside should be joined to the other acts of grace for which we were to give him the thanks of the House; many excellent speeches were made against it by Sir Robert Atkins, Sir John Maynard, Mr. Marvell, Mr. Dowdswell and the two Goodricks and Colonel Birch, intimating that it was a precondemning him before any crime was laid to his charge.[1]

On the other hand many as good speeches were made for it by the Lord Vaughan with one eye, Sir Thomas Littleton, Mr. Trevor, Sir William Coventry, Mr. Waller, Mr. John Vaughan and others, that it was necessary and that the House was obliged to give the King their humble thanks for it, it being an act that besides the justice of it the King had done it to gratify the people and whole kingdom. Mr. Solicitor declared himself to be of the same judgment. In conclusion it was put to the question and it was carried in the affirmative without dividing the House.

Before this debate it was moved in the House to petition the King to put a stop to the transporting men and horses to serve the King of France, great complaints being made that great numbers both of men and horses that were already gone over to him and daily were still going away, especially of such men as were lately disbanded.

OCTOBER 15TH. This day a petition was brought into the House against the Quakers[2] who deny to pay their due tithes out of conscience, urging the unlawfulness of tithes, and this is to the prejudice of parsons and vicars under whose charge and cures they dwell.

---

[1] See Appendix II for some expansion of this.

[2] *C.J.* IX, 3. Quakers not mentioned.

This is so great an inconvenience that if it should be suffered and that a Quaker may be excused from paying due tithes, because his conscience tells him that tithes are unlawful, many men will pretend to be Quakers only to save their tithes.

The bill for prisoners lying in for debt was read this day, and it admitted a great debate; some were very much for it, as a very charitable act, others as much against it, and said it would prove very destructive to charity, in giving men just cause not to trust or lend, since every man whose large conscience will serve him to be unjust may pay his vast debts by taking his oath that he is not worth £5 above his wearing apparel, working tools and utensils.

Sir John Maynard said that there was great deceit in this word "utensils" and that it was a word of large extent, as thus: a professed gamester that hath an hundred pieces of money in his pocket will swear that he is not worth £5 besides his utensils and necessary working tools, for he accounts his hundred pieces the utensils and necessary tools of his gaming.

There were this day brought into the House many [*potestatem*] *dedimus* to be sent into the country to commissioners to tender the oaths of allegiance and supremacy to Popish recusants.

Sir George Downing brought a bill in to encourage the lending money into the Exchequer, and upon this ground or reason, because it was lawful for any man that shall lend any money to the King, and enter it into the Exchequer, to assign the same to any other in discharge of debt bargain or otherwise, and that assigned to any other, and so from man to man, with as much lawfulness and security as may be done in any bargain or sale of land.

It was voted to fall upon the accounts, and a committee was nominated and appointed to examine the former proceedings of those men that had inspected the accounts, and to bring in a new way or method which may be more effectual or expeditious.

It was moved to inspect the abuses in the rate of coals, corn and hay, and to moderate and regulate the prices of them.

This liberty and freedom of speech in the House was taken into debate to prevent that no man should be called in question after the end of the Parliament in any inferior court for words during the session, unless they extend to treason, it being the privilege of the members to speak their minds freely, to have access to the King freely and to enjoy their liberty freely.

A case was brought out of Judge Crooke's[1] reports to which his hand was subscribed, where Elliott and Valentine were convented at the King's Bench Bar for words spoken in Parliament, and that treasonable words are not privileged.

In the afternoon the Lords and Commons attended the King in the Banqueting House, where the Lord Keeper presented His Majesty the humble thanks of both Houses for his acts of grace done since the last prorogation, and particularly for laying aside the Lord Clarendon. The King was pleased to say, "I thank you for thanking me, and am glad I have done such acts as are acceptable to you, and for that particular that concerns the Lord Chancellor, I do assure you I will never trust nor make use of him in any public employment."

OCTOBER 16TH. This day a bill was read for the more strict observation of the Lord's day.[2]

A large bill and oath was brought in for the conviction of Popish recusants, indeed little inferior for its severity to the Spanish Inquisition, a very direct persecution. It was very much disliked and spoken against by many in the House, but ordered to be read again the second time on that day fortnight.

The Lord Chief Justice Keeling was complained of by some of the House for his severe and illegal fining and imprisoning juries, both the grand and petty juries, for their verdicts, and also for giving some worthy gentlemen that served uncivil and insolent language, as Sir Hugh Windham and others. A committee was nominated and appointed to enquire into the matter and complaint and to make a report thereof to the House, to the intent that a course may be taken that judges may not at their

[1] The reports of both Crook, judge and law reporter, and Coke or Cook were freely quoted at this time. I am not quite sure that Milward always distinguishes between them.

[2] Grey (p. 2) reports Denham's story of the Miller on 16 October, whereas Milward reports it on the 30th. The first reading of a bill to prevent the Growth of Popery took place on the former, the second on the latter date (C.J. IX, 4, 10). It seems more likely that the debate took place on the second reading.

own wills and pleasures impose fines and imprison or affront either grand juries or petty juries for giving and adhering to their verdicts.

OCTOBER 17TH. This day Sir John Holland presented to the House the petition of the Lord Horatio Townshend; it was read, he having taken in a park and had exchanged some lands for some church lands that lay conveniently and within the compass of the park, belonging to the Rector of Rainham,[1] in Norfolk, and having the consent of the bishop of that diocese and of the Rector also, prayed an act of Parliament to confirm the exchange, he having given other lands for it and to the full value, he prays to be secured by an act against all succeeding incumbents. The petition was read the first time.

A bill was brought in to take into consideration a way and means to preserve and increase the growth of wood and timber in this kingdom.

It was moved in the House that a committee should be appointed to examine the miscarriages of the late war; the committee was ordered to sit on Saturday next about it, and especially to enquire into the abuse of paying the seamen with tickets.

Also a committee was appointed to enquire after the sale of Dunkirk and of all such persons as had received money for promoting that sale.

The House adjourned until Saturday because Friday was St. Luke's Day.

OCTOBER 19TH. This day[2] the House took into consideration the best way and means how to prevent robbing by the highways. One way was proposed, the sending away all such as should be taken to the plantation, in regard that many do escape hanging which do so much encourage others, whereas if they were certainly to be sent away without any hope of escaping it would be of more force than the present law of hanging.

It was taken into consideration the trade with Scotland, to prevent the Scots from carrying their commodities to Holland or France.

[1] *C.J.* IX, 4. East Rainham. MS. gives Raman.
[2] Although Milward mentions the Friday holiday above, the MS. gives 18 October for the 19th.

This dividing the Fleet was taken into debate and the true cause of their dividing was endeavoured to be found out.[1] Sir William Coventry by his papers endeavoured to satisfy the House that the Fleet was not divided upon any intent but upon good advice and counsel.

Sir Edward Spragg questionable for it.

For the business at Chatham, it was affirmed that the Duke of Albemarle had sent to the King and did give him some assurance that he had done as much as was possible in so short a time to fortify the river by drawing a chain over it, and hoped it would be sufficient to keep off the enemies from doing us any great harm.

There was a great debate in the House of the cause that should obstruct the Duke of York's prosecuting his victory over the Dutch.

This fell foul upon Mr. Brouncker, for it was plainly proved that the Duke (after his extraordinary toil and service in the fight), going to take his rest, gave order that the ships should be in readiness to pursue the victory as soon as it was light, but when the morning light appeared, the whole Dutch fleet was gotten a league or more before our fleet: and as it was affirmed in the House of Commons that Captain Cock had order to lower or slacken the sails, which was contrary to the Duke's order, which was that he should lie as near the Dutch ships as possibly he could and his sails fully drawn up that so he might fall upon them as soon as it was light. Whereupon Mr. Brouncker, Captain Cock, Captain Penn and Sir Edward Spragg was commanded to attend the House on Monday next by nine of the clock in morning.

OCTOBER 21ST. This day the Lord Townshend's bill was read the second time.

A remedy was proposed for speedy recovering the tithes, viz: by a hearing and order of two justices of the peace but so as that the party complained of might appeal to the quarter sessions.

The bill against duels was read the second time but spoken against in regard of forfeiting estates and some other inconveniences.

[1] Cf. Appendix II and Rawl. A, 195, f. 6, etc., on Miscarriages.

Sir William Penn was examined about the miscarriage of the Fleet, when the Duke of York had given that great overthrow to the Dutch, but said not much to the purpose. Captain Cock affirmed that Mr. Brouncker came to him and persuaded him to lower the sails, which he excused, having received that night the Duke's orders to be in readiness to attack the Dutch in the morning; Mr. Brouncker went from him and returned with Sir John Harman, who was superior officer to Captain Cock, who gave him orders to lower his sails, which he obeying, gave the Dutch opportunity to escape.

Sir Allen Apsley affirmed the same.

Mr. Pearse, the Duke's surgeon, affirms that when Captain Cock refused to slacken his sails, that Harman and Brouncker said that if the Duke should miscarry the King would take it ill and require it of him.

Sir Robert Holmes blames Harman and Brouncker, and said that if it had not been for that advice of lowering the Duke might easily have got before them, and Prince Rupert being in the rear of them and in their pursuit in all probability they had destroyed the whole Dutch fleet.

Mr. Brouncker excuseth himself and saith that what he said to Cock was only his advice, and it was out of his special of the Duke's safety, but denyeth that he brought any orders from the Duke, nor from any man, but that it was merely his own innocent advice.

The sum of the whole matter is this: a most notorious fault was committed, let it fix where it will: for [the] Duke having sunk Opdam the Dutch admiral, and the whole Dutch fleet being in a fleeing posture, and the Duke being close upon them at night when he went to rest, and then gave his orders to Captain Cock to keep as near to them with his full sail as possibly he could that so they might fall upon them with the first morning light, but contrary to His Royal Highness's orders, the sails being lowered, and the Dutch had the opportunity to get so far away before us that our Fleet could not overtake them the next day; which as soon as it was light and the Duke perceived it, he was highly displeased, but this was the true cause that we lost the effect of the first victory: but where this fault will fix, whether upon Cock that did not obey the Duke's orders, or on Sir John Harman, who gave that order without the Duke's command, or on Mr. Brouncker, who gave the first advice, it is not yet determined, but rests upon farther enquiry, but [at] present it reflects most on Harman, who is now at sea, and so it will rest until his return.

OCTOBER 22ND. The first business of this day was concerning a survey of the levels that the value of them may be truly known and so the taxes may be equally stated and levied; and Colonel Sandys's wrongs and grievances there sustained may be redressed.

Then was Sir John Winter's petition in order to the enclosing and fencing in ten thousand acres of wood in the Forest of Dean for the increase of timber, and preserving the young wood from spoil, and that he may have to his own use eight thousand acres more of that forest.

The petition was well approved so far as it concerned the preservation of wood and increase of timber, but it is disliked as it concerns his own quantity of acres, for it is affirmed that the whole forest is but twenty-two thousand acres, and if the King have ten thousand and he eight thousand, and the commoners but four thousand, the commoners are not satisfied, supposing that their proportion is too little and Sir John Winter's too much a great deal.

Also it was proposed to make the river navigable between Teme and Avon in the West Country.[1]

Then the House took up the business of the day into debate, which was to enquire into the dividing of the Fleet. Sir Edward Spragg was sent for and examined concerning it and what he could say in that business. He did not say anything very material; he only said that he complained to Sir William Coventry that there wanted seamen, who made him this answer, that there were coming a great fleet of colliers' ships and then they should have seamen enow, but in the meantime he said he was not supplied with men, which was a great disadvantage to their present business.

[1] *C.J.* IX, 6. "A river navigable from River Severn to London."

It is believed that the officers of the ordnance did not perform their offices and trust in the fortifications at Sheerness.

Prince Rupert found great fault with the neglect when he came to Sheerness, but afterwards he made excellent works there.

Sir John Duncombe pretends to excuse and clear himself and the rest of the officers of the ordnance from any neglect of their duty. The workmen employed for making of boats neglected their work, and being reproved for it by Sir Edward Spragg they fell into a mutiny for want of pay.

Sir Edward Spragg said there were three of the King's ships burnt at Chatham, and the *Royal Charles* taken away by a sorry boat and six men.

He also said that certain fire-ships were ordered to be sunk to stop the channel, and he being commanded to sound the channel, he found that there was two channels by which the Dutch ships might come in, and thereupon gave the Duke of Albemarle this account, that those fire-ships might be a terror to the Dutch and of good advantage to ourselves in service, but of no advantage at all if they should be sunk as they were appointed to be; but he advised to sink all the great ships in another place; which advice if it had been followed had prevented all the harm and loss that we afterwards sustained. But instead of sinking those great ships they sunk a few small vessels, between which the Dutch came in and burned up our great ships and did us all that great harm we sustained.

Sir Edward Spragg refers the farther discovery of this business to Commissioner Pett, who was chiefly entrusted with the ships at Chatham; Pett is to be examined this day at a committee or to-morrow at the Bar.

In all this discourse of Sir Edward Spragg concerning the dividing of the Fleet he doth not give any hint as though there were any ill design in it, but that all the ill proceeded from a false intelligence; for they had intelligence that the Dutch fleet would not be out six weeks, whereupon the Prince with his squadron went out in hopes to fall upon some of the French ships, which they said lay open to his ships, but the Dutch came out within a day or two, and finding our Navy divided fell upon the Duke in the Prince's absence and so did endanger the whole Fleet:

it is [said] the Duke might have avoided that fight, but he seeing the Dutch could not forbear, but presently sailed up to them and willingly engaged, which was not discreetly done.

OCTOBER 23RD. The first thing moved this day was Sir John Prettyman's petition, who being a member of the House, but now a prisoner in the Fleet for debt, desired his liberty to attend the House and to serve for the place for which he was elected. His petition was referred to the committee of privileges to enquire whether he was a prisoner upon an execution, and if he was so, then to consider whether he was taken upon that execution in the time of privilege of Parliament or in the vacancy; if it was in the time of privilege then that he should be set at liberty to attend the House and his service as a member, but if he was taken in the vacancy then he ought not to have his liberty.

It was also moved that the condition of our English prisoners in Zeeland should be taken into consideration, for we having set at liberty (according to the article) all the Dutch prisoners that were not commanders without ransom, the Zeelanders delayed ours and stand upon their ransom most unjustly. To this Sir William Doyley informed the House that he and some others appointed by His Majesty had lately and within a day or two had conference with the Dutch Ambassador, and that it was agreed by them that our prisoners should be immediately set at liberty.

A bill was brought in about the repair of highways, and against the supernumerary teams of horses, according to the article, and that the fines imposed and levied upon those that had more horses in their carriages than was allowed should go to the poor.

A bill was brought in for selling and that there might be no failing in the payment of excise, nor abuse in them that gather it, it was moved that all vessels should be marked, and that the sellers should sell a wine quart of the strongest ale for two pence and the smallest for a penny.

Mr. Hilton's gift for charitable uses was read; some said all parties concerned in that gift were agreed; others said they were not all agreed, and therefore it was referred to a committee.

This day the Lord Buckhurst, Lord Ancram, Mr. Waller, Colonel Kirby, Mr. Trevor and Sir Robert Brooke, who was Chairman of the committee for enquiring into the miscarriages of the late war, were sent to Prince Rupert and the General to give them the thanks of the House for their eminent service in the late war, and humbly to desire them to inform the House as far as they shall think fit of the whole business of Sheerness and Chatham, and especially of the dividing the Fleet in '66 and of the whole business of the Dutch war.

The bill for payment of tithes was read the second time and much spoken against by some, and as much defended by others, but it was laid aside upon the account that it was interlined, which it was affirmed ought not to be suffered, but that a new bill fair written should be brought in. The bill did intend the more speedy recovery and paying of tithes, and with the least charge.

Sir Thomas Littleton moved that the House would appoint a day for the bringing in an accusation and charge against the Earl of Clarendon; this motion was not well taken by some, and many speeches were given both for it and against it, and at last it was laid aside with this resolution, that it was more agreeable to the honour and rules of the House to bring in an accusation and impeachment against any man, and at a convenient time, than for the House to appoint a set day beforehand, because to appoint a set day was to invite all men to bring in a charge against any person when at present there appeared no just cause to accuse him.

They that spoke for the Earl, as Mr. Henry Coventry, Secretary Morice and many others, moved in his behalf that since he was cast off and laid aside by his master and was so low and on the ground that he seemed buried in the law that they should not further prosecute him nor trample on him.

It is believed that an impeachment will be drawn up against him.

OCTOBER 24TH. This day[1] it was moved that His Majesty should be petitioned to put a stop to all of horse and men that

---

[1] *C.J.* IX, 7. MS. omits the date here.

are going to serve the King of France; many they say are in a body, and some of them are of those that were disbanded out of my Lord Frechville's troop.

Mr. Prynne made a report from the woodmongers that the Clerk of the Company refused (upon order of the committee) to show his book of accounts. Whereupon it was ordered to send for the Clerk and Master of the Company by the Serjeant, to attend the committee with that book on Friday next.

It was ordered that the Lord Mayor for London and the Bailiffs for Westminster and Southwark[1] should search all the woodyards, and where they find the billets and faggots under the size and measure according to the statute to seize and distribute them to the poor.

It was also moved to set a rate upon the price of coals, but that was suspended in regard that coals were scarce, and if the price now should be lessened it might hinder the bringing in of them, and so obstruct a supply and hopes of greater plenty, which would be the only way to bring down the price of coals.

It is said that the full provision of coals for the supply of London for one whole year is usually three hundred thousand chauldrons, and that there hath been brought in as yet in order to that supply but 100,000 chauldrons.

Sir John Holland's report of Lord Townshend's bill from the committee with its amendment, which was agreed to by the House.

Colonel Sandys's bill was read, for restoring him to his lands in the levels, and was agreed to and committed, though spoken against by the Lord George and Mr. Pepys.

The members that the House sent to Prince Rupert and the General brought this report to the House from them, that they gave the House thanks for their thankful acknowledgement of their service, and that they would peruse their papers and prepare a narrative in writing of the whole business, and when they had it in readiness they would send for the members again and present it to the House by them, and will readily give the House any further satisfaction in what they shall be able.[2]

---

[1] *C.J.* IX, 7. Southwark, not Surrey as in the MS.
[2] Cf. Add. MSS. 36916, f. 4. Starkey reports on this report.

Secretary Morice was desired to give the House an account of His Majesty's pleasure concerning their humble address, that he would give leave to the Secretary to declare to the House what he can say as to the dividing the Fleet in '66. The Secretary told the House that His Majesty is pleased to give him leave to give the House an account to the House [sic] as to matter of fact, but not to publish and reveal the secrets of Council.

The Secretary thereupon gave this account to the House, that he had employed an agent into Holland to give him notice in what readiness the Dutch fleet was. His agent writ to him that the fleet would be in readiness to come forth within a week or thereabouts, and accordingly it did so, but as to the dividing of our fleet, and the cross intelligence of the Holland fleet not to come out in six weeks, he could not give any full satisfaction.

Therefore the House ordered that the Secretary should give an account to the House of the dates of his letters in reference to the orders given for the dividing the Fleet, and the time when those orders were given, and whether the Fleet was divided before or after those orders were given them.

It was moved that if the Secretary's letters did not contain some secrets of the Council that the letters themselves should be produced; but the motion was not approved, because it might be to the prejudice of the Dutch agent, by discovering him.

OCTOBER 25TH. This day Mr. Vaughan brought in a bill of the discharge of Sheriffs Sir Robert Viner and Sir Joseph Sheldon and the keepers of the prisons that were burnt in the last dreadful fire, and the other sheriffs to whom they did pass over their prisoners; and to free them from actions and suits for escape of prisoners and removing others, which is an escape in law, and that it shall be lawful for any persons to renew their executions for the seizing and imprisoning again any that shall pretend to this escape. This bill was read and ordered to be read the second time.

The petition of prisoners that lay in for debt and are not worth five pounds was read but much spoken against.

There was a debate in the House of a way to prevent the extraordinary robbing upon the high-way; it was moved that the King should be humbly desired to give the Lord General orders to consider of some speedy course to be taken for redressing this grievance: in the meantime that an act is preparing for it.

Mr. Taylor's petition was read against Lord Mordaunt with the particulars of his charge; there are some new ones added to the former. One was that he caused a man to be beaten and knocked down, and when he was on the ground he caused some of the soldiers standing by to piss on him, which was done; the man died within a year after, and told it upon his death that those blows were the cause of it.

The woodmongers [petitioned] that the order for seizing wood that was under measure might be respited until they were heard to speak for themselves; it is hoped that their patent will be called in.

Lord Arlington is to be sent to by Colonel Kirby to bring in his letters of intelligence as Secretary Morice had been ordered the day before.

Sir William Coventry acquainted the House that the King had given order to the General to send to all the posts to stop all men and horses that were going to the King of France, and it is said that the General had done it accordingly.

The petition and bill for enclosing 40 acres of common about the pest-house at Cambridge was brought in and read. The bill sets out the want of room to place the infected and to remove them that recover into fresh lodgings; they desire that 40 acres may be taken out of the common, and that a wall may be drawn about it, to keep out any from coming in to the infected and to keep in the infected from breaking out to those that are sound; and in time of no infection the profit of the enclosure and rent of the house shall go to the poor and be as a stock to set them on work.

OCTOBER 26TH. A bill was brought in for the preventing the exacting of fees in all courts and offices, and that a table of fees may be made and hung up, that every man may see and know what fees are due to be paid.

The bill of certioraries being engrossed was brought in and read, and amended in some particulars was sent up to the Lords.

The bill of accounts was reported from the committee by Sir Charles Harbord; it is a pretty severe bill and was allowed.

This day[1] Mr. Seymour first opened the accusation of the Earl of Clarendon: the accusation consisted of many foul crimes, of bribery and taking great sums of money, abusing the Great Seal at pleasure and commanding the treasure at his own will for building his house. Of the Canary Company he is accused to receive four thousand pounds, for which he undertook to support and justify it so long as he stood. That he passed the Seal illegally in Lord Mordaunt's and Lord Sandwich their cases; that he had a third part of three hundred and sixty thousand pounds that was brought into the treasury.

For passing patents in Ireland he had fifty thousand pounds.

When the kingdom was in the greatest danger, even at the time when the Dutch fell into Chatham and burned our ships, the King then resolving to call the Parliament, as the best counsel and means to consult with at that time and in that extremity, and accordingly sent out his proclamation to summon it, and accordingly when it met, he was the only cause why the King suddenly prorogued it; and to move His Majesty to it he used these words, that the four hundred men, meaning the Parliament, were only of use to raise him money, but were not fit to meddle with state affairs.

The King thereupon asked him what he must do, and what course he was best to take in this extremity; he answered, dissolve this Parliament and set up a standing army. The King asked him, "How shall I then have another Parliament, and how shall that standing army be paid?" He answered that another Parliament was not necessary, but that he should govern in an arbitrary way by that army. The King asked him how shall he pay that army; he answered with free quarter and contribution.

Sir Thomas Littleton said that these miscarriages being charged upon the Chancellor, and he being chief Minister of State and taking upon him the sole management of the government, must either be guilty or be able to clear himself by laying it justly upon others that are guilty.

---

[1] The *Proceedings* commence with this date—26 October. Notice too Cobbett, IV, 370 f. *State Trials*, Grey, etc.

It was farther charged upon him that he had abused the King in all his treaties, especially in those of France, making the King believe that he was certain of a peace with the French King, which was the cause that the preparations for our war and defence were neglected until the King of France came out and joined with the Dutch.

The like he did this year with the Dutch, until they came out with their fleet and we had not one ship in readiness to meet them.

That he set on foot a plot at a committee of Lords and Commons merely on purpose to move the King to set up a standing army.

It was moved in the House to draw up an impeachment of treason against him and to send it up to the Lords and to move for his commitment.

Sir William Lewis moved that the House would proceed legally in the execution of this business against him: and in order thereto to send the Serjeant into the Hall with the Mace to call up all the members of the Long Robe from all the Bars and Courts then sitting, to be instructed by them and to give precedents how they ought to proceed.

Sir Charles Wheeler said that the Lord Clarendon[1] had been the only obstructor of the settlement of the government both in Church and State; and that he had supported the nonconformists and countenanced them in their stubbornness; that he had hindered the poor Cavaliers from preferment and had diverted the King from his gracious looking upon those that had served and suffered for him and his father.

And that when he was beyond seas with the King, and was returned from Spain, whither the King had sent him to negociate his affairs, he bore the King in hand that he had done all his business effectually with the King and had brought with him ten thousand pounds, by which he secured himself into the King's favour more closely, and by that means had the management of the purse, and others were displaced, when indeed he

---

[1] Cf. Clarendon (*Cont.* p. 1035) and K. Feiling (*English Historical Review*, XLIV, 289 ff.). See Grey (p. 22) for a similar debate on 6 November.

had got no such sum nor any considerable part of ten thousand pounds.

That he held correspondence with Cromwell and received several sums from him, and that Cromwell had one of the King's seals from him to make use of when he had occasion or opportunity.

That he did ill offices between the King and Duke of York, incensing the King against his brother by his insinuations that the people's affections were more to the Duke than to His Majesty, which caused the Duke to be sent away from the King, and so continued under the malice of Lord Clarendon until in the end he married his daughter.

Sir Edward Walpole advised to deliberate in the prosecution of Lord Clarendon, and to proceed in a just cause justly.

Sir Thomas Osbourne[1] charged the Earl that he had fraudalised the King as not to be a true Protestant but a Papist in heart, and that the Earl did endeavour to subvert the laws both of Church and State.

It was also charged against him that he swayed and ruled all at the Council board, and if any Lord opposed him in any of his counsels he did carry himself imperiously both in his words, looks and gestures.

The Lord Treasurer complained that he was Treasurer in name but the Chancellor disposed of the treasure at his pleasure.

This charge Sir Allen Broderick excused, as also receiving money on the Irish account, as was said before.

Sir Philip Warwick that he had never heard the Lord Treasurer say anything against him for commanding the Treasury.

Mr. Harry Coventry spake against him his commitment and all undue proceedings against him.

It was moved in the House that before any impeachment be sent up against him, that witnesses should be examined, and that the House might be satisfied of the proofs of those things that were laid to his charge.

---

[1] Add. MSS. 28045, ff. 1–18, includes some notes by Sir Thomas Osbourne, some correspondence with possible witnesses against Clarendon, votes of the House, etc.; on f. 11 v. is a note pointing out that 11 November is the anniversary of the impeachment of Strafford.

Sir Robert Howard was against the examining of witnesses before he was brought to the trial, and said that if witnesses should be examined before a committee, as Mr. Prynne and others moved, they being known may be practised upon, and either by bribes or threats be taken off, and be exposed to the revenge and malice of some greater ones, or to the fury of some desperate persons.

Also he said it was against the rules of proceedings against criminals to produce witnesses before they be brought to trial.

Mr. Vaughan also spoke to the same purpose that witnesses should not be produced before the impeachment was brought up.

All that was hitherto done amounted to no more but a bare accusation.

OCTOBER 29TH. This day Sir Robert Atkins carried up the engrossed bill concerning the restraint of certioraries, on whom I attended.

Mr. Vaughan made his report from the committee which was appointed to search the Journals for precedents of impeachments:[1] he said that he could find no precedent for any crime that was capital until that of my Lord Strafford, Archbishop Laud and Mr. Chief Justice Finch. Lord Strafford was impeached by the Commons, and upon his impeachment at the desire of the Commons he was removed from the Parliament and committed to the Tower. And after his commitment the Commons brought a charge against him, which was proved by Sir Henry Vane. A committee was appointed to draw up a charge against the Earl of Strafford and voted Mr. Prynne to carry up the charge against him unto the House of Lords.

In like manner they proceeded against Archbishop Laud and Mr. Chief Justice Finch by Mr. Prynne.

It was [said] that there were three manners of impeachments.

First by the King, as in case of Earl Godwin, Archbishop Anselm and the Earl of March.

[1] Miss M. V. Clarke gives the best account of impeachment in a paper included in *Oxford Essays in Medieval History* (1934), pp. 164 ff. No exact precedent could be found for Clarendon's impeachment, and protests like Holland's speech given in Appendix I were not wanting.

Secondly by the Lords, and thus they have impeached one another.

Thirdly of the Commons, in the 50th of Edward the third against Lyon. And also against Neville, and William and Michael de la Pole.

Also the Commons have impeached divers for basely and cowardly delivering up places of strength to the enemy. And others also for selling the King's forces.

Michael de la Pole was impeached by the Commons in Richard II's times and was committed upon it and afterwards brought to his trial, but his offence did not prove capital.

Thomas Arundel, Archbishop of Canterbury, was impeached by the Commons and his goods forfeited and himself banished without naming the persons that accused him.

The Lord St. Albans, Lord Keeper Bacon, was accused of bribery of the Commons without any charge drawn up in writing, and was ordered to answer to the charge.

Criminal offenders may be charged by word of mouth and may be ordered to answer to the charge.

But capital offenders are to be proceeded against by impeachment and witnesses.

To bring in a charge upon public fame is Parliamentary.

The rest of this day until after four of the clock was spent in debate of the manner how to proceed against the Earl of Clarendon; some moved to have his accusation committed (and a committee to be nominated) or to the committee of grievances and witnesses to be examined to prove the several things in the charge, but this was not liked.

Others moved that his accusation should be referred to a particular committee to draw up the heads of the charge into form and report them to the House and there to debate of the nature of the crimes and to resolve whether they were treasonable and capital, or whether they be only criminal: this was put to the question, which was carried in the affirmative, and the committee ordered to sit to-morrow in the afternoon.[1]

OCTOBER 30TH. This day the bill was read for high-ways the second time, only it was moved that the clause in the former

[1] Cf. Grey, who however omits the 30th, 31st; and Appendix II.

act (which did empower justices and officers to lay a charge of sixpence an acre for their repair) may be left out, and because that market towns have few or no draught to send to the highways that there may be a charge of money imposed.

The bill for lending money upon the twelve hundred and fifty thousand pounds and for the advancing the credit of Exchequer was read; and for confirmation of assignments, and that it may extend to executors and assignees *toties quoties* from assigns to assigns without limitation; and so making the Exchequer the best security imaginable.

This was well approved, but not that it should be established by an act to perpetuity.

Lord Townshend's [bill] was brought in engrossed, and read and passed and sent up to the Lords by Sir John Holland.

The bill against exacting of fees was read, by which the Lord Keeper, Chief Baron, Chancellor of the Duchy and others of the chief judges were desired to cause this to be enquired into by attorneys and others in their several courts and make search into the fees allowed in the 30th of Queen Elizabeth, and that a table of fees shall be established and hung up in every court, but yet notwithstanding there should be regard had both to the former times and the fees then allowed, and these present times, which are of double expense, which cannot possibly be maintained by the fees in Queen Elizabeth's time.

The bill against recusants was read the second time and generally spoken against, and particularly by Lord Ancram, Colonel Sandys and Sir John Denham.[1] Indeed it was so clogged with unreasonable penalties and severities that it was no other but a persecution and not a good law to reform them. Sir John Denham, speaking against the severities of it and that it was not safe to exasperate thereby the Papists, told a merry story of a miller whose mill was on fire. His wife bade him to call to God to send water to quench the fire, and withal advised

---

[1] Cf. p. 88, n. 2 above. Should Grey's *Debates* ever find a new editor, their dating, in this first volume at any rate, will require very precise verification. It is my distinct impression that the notes for the early period covered by his reports must have been rather confused and not always clearly dated in the original unless indeed the eighteenth-century editors badly mistreated them.

him to renounce the devil and all his works; the miller told [her] that he liked her counsel well and would follow it as to the first part of it, but he did not like the latter part of it, nor would he at that time create more enemies.

Sir Solomon Swale and Mr. Waller spoke excellently against the unreasonableness and severity of the bill.

Secretary Morice seemed to countenance the bill, but yet spoke against the new oath in it.

Some spoke for the casting out of the bill, but at last it was voted to be committed, but to leave out the oath, and to endeavour to prevent the growth of Popery, but not to destroy all Papists, and to moderate the severity of the bill.

OCTOBER 31ST. This day a bill was read for denization of four persons born out of the King's dominions.

The petition of Bulckeley [and] Barker[1] was brought in and read concerning the purchasers of the Irish rebels' lands; they were called in and owned the petition.

The bill to enable the Bishop of Durham and his successors to make a lease of the barmaster's office to Mr. Wharton for three lives, and of the mines within the bishopric, he undertaking to drain the mines, which he saith will cost him ten thousand pounds, was brought in, engrossed and passed, and sent up to the Lords by Sir Gilbert Gerrard.

Lord Arlington's letters and papers relating to the dividing the Fleet and other miscarriages in the late war were brought in by Mr. Williamson, who was desired to attend the committee with them.

Mr. Seymour's affront by Mr. Coventry was referred to a committee, but nothing came of it, for it proved to be an old quarrel at sea and no affront in anything done or spoken in the House against the Chancellor by Mr. Seymour, though Mr. Coventry drew upon him in the palace yard as soon as he was gone out of the House.

---

[1] *C.J.* IX, 10. The petition of William Bulckeley and William Barker on the subject of lands in Ireland was to recur throughout this winter and Milward reports debates in the House upon their business, 19 February, 20, 23 April, etc.

Lord Ancram brought in Prince Rupert's narrative, and Sir Robert Brooke the General's narrative of the miscarriages of the war.[1]

Prince Rupert saith that if the Duke of York's orders had been obeyed when he had beaten the Dutch, the victory had been completed with the utter destruction of the Dutch fleet.

And as to the division of the Fleet in '66 it was chiefly caused by the intelligence that they had from France, viz: that the squadron of the Fleet commanded by the Prince might do very good service upon the French ships that lay in such an harbour, and also might probably fall upon Banckert before he should join with the Dutch. It was also assured that the Dutch fleet would not be out until some long time after and that the same wind that must bring the Dutch fleet out to sea would bring the Prince to the General and Fleet again.

The Prince complained of great want of all manner of provision for the Fleet and necessary supplies, though they timely went to Sir William Coventry and Sir George Carteret, who were Treasurers of the Navy. And when after a long time they did send provision, and after long delay, they being in want of it, the provision was both short and wanting and unwholesome and naught. In the second fight that summer he saith their supplies were greatly defective, and the blue squadron fought not at all, but behaved themselves basely.

The supply of fire-ships at the second fight and some other great ships, as the *Royal London* and others that were ordered to be sent, were not sent in upon the first orders, but the Prince and Duke was forced to send for them by a second order when they were ready to fight.

Orders were likewise given to make some defences at Sheerness and Harwich, but there was nothing done, which gave the Dutch opportunity and advantage to do us all that harm at Chatham.

But the greatest cause of our loss both of reputation, the firing of our ships and all other damage this summer, was our not setting forth our Royal Navy, for although we had certain intelligence that the Dutch would be out with their fleet yet

---

[1] *C.J.* IX, 11 ff., for Prince Rupert's and Monk's narratives. Many manuscript copies of these narratives were circulated. See Bibliography.

we made no preparation to meet them, nor had we any one ship manned and in readiness.

The Duke of Albemarle in his narrative tells us that Sir George Carteret and Sir William Coventry came to him and moved it to him to spare a squadron out of his fleet to fall upon the French, for they had certain intelligence that the Dutch would not come out with their fleet as yet.

"This motion," said the Duke, "did amaze me, being it tended to the dividing the Fleet, since on counsel it was resolved to the contrary."

The Duke also saith that when the Dutch and he engaged his was but fifty-four sail, and the Dutch fourscore sail, and yet he lost but ten of his ships and they lost twenty of theirs.

"We finding our disadvantage endeavoured to get into the river until the Prince came in with his squadron.

"The commissioners of the Navy were sent to, when we lay at the buoy in the Nore, to recruit us (our ships being very sore shattered), but no supply came from them." He farther saith that the 10th of June he went to Chatham, where he found very few guns mounted, and scarce twelve men to be found there, although the commissioners of the ordnance were strictly charged to send down guns for that service and supply.

And whereas there was 800 men in pay for the King's service at Chatham, scarce twelve men were to be found there; all the rest were run away or at least absent when they should have been put upon duty.

Of thirty boats that should be ready for the service of the ships there was not to be found there above six in readiness; all the rest were carried away by Commissioner Pett and other men and he gone away with his own goods in some of those boats.

And that there was no defence made for securing the chain.

Pett was sent to for boards, and there being store of thick oak planks he sent none but thin deal boards that were of no use.

"Nor did he furnish us with any tools, spades and picks until we were forced to break open the storehouse and to furnish our own selves."

No guns as yet sent down, although he gave order to have some speedily sent down.

Pett was commanded to draw up the *Royal Charles* further into the river at the next tide, to secure it, which after ten weeks' command he neglected to do.

The Duke also saith that after that he came to Chatham he commanded Pett to secure the *Royal Charles* by hauling it up the river the next tide, which he refused to do. Also he gave him express orders to sink the *Sancta Maria* in the passage between our ships, which if he had done the Dutch ships could not have come up the river to ours; but instead of sinking her he ran her aground, and so the Dutch ships came in at that very place where he had order to sink her, and so did us all the mischief.

If we had had those boats that Pett took away with him and had suffered to be taken away they had preserved the three great ships from being burnt.

Pett was brought into the House of Commons and his charge laid open before him: he said it was new matter to him, and therefore desired to have time to make his answer for it; which was granted, and so he was committed to the Serjeant in order to his imprisonment in the Tower, and Sir John Robinson ordered to take care of him that he did not make his escape, but that he might be brought to the committee as occasion required.

Sir John Robinson had formerly taken bail of £5,000, he being committed by the Privy Council, which bail was now delivered up, being committed by order of the House. Swinsen, Boscawen and Marvell spoke for him and against sending him to the Tower.[1]

We adjourned until Monday because of All Saints' and All Souls' Days.

NOVEMBER 4TH. This day the bill was read the second time for reliefs of the sheriffs for the escapes of prisoners out of Ludgate, Newgate, the Fleet and other prisons by reason of the dreadful fire, both as to their escapes by running away, as also by their removal from one prison to another and from one sheriff to another, all which amounts to an escape in law: for it was

---

[1] Cf. Grey (p. 14), who mentions a speech of Marvell's on Clarendon on 29 October, but has nothing about the defence of Pett by Marvell and Boscawen, or indeed about the matter of miscarriages. MS. puts Suniton for Swinsen here.

affirmed that there were already suits commenced of this nature, and therefore this act was desired and that it might be passed in as convenient time as may be for their relief. The Warden of the Fleet was to be included among the sheriffs in this act, to which a proviso is to be added, that none shall be relieved by this act for an escape but only such as were removed by reason of the fire.

It was moved that the custom and money raised or levied upon the pretence of the lighthouse at Milford Haven should be looked into as a grievance, and the bill that was formerly brought in to empower the collecting of that money for that lighthouse was rejected and cast out. Also it was informed by Sir John Knight, and others confirmed it, that Mr. Brouncker and certain other officers had a patent, by which they have received and raised many sums of money, and say that they have a patent from the King for it.

Colonel Sandys's bill for Bedford levels was read and ordered to be engrossed.

The bill for weights and measures was read again, but was not fully agreed to.

Secretary Morice brought in his letters of intelligence out of Holland, and he affirms that orders upon them went from him to the Fleet.

But the orders that were sent, the Duke of York sent them by Sir William Coventry.

It was moved to look over the book of rates and to make a new one, and to lay a greater custom and imposition of wine and linen and other French commodities, because the King of France hath so much raised the English commodities, which is indeed in a manner to prohibit them, that so they may have coin and ready money and none of our manufactures for theirs, which in the end will carry all our coin out of the kingdom; and at present they have good part already, for notwithstanding that the King of France hath ordered to melt our coin and to put his stamp upon it, yet there is ten pieces of gold of our coin, yea, of our newest coin, seen and current there, for one piece with us.

We adjourned until Wednesday because of the Gunpowder Plot the 5th of November.

NOVEMBER 6TH. A complaint (by way of petition)[1] from the blacksmiths of Cirencester against the farmers of hearth money was brought in this day for exacting money for the smithy hearths; whereupon it was ordered that the act be consulted, whether smiths' forges be excepted or not; by this means the abuses of the farmers (and their officers), which are great, will be questioned and enquired into.

The complaint against woodmongers and their abuses in the price and measures of coals was debated, their patent voted illegal and a grievance to the people, and therefore to be called in.

They by their charter are not to sell coals, and those that are allowed to sell by that charter are to sell by sacks sealed at Guildhall, and yet contrary to that charter they sell by sacks sealed at Woodmongers' Hall, 3 inches shorter and 3 inches narrower than the other sacks sealed at Guildhall.

Also they are complained of for imposing fines and illegally imprisoning car-men at their pleasure, that they have exacted £5 of a car-man, whereas there was due but 15s., and in another case 18s. for 8s. This charge of the car-men against the woodmongers was proved and made good at the committee.

The Lord Mayor was spoken against in the House for not executing the Parliament's order for setting a price upon coals, to which he gave these reasons, as was affirmed in his behalf:

First because he was prevented by the violent plague following.

Secondly because it was a means to make coals scarce, and then of necessity coals must be dearer, whereas if the coals take a good price here there will be the greater plenty brought in, which in the end will make them cheap.

Thirdly because it was not practicable to set a price upon coals.

A woodmonger was complained of that sold half a chauldron of coals by his own sealed bag, which in measuring proved to want four bushels of the Guildhall bag, for which the party cheated sued and cast him, and the woodmonger was fined £40; this was affirmed by Sir Charles Harbord.

[1] This complaint started a new discussion of hearth money, which was unpopular throughout the period. An earlier attempt to remedy grievances aroused by it was reported during the debates on supply in 1666, when its abolition was proposed.

The engrossing coals by the woodmongers voted illegal and a grievance.

There was this day brought in divers heads of a way to prevent robbing by the high-way.

This day[1] Sir Thomas Littleton brought in the head of the accusation against the Earl of Clarendon which was read in the House. Many hours were spent about the order of proceeding upon them, whether an impeachment should be drawn up against him upon this first reading of the heads of his accusation, or whether they should be committed to a private committee, or to a committee of the whole House, that so they might be proved by witnesses to give satisfaction to all men. Some spoke against examining witnesses beforehand, say[ing] that it was not meet that the defendant should be acquainted beforehand that he came to his trial with those that should witness against him. And besides that it is not safe for witnesses to be made public beforehand, because when their persons are known, they may be in danger to be took off by bribery or by violence offered or threatened to their persons, for it is said that some have been already threatened and terrified that have appeared in his prosecution. Also by admitting witnesses to be examined by a committee the House deprived themselves of one of [the] greatest privileges they had, which was to draw up an impeachment upon the testimonies of their own Houses.

Others said that it was against the justice of the House to draw up an impeachment without examination of witnesses.

Sir Thomas Littleton made his report from the committee that five papers of heads of the charge against the Earl of Clarendon were brought to the committee, which he had drawn up into

[1] Cf. Grey (pp. 27 ff.) for another confusion of dates. Cobbett, IV, 377 f., reports the XVII charges on 6 November. Many versions of these charges exist in manuscript, but the variations are on the whole unimportant. Some are noted below, p. 112, n. 2. Speeches like that by Holland in Appendix I, and those reported in Appendix II, show how the rather unusual procedure adopted was decided upon. Members standing in their places to vouch for the charges preferred, represented a compromise between the arbitrary plans of the committee, and the feeling of more moderate men in the House that impeachment without something more than a mere accusation could not be justified either to the Lords or the country.

one paper, which was read in the House and contained all the articles of his accusation.

The articles seemed to be of so high a nature that none can be greater but the assaulting the King's person.

Sir Thomas Littleton made a distinction of crimes: first crimes that proceed from without doors and are criminal only, and these ought to be proved by witnesses at the committee, and crimes that are capital and within doors by members of either House, and that the House hath power to proceed against him by way of impeachment without examining witnesses before the impeachment.

This accusation and charge is in some part of it to be made good and proved by some of the peers and members of the Privy Council whom the House of Commons have no power to summon before them, neither have they power to examine witnesses upon oath.

After all this long debate it was put to the question whether the heads of the charge should be referred to a committee; the House was divided upon it; the ayes that went out were 128, the noes that stayed in were 194, of which I was one.[1]

Then it was put to the vote whether we should proceed presently upon to debate of the heads of the charge and take them in order severally or to adjourn the debate until to-morrow.

It was voted and carried to begin presently.[2]

[1] *C.J.* IX, 15, 128–194, Birch and Clarges, Seymour and Osbourne.

[2] The *Proceedings* gives the debates on the Charges on the 6th, and has no entry for the 7th. Cf. also Appendix II, and Grey for 6, 7, 9 and 11 November. There is again a confusion about an incident—one in which Marvell was concerned—reported on the 7th in Milward, 6th in the *Proceedings*, and 11th in Grey.

C.J. IX, 17, breaks the debate on the charges at article 5, continuing with article 6, as in Milward, on the 7th. Milward's numbering of the Charges does not agree with the final list of them as printed in the *Journals*, etc., as of course he was taking them down as read and debated. Some like article 7 were included in another (6) in the final version.

About articles 1 and 2 accounts do not seem to differ.

Article 3, proved by Seymour in the *Proceedings* (p. 21), by Seymour and Osbourne in Appendix II and Add. MSS. 38175, f. 63. In Osbourne's notes in Add. MSS. 28045, f. 9, there is a letter from Mr Read of the Canary Company in Mark Lane, endorsed with a note

1. The first article was read, viz: that the Earl of Clarendon did counsel the King to dissolve this Parliament and to raise a standing army, to pay them with free quarter and contribution

by Seymour to Osbourne, and in Mr Read's letter, charges similar to those in article 3 are preferred against Mr Solicitor, Mr Attorney, Lord Ashley as well as Clarendon.

Article 7 here includes 6 in *C.J.* IX, 16. Milward's numbers used hereafter.

Article 8 proved by Carr in the *Proceedings* (6), Add. MSS. 38175 (7), Appendix II (7).

Article 9. Add. MSS. 38175 adds Vaughan and Seymour to the name of Littleton as provers.

Article 10. Proved by Wheeler in Add. MSS. 38175, by Littleton and Osbourne in the *Proceedings*.

Article 11. Proved by Wheeler in the *Proceedings*, by Osbourne in Add. MSS. 38175.

Article 12, about correspondence with Cromwell, not listed in Add. MSS. 38175, proved by Wheeler in Appendix II as here. *Proceedings* (p. 23) gives speeches by Swinsen, Vaughan, Wheeler, Howard and Hampden, Vaughan, Swinsen, Maynard, Vaughan. All the MS. versions of the *Proceedings* I have seen and collated insert between Howard and Hampden above a speech by Dowdeswell, reported in a similar position by Grey, but on 11 November (p. 34). The speech is as follows: "Mr. Dowdeswell speaking against this article and comparing the proceedings of the House to a violent stream, it was moved by divers to call him to the Bar to explaine himself, but was permitted in his place to do it, and so it passed." (Stowe, 368, f. 39; 369, f. 36; Harl. 1218, f. 39; Harl. 881, f. 39; Rawl. A, 131, f. 41.)

Article 12 is affirmed in all by Osbourne.

Article 14, about Dr Crowther, is proved by Thomas, Add. MSS. 38175.

Article 15, proved by Thomas in the *Proceedings* (13), and by Littleton in Add. MSS. 38175 (13).

Article 16, proved by Littleton in Add. MSS. 38175 and the *Proceedings* (14), but in Appendix II by Sir Edward Masters (15).

Article 17, about Ireland, proved by Temple in Add. MSS. 38175, and by Howard in the *Proceedings*.

Article 18, the famous article 16 of the charges in their final form, on which a speech by Holland is in Appendix I, proved by Littleton in all accounts.

Article 19, about the division of the fleet, proved by Thomas in Add. MSS. 38175, by Thomas and Littleton in the *Proceedings*, and by these and Howard in Appendix II. After mentioning the Marvell incident already commented on, the *Proceedings* returns to the article about the customs and reports speeches by Temple and Osbourne (p. 27).

and to think no more of future Parliaments, but to govern in an arbitrary way by an army.

Sir Robert Howard and Lord Vaughan affirm that this will be proved.

2. The second article was that the Earl should say that the King was already a Papist in his heart and was altering his religion.

This the Lord St. John affirmed will be proved.

3. The third article was that the Earl had taken a great sum of money for passing the Canary patent, and gave assurance to the patentees that so long as the King lived and he was Chancellor that he would uphold the patent.

This Mr. Seymour affirmed will be directly proved.

4. The fourth article, that he had caused divers to be imprisoned in the Barbadoes and other foreign parts merely for disobeying his orders.

This Sir Richard Temple saith will be proved.

5. The fifth article that he had sold many offices for great sums of money.

This Sir Richard Temple saith likewise will be proved.

NOVEMBER 7TH. This day the House proceeded upon the sixth article, which was that he procured the King's customs to be set at under rates, and for that he had given him great sums of money.

7. The seventh article, that he had great sums of money to procure the King to pay certain great debts which the King ought not to have paid.

8. The eighth article, that he received certain sums of money from the vintners to protect them from being punished for selling wines at unlawful prices.

9. The ninth article, that he had got a greater estate than possibly he could do honestly in so short a time, out of his offices and places, and that he hath under the Great Seal got lands and leases that belonged to the King, which is contrary to his oath, as being a Privy Councillor and Chancellor which oath did oblige and restrain him from doing anything to the King's prejudice or damage.

Sir Thomas Littleton asserted many great purchases made by him.

10. The tenth article, that he had introduced an arbitrary government in the foreign plantations and that he imprisoned many that came hither to complain of it.

This was affirmed by Sir Thomas Littleton and Sir Thomas Osbourne, and that one Farmer was imprisoned by him.

11. The eleventh article, that he did obstruct the securing Barbados Nevis and other plantations: Sir Charles Wheeler affirms this.

12. The twelfth article, that he had correspondence with Cromwell and received divers sums of money without His Majesty's privity.

This likewise Sir Charles Wheeler affirms, but this was taken off by the Act of Oblivion; which was a great disgrace to him.

13. The thirteenth article, that he was the sole instrument of the sale of Dunkirk and all the guns, ammunition and stores there, and that the guns and ammunition were worth more and of better value than all the money the King received for it.

It was said to this article that another Lord was acquainted with the sale of Dunkirk as well as the Lord Clarendon, but that other Lord said that the Lord Clarendon had made that contract for it three quarters of a year before he was acquainted with it.

This was affirmed to be proved by Sir Thomas Osbourne.

14. The fourteenth article, that he altered letters patents passed under the Great Seal at his own pleasure, as in Dr. Crowder's case.

15. The fifteenth article, that by an arbitrary way he hath stopped proceedings at law at the Council table that concerned men's rights and titles.

This Mr. Thomas affirms to prove.

16. The sixteenth article, that he made *quo warrantoes*, to invalidate charters, that he might force men to renew them thereby to get money.

17. The seventeenth article, that he had great sums of money of the purchasers of lands in Ireland, for selling those purchases.

18. The eighteenth article, that he hath deluded His Majesty and kingdom in foreign treaties both with the Dutch and French

and other foreign states, especially in the late wars. This Mr. Harry Coventry seems to excuse.

19. The nineteenth article, that he was a principal agent and cause of dividing the Fleet, by his intelligence that the Dutch would not come out with their fleet of so long and that the French were already come out, when after it proved that the French were not come out but the Dutch were.

Sir Edward Littleton, Mr. Thomas and Sir Edward Spragg to prove this.

Sir Robert Howard said that the General speaking of the dividing the Fleet, the Lord Clarendon replied that he might have chosen whether he would have engaged with the Dutch or not. The General replied that he were forced to fight them or to have give up his ships to them.

After all the articles of the charge had been debated,[1] Mr. Marvell pressed that the words that were said to be spoken against the King should not be passed over in silence but be declared; the words as it [is] said are these:

"The Chancellor should say that the King was an unactive person and indisposed for government." Sir Robert Howard pointed at Mr. Seymour, who indeed gave the first hint of them. Mr. Seymour produced Sir John Denham and Sir John Denham he affirmed that he had it from another who would justify that the Chancellor said so, and made a most rational and excellent speech.

It is said that the Chancellor spake these words in France before that the King was restored.

Colonel Sandys's bill was read and engrossed and passed and sent up to the Lords by Lord Ancram.

Sir George Downing made his report from the committee that it was agreed there that the assignment of money lent to the King into the Exchequer should be entered into the book for 6d. an assignment if the sum was less than £100 and but 1s. if the assignment was above £100.

Several heads were read to be put in execution for preventing robbing by the high-way.

First that all innkeepers and victuallers should give an account weekly of all their guests that they take into lodging.

---

[1] See p. 108, n. 1 above.

Secondly that none ride with firearms.

Thirdly that six or eight soldiers of the militia be continually upon the high-ways instead of watch and ward.

Fourthly that he that apprehends a thief for robbing by the high-ways or for burglary shall have ten pounds.

Fifthly that he that is robbed shall not recover it of the country, which will make them more careful and diligent to get out hue and cries.

Sixthly that a thief taken for robbing shall be hanged in chains of iron in the place where he did the robbery.

Mr. Prynne brought in his bill against plurality of benefices and offices, which was this:

That after the year '67 no clergyman should have above two livings or two offices or dignities, and if two livings they shall be within some reasonable distance one to another; that the minister shall make his choice of one of them which he likes best, where he shall constantly approach and keep hospitality, and shall allow to his substitute in the other living the full half of the revenue with the houses and gardens upon it. And if after the year '67 any minister shall be possessed of more than two livings, another minister that is destitute of one living may be put into one of them as if the present minister were dead. If any man after this session of Parliament shall get a plurality of livings and hold them he shall pay £200 towards the building of the churches in London.

Bishops that have impropriations shall be compelled to allow sufficient supplies to their substitutes, and in case it be not so allowed it shall be lawful for the incumbent to show for half of the profits of that living in that which he doth officiate and shall recover it from the Bishop.

This bill extends to the plurality of offices and dignities in ecclesiastical courts.

NOVEMBER 8TH. This day[1] Mr. Prynne brought in a bill against granting licences and clandestine marriages under these four penalties:

---

[1] Grey omits the 8th, but gives Strickland's speech on the 9th (p. 29), in much the version given here on the 8th.

First, suspension for three first years for the first offence both of the priest that marryeth any persons and officer that granteth such licence.

Secondly for a second offence they shall suffer a total deprivation.

Thirdly that man that shall be so married shall lose the benefit of the courtesy of England, and the woman her dower.

Fourthly, all such clandestine marriages for the three first years to be void.

Sir Job Charlton made his report of Lord Fitzwilliam's election for a burgess place of Peterborough to be a good election.

I was at the committee of privileges when the election was debated and it was very clear for Lord Fitzwilliam.

Then came on the business of the day, my Lord Clarendon's case. It was moved that an impeachment should be drawn up against him and that there was sufficient ground for an impeachment upon the heads of his charge and accusation.

This was moved by Sir Robert Carr and Mr. Seymour. Sir Edward Windham likewise moved that he should be impeached and the impeachment sent up to the Lords.

Mr. Prynne moved that the impeachment should be named and for what he is impeached, whether for treason or misdemeanour. Sir William Lewis seconded it.

Sir Robert Howard was for an impeachment.

Henry North made a very good speech against it unless there were plainer proofs of it than (he said) he yet saw; also moved that the articles might be particularly examined that we may be informed whether they extend to treason or but misdemeanours.

Sir Robert Atkins spoke against the impeachment, because the accusation came from without doors and to the House but at the third hand.

Sir William Lowther informed the House that by a precedent in the Duke of Buckingham's case (as it is recorded in Mr. Rushworth's Journal book)[1] it was there resolved that an impeachment may be justly drawn up by the Commons against a Peer by public fame.

---

[1] Rushworth, I, 302 ff.

Sir Thomas Strickland made a very good speech and cited the Lord Strafford's impeachment and trial, and said although he abhorred the rigour of that proceeding, yet the easy part of it (he said) might be drawn into a precedent and made use of, and that the Lord Strafford did not find fault with the proceedings of the House of Commons before his trial, but at the prosecution of his trial and judgment.

It was voted that an impeachment be drawn up and to-morrow to debate the crimes, whether they be treason or but misdemeanours.

NOVEMBER 9TH.   This day complaint was made of the abuses [of] the post office, both of the delay of sending away letters, and in suffering letters to be opened, and in exacting unreasonable payment for them; and that the same be referred to a committee to examine it and to consider of a way how to redress it.

Dr. Burwell brought in Perkins his petition. It seems that Dr. Wharton had bought land of another Perkins to the value of two thousand four hundred pounds, and caused twelve hundred pounds of it to be kept in the hands of one Mr. Bierley until some cumbrances were cleared and all things perfected. Perkins his conveyance afterward proved fraudulent, whereupon the £1,200 is still kept from this complainant, to whom it seems it is due; he desires to be relieved in this case and to have the money out of Mr. Bierley his hands for his present subsistence.

The abuses in making woollen cloth is complained of and referred to a committee.

Sir Robert Brooke made a report from the committee for the miscarriages in the late war, and desired that the Duke of York may be humbly desired to be pleased to acquaint the House to whom he commanded the fortifying of Sheerness and at what time.

Also Sir Robert moved that some of the members should be sent to Trinity Hall, to be informed of the tickets by which seamen had been paid.

Sir John Goodrick informed the House that where it is said in the first article of the Earl of Clarendon's charge that he designed to alter the present etc., that the word "designed" cannot extend to treason.[1]

Sir William Lewis that the time may be asserted when the words were spoken to the King.

Mr. Steward made a long speech, and indeed did well state the nature of treason, whether this first article were a treason before the statute of the 25th of Edward III and also whether it is within the treasons of that statute.

Colonel Birch said that the miscarriage at Chatham is excused by some that it was not through any treachery, but that the men there were distracted and amazed, which made them so unserviceable in the defence, and if so, then might the Earl of Clarendon in the like distraction advise the King to dissolve this Parliament and to raise a standing army.

Sir Francis Goodrick said that these words of the Earl were not treason because they were not felony, and that there can be no treason but what is felony in the first place. But this Mr. Vaughan said was not good law, for that may be treason that is not felony first.

For first, to deflower the King's daughter is not felony, but yet it is treason and is punished with death, whereas if it was not treason it should be punished no otherwise than adultery.

John Emperiall, the Genoese Ambassador, was killed in London, and it was adjudged treason.

Secondly, to bring in false coin is not felony and yet it is treason.

It was farther objected that crimes of the Lord Clarendon cannot be treason because they are not misprision of treason, and misprision of treason they cannot be, because they were spoken and not concealed.

Again, to advise the King to dissolve the Parliament cannot be treason, because it was the advice only of a Privy Councillor, and a Privy Councillor may give advice which to himself may seem good and yet not prove well. To which it was answered,

---

[1] This is the "great debate on treason" frequently referred to. Appendix I gives a speech by Holland on the matter. Appendix II gives some additional speeches, for example, one by Sergeant Sise or Seys (member for Gloucester with Massey), not mentioned elsewhere.

a Privy Councillor may give advice of several things, both of things at home and affairs abroad and of war also, but he may not give counsel against the known laws, or to the subversion of established government, or against his fellow-subjects and his oath. If the King want money he may not advise the King to set up thieves to rob by the high-way to supply him.

Mr. Vaughan informed the House that in Henry II's time there was a treason called *seductio regis*, to advise the King to do things against the laws, to make him odious to his subjects and an enemy to the government of the known laws. That this counsel or advice of Lord Clarendon was to make the King break his oath at his coronation, and to set up an arbitrary government contrary to his laws, and after his people had manifested so much loyalty and true care of His Majesty, and the King had not at that time the least displeasure against his people, and having a Parliament of as much loyalty and true care of His Majesty and his kingdom's welfare and good as any Parliament before them ever had. And now to give the King advice to do such things as would certainly bring him into the highest of dangers is a crime of the highest nature that can be.

The statute of the 25th of Edward III belongs to the inferior courts and was a standing rule for them to judge what is treason, but yet doth not take away the power of Parliament to declare [what] is treason.

Sir Richard Temple said that to give advice against the government established to overthrow it is treason, contained in that 25th statute of Edward III.

The Spencers' advising the King to raise horse and arms against the people was adjudged treason, although no hostile act followed.

The insurrection of the villains, to overthrow the tenure of the villeinage, was adjudged treason.[1]

---

[1] Cf. Grey, p. 31. Temple mentions the villains and the enclosure rebellion. Much light is thrown on these references by a note in Stowe, 425, f. 91 v., where amongst other references to the examples cited on this day is one to the insurrection of the villains, 5 Richard II, and another to the rebellion of Bradshaw and Barret in 39 Elizabeth. Milward perhaps remembered tales of the incident from older friends, as it occurred in Derbyshire. See Tawney, *Agrarian Problem*, p. 327.

Bradshaw and Barret for raising forces to throw down ditches and enclosures were adjudged traitors.

Whatsoever is done against the King's authority is treason, as well as what is done against his person, by a new and late statute made in Parliament in our present King's reign.

Story practised with foreigners to betray the realm, and was executed for treason, though no act followed.

If the Earl of Clarendon be not impeached of treason and secured these inconveniences will follow:

First, he hath liberty to flee and make his escape, if the Lords shall find it treason.

Secondly, if but misdemeanours, then he shall have counsel assigned him to plead for him: Sir Richard Temple.

After five or six hours' debate this day, whether the House of Commons had power to declare this first article treason or no, it was resolved that the House had power.

Then it was put to the question whether he should be impeached of treason upon the first article. The House was divided upon it; the ayes that were for it went out, and were 103; the noes that stayed in were 172, of which I was one;[1] and so it was carried that he was not impeached of treason upon the first article.

The other heads were to be debated on Monday next.

NOVEMBER 11TH. There was a petition this day brought in by Sir Edward Windham concerning an estate where the Lord Clarendon's servants made a forcible entry, wherein Peroon, Allen and Lord Caron[2] were concerned.

The King's tithe also seems to be concerned. Upon the reading of the petition it is ordered and licence is given to bring in a bill.

Dr. Chamberlayne's petition was read; he petitioned that he and his heirs may have a grant to them and their assigns for

---

[1] *C.J.* IX, 18, 103–172, Osbourne and Seymour, Clifford Clifton and Brooke.

[2] The MS. is clearly not Caron here, but the *Journals* make it clear that someone called Caron was involved. Clarendon acquired Caron House, formerly the property of Caron, a Dutch ambassador (Lister, II, 538). I cannot identify Peroon or Allen.

ever to have the sole benefit and patent and management of a new way of navigation, in a straight line with all winds; he hath already obtained a patent from the King of France and from the state of Holland. His petition is referred to a committee of the Long Robe and physicians, and ordered to be read a second time.

The House then fell to the business of the day, and read the second article of the Earl of Clarendon's accusation, which was this, that he said the King were a Papist in heart and popishly affected.

To this some answered by way of excuse that these words were pardoned in the Act of Oblivion, and also that this accusation was not brought within six months.

Mr. Vaughan and Sir Heneage Finch said that the time of six months might excuse as from being judged in inferior courts, but it did not take away the guilt of it; but that still it was treason, or such a crime as the act and statute held it out to be, and so liable to the law.

For setting and farming the customs at undervalues and for taking money in that case, he was charged by Sir John Shaw and Sir Philip Warwick, who affirmed to the House that the customs were set at £390,000 by the year, which was much and more than could be got for them from other merchants to whom they had been formerly offered, and they did verily believe he had no bribe in that case, because the bargain did not deserve it.

The next article was the sale of Dunkirk; the sale of this town was disliked and condemned by all.

It was affirmed that the advice given to sell it was treason, because it was a part of the King's dominions annexed to the Crown, and if so then he might as well have given counsel for the sale of England or any part of it as well as Dunkirk; and therefore if it was sold by the Chancellor without King, Lords and Commons it was treason.

That there may be a treason declared by the House of Commons though not contained in the 25th statute of Edward III is asserted by Mr. Vaughan.

But then saith Sir Heneage Finch it must be prosecuted by way of bill.

The Parliament gave the King £120,000 as a free gift, and therefore it was not probable that he should be constrained to sell Dunkirk for want of money.

Mr. Henry Coventry affirmed that although Dunkirk was the King's, yet it was not annexed to the Crown and revenue, and therefore he may increase or diminish them at his pleasure.

Sir Robert Howard answered that if any man should sell the King's guard to a stranger, though they are not annexed to the Crown, yet it is treason.

It is reported that the King of France should say (when he had bought Dunkirk) that the next thing he should buy of the King of England should be London.

Mr. Prynne, to justify the sale of Dunkirk, said that the King was privy to the sale of it, and therefore it could not be betrayed and therefore no treason.

Mr. Vaughan made this reply to him, suppose the King was acquainted and gave his consent to the sale of Dunkirk, yet the party counselling and advising him to it may be guilty of treason, because Dunkirk being a part of the King's dominions cannot be alienated or sold without an act of Parliament, and therefore to persuade the King to the sale of it without an act of Parliament was the greater fault.

Sir Edward Harley said that the King gave commandment that an act of Parliament should be made and passed to annex Dunkirk to the Crown. And accordingly the House of Commons proceeded and passed the bill, but the cause why it stopped in the House of Lords is not yet known.

He also affirmed that the charge of maintaining and keeping Dunkirk was not so great as is reported, for when he was commanded to quit the place he left in current money nine thousand six hundred and forty pounds, and that the advantage of the place, both as being a place for retreat, being beyond the seas, and proper to infest an enemy, and many other conveniences, was much more advantageous and considerable to the King and kingdom than the charge could be of keeping it.

Sir Charles Wheeler also confirmed the same.

The Lord Brandon told the King of France that the buying of Dunkirk was the best bargain that ever he made.

Sir Edward Walpole, in favour of parting with Dunkirk, that it was not conquered by the King of England, but surrendered by contract by the King of France, and therefore the sale of it again to him cannot be said to be betraying it.

The next article taken into debate was that of the Lord Clarendon's betraying the King's counsels to his enemies, which is treason.

Sir John Maynard and Sir Heneage Finch affirmed that if he had betrayed the King's counsels to the King of France, being then in actual war against him, it was treason of the highest degree.

There was exception against the article, that it did not as yet appear that the Earl had betrayed the King's secret counsels, for these words were not in the article.

The Lord Vaughan moved that those words, "his secret counsels" should be put into the article, for he was ready to produce witness to prove them.

After a long debate of three hours, and many frivolous exceptions and cavils by the Earl's friends (one was, it should be declared whether the witness to prove this article were a foreigner or a natural subject; it was put to the question, whether the question, "or a foreigner" should be put or not; it was carried by the noes, of which I was one), then it was put to the question whether he should be impeached of treason upon this article or no. The ayes that were for the impeachment went out and were 161, of which I was one; the noes that stayed in were 89.[1] It was then voted that the Speaker should carry the impeachment to the Lords.

NOVEMBER 12TH. This day the bill that concerned Perkins, Dr. Wharton and Mr. Bierley was read the second time and committed.

A petition was brought in by the commoners belonging to the Forest of Dean by Mr. Hall and Captain Colchester in opposition to Sir John Winter his design in taking in ten thousand acres of the forest for the King, and he to have eight thousand more for himself; and the commoners to have but four thousand acres, for the whole forest is but 22,000 acres.

They complain in their petition that Sir John Winter hath

[1] *C.J.* IX, 18, 161–89, Carr and Wheeler, Brooke and Allen.

been principal in cutting down and wasting all those many thousands of goodly oaks, most proper for ships, and now he aims at the soil also.

It was referred to a committee both to consider of the petition and abuses.

Mr. Vaughan brought in his report from the committee of grievances, in reference to an act of judicial proceedings and calling the members of this House into question for words and votes spoken and passed in this House, by any of the courts in Westminster Hall.[1]

The case of Mr. Elliott and Mr. Denzil Holles was repeated and the proceedings against them in the King's Bench Court reported, and it was adjudged to be a breach of the privilege of Parliament, and [they] were voted to have reparation for their sufferings against the Lords of the Council, the judges and lawyers that pleaded and gave judgment against them.

Also Mr. Stroude's case in Henry VIII's time was brought in for a precedent and made a standing law for maintaining the privilege of the members of Parliament.

It was ordered that this report should be reassumed on Thursday next and the King's Counsel to be heard if they have anything to say justly against it.

There are three heads of act of Parliament.

First, general, when the act concerns the whole nation, or the general government of bishops and ecclesiastical jurisdiction.

Secondly, special, when it concerns a corporation or a particular body corporate.

Thirdly, individual, when it concerns a particular and individual person.

The House altered the former order of sending the impeachment by the Speaker, and they sent it up by Mr. Seymour. The ground of this alteration was a debate taken up in the House concerning the manner of the Speaker's going up to the House of Lords, whether with his mace carried before him on the Serjeant's shoulder, or whether with the mace lowered. If he should have the mace carried before him and the Lords should question

---

[1] *C.J.* IX, 19. These precedents widely noted in MS. books as well as in Grey, pp. 37–8, etc.

it we cannot make it good by any precedent since the time of Michael de la Pole, and if he should go in with [it] lowered it might be a lessening of our just power. By reason of this uncertainty it was resolved to send it up by Mr. Seymour.

The words that he was ordered to say to the House of Lords were these:

"My Lords, I am commanded by the Commons to impeach an honourable person of this House, the Earl of Clarendon, of high treason, in the name of the Commons of England, and that he may be sequestered from this House and committed to safe custody and that within a reasonable time the Commons will be ready to make good this impeachment."[1]

NOVEMBER 13TH. This day[2] Mr. Seymour made his report from the Lords that they would take their message and impeachment into consideration and would return their answer by their own messenger.

Sir John Knight made his report from the committee of trade, as it concerned the commodities and settlement of trade between England and Scotland. This being a business of great consequence the House ordered that two days in a week, viz: Wednesday and Friday, the House should resolve into a Grand Committee, to consider the best way how to settle and establish the trade between England and Scotland and of the trade in general in England.

Sir Robert Brooke made his report from the committee of miscarriages in the war; of the examination of Commissioner Pett and of the answer he made to the General's narrative; which was very unsatisfactory to the House, and therefore it moved to draw up an impeachment against him. And especially for his disobeying the Duke's orders, and not securing the *Royal Charles* by drawing it up the river nearer its safety in ten weeks' time; this neglect he doth not nor can he truly and fully excuse.

The sectaries[3] do very much favour Pett.

[1] Seymour's speech at greater length was printed amongst other places in *Articles of Treason exhibited in Parliament against Edward, Earl of Clarendon*, 1669.

[2] Cf. Grey, p. 39; Marvell to Hull (*Letters*, p. 58), etc.

[3] MS. reads "secretaries", but surely "sectaries" is meant here, and means the Swinsen-Marvell-Boscawen "gang", I think.

NOVEMBER 14TH. This day the inhabitants about the Tower whose houses were pulled down at the late dreadful fire brought in their petition to the House craving their assistance in their relief. The House being informed that they were the King's tenants and had leases of 80 years from the King, and had as yet 20 years in being, and their houses were pulled down by the King's command for the safety of the Tower, do judge it the most proper way for them to petition the King, it being improper for the Parliament to meddle with it.

Mr. Palmes brought in his bill to enable him to sell £400 per annum in Derbyshire and other places that are entailed lands, for the payment of debts, and in lieu of it he offers to settle £500 per annum in the same tenure and estate which he hath power to sell; it was appointed a second reading.

An ancient bill was revived and brought in for the draining of Lindsey levels.

This bill was mainly opposed by Sir Robert Carr and as stoutly maintained by Sir William Killigrew and others; it was laid aside for the present.

The rest of the day was spent in debate about impeachment of Pett; it is believed [he] will prove a very great criminal, but much friended by the old gang.

NOVEMBER 15TH. The Lords this day resumed the debate concerning the commitment of Lord Clarendon, but not yet resolved whether to commit him or not.

This day we had a conference with the Lords; the Earl of Oxford there brought the Lords' answer and resolution in writing, viz: that they have not agreed with us to commit the Earl of Clarendon, because the impeachment was general, and there was no special matter sent up for an impeachment.

The Lords urged the precedent of William de la Pole in Henry VI's time. He was impeached but not committed, until the House of Commons sent up a special charge against him, and then the Lords committed him.

This Sir Robert Holt urged and withal moved to send up a special charge, and Sir William Lewis seconded him.

Sir John Denham and Mr. Garroway spoke against it.

Sir Robert Holt and Mr. Trevor moved to adjourn this debate until to-morrow.

Mr. Vaughan was against the sending up the article, but rather to prepare some precedents and reasons to justify their proceedings.

Sir Charles Harbord agreed with him.

Sir Heneage Finch said it was undoubtedly true that the House of Commons hath power to impeach and the House of Lords have power to imprison upon that impeachment, but yet they were not obliged to do [it] in this case, for they have power to imprison or to bail by an inherent power in them, and so also hath the King's Bench, and have bailed men indicted for treason.

In the end the debate was adjourned until Saturday morning.

NOVEMBER 16TH.   This day[1] Sir Edward Windham made a long speech in order to the sending up the article of impeachment to the Lords. Sir Robert Carr spoke against it.

Sir George Reeves moved to send up reasons to justify our proceedings, and if the Lords would not be satisfied with them, then to send up the article.

Mr. Vaughan said that the King's Bench had power to bail a person indicted for treason, but only in the case where there was an undue delay of prosecution, because a prisoner should not long lie in prison and not be brought to his trial.

It was also alleged that if the article should be sent up and made public it might give alarm to all that were engaged in the treason to make their escape and go away.

Mr. Vaughan also affirmeth that the House of Lords and Commons in a Parliamentary way have an unlimited power.

If the King had been in the House of Lords and had commanded the article, the Commons had been obliged to bring it up, for the King had power then to commit or to bail him, and that because the King had power to pardon him, which the Lords had not.

It was again moved to send up the reasons and with it the article put into a due form.

---

[1] Cf. Grey, pp. 41–4.

To which Sir Heneage Finch agrees, but differs with Mr. Vaughan about the power of the King's Bench; for he saith after the Grand Jury have indicted a man of treason, the King's Bench upon good security may bail him, and though they do not or will not bail all men in case of treason, yet they have a fundamental power to do it. Nor is it in regard of the King's person whom the Lords do represent that they can bail a man in this case, but from an inherent power committed to them.

Sir Heneage Finch also further saith that the article as it is now penned is so defective that the party indicted may demur to it, but it ought so to be drawn that the party must unavoidably plead to it.

In impeachments of misdemeanours times and places are sufficient to be nominated, but in treason the subject matter must be clearly stated.

Sir Richard Temple saith that the Lords ought to have committed him upon the impeachment of the House of Commons, because their power is in reference to the Parliament, for if it were not so, they might at any time acquit or condemn any man at their pleasure.

The King's Bench is so limited in their power that they cannot deny bail where it is to be granted.

If the Lords may stand upon the article to have it specified they may by the same power and rule require that witnesses be produced to prove the article, and so also may choose whether they will proceed upon the impeachment.

It is said that the impeachment itself, being an impeachment of treason, is a special matter, and so differs from a general impeachment, for it sets forth the crime, which is treason, and so distinguisheth it from felony and other criminal offences. So far Sir Richard Temple.

Mr. Prynne said that a man that is a free man is not to be committed upon a bare impeachment of treason; but if he be not a free man, but in prison or under restraint for any crime, he may be committed upon a bare impeachment of treason.

Earl Godwin was a freed man and impeached of treason by the King himself, yet he was not committed upon that impeachment. For the Lords took him in their arms and presented him to the King and procured his pardon.

Whereas it is alleged that if the Lords should commit Earl

Clarendon upon this general impeachment the Commons may by the same rule impeach all the Lords that sit in the House and the Lords may impeach all the Commons.

This Mr. Vaughan said was a needless objection, for the House of Lords cannot impeach a member of the House of Commons without the consent of the Commoners.[1]

After some hours spent in this debate it was ordered that a committee should be nominated to draw up some reasons to justify our proceeding to the Lords at a conference.

NOVEMBER 18TH. This day[2] Mr. William Palmes his bill was read the second time.

Sir Robert Howard informed the House that a member of the House had received a bribe of £400 for the procuring a licence for the wine merchants to land their French wines, which were prohibited by a former act, and indeed confiscated by the act. He affirmed that he could name two persons to accuse a third that was criminal. Some moved that he should name them, but he came up to the table and writ the names both of the accusers and the person accused.

Sir Thomas Littleton made his report of the reasons that were drawn up to be tendered to the Lords, why the Commons desired their concurrence in the committing the Earl upon the impeachment. The reasons are these six:

First because it appears by precedent that the Lords have committed a person upon a general impeachment of treason.

Secondly because a general impeachment is a legal way of proceeding to a commitment.

Thirdly because accomplices might escape.

Fourthly because if this general impeachment be judged insufficient to satisfy the Lords as to the Earl's commitment the Commons will be at a loss how to draw up future impeachments that may satisfy.

Fifthly that the precedents of Strafford, the Archbishop Laud, Finch and Sir George Ratcliff are sufficient precedents to justify the impeachment for this commitment.

Sixthly because inferior Courts are limited by the discretion of Parliament.

---

[1] Cf. *Proceedings*, p. 60 f.; Eg. 2543, f. 196, etc.
[2] *C.J.* IX, 18. MS. omits the date here.

NOVEMBER 19TH.   This day Sir Allen Apsley brought in a bill
for the selling of the King's lands for the payment of a debt of
£2,300 laid out by Sir Allen's father and another person for the
furnishing the King's ships. The bill had like to have been cast
out, but in conclusion it was ordered a second reading.

Then the House took up the complaint of bribery, and Sir
John Ashburnham was accused of receiving a bribe from the
wine merchants of £500.

Two witnesses were produced, but they did rather excuse
than accuse him, whereupon Sir Edward Walpole spoke for his
acquitting, but the House would not admit it.

Some that were for him said that he took not the £500 as
a member of the House of Commons but as a Courtier.

The matter was ordered to be examined by a committee.

The reasons for the impeachment were carried up to the
Lords at a Conference; the Lords will debate them to-morrow.

NOVEMBER 20TH.   This day Mr. Beckam's bill was read; it
was to enable him to sell part of his land. His case seems to
be this: his whole land is the value of £300 per annum, out of
which a part was appointed for the payment of debts, and for
present maintenance of several younger sons and daughters,
until so much money was raised for portions for younger
children, so that there is almost nothing left to the heir for his
maintenance, nor can there be any portion raised out of the
estate that is undisposed of, without selling some part of the
land.

Sir George Downing's bill for settling fees in the Exchequer
for recording assignments, being engrossed was read.

Sir Job Charlton made his report from the committee of
privileges that Sir John Coventry's election was good.

Sir Thomas Higgins made his report from the committee
for the abuse of the price of coals that the merchants and owners
of the great ships that are in the river laden with coals refuse
to sell any without a ticket from the woodmongers, and that they
refuse to land their coals, but say they will make their great
ships their warehouses and there sell their coals at their own
prices.

The colliers complain greatly of the officers of the ballast.

First, that they raise the price of their ballast at their pleasure.

Secondly, that they delay to furnish them with ballast, but make them wait, it may be, ten days, which hinders them in their return with a fresh supply.

Thirdly, that instead of an hundredweight of ballast they give them so much too short that many times wanting their due weight of ballast their ships are in danger, and sometimes both ship and men are cast away.

The residue of this morning was spent wholly in the case of bribery.

A paper was brought in and the names of many members which had received money and wines.

NOVEMBER 21ST. This day[1] Sir Charles Harbord made his report from the committee of accounts; it only reported the amendment of the bill.

The Lords sent a message to the House that they would meet us at a conference in order to a debate concerning the commitment of the Earl of Clarendon.

It was debated whether we should admit of this conference or by messenger of our own desire a free conference, which was more proper for the debate as some of our members did conceive, and they gave this reason, because this being a second conference, the Lords may afterwards rightly deny a free conference.

Of this opinion was Sir Robert Howard, Sir Thomas Littleton and Sir Richard Temple and others.

Sir Robert Holt and the Speaker were for a present conference and Mr. Vaughan not much against it.

This debate held until one of the clock, and in the conclusion they agreed to the present conference.

The Lords at this conference told them they did not agree to their reasons, but would adhere to their own resolutions; the Commons then desired to debate their reasons at a free conference; the Lords will take time until to-morrow to consider of it.

[1] *C.J.* IX, 23. Colonel Milward added to the committee of elections, 21 November. Starkey, f. 22, notes the strictness of the Commons upon the bill of accounts. On the Lords' debates on this and other days at this crisis see Bibliography.

It is reported, and I believe it is true, that upon the debate of our reasons given in on Monday the Lords were divided whether they should agree to them or no, but it was carried by the major votes not to agree. All the bishops were against the agreement but the Bishop of Durham, the Bishop of Hereford, the Bishop of St. David's and the Bishop of Asaph; above twenty Lords were for the agreement, most of them of the royal party.

When it was carried against them [they] entered their protestation into the Journal that not to agree with the reasons was against their vote and judgment. The Duke of Albemarle entered his protestation, and so it is said Prince Rupert would have done had he been in the House.

I went to the committee of privileges, where I stayed till eight of the clock at night; it was concerning the election: Sir Fretchville Holles by his petition questioned his election and proved it illegal and himself to be duly elected, and so carried it at the committee.[1]

Sir Philip's cause was very ill managed by himself and his agents, but especially by his counsel, or else it might have gone better with him.

Sir Philip had twenty-six voices and Sir Fretchville had but twenty-three, but they proved nine of Sir Philip's to be bribed and threatened into the election, and so Sir Fretchville Holles carried it as having the greater number of legal votes.

NOVEMBER 22ND. This day I came late into the House, being misinformed that the Speaker was not come. After I came the House fell into debate of Sir John Ashburnham's bribery.[2]

The merchants were examined, and denied there were any contract between him and them.

The witnesses Hartlip, Cresset and Bennet were examined. Hartlip denied any contract to be made with Mr. Ashburnham, but Cresset did justify that Hartlip did say that there was a fore-promise made to Mr. Ashburnham of £500 and afterwards paid and carried by Mr. Sawtin, or a bill for it.

[1] Something omitted from the MS. here referring to these rivals. Sir Philip was Tirwhit (or Jerret in Milward's spelling).

[2] Cf. Grey, p. 46; Marvell, *Letters*, p. 60; *C.S.P.D.* 1667/8, p. 58, etc.

Doubtless Hartlip is an egregious knave, and abused the merchants by putting them upon giving of bribes, and shamefully abused many members of Parliament, by making a list of them and of their several bribes both of money and wine.

To the Serjeant £50 in gold; to Marsh, the under-clerk £11; to divers members several jerses of wine; and named some that never received one drop of wine, as Sir Edward Windham and Colonel Kirby and others.

After all the long debate it was not to be denied but that Mr. Ashburnham had the £500, but indeed it was never proved clearly, in my judgment, that there was any contract made aforehand with him for it.

It was proved that he told the merchant, "Since the King hath done so much for you, it is fit you present His Majesty with a New Year's gift of £1,000," which sounded very ill, and showed a great deal of corruption in him, who like enough intended most of it for himself.

In the end he was voted to be expelled the House and a writ sent out for a new election of another member in his place; that he should be sent to the Tower and to receive the sentence upon his knees at the Bar; but all was pardoned but his expulsion.

Sir Job Charlton made his report from the committee of privileges of the due election of Sir Fretchville Holles, whereupon the sitting member, Sir Philip Jerret, was removed, and he took his place.

NOVEMBER 23RD. This day Captain Lawe's[1] bill was brought in for the sale of his wife's lands in her jointure; it found opposition, but yet it got an order that it should be read a second time. The opposition did rise from the great charge upon the estate, for debts are said to be £13,000. Madam Lawe demands for recompence of her dower £4,000; a brother demands £900 and the daughters' portions to be £6,000, and the whole estate is £1,000 per annum, so that if all the demands be satisfied the creditors must fall short of the payment of their debts.

---

[1] *C.J.* IX, 24. Lawe, whom I believe to be Capt. Henry Dawe, not mentioned. The petition below was from Sir William Ryder, or Rider. Cf. also for debates on this day, *Proceedings*; Add. MSS. 22263, ff. 10–23, etc. Grey is brief.

It was therefore advised that the creditors be satisfied in their demands, and then the bill will be more like to pass.

There was a petition brought in [by] certain merchants by way of complaint against Carpenters and Andrews for exacting undue customs in the Water-bailiff's office.

The petition was much spoken against by Sir Richard Brown and Sir John Birkenhead as unjust and causeless, and that it was brought in on purpose to obstruct a trial at the Exchequer Bar on Monday next, where the merit of the cause would be determined. It was therefore moved to lay aside the petition until the cause had been tried there, and then if the petitioners cast the officers then there would be no need of the Parliament's relief.

Mr. Hobby brought in a letter of complaint that the only son of one Mr. Reeve should be seduced by certain Jesuits and priests and sent away to Douai in Flanders. To this one Mr. Bennet made answer that the complainant had married the young man's mother and proved an unkind father to him, wasted the estate and forced the young man to pray Mr. Bennet to be his guardian, the estate being £300 per annum; which Mr. Bennet refusing, the young man went to his own uncle within few miles of him, and there he is at present time.

The Lords sent us a message to desire a conference, at which they gave their reasons why they did not agree with our reasons, and also said that our denying them a conference upon their demands upon our former conference was not Parliamentary.

At their return from the conference Sir Robert Howard made his report of it. The House took their reasons into debate, and concluded to agree to a conference as the Lords had desired.

But it was first stiffly debated, which debate held very long, whether we should singly yield to a conference or with it to send an excuse or reason that we did demur, because we did believe that the Lords, if we admitted this conference, would not give us a free conference to debate and justify our reasons which we had given to them to make good our general impeachment sufficient for the Earl's commitment.

There was divers opinions on this debate; some were for a conference, some against it. My judgment was to agree to

a conference without any insinuation or excuse, but I stayed
not the end of the debate for I liked it not.

NOVEMBER 25TH.   This day Mr. Beckam's bill was brought in;
he is a Norfolk man and hath four or five brothers and one
sister, and great debts are upon the estate, the interest much
and the younger children's portions very considerable, insomuch
that the yearly revenue of the land will not be able to discharge
all, and therefore it was moved that an act of Parliament may
be had to enable him to sell so much land as to pay the debts and
the younger children's portions and then the heir to have the rest.

The Heralds sent their bill to have descents to be recorded,
because, as they allege, the Court of Wards being taken away
and offices not being found, men of good descent were liable to
lose their derivations and houses and families from which they
are descended.

This seemed to me to be a design of the Heralds to gain fees
to their office.

The House took up the debate of the information of the taking
of bribes.

The Serjeant being formerly accused and in the list of those
that had taken bribes for taking £50 in gold of the merchants,
said that he had not any £50 in gold, but he had received £40
in silver as his fees, as being a counsellor and barrister-at-law,
and for giving them advice how to manage their business at
court.

The Senior Clerk, Mr. Goldsborough, confesseth that he had
received three jerses of base French wine, but not as any bribe,
but as part of his fees which would come to a full £100, which
fees he did [not] expect to receive.

Divers more could not deny but that they had wine given
them, but not as bribes, but out of the vintners' own kindness,
as Lord Fanshawe and others, but it was moved that the wine
should not be any further taken notice of.

NOVEMBER 26TH.   This day Sir Charles Harbord's report was
read and the amendments added to it.

There was a debate of the salary, how much to be allowed
to the commissioners that were employed to inspect the accounts,

for it is supposed that in regard they must be many officers and attendants the salary ought to be of a very considerable value.

It was then moved in the House to send up to the Lords for a free conference upon the reason we had given them; Mr. Prynne was against it because we already had a conference with them about it; the Lords notwithstanding refuse to commit the Earl upon the general impeachment. But notwithstanding the House sent up a message by Sir Thomas Littleton to desire a free conference. The Lords said they would consider of it and send us an answer by a messenger of their own.

Colonel Sandys informed the House that he had good information that a certain man, now being sick and likely to die, would discover a man (now out of office) that had cheated the King of £65,000 if the King or Parliament would secure him £1,000 to leave to his friends.[1]

Sir Thomas Bludworth, Colonel Sandys and Mr. Love were appointed to go to the man and to know of him what he could inform and to make report of it to the House.

Sir George Downing brought in his bill for the exportation of hides and leather, which was allowed and appointed a second reading.

The election of Sir Frederick Hyde[2] was reported and made void by the committee of privileges, but upon the debate and report the House was divided and it was carried in the affirmative to be a good election, and therefore not to agree with the committee; I gave my voice for him.

NOVEMBER 27TH. This day[3] the bill for suppressing and preventing robbing by the high-ways was read; it did contain these heads:

First, that whosoever shall apprehend a thief that hath robbed by the high-way or one that hath committed burglary in the night shall have ten pounds.

Secondly, this ten pounds shall be paid by the Sheriff upon a certificate from two justices of the peace or the judges of an assize.

---

[1] Cf. Grey, p. 53, notes in a bracket on this.

[2] *C.J.* IX, 26. Hyde's opponent was Hugh Owen, and the figures on the division, 57–95, Seymour and Weld, Holt and Kirby.

[3] Grey omits 27–29 November, but Cobbett, IV, 387–91, full.

Thirdly, if the Sheriff refuse to pay the ten pounds upon such certificate within ten days after it is demanded, he shall pay ten pounds more to the party than the former ten pounds, and that ten pounds he shall pay out of his own estate, but the other ten pounds shall be allowed by the King upon his accounts.

Fourthly, if the justices refuse to make such certificates they are likewise to pay ten pounds to the party requiring the certificate.

Fifthly, the parties that shall commit a robbery, if it be not burglary by night nor any murder committed in the robbery, shall be transported into some of the foreign plantations.

Sixthly, if a man that hath committed a robbery shall of his own free will confess the said [robbery], if no murder be committed in the robbery, he shall be pardoned.

The General's letter was read, which advised to make an address to the King to send out his proclamation against robbing until the act can be perfected, and that no soldier or officer under the degree of a captain shall travel without a pass under the penalty of cashiering; if he have a pass he shall not travel with firearms; if they do they may be seized by the Mayor of any corporation or other officer in any place where they shall make their stay.

Sir John Knight moved to the House to naturalise prize ships taken in the late war.

Many arguments were used for and against it.

They that moved for it said that many ships belonging to the out ports were lost and spoiled, by which loss the merchants want ships to carry on their trade.

Others were against and said that it would be a means to let in all the Dutch ships, and by that means totally destroy the art of making ships in England, for if that trade and art of making ships should be neglected but one year in England it will be in danger to be wholly lost.

The House resolved into a Grand Committee; Mr. Seymour was chosen Chairman; it was for settling trade.

Sir George Downing began with the bill that had been read concerning the settling of a trade with Scotland; his judgment was that we should not be too hasty in settling it by a bill and committee, but rather by commissioners, because the commodities of Scotland were of such a nature that we might well be without them, as coal, salt, corn, cloth and cattle, sheep and hides, and their whole custom to the King was but £12,000 in the year; that Scotland was not our Indies, as Sir Thomas Clifford had said, for they greatly exhaust our coin and we have not any Scotch money, but they carry away our coin for their inconsiderable commodities.

Sir Thomas Clifford spoke for a speedy settlement of the trade with Scotland, contrary to what Sir George Downing had said before, and affirmed that the King's customs for their commodities were above £12,000 in the year, and that we got much by their commodities; we had them in gross, hides and tallow, and sent them in again in boots, shoes and candles.

While the House was in this debate Sir Robert Howard acquainted the Speaker (who beforehand had resumed the Chair) that if the Lords should send to us that they would admit of a free conference as we desired possibly they might require it at that very instant, it being proper to them to appoint their own time, and the House being then very thin and most of the members absent that should manage the conference, and to avoid a sudden surprise, he advised to adjourn the House, which was accordingly done. When the House was up we heard that the Lords were resolved to give us a free conference to-morrow.

NOVEMBER 28TH. This day the Cambridge bill was brought and read the second time for the enclosing 40 acres of common for the pest-house, and was ordered to be engrossed.

The bill for Lindsey levels was read and ordered to be committed, though very much opposed by Sir Robert Carr, who indeed spoke very much reason.

The men that were concerned for it were Sir William Killigrew and Sir Henry Horn, who are to have 114,000 acres for their shares for draining it.

The Lords sent two judges, Windham and Rainsford, in their furred gowns with their answer to the Commons that they did consent to a free conference, and would presently meet them in the Painted Chamber.

NOVEMBER 29TH. This day[1] the bill for preventing robbing by the high-way was brought in; some were for the sending away those that were taken for robbing (if it was not for burglary in the night and where no murder is committed) to foreign plantations; others spoke against it and said it would be encouragement to thieves and robbers to do it to get a stock to carry to the plantations and to others that might be in hopes to make an escape and so get back.

Others moved that the law may be altered which orders the county to pay the money taken from any man by thieves, and that the county should pay but half, to cause the party robbed to be more active to get out hue and cries to apprehend the robbers.

But the bill was passed as it was first brought in.

Colonel Sandys made his report according to his orders for finding out the person that said he would discover where the King had been cheated of £65,000, but he referred it to Sir Thomas Bludworth and Mr. Love to report it, but none of them made anything of advantage by the sick man's report, but that the store that was formerly but £20,000 for setting forth so many ships was now got up to £80,000.

They examined a brother of this sick man who told Sir William Batten, who was a chief officer and had command of soldiers, being told of the abuse of half musters and stores replied, "What is that to you? Meddle you not with that."

Mr. Love said that the man that offered to give this information was in a manner a dead man and not likely to live two days, and yet he did protest, as he did expect mercy, that being clerk to Batten did know that they gave in a list of 3,000 when they had not above 2,000 and that he could say more, but for fear of the money and pay that was behind should be taken from him.

He said that the commanders would give leave to the soldiers to go abroad and then give in a muster of 2,000 when there was not so many, and so the King's forces were weakened and he deluded in his payments.

And that officers would give an account of seamen who ought

[1] *C.J.* IX, 27. MS. omits this date. Milward on the committee for the bill for preventing robbery.

to have but 19s. per mensem to be men of that rank that ought
to have 30s. a month.

Sir William Warren, who undertook to find the King masts
and other necessaries at the rate of £20,000, and to do it within
such a time, delayed the same until the Dutch and we were
engaged, and then he gave in an account of £80,000.

The sick man told them of several persons that could inform
the committee of great abuses and cheats, if they may be secured
to have their pay that is due to them.

The House gave assurance to these persons that do discover
(and make it good) these abuses they should be indemnified
from all that would do them wrong.

Colonel Birch said that seven commissioners were sufficient
and enow to inspect the accounts.

Sir Richard Temple he moved for a few clerks to attend those
commissioners, but no sum was agreed upon for the clerks and
under-officers.

It was once thought that a certain sum should be allowed for
clerks and under-officers for one year. Others moved that the
sum of £20,000 should be allowed the commissioners and officers
for one year, and the commissioners to give an account how the
money was laid out.

The gentlemen that were employed to manage the free conference[1] with the Lords were Mr. Vaughan, Sir Robert Howard,
Sir Thomas Littleton, Mr. Seymour and Mr. Waller; they made
their report of the conference as followeth:

Mr. Swinsen began the report, and reported the first argument
that we used for the commitment of the Earl of Clarendon upon
a general impeachment, which was the usage of the Parliament
in that case for which we gave them precedents, as Lord
Strafford, Archbishop Laud, Chief Justice Finch and Sir George
Ratcliff. And that the Lords had not one precedent that can
make it appear that upon a general impeachment of high treason
against any man by the House of Commons that ever it was
refused to commit such a person upon the demand of the House
of Commons.

[1] Cf. Add. MSS. 22263, ff. 15–16, on conference in the Painted
Chamber.

To this the Lords reply and say that these precedents were in troublesome times and they are not convincing, and the precedent of the Earl of Strafford was so much abhorred that that proceeding against him was made unexemplary, and wholly reversed by an act of Parliament.

And they allege the precedents of Michael de la Pole, who was impeached of treason but was not committed, because no special charge was brought up against him.

To this we answer that Michael de la Pole was not committed, and the reason was because he was not impeached by the Commons; but he hearing of a general accusation and a common fame of his miscarriages desired of his own accord to be brought to his trial.

Lord Holles said that the act had made null the impeachment of the Earl of Strafford and all the whole proceedings of that trial, because all that belonged to that attainder was discharged by that act.

Lord Anglesey also said that these precedents were new, and that new precedents were not so binding and authentic as those that were more ancient.

To which we replied that new precedents were most forcible and binding, especially where there were no old ones to cross (or to be produced against) them.

The Lords insisted upon it that those precedents were in evil times. And this committing Lord Clarendon was against the Petition of Right and the law of the land.

Then Mr. Vaughan proceeded in the report and replied to the Lords that by the Petition of Right no man ought to be committed to prison without a special charge brought against him, that so he might know whereof he was accused and imprisoned, and so might be brought to his trial. But the ground, saith Mr. Vaughan, of this Petition of Right was this: where the King by his own command or Privy Council shall commit a man there the judges cannot bail him, but if he procure his *habeas corpus* and his trial delayed, there the judge may bail him, but also may at any time remand him to prison again.

The Lords notwithstanding insist still upon a special charge, but withal say it shall be sufficient without any proofs.

To which we answered that if the Lords might commit him without bringing any proofs against him of the treason, they might with equal justice commit him without any special matter of charge.

The Lords once more alleged that these new precedent[s] were not to be insisted upon, because they were precedents of bad and turbulent times.

To which we again replied that if laws made in those bad and turbulent times were and are still retained and received why may not the same be still executed and the precedents of the same times allowed.

The judgment and proceedings of all inferior courts were allowed and their sentences and rules binding, and why then may not the judgments and proceedings of the Parliament, being the highest court, be also in force and justified.

In the wars in the Low Countries the laws were always in force and duly executed.

The Lords brought a second precedent of the Spencer in the 14th of Edward III, who being impeached, his commitment was demanded; to which the King replied that it ought not to be done, because there was no special charge brought against him.

To this we answered that the charge against Spencer was not an impeachment of the Commons, but a bare allegation only.

The Lords brought a third precedent of the Lord Stanley, against whom when they sent up an impeachment the King did not commit him, but said he would advise of it.

To this we answered first that although the King did not commit him, but said he would advise of it, yet he did not refuse and deny to commit him as the Lords now do.

Secondly, the Lord Stanley's crime was not treason.

Thirdly, this was an act of the King's own immediately, who had an absolute power of himself to bail or imprison him at his own pleasure.

The Lords urged a fourth precedent, of Thomas Arundel, Archbishop of Canterbury in vincesimo of Richard II, who was not committed but impeached.

We answer that he was not impeached of treason, but for granting a commission from the King, whereby divers miscarriages in government were committed in the kingdom, whereupon the King sent to Judge Belknap and some other judges, and straitly charged them to answer him truly whether the granting such a commission was treason or not. The judges said it was treason, but yet that treason could not be charged upon the Archbishop, because the judges' opinions were not published until after his impeachment, and therefore at the time of his impeachment he ought not to be committed.

The Lords notwithstanding would not be satisfied, but said they could not consent to his commitment without a special charge, because the House in this their demand did break in upon their judicial power, and that the Commons would be equal judges with them and of this they were very tender to preserve entire.

We replied that we were so far from lessening their power that we were most careful to preserve it, and not in the least to encroach or break in upon it.

The Lords further objected that the Commons took upon them to judge of treason, which they themselves have not power to do.

We answered, if justices of peace have both knowledge and power to judge of yea and to commit a Peer of the Realm for treason out of the session of Parliament, and that every one of the King's subjects ought to know what is treason that so he might avoid the committing it, how much less can it be imagined that the House of Commons, being such a convention of all sorts of able men, should be ignorant in point of treason, nor can that assertion or argument be made good that because the House of Lords have power to judge of treason and to condemn it therefore the House of Commons ought not to take cognisance of treason.

Here the Lords moved (that in regard the conference had held long) to put it off until another day.

We answered that we had not much more to say nor did we believe that their Lordships could add to that which they had been pleased already to allege, and therefore we desired their

Lordships to go on and make an end of the conference at this time.

The Lords very much pressed the necessity of specifying the treason that so the party impeached might be acquainted with it in order to make his defence.

We answered that there were many inconveniences that might follow if the treason were specified; it gave the party impeached occasion and opportunity to flee, and it gave opportunity to all others concerned in the treason to make their escape from justice.

And that neither their Lordships nor the party impeached could be better instructed by specifying the treason without proofs than already they are by the general impeachment.

There was an instance of a man that had a patent granted under the Great Seal and that had fastened a blank parchment to it, labels and every way made fit so cunningly that it could not be discerned. Afterwards he could separate the blank parchment from the other and keep the Great Seal to it and then write in the blank parchment what would serve his turn and had the Great Seal to it to justify it. For this he was impeached of treason and committed, and yet when he came to his trial this did not prove treason; so that then if a man may be committed upon an impeachment of treason when indeed it is not treason, much more may a man be committed upon an impeachment of treason when indeed it is treason, without a special charge.

As for Lord Finch, though he was gone away out of the kingdom, yet upon his impeachment he was censured to be committed.

But most certain it is, if upon an impeachment the treason should always be specified and published, it were the most probable way and means to render the Commons incapable of doing the King and people service in prosecuting and punishing such heinous crimes and great offences.

The Lords further replied that there could be no inconvenience in publishing that to them which was made known to four hundred men in the House of Commons.

We answered that the House of Commons might proceed with what secrecy or openness they thought fit or saw cause, and the Lords were not to take any notice of it.

To this the Lords made no reply.

In the time of no Parliament abuses criminal may be brought to the Council, but in time of Parliament sitting they are most proper to be brought to it.

Then Sir Robert Howard proceeded in the report.

The Lords said that the Commons ought to take care of the liberty of the subject, since they took upon them to be the principal lookers to at that liberty.

They said that Archbishop Laud was committed upon a general impeachment and was kept in prison many years, which was contrary to the liberty of the subject.

We answered that he lay no longer in prison upon his general impeachment than he should have done if the crime had been specified; it was the great troubles of the kingdom that caused that delay in his proceedings.

Then Mr. Waller he proceeded in the report, and said that the Lords asked whether the Commons did not conceive that their Lordships' consciences were not concerned in making an unjust commitment of any person.

We answered that it did not concern their Lordships' consciences at all, for the Commons impeached and demanded the Lord Clarendon's commitment, and if the Commons failed in their proofs the guilt lay at their door and their Lordships were clear.

Lord Ashley said if the Commons had been required to have given a special treason against the Earl of Strafford they could not have done it, and so the business would have been laid aside.

We answered it was very true no single act of treason could have been laid to his charge, but it was an accumulation of many crimes, and so in the impeachment no crime could be specified, and yet he was committed upon the impeachment; but in this against the Earl of Clarendon a particular treason is brought to the House, and good assurance given to the House that it will be proved and made good against him.

The Lords said that when the five members were impeached the House of Commons thought it not sufficient to impeach them only, but that proofs also ought to be brought against them, and this was in the face of war and rebellion.

The Bishop of Rochester cited a case in Judge Cooke, where he saith that no man ought to be committed but upon especial matter.

To which we answered that by special matter the Judge means that no man ought to be committed but for felony or treason.

The Lords replied that if a Peer may be committed upon a general impeachment the Commons may impeach all the Lords one by one, and so take them all away or leave the House very thin.

We answered that the Lords had no reason to suspect the Commons of any such injustice and miscarriage towards them, and especially the bishops, for they were so far from thinning their House that they were the only (or chief) means at the least to bring and restore them to the House when the Lords endeavoured to keep them out.

We acknowledge the Lords to have the chief power of judicature and therefore have no thoughts to thin their House or to weaken their power but to keep it as strong and entire as we can.

Then the Lords told us that it was a favour to give us this free conference, it being in their power to have denied it, and that in yielding to it they had gone from their privilege which they might justly have stood upon.

We answered that they received no disadvantage by it; the disadvantage, if any, fell upon us, for we had given their Lordships our reasons in papers which they had consulted and came prepared to the conference to debate them; but we had no other reason from them but their positive resolution that they would not commit the Earl without special matter, and so we came to the conference without any preparation at all, but such only as our own reasons and the justice of the cause did arm us with.

DECEMBER 2ND. This day Mr. Wood's[1] bill was read the second time to enable him to sell lands, which were formerly appointed to be sold by deed, which deed was lost, though the counterpart be in being; and Wood himself being dead, the bill is brought in to enable the present heir to make good that former sale.

[1] *C.J.* IX, 28. Mr Wood not mentioned. Grey and Cobbett are brief for this date. See p. 154, n. 2 below.

Also Mr. Paston's bill was read to enable the enclosing some commons in the manor of Hopton in Gloucestershire for the increase of timber.

A petition was brought in by Colonel Sandys which had discovered that Mr. Blackwell and others had received the sum of £40,000 whereof the King had been defrauded. Sir John Ashburnham to clear or rather to excuse this affirmeth that £28,000 of this came at one time into the King's Exchequer, and afterwards as much more as to make it £50,000, but upon examination it proved that the King had not received above £80,000, and the Colonel affirmeth that this informer had never had one farthing of recompense.

The Lords sent a message by two judges in their robes, Sir William Wild and Judge Archer, viz: that upon the debate of the late free conference they were not satisfied with our reasons, therefore could not agree with us to commit the Earl of Clarendon without a special charge of treason.

The Lord Torrington moved the House not to depart from any of these just privileges; Sir Robert Howard declaring the substance of the conference moved that we should adhere to our privileges, for, said he, the Lords of the Privy Council have power to commit any man that shall be brought before them upon a bare information: and then much more may the Lords sitting in Parliament, being the highest Council, do it.

Mr. Waller told us that he did observe how readily the Lords did oppose and contradict what power the Commons did propose or offer to them.

First in the former case of the militia, which is a great charge to the people, the Lords did exempt themselves from joining with the Commons in that charge, and would charge themselves, and not be charged after the ancient way by the lieutenancy.

Secondly in the Lord Mordaunt's case they would not suffer him to be tried at the Bar, at the demand of the Commons, but did assume the sole power of judicature to try him where they please.

Thirdly they denied the Commons a free conference at their request, until it was their own pleasure to give it.

If the Lords have power at their pleasure to deny anything

that we require *in ordine judiciali* we cannot be in hope or
expectation to obtain any desires or requests from them, let
them be never so just or necessary.

And therefore we have no reason to agree with them, because
we have no hopes to give them satisfaction.

Mr. Vaughan did affirm that the Lords did not want sufficient
reason from them at the conference, nor did those reasons
want true grounds to justify them, to have persuaded them to
have agreed with us, but they were absolutely resolved not to
do it. When we gave them precedents they said they had the
law on their side against them, but they never produced that
law that made against the precedents.

Mr. Vaughan said they used the law as a sword in a lady's
hand: it was a law indeed, but when they came to use it there
was no hand to guide it.

They insist much upon Magna Charta, which saith that no
man shall be condemned or tried but by his peers and the laws
of England, nor shall any man be imprisoned but by due process
of the law.

Mr. Vaughan answered that there are divers cases in which
a man may be imprisoned which are not with the Great Charter.

1. First the Crown or prerogative law, which differs from
common proceedings.

2. Secondly the law of the Parliament, by which it hath
power to imprison its own members without process.

3. Thirdly the common law to inflict and enjoin penance.

4. Fourthly the law of admiralty.

5. Fifthly the law of merchants.

6. The law of arms.[1]

All these have power to imprison men upon bare accusations without legal process or special charge or indictment
and are not comprised within Magna Charta.

If a man receive the King's money to serve him and afterwards he refuses to serve he is to be imprisoned without any
legal process.

Also by a writ *de excommunicato capiendo* a man may be
imprisoned.

[1] *Proceedings*, p. 84, gives also Forest Law.

And by a writ *ne exeat regnum* a man is bound to find sureties that he depart not the kingdom or else he is to be imprisoned.

If the Parliament have not power to imprison a man without a special charge all privileges of Parliament for imprisoning their members is taken away.

If a man be said to be guilty, or is defamed for treason in general, any man may seize and commit him to custody, or upon hue and cry may apprehend him, and this is a due process in law.

If the Commons in Parliament should accuse and commit any of their members, though the crime be not proved or made good, yet this is not fault in them, nor shall the party imprisoned have any remedy, because the Parliament can do no wrong.

If this impeachment of the Earl of Clarendon be avoided, as it seems the Lords do endeavour it, there is no proceeding to any other, but of necessity must let this fall.

The House of Peers were called anciently the Upper House, and the Peers had that name not as noble men, but as equals to those that they were to try, and in this respect every commoner is tried by his peers as well as a nobleman.

The judicial power of the Lords ariseth from the Commons, who bring the accusation or impeachment of any man before them.

And the Lords are but triers of the fact and party; the judge that pronounceth sentence and judgment is the High Steward whom the King appoints at that time; and therefore their jurisdiction and judicial power is not so great as they pretend to.

After all this long discourse and debate in the House it was moved that a committee should be appointed to draw up a protestation against the proceedings of the Lords and their invading the privileges of the Commons, to the danger of the kingdom. This was done accordingly, and this it was:

"Resolved, that the Lords not having complied with the desires of the Commons for the commitment of the Earl of Clarendon upon the impeachment of treason is an obstruction of the public justice of the kingdom in the proceedings of both Houses of Parliament, and that the precedent is of evil and dangerous consequences."

DECEMBER 3RD. This day Sir John Morton brought in a petition against the exportation of leather, which was rejected by the House.

Whereupon it was moved that no printed papers of any kind should be licensed to be printed and delivered to the members at the Parliament door, as was too frequently done. The House was divided upon the question, viz: whether papers should be prohibited to be printed or not; the ayes that went out lost it [by] 20 voices, of which I was one.

Mrs. Stonehouse petitioned the House against the Earl of Clarendon for cheating and violently getting a lease from her of the Bishop of Winchester when she had a right to it.[1] Although the Lord Cornbury spoke in defence and justification of the business on his father's part, and affirming that he had the tenant right from Bryce, yet it was affirmed that that tenant right was gotten from Lenthall by imprisoning him (who had Bryce his tithe) and charging him with treason, and threatening to hang him if he did not yield up his right and title to him, and after he had thus forced him to yield the same, he was set at liberty and so the Earl got the lease from them all.

The bill for general naturalisation was brought in and read and well debated; some commended it to be an excellent bill and that it would fill the kingdom full of people (of which some said there was a want), which would raise the price of land. Others spoke against it, and said it would prove dangerous to the government established in the Church by bringing in sectaries and men of all judgments, and it was designed, as some think, to usher in a toleration of all religions.

Whilst this was in debate the Lords sent two judges, Judge Twisden and Judge Brown, with a message that they had received a large letter or paper from the Earl of Clarendon which acquainted them that he had withdrawn himself.

[1] *C.J.* IX, 74, clears up the intricacies of the Stonehouse Lenthall case. The manor of Witney, like Caron House, had been one of Clarendon's post-restoration acquisitions, and had been let by him to a Mr Granger (Lister, II, 538 ff.). Lenthall, who was the son of the Speaker and nephew of the Warden of the King's Bench prison, was a thoroughly bad character, and here evidently was running true to form and attempting a double cheat upon his wife's family and upon Clarendon.

The House immediately voted that an address should be made to the King humbly to pray him speedily to give order to all ports to stop him.[1] The address was to be sent by Lord Fitzharding, Mr. Controller and Secretary Morice.

The House voted that a declaration should be drawn up by a committee to be chosen for the same to show all the proceedings against the Earl of Clarendon, in order to bring him to a legal trial, and so to give satisfaction of their fidelity both to King and people.

DECEMBER 4TH. This day Mr. Palmes his bill was brought in engrossed and read for the selling some lands in Derbyshire, Nottinghamshire and for the preserving lands in Yorkshire at better yearly value which he had power to sell; this bill was this day passed.

Lord Fitzharding reported to the House that the King graciously accepted our address in stopping the ports, in order to seizing the Lord Clarendon, and that he would immediately send orders to the several ports.

The bill for a general naturalisation was debated as that it would make the land populous, which would be a great help to making land dear; others spoke as much against it, and the main objection that I and many more did urge is that it may prove dangerous to the government established in the Church and so scandalise our religion; and it is much suspected that this bill is brought in by the Presbyterians and sectaries to usher in a toleration.

Mr. Solicitor made an excellent speech and showed that the best and only way to make a kingdom flourish and to receive the benefit of foreigners that shall come in and plant among us is first to settle a peaceable government in the nation; for who will come and plant themselves and live in a disordered government and discontented people? And as for our religion and church government established, our act of uniformity reacheth neither the French nor Dutch that dwell amongst us.

When the debate was ready for the question the Lords sent down a message by two of the judges, Twisden and Tyrrell,

---

[1] Cf. *Proceedings*, p. 98, where Tomkins makes this motion.

to desire a conference about the Earl of Clarendon's letter or paper.[1]

At the conference the Lords delivered to us a copy of the paper, which was publicly read in the House; it consisted of two heads:

First that he was accused of too hastily getting a vast estate.

Secondly that he had been the only and chief minister of state and that the government had been ill managed by him.

To the first he protested his integrity, that he had not taken any bribes to the value of £5, or one shilling; that he had not sold any places but such as he might lawfully sell, as the Lord Keeper Elsmore and Coventry had done before him.

That he had served the King thirty years, and that the greatest part of his estate was that that the King had graciously given him; that he never had a farthing of any foreign prince or state, but only for the books and papers of the Louvre.

For the second, his acting as chief minister of state, he said that he did nothing but what was beforehand debated at the Council, and that after Secretary Nicholas was put out of that place and others put in he saith that he acted very little, and that his credit was blasted, and that the counsel of some unworthy loose persons was followed and embraced to lay him aside.

When the letter had been read in the House it was voted to be a seditious and scandalous libel with some other expressions that it should be burnt by the common hangman.

DECEMBER 5TH.   This day[2] the bill for enclosing the 40 acres for the pest-house at Cambridge was brought in engrossed, and should have been read, but was spoken against by Sir Robert Holt and Colonel Sandys, who affirmed that they had a petition under the hands of many commoners who have right to the common there, whose right will be taken from them if those 40 acres be enclosed.

---

[1] See Bibliography above for Clarendon's Petition.

[2] *C.J.* IX, 32. MS. omits date here. On the woodmongers see *C.S.P.D.* 1667, p. 68, 8 December 1667. On the debate on the Lords' behaviour see a speech by Holland in Appendix I, and Grey, p. 61; *Proceedings*, p. 116 f., etc.

It was therefore put off at that time and not read, and referred to be debated at the Bar by counsel on both parties.

Sir John Knight's bill for naturalising ships taken in the war was spoken against and put off at that time.

Then the House entered upon a debate of sending up that Earl of Clarendon paper that came from the Lords, and whether the vote that was passed for burning it by the common hangman should be sent up with it.

Some were of opinion that it had been more prudence not to have passed that vote; they said it was [not] fit it should be sent up to the Lords.

It was resolved that a copy of the paper should be taken and examined to be a true copy, and then to send both the vote and paper up to the Lords to-morrow morning.

Mr. Vaughan brought in two votes to be offered to the Lords from the Commons.

The first was that when any subject shall be impeached of treason in general by the Commons, and the impeachment sent up to the Lords sitting in Parliament, and with demand to have him secured, that the person so impeached shall forthwith be secured, both for the safety of the King and kingdom.

Secondly that when such person is secured the Lords may limit a convenient time for the Commons to bring in his particular charge, to avoid all unnecessary and undue delay of justice.

It was very much debated whether these two votes should be sent up to the Lords before the declaration was drawn up and perfected that was formerly agreed on.

Mr. Swinsen was of the opinion that these votes for the present should be respited, being the Earl being fled justifies our proceedings and is very much to our advantage, for if the Lords would not commit the Earl upon our impeachment, by what reason have they to send a bill to us for his banishment, not having any more of special matter to banish him than they had to secure him upon the impeachment, and therefore he moves that these two bills should be laid aside and the whole matter left as it was.

Sir Robert Howard was for the sending up the two votes,

but withal first to perfect the declaration for justifying our proceedings, and then to send up the votes, and though the Lords do agree with us yet to justify and publish the declaration to all the world.

Sir Richard Temple was against the sending up the votes, but to go on with the declaration, and at that time to make it appear to the world that the Lords' delaying to imprison the Earl gave him the opportunity to make his escape, and then humbly to pray His Majesty to send out his proclamation to apprehend him as one that flees from justice, and then to send up the votes.

Sir Thomas Lee was against the declaration, for, saith he, it may beget a reply from the Lords, and then another reply from us and so to remonstrances without end.

Sir Thomas Littleton was against the sending up the votes, because if the Lords should quarrel and not agree to them it may obstruct the proceedings by bill of attainder.

This debate held a long time. I went out, because I would not give my vote in it, for though I approve of the votes, yet I am against the sending them up at this time. In conclusion it was resolved that the votes should be entered into the Journal, but that the time should be respited for sending them up.

DECEMBER 6TH.   This day[1] the Yarmouth bill was read, which informed by the inhabitants that their pier was very much out of repair and that it would cost more to repair it than they were able to lay out, that they were much impoverished, and they therefore did petition the House that they may be authorised to lay a tax on all such goods as shall be imported thither, at so much per ton, except provisions for fishing.

The Speaker left the Chair and the House went into a Grand Committee to debate the settlement of trade.

Sir Robert Atkins was called to the Chair in Mr. Seymour's absence, and first they began with the settlement of the trade between England and Scotland.

It was moved as a good way to settle a common and free trade betwixt England and Scotland to choose commissioners

---

[1] Grey omits 6, 7, 9, 10 December.

and to put it to them, these commissioners being chosen by the two Parliaments of England and Scotland; to give them power to treat and conclude this settlement; and that what shall be concluded by the commissioners should continue in force until the end of the next session of Parliament, if it stand with the consent of the King.

Some are against giving power to commissioners to conclude, as it was settled primo of James, for then the Scots had liberty by that act to trade in our plantations.

The strength of this debate was whether we should delegate an absolute power to commissioners to conclude and so put the whole power out of Parliament.

I did not stay out this debate.

The Speaker took the Chair again, and the House sent up Sir Robert Howard to the Lords to desire a conference, which the Lords immediately granted. We sent up the Lord Clarendon's letter and with it our vote to burn it by the hangman.

DECEMBER 7TH.   This day[1] the bill was read for the enclosing 500 acres of common near unto Wakefield which was formerly Sir Gervas Clifton's; he with the consent of the freeholders and commoners thereto belonging made a division by consent, and the 500 acres which belonged to Sir Gervas he did enclose, and so might all the rest enclose that which did belong to them when they pleased. Sir Gervas having enclosed these 500 acres, the wars then falling out and Sir Gervas for his loyalty being sequestered, the rude people threw open the enclosure and laid it to the common again.

These 500 acres Sir Gervas sold to Sir Christopher Chapman, who by petition brings in his bill to pray the House that he may be empowered to enclose it again, and he will allow an eighth per annum to the vicar or Rector of Wakefield.

The Yarmouth bill was read and after much debate both for and against it it was committed.

The House received Mr. Crouch his report from the committee for inspecting the grievances and abuses of the collectors or

---

[1] *C.J.* IX, 33. MS. omits the date, and also the long report on hearth money. Cobbett omits the 7th.

farmers of the hearth money. He reported 16 or 17 several grievances, which when they are particularly examined it is moved that a bill be brought in to explain the act, that so all abuses may be prevented for the future.

DECEMBER 9TH. This day[1] the Cambridge bill for enclosure of 40 acres of common of Coldham, to be laid to the pest-house, was reported and debated, and counsel heard at the Bar for both sides.

Sir William Scroggs with others for the defendants against the bill opened the case, and his plea was that there were two commons and two manors, viz: Coldham and Barnwell. Coldham belonged to Jesus College and Barnwell belonged to the town of Barnwell, but neither of the commons to the town and University of Cambridge, nor could the town or corporation of Cambridge lay any claim to it as lords of the soil. Mr. Winnington, who is of counsel for the plaintiffs, saith that the King granted these commons to certain freeholders, and that this of Coldham is no manor, and that neither Jesus College nor Mr. Butler, who is, they say, the only man that obstructs this enclosure, and a few other inconsiderable persons that lay claim, have any right to the common as it is a manor, but only are against the enclosure to hinder the benefit of the public and other good uses.

Sir William Scroggs replies and saith that it is not Jesus College only and Mr. Butler, but above twenty freeholders that oppose the enclosure and this bill.

Mr. Winnington pleaded that no man ought to obstruct the taking in of those acres but those that have right of common there, but many that oppose this bill and enclosure have no right of common there.

He also pleaded that in point of law a Lord of the Manor may enclose a common, so that he lay out sufficient of common to satisfy the freeholders and all other interests. And that the owner of a large waste, though he be not Lord of a Manor, may do the like.

Sir William Scroggs pleaded that the common of Coldham,

---

[1] *C.J.* IX, 34. MS. omits the date again.

out of which they would enclose these 40 acres, was in all but 80, so that there was not sufficient of common left to the freeholders and commoners. And besides, if they should enclose those 40 acres it would wholly exclude and hinder the inhabitants of Barnwell from driving their cattle to any other common, their usual and direct way lying through Coldham Common.

Mr. Winnington answered that there are two commons, viz; Coldham, which is eightscore acres, and Barnwell, which is 600 acres; that they deny to enclose any of the 80 acres but they claim a right to the eightscore acres.

Sir William Scroggs produced a witness who affirmed that the common of Coldham was not eightscore acres, but only fourscore.

And a second witness that affirmed that it was but 80.

And a third witness that affirmed that Barnwell only had right of common in Coldham.

Mr. Winnington replied that Barnwell hath right of common both in Coldham and Barnwell, and that the town and corporation of Cambridge have right of common in Coldham.

It was said that Jesus College hath right of common in Coldham but not in Barnwell, and that their horses and cattle have been impounded out of the common of Barnwell. The plaintiffs' counsel failed much in their proofs, and so it was cast out by vote.

Then came on Chief Justice Keeling's charge and accusation, which consisted of these three heads:

1. First for his severity to the jury in Old Bailey.
2. For his severity to the jury in Somersetshire.
3. For his severity in Cornwall.

First his charge for his severity to the jury in Old Bailey was this: certain Quakers found at a conventicle who had been twice imprisoned for the like offences and now they were found together again at the usual meeting place, and being asked what they did there they answered, "To seek God in the spirit," but notwithstanding these circumstances the jury would not find them guilty, because they had not full proof that there was not any religious worship performed. He not approving their verdict caused them to go forth again, and told them the evidence was plain and therefore they ought to find them guilty. The jury would not alter from their verdict, and therefore he imprisoned and fined some of them one hundred marks apiece, which fine some of them paid.

Sir William Wild moved him to delay the fine and again to try if they would be wrought upon to alter their judgments; he answered that he would make them know themselves, and said they were peremptory saucy fellows.

The next thing charged upon him was a business in Cornwall: a man was arraigned for killing a boy; this was the head man to a weaver. The master in his shop gave him power to oversee the rest and correct them if they neglected their work. This boy had neglected to wind some spindles of yarn, and therefore this man beat him about the head with a broomstaff, of which he died within a day or two. The jury found this manslaughter, and because they did not find it murder nor would be persuaded to alter their verdict he told that if they would not go out again and find murder he would fine them £2 a man. The jury for fear went out again and found it murder and the man was hanged.

The third thing laid to his charge was this: there happened a fray in which one man was slain; it was proved that the man that killed him was set upon and so did it in his own defence, and thereupon the jury found it *se defendendo*. The judge would not take this verdict, but caused them to go out again, but still they brought in the same verdict. He caused them to go out again, and threatened them to fine them if they brought in the same verdict; they being fearful brought it in manslaughter.

The King sent in a paper by Secretary Morice that it was his pleasure the Parliament should adjourn the 17th of December until the beginning of February.

DECEMBER 10TH. This day the Irish bill was read for preventing the importation of foreign cattle, and so it was, that they that have formerly brought in any such until such a day shall be indemnified, but if any bring in any after that day, they shall be forfeited and the vessels which brought them over.

Sir Robert Brooke brought in a bill from two or three adventurers and purchasers of the Irish rebels' lands in the name of the rest of the adventurers.[1]

Sir Heneage Finch spoke against the petition, as a thing most unjust and of very ill consequence. He said there were already a settlement of that business in Ireland and to recall it or ravel into or undo that settlement might endanger the King's revenue already established by quit-rents, which are to the value of £70,000, and likewise to unsettle the Duke of York's estate, which was out of the lands of the rebels and regicides there, which are to the yearly value of £10,000, and also to endanger the quiet possession of the loyal soldiers and their right which they had for their faithful service to the King; and lastly it was the most likely way to gratify the Papists, which look for a disturbance there.

And whereas these adventurers claim the benefit of the two statutes of the 17th and 18th of Charles I, he asserted that the conditions upon which these two statutes were grounded were never performed.

Colonel Massey affirmed that not the twentieth man of the adventurers was acquainted with (and assenting to) the petition, but that a few persons of their own heads brought in this petition. This Sir Robert Atkins said ought to be enquired into, and if it proved to be true then to punish the offenders severely for such impudency.

Sir Edward Walpole moved to lay this petition aside, that came in so unjustly in the name of all the adventurers, and these persons that do personally appear, if they have any just cause to be relieved in their particular interests, that they may make it appear in their addresses to the House.

The report of hearth money was brought in this day, and the grievances and abuses reported by the committee; the House agreed with the committee.

It was resolved that smiths' forges are not to pay; and that

---

[1] Barker's petition has already been noticed above, p. 105, n. 1. The adventurers in Irish lands, in spite of very preferential treatment in the Act of 1662, remained dissatisfied and fought every concession made by the Commissioners appointed under that Act to the so-called innocent Irish.

order be taken and due punishment inflicted on all those collectors that have unjustly and vexatiously served persons (even hundreds) into the Exchequer, notwithstanding that they have paid their due hearth money and have acquittances to show for their discharge. Also all such as are in such a capacity by reason of poverty are not to pay hearth money.

The Lords sent us two messages.

One was a bill to enable Lord Clare to sell land for the payment of debts and to raise daughters' portions.

Also that they did agree with our vote to burn Lord Clarendon's paper, and that it should be burned at the Exchange at Gresham College by the hangman on Thursday next in full Exchange.

The second message was that they consent to a conference as we desired concerning an act against calling in question the members of our House by any inferior court after the end of the Parliament for words spoken in Parliament.

DECEMBER 11TH. This day the Lord Clare's bill should have been read, but was put off by bringing in Fitton's petition.[1]

Sir John Knight moved for the naturalising of the prize ships and the bill was read the first time.

The petition of indigent officers was read and a committee was ordered to examine Sir John Bennet, who was treasurer for that money, and Mr. John Cooper, of what money they had received of the £60,000 and when they received it, and how much of it they had paid and to whom and when.

The Lord Chief Justice his business was reported by the Chairman of that committee, Mr. Crouch.

In the business that related to Somersetshire Sir Hugh Windham declared his proceedings to be very illegal, both against himself and others; he being returned on the Grand Jury and finding a bill according to its best proofs, and because it did not agree with his Lordship's sense, and they would not alter their opinions upon his will, he fined them £20 a man, and told Sir Hugh that he was the head of a party. Sir Hugh told him he was a member of the House of Commons and the King's servant, and therefore claimed his privilege; the Chief

[1] Cf. Grey, pp. 61 ff. Grey identifies the reporter of the Magna Farta incident as Gower.

Justice told him that he would make him know that he was now his servant and that he would make him stoop.

Then was reported the business in Devonshire, that of the weaver's man for killing the prentice boy: the petty jury found it but manslaughter, but he threatening them made them go out and find it murder, whereupon they went out again and brought it in murder and the man was hanged, although Sir Thomas Clifford and other gentlemen earnestly moved for a reprieve.

This rigour and miscarriage of his both to Grand and Petty Jury hath so much discouraged the gentlemen that they are resolved to stand and submit to any fine rather than that they will serve upon any future juries if he be judge at that circuit.

Also it was reported that a certain man claiming the privilege of Magna Charta, he called it Magna Farta.

The Chairman in the end reported the sense of the committee, which was that these proceedings of the Chief Justice were extra-judicial, and that he used an illegal and arbitrary power, that he slighted Magna Charta and therefore that he should be speedily brought to his answer, and if it be made good against him to receive condign punishment.

The Lords sent us a bill for setting the prices of wine and for the preventing the blending and adulterating wine and other abuses in the selling of their wines.

Sir Thomas Higgins made an excellent speech in the defence of the Chief Justice. That although his passions might lead him a little out of the way sometimes, yet he was a very good and just judge, and had done nothing against the law.

Mr. Streete and some others moved that before the House proceeded to an impeachment of the Chief Justice, that he might be heard to make his defence at the Bar, whereupon it was ordered that he should be heard at the Bar in the House of Commons on Friday next.

The Lords sent in the bill for banishment of the Earl of Clarendon.

DECEMBER 12TH.   This day it was ordered that the surveyors-general shall give in an exact [account] of all the King's lands, fee, farm and chief rents both in England and Ireland, and how they have been alienated and since March the 25th in 1640, and to whom and for what; and also to give an account of the forfeited rebels' lands, to whom they have been granted, for what term and for what.

Mr. Jolly brought in Mr. Fitton's petition against the Lord Gerrard, to pray the House for his enlargement out of prison, having been committed by the Lords of the Council for saying that the Lord Gerrard had suborned a witness, one Granger, to swear that the deed that Mr. Fitton produced was a counterfeit deed, by which testimony Lord Gerrard recovered Sir Edward Fitton's estate from this Mr. Fitton. There was a long debate about this petition and many speeches made both for and against it, but in conclusion it was voted to be committed.

The Lords sent down a message to us that they did agree with our vote for the freedom of speech in the Parliament.

Sir Robert Howard moved that Simmons, who conveyed away the Lord Clarendon, should be sent for into custody; they say he doth belong to an office in the custom house, to manage his ketch[1] and vessels.

Sir George Downing made his report from the committee for transporting leather and hides out of England.

Sir Charles Harbord made his report of the twenty commissioners' names[2] selected by the committee that were to be employed in the taking account of the kingdom's moneys raised for the carrying on the war; the panel was very much disliked (and very justly) because many villains and enemies to the late King were nominated, especially Colonel King and Major Wildman. It was ordered that a new list of names should be brought in, and nine of them to be a committee and five of the quorum, but before this was resolved I went out of the House.

DECEMBER 13TH. This day a bill was brought in for the naturalisation of certain persons born beyond sea, which was read and committed.

The additional or explanatory bill for the preventing of the importation of foreign cattle was brought in and read; it consisted of these heads:

[1] MS. has Calsh.
[2] *C.J.* IX, 36; Marvell, *Letters*, p. 63.

1. First that all those that have formerly abused the former made act by any underhand buying and selling such cattle shall be called to an account for it.

2. Secondly that the ship or vessel that brings in any cattle prohibited after such a day in February next shall be seized on and forfeited, and all the cattle shall also be seized and brought in and sold in the public market, and so to be seized in all markets where such cattle shall be found. He that seizeth them shall have one half and the poor of the parish where they shall be seized shall have the other half.

This extends to the seizing both of cattle, beef and sheep and pork.

The bill for the banishment of the Earl of Clarendon was read; it runs thus: "Whereas the Earl of Clarendon is fled upon his impeachment of treason by the House of Commons, it is that he shall be for ever banished this kingdom of England, and all other His Majesty's dominions; that he shall be uncapable of any place of honour, trust or employment; that if he return into England or into any other place of His Majesty's dominions he shall be prosecuted as a traitor. That he shall not be capable of pardon, without an act of Parliament, and that if any person shall have correspondence with him (except his own children and by licence from the Council) they shall be proceeded against as persons that hold correspondence with a traitor."[1]

The bill was generally disliked by the whole House.

Sir Robert Holt in his speech justly reflected upon the Lords for their refusing to commit him upon his impeachment, and now without any conference with us, or having any other special matter for it, have sent us in a bill for his banishment, upon his flight to avoid that impeachment.

Lord Cavendish spoke very well, and said that this bill was in favour to him, for he being fled to avoid his trial and the hand of justice should now go away with that large estate and consume it in a foreign country, which he had unjustly got from us here.

It was ordered that an humble address be made to the King

[1] Add. MSS. 22263, f. 23, contains Judge Francis Pemberton's opinion on the legal effects of this Act.

that he will be pleased to send out his proclamation to summon him by such a day in order to his apprehending, that so he might come to his trial, and if he come not in by that day then to proceed to a bill of attainder.

The Lord Chief Justice Keeling came to the Bar; a chair was set for him and [he] was desired to repose himself, but he stood all the time of his speech. When the Speaker had acquainted him wherefore the House had sent for him, viz: to answer to some things charged upon him acted by him in his circuit and seat of justice, he with very great reverence and respect to the House did acknowledge it as a very great favour to him that the House of Commons would give him leave to declare to them his own justification, which he protested to do with all clearness and sincerity, and then wholly to submit himself to the determination and judgment of the honourable House.

First he began with the business of the three Quakers in the Old Bailey. He acknowledged that he fined some of the jury an hundred marks a man, and imprisoned them because they would not find the bill against the Quakers. And the ground of this his proceeding against the jurors he said was this: the jurors pretended that they had not full evidence that they met about any religious act; after that the jury had heard their evidence and stayed long before they came in with their verdict the judge sent to know why they stayed so long, and whether they were not agreed on a verdict; they sent him word they was not, but at last they came in and gave up their verdict not guilty. He asked their reason; they answered that they had not full evidence to prove them guilty. He asked them whether these three men had not been twice convicted before for the same unlawful meeting; they answered yea. He asked them whether these were not the same men and known by the same names; they answered yea. He asked them whether [there] were not above the number allowed by the act; they answered yea. He asked them whether these men were not above the age of sixteen years; they said yea. He asked them whether the place called the "Bull and Mouth" where these persons were taken was not the usual place where Quakers met; they said yea. He asked them whether this meeting was not on a Sunday, when these should have been at the church at the public worship of God; they answered yea. He asked them whether they did believe these persons were at a religious service, since it appeared by the Quakers' own confession that they met to seek God in the spirit; they answered yea. He then asked them why then they did not find the bill, and caused them to go out again, which they did, and after a long stay came in again with the said verdict not guilty, and said they wanted full evidence that they were met at a religious act, whereupon he did fine some of them as aforesaid.

And yet he affirmed that he promised the Quakers that he would not only pardon the offence, but that the other two convictions should be absolutely taken off, if they would repent and come constantly to our church, which they absolutely refused, and said they would not come to our church because it is not a true and lawful church.

In the full of this of the Old Bailey the Chief Justice did say that if he had not thus far proceeded against the Quakers and the jurors he did assure himself that he had not proceeded justly according to the act of Parliament.

As to the slight speaking of the Magna Charta, he affirmed that it being long since he did not remember, nor believe that he said those words, yet he was not absolutely certain that he did not speak them, but it might be possible, Magna Charta being often and ignorantly pressed upon him, that he did utter that indecent expression, but as he doth not remember, neither can it reasonably be imagined that he should speak these words in any dishonour to that great Charter, for it is evidently known to all men his great loyalty to his Sovereign and laws by his suffering for both.

For that case when the jury brought in the bill or verdict *se defendendo*, it was this. Two men fell out, had their swords drawn and were parted, and after a while fell to fighting again. One of them was slain, but because it was said he that killed the other fled to the wall and afterward slew him therefore the jury would not find it murder, and for this he fined them.

A third case was this: a smith struck his prentice with a bar of iron, broke his skull, and the prentice died of the wound

within two or three days. The jury would not find this murder
at the first, whereupon he threatened them and made them go
out again, and told them that they ought to find it murder, which
accordingly they did; and of this the judges in Westminster
Hall gave their opinion that it was murder, for, say they, a parent
may correct a child and a master his servant, but not with a
sword or a bar of iron, nor any other weapon or instrument to
kill them. But although this man was condemned yet because
he was very well spoke of (and for) by his neighbours he procured
his pardon from the King.

The case in Devonshire was this: a weaver having divers
servants and apprentices gave order to a servant and authority
to oversee them and in his absence to correct the younger
prentices if they neglected their work. A prentice boy not
winding his pins appointed to him, but neglecting his work,
this servant beat him about the head with a broomstick, and
(as the Chief Justice affirmed) until the blood gushed out of his
nose, mouth and ears, of which the boy died within two or three
hours.

The jury would find this manslaughter; he caused them to
go out again and bring it in murder, which accordingly they
did, for which the man was condemned and hanged. "And
although I was petitioned," said the Chief Justice, "by Sir
Thomas Clifford for his reprieve, yet I confess I did not grant
it, because I do acknowledge I am very strict and severe against
high-way robbers and in case of blood."

That case in Somersetshire was this: the Grand Jury was of
persons of great [wealth] and quality, as Sir Hugh Windham
and others; they brought in a bill of a man that was killed *per
infortunium*. The Chief Justice told them they ought to bring in
the bill either *billa vera* or else *ignoramus*. "I also told them,"
said he, "they had two kinds of duties or directions to go by;
first, they might make presentments of those things that came in
their own knowledge. Secondly, to examine anything that shall
be brought before them by proofs; and if they find the proofs to
be slight or not material, then to find it *ignoramus*, and if it be
sufficiently proved then to bring it in *billa vera*, and then to
leave it to the trial of the court.

"I also told them that a Grand Jury may judge of matter of fact, but not of point of law; notwithstanding the Grand Jury would not alter, but still brought it in *per infortunium*. I desired them better to consider of it that night, but at the next day they were of the same judgment and told me they were resolved not to alter from it, whereupon I fined some of them £20 a man, bound them to the good behaviour and to appear at the King's Bench Bar the next term.

"Notwithstanding I offered them to withdraw their fine and recognisance for the good behaviour if they would submit, which they refused, and the matter came to an hearing, and the judges with one consent said that I was in the right and had done no more but what was just and lawful.

"Afterwards I caused the clerk of the assize to remit their fines."

Sir Hugh Windham had former affirmed to the House that the Chief Justice had given him some unhandsome passionate speeches, as that he was the head of a faction and that he would make [him] know he was now his servant, all which is believed was very true; but the Chief Justice took no notice of that in his defence, and Sir Hugh very nobly said that since the Chief Justice did forget it, he would also do it and forgave it, which was very much for the Chief Justice's advantage.

He was also charged with denying bail to a prisoner upon *habeas corpus*; to this he answered that he did it in a time of danger, and the person whom it was denied was a dangerous person and had formerly been in rebellion, and although the Act of Oblivion had pardoned his former offences, yet he did not think it safe to suffer a person of such ill principles to go at large in a time so full of danger.

Mr. Scawen would have brought on his son's business against him. The case was thus: Mr. Scawen's son was indicted for stealing a mare and was arraigned before the Chief Justice. The fact was proved, and he found guilty by the jury, and was condemned and the sentence of death given against him. Mr. Scawen the father came to the Chief Justice and entreated him that he would move the King for his pardon, and to inform the King that the evidence against his son was not full; the Chief

Justice told him that he could not well do that, nor to inform the King an untruth, for the evidence (whether true or false) was as full as possibly could be, but notwithstanding he did intercede for him and procured pardon. But old Mr. Scawen thought his son to be falsely accused, and was angry with the judge, and now would have laid some fault to his charge concerning the judgment, although the Chief Justice for anything that appears did nothing but what he ought to do.

When the Chief Justice had made this large declaration and particular defence, no man speaking against him, he said, "Mr. Speaker, I have infirmities sufficient not only to desire grains but greater weights of the charity of this honourable House. I acknowledge I have the failings of a man, but I cannot accuse myself of injustice, bribery or perverting or acting against the known laws, nor do I believe it can by any man be justly laid to my charge, and therefore I humbly crave and hope to obtain the favour and charity of this honourable House upon which I cast myself."

I did attend his narrative with all diligence, and am very confident that he made a very good and sufficient defence to everything charged upon him as to the point of integrity and justice, but without doubt he had failed in point of passion and discretion.

After he was withdrawn it came to a debate of four hours at least; many did aggravate, others did extenuate his failings. In the close the House passed two votes.

1. First that the late proceedings and precedents in fining and imprisoning juries for giving in their verdict was illegal, and that a bill be brought in to prevent the like for the future.

2. Secondly that there shall be no further prosecution or proceedings against the Chief Justice upon this charge.

DECEMBER 14TH. This day the House sent up a bill to the Lords for naturalising certain persons born out of the King's dominions; Lord Richardson carried it up.

And another bill for the exporting of leather by Colonel Birch.

We sent up a vote to the Lords for their concurrence in a petition to the King that he would grant out his proclamation to summon the Earl of Clarendon to come in by such a day to

answer to his impeachment; Lord Cavendish carried it. Lord
Cavendish reported that the Lords received the vote and would
return their answer by their own messengers.

The bill for naturalising prize ships was read.

It was moved to add a proviso to that bill for the tolerating
all ships of any nation to bring in timber for one year in order
for the more speedy rebuilding in London. Very many spoke for
it, as Mr. Henry Coventry and others, as being a means to be
speedier and better supplied with timber and at better rates;
others spoke against it, as Mr. William Coventry and the citizens,
saying that it would be a very great inconvenience to the kingdom, both in the trade of shipping and by carrying away the
money out of the kingdom, nor would it make timber any whit
cheaper to us when we had counted all charges.

The Lords sent down a message to us that they would adjourn
for an hour or two and sit again at four of the clock; we then did
likewise immediately adjourn to the same hour.

When we met we looked that the Lords would have sent some
message to us. I stayed till six of the clock and none came, and
so I went away.

During the time of our adjournment I went to Lambeth and
dined there.

After I left the House at six the House sat until nine, and at
that hour the Lords sent to desire a conference, at which they
gave two reasons why they did not agree with our vote to move
the King to send out his proclamation.

The Lord St. John was ordered to report it on Monday morning.

DECEMBER 16TH. This day Sir Thomas Higgins made his
report from the committee appointed to look into the abuses
of wood and coals.[1] He divided his report into three heads,
viz: wood, ballast, coals.

Concerning wood he said that it was complained that the
woodmongers abused the buyers by the cleaving and notching
billets; a billet that they bought of three notches they would
cleave into three billets and so make nine notches of it.

[1] Cf. Grey, p. 68, where Higgins's report is mentioned, but omitted.

Also that they have refused to buy of gentlemen billets that were made longer and of true size wood, and say it doth hinder and disparage the sale of their smaller sized wood.

It is voted that the selling of billets by notches is deceitful and not fit to be continued.

It was moved at the committee that billets should be sold by weight and measure and not by notches, but this motion would not pass; then it was further moved that billets should be sold by stacks, a billet to be three foot long, and the stack to be eight foot high and four foot broad.

If any woodmonger sell by any less measure he shall forfeit his wood for the first offence, and his wood and five pounds for his second, and for his third offence his wood and £10, half the wood and fine to the informer and half to the poor. And that one justice of the peace may grant out his warrant to seize and dispose of it. And if any man's wood shall be unjustly seized of, he may appeal to the next sessions.

As for faggots, it was voted that they should be of the same size they now are, but whereas they put a short faggot stick, very short and very thick, to make the faggot hold out in the middle, though it be very small at the ends, it is ordered that the faggot still shall be a full foot in length, and but four inches in thickness, to avoid that cheat.

It was ordered that a bill be brought in to settle the measure of faggots and stacks of billets as aforesaid.

The second head of the report was concerning ballast for ships. It was complained of the Trinity House of that company that furnished ships with ballast that the seamen were cheated in the weight of their ballast: whereas they were to have 2,000 weight by the ton they had not above 1,500 ton, and for want of true ballast many ships were in danger and some both ships and men cast away.

Also they complained that they had not their ballast in due time, but with ill language were forced to stay some times and days, in which time it hath so fallen out that the wind hath changed, and so have lost a voyage which otherwise they might have made.

Thirdly they complained that they were abused in the price,

for whereas the usual price was sixpence a ton they now made them pay ninepence.

Fourthly they complained that the lighters were unmarked and so they were furnished with unlawful lighters, which did not hold measure, whereas none but such liters as were marked out to be employed in bringing them their ballast and these lighters ought to be new marked every two years, because the marks are apt to be washed out with rain and weather.

Although these complaints were made, yet the first complainers did not come in to justify their complaints, but they were sufficiently proved by others.

Whereupon it was ordered that the shipmen be speedily supplied with the ballast. And they that buy the ballast may cast it away and dispose of it as they please.

It was complained against the engrossing coals as the only cause of raising the price of coals.

Some moved to set a price of coals at 30s. a chauldron until the 25th of March, alleging that there were no such scarcity of coals to keep them up at so high a price as now they see them.

But in the end this debate and vote ended in nothing, but the resolution and further debate was adjourned.

Carr's fraudulent petition against the Lord Brandon was debated but left unresolved.

The Lord St. John made his report of the two reasons that the Lords gave at the conference why they did not agree with our vote to move the King to send out his proclamation to summon in the Earl Clarendon.[1]

The first was this: they conceive that a proclamation in the way proposed would be ineffectual, since it is not *sub poena convictionis*, which cannot be until there be particulars declared in order to a trial.

Secondly because that which the House of Commons hath proposed and do now propose at present is in a general way of proceeding, but the Lords upon consideration of the whole state of affairs of the kingdom (since the Earl's flight) have upon

---

[1] Grey (p. 68) gives this report by St John before Higgins's report above mentioned, and dates it the 14th. The *Proceedings* mentions the reports on the 16th, and then reports the debate on it.

grounds and prudence and justice thought fit for the security of the kingdom to proceed in a legislative way against the Earl, and have to that end passed and sent down to the Commons a bill for his banishment and incapacitating him, with which this vote is inconsistent.

Upon this report the House adjourned until three of the clock, at what time the House met, and sat until almost ten of the night. After the House adjourned I came not in again that day.

The great debate which held the House so late was first about the two reasons which the Lords gave at the conference, whether they were satisfactory or not.

Mr. Grey told me they were voted satisfactory, but Sir Thomas Osbourne told me that that vote did not pass, which I rather believe, and that it was only put to the vote whether that vote (viz: whether the reasons were satisfactory or not) should be put to the question or not, and it was carried in the negative that that question should not be put.

After a very earnest debate it was put to the question whether the bill sent down from the Lords for the Earl of Clarendon's banishment should be committed or no; it was carried in the affirmative and a committee nominated to consider of it.[1]

DECEMBER 17TH.   This day Carr came to the door and brought in his petition in writing and delivered it to Sir Thomas Tomkins, who presented it to the Speaker, and it was ordered to be read. It agreed with printed paper *verbatim*. It was condemned by most, but notwithstanding it was put to the question whether it should [be] committed to a committee to examine the particulars or to lay it aside.

The House were divided upon it and the noes that were against the committing it went out and carried it; I was one of them.

Secretary Morice acquainted the House that the King intended to adjourn the House this day, but in regard he understood that there were bills ready to be passed he is pleased that the House sit until Thursday for the perfecting those bills. And that it

---

[1] *C.J.* IX, 40, 65–101, Carew and Carr, St John and Howard; 109–55, Talbot and Trevor, Cavendish and Carr.

was his pleasure we should begin with that bill that concerned the settling the trade between England and Scotland and commissioners be chosen both for England and Scotland, and that a place be appointed and approved of by the King, and the treaty to continue for twelve months or to the end of the next session of Parliament, which shall fall out first.

It was moved that it should be stood upon in the treaty that the Scots shall import into England no commodities but those of their own growth and manufacture, but that England may carry into Scotland all commodities whatsoever.

Sir John Knight made his report for naturalising prize ships with the amendments of the bill.

Colonel Birch moved the taking into consideration the settling of trade between Ireland and England, to prevent their carrying their trade to foreign nations; it was therefore ordered at the next meeting of the Parliament to take it into consideration.

The bill for accounts was brought in engrossed and was read; it contains first that there be nine commissioners elected to examine these accounts; that five be of the quorum; that they be authorised to sit three years.

It was ordered that Sir Robert Howard bring in a proviso to-morrow morning for the relief of seamen that have been paid by tickets and have been forced to sell them at under value.

DECEMBER 18TH.[1] It was ordered this day that the militia of the kingdom be taken into consideration in the first place at the next meeting of the Parliament, and an account of the money that hath been raised and received for the discharge of it and how it hath been laid out, and also to consider wherein the militia is defective and how it may be amended.

The amendments of the bill for the trade with Scotland was reported by Sir Thomas Meers and sent up.

The bill of accounts with two provisoes, one for the relief of the seamen that have been paid by tickets, the other to make a false oath in that case perjury, was sent up to the Lords.

The bill for naturalising ships was sent up.

---

[1] The account of this session in the *Proceedings* ends with the debates of 18 December.

The House sent to the Lords that they would sit that afternoon and desired the Lords that they would likewise sit; the Lords sent to us that they would likewise sit that afternoon. We thereupon adjourned and met again at four of the clock, and fell upon the debate of the Earl Clarendon's banishment. The bill was brought in with this proviso, that he render himself by the first of February; some would have it the 10th; and if he come not in by that day then the bill for his banishment to be in force. This displeased some of the members, but it was put to the question whether that proviso being put to the bill should pass. The House was divided upon it; the ayes went out and carried it; I was one.

Sir Job Charlton made his report from the committee to whom the bill for banishing the Earl was committed; some amendments of the bill were agreed to.

But first it was put to the question whether after the word "misdemeanour" in the preamble these words shall be inserted, "and not being committed and secured by the Lords at their desire for the same." It passed in the negative.

Also in the first skin, line the fourth, after the word "himself" these words, "and is fled" be inserted. It was carried in the affirmative.

The bill with the amendments was read the third time.

It was put to the question whether the time of his coming should be enlarged from the 1st of February to the 10th; it was carried in the negative.

Then it was put to the question whether the bill with the amendments should pass; the House was divided upon it. The ayes went out; their tellers were Mr. Cheyney and Sir John Talbot; they were 65. The noes that stayed in, their tellers were Sir Robert Carr and Sir Nicholas Cary; they were 42.[1]

The title of the bill was "An Act for the Banishing and Disabling the Earl Clarendon."

DECEMBER 19TH. This day there was a debate concerning the £60,000 given to the indigent officers; it was ordered that the

---

[1] C.J. IX, 42. The figures agree, but Trevor appears instead of Cheyny.

Speaker send his letters unto the several countries where any of that money is unpaid to find out in whose hands it is, and if present payment be not made of it, then to send down the Serjeant and to take such persons into custody; and if any person that hath any of that money in his hands prove to be poor and not responsible, then to repose that money in the place where it was first laid.[1]

The House took Pett's articles into debate, which are these, upon which he is to be impeached:

First, he having orders from His Highness the Duke of York to draw up the river the *Royal Charles* to secure it, did neglect to do it after ten months' time.

Secondly, he having new orders from the Duke of Albemarle (after the Dutch were come out) to draw it up the river, he still neglected to do it, and never gave any account why he did it not.

Thirdly that the General gave him orders to provide lighters for drawing up the *Royal Charles* into safety, which he also neglected, although several persons offered their assistance to do it.

Fourthly, the General commanded him to sink the *Sancta Mary* in the deep part of the channel to stop the passage of the enemies' ships, which if he had done they could not have come in and fired our ships and done us so great damage as then they did; this he carelessly committed to another to do, who, as it is said, was drunk, and ran the ship aground, and gave the Dutch way to come in and to do us that mischief which they did.

He seems (or his friends for him, of which he hath too many) to excuse by laying the fault on another whom he trusted to sink the ship.

Fifthly, the General gave him order to make ready the boats to attend the ships, but instead of obeying those orders he employed those boats another way, and sent away his own goods in them.

---

[1] Marvell on 19 December (*Letters*, p. 63). Starkey (f. 58) gives gossip of a comprehension bill. *C.J.* IX, 42–3, articles v. Pett. An interesting note of enquiries in committee about Pett is given in S.P.D. 29, CCXXV, no. 42, five pages in Williamson's writing. Pett said that any number of ships would not have saved anything.

Sixthly, he had the General's command to have all the officers and soldiers in readiness, and when the General came to command them of eight hundred men that were in the King's pay there were not in readiness to serve [ten] of them.

Seventhly, the General gave him orders to have picks, spades, shovels and other necessary tools in readiness for service, but only a few shovels he had now prepared of all those when they were to be used.

Eighthly, the General sent to him for good thick oak boards for the service; instead of them he sent a few deal boards, when as it is made good he had good oak boards in store.

The impeachment was voted to be sent up to the Lords.

The title of the impeachment was this: "An Impeachment against Commissioner Pett for many high Crimes and Misdemeanours committed by him."

The Lords sent down three bills, and also they acquainted us that they would sit this afternoon and desired us to do likewise.

We adjourned till three of the clock, and when the House met it took up the debate for coals; as soon as the House was entered into that debate, the Black Rod came and summoned us to attend the King's Commissioners in the House of Lords. The King not coming to the House in person appointed these four Commissioners: Lord Keeper, Duke of Buckingham, Lord Privy Seal and the Duke of Albemarle.

These Commissioners passed five public bills:
1. First the bill for accounts.
2. Secondly the bill for assignments in the Exchequer.
3. Thirdly the bill for naturalising ships.
4. Fourthly the bill for settling trade with Scotland.
5. Fifthly the bill for the banishment of the Earl of Clarendon.

They also passed six private bills:
1. First the Earl of Clare's bill to enable him to sell some land.
2. Secondly the Bishop of Durham's bill to empower him to make a lease of the lead mines to Mr. Wharton for three lives.
3. Thirdly Mr. Palmes's bill to enable him to sell some lands in Derbyshire, Nottinghamshire and in other places.

4. Fourthly a bill for naturalising certain persons born out of the King's dominions.

5. Fifthly the Lord Townshend's bill to confirm his exchange of lands with the Rector of Rainham in Norfolk, he having taken some of the church lands into his park hath given a full proportion of other lands for it; he is the patron of that church-living.

6. Sixthly. [Wiseman's bill.]

At our return from the House of Lords Secretary Morice delivered the King's paper to the Speaker, which acquainted us that it was the King's pleasure that we should then adjourn the House until the 6th of February next.

FEBRUARY 6TH. This day the Parliament met; the King was expected but came not to the House. It is supposed he came not because he thought the House was not full and he would speak to a full House.

We only passed one vote this day, viz: that the House should receive no new business before the House was called, that so the House may be full before any new business be debated, which was accordingly ordered, and the House to be called on Thursday next.

This vote was passed to prevent the bringing in the bill of comprehension, which will be brought in and countenanced by very great persons.

After we had sat half an hour the House adjourned until Monday.

FEBRUARY 10TH. This day[1] Colonel Grey complained to the House that his menial servant was arrested at one Mr. Payton's suit, and that the serjeants carried him to prison, although they were informed that he was his menial servant, and that against the privilege of Parliament; and also that they gave ill languages against the authority of the Parliament. It was therefore moved

---

[1] MS. misplaces the date two lines above. Cobbett gives the King's speech, which asked for supply and a measure of comprehension or leniency, on which see an undated speech by Holland, Appendix I below. Grey does not begin until the 13th. *C.J.* IX, 44, gives Edward Kenwrick as Grey's servant, and the offenders as Hull, Husband and Chandler.

that Payton and the serjeants should be sent for into custody, but the Speaker informed the House that for arresting him they might not be sent for into custody, but the serjeants for contemptuous speeches might be sent for into custody, and Payton be sent for to make his defence, and then if he continue in his error and do not release the prisoner he is liable to the severity of the House, and the prisoner to be set at liberty.

A committee was appointed to examine all bills before they be brought into the House.

It was voted that the King be petitioned to send out his proclamations to restrain the disorderly and tumultuous meeting of dissenters to the act of uniformity and from the government of the Church, and to put the laws in execution against conventicles. It was ordered that the petition should be carried up this afternoon and presented to His Majesty by the Privy Councillors and Sir Philip Musgrave and some others.

It was moved that a committee be appointed to inspect the cause and grounds of the mis-spending the moneys raised and of our present poverty throughout the whole nation.

The King sent the Black Rod to command the Commons to attend him in the House of Lords. He only made a short speech to us. We are to consider of it and to give him a speedy account of it and to present our humble thanks to His Majesty on Friday next.

FEBRUARY 11TH. This day[1] it was moved that Mr. Harbord the Chairman should make his report from the committee of the business of the Forest of Dean between Sir John Winter and the commoners. It was objected that the committee could not determine it, because there was at present a suit or trial depending between the King and commoners whether the common did belong to the King or to the commoners; this trial should have been heard this term at the Exchequer Bar, but the Chief Baron, hearing that the Parliament had taken it into consideration, suspended the trial. Whereupon it was moved that the House

---

[1] *C.J.* IX, 44. MS. omits the date. Starkey (f. 66) talks of comprehension and the agitation newly stirred up for the enforcements of the acts against dissenters.

should send to the Chief Baron to hear and try the cause, that the House being informed rightly to whom the soil did belong they might with more justice take the waste wood into consideration.

Sir Benham Throckmorton informed the House that there was not now in London above six of the commoners to appear in the business, and therefore desired that the trial might be put off this time at the Exchequer Bar, to which it was replied, the cause between the King and commoners might as well be tried against one commoner as against twenty or the whole body of them. It was therefore ordered to send to the Chief Baron to hear the cause at the Exchequer Bar, and then that the House should hear the cause reported from the committee.

A complaint was made to the House that horse and men that were already gone and were now agoing to serve the King of France. Upon further enquiring into the business it was proved that very few horse and men were gone, but that many seamen for want of pay were gone to him and to Holland. Upon this the House fell into a long and serious debate about the conveniency or inconveniency of conveying horses into France. At last it was ordered that a committee should be appointed to consider of the free exporting horses, beasts and corn, as much to our advantage and a means to increase coin amongst us, that by the breeding of more cattle and horses land would take better price and rents be better paid.

In the afternoon I went to the committee of privileges, where was debated the election of Trevor Williams, who being the sitting member for the County of Pembroke, his election was questioned by Mr. James Herbert, and countenanced by Lord Herbert, Marquess of Worcester; but the election was clear for Sir Trevor Williams, he voted to be lawfully elected and his return also lawful.

A complaint was made against Lord Clarendon, that he had got a lease of the Bishop of Winchester, Dr. Duppa, from another person, Mr. Lenthall, by violence and injustice, and it was moved that the Lord Cornbury take notice that the matter should be heard at the Bar before the Commons the next week.

FEBRUARY 12TH. This day Colonel Sandys made a complaint against the abuse of the car-men, that they affronted and stopped the coaches that brought the members to the Parliament, whereupon it was ordered that the justices of peace between Westminster and Temple Bar should be desired to take notice that no cars should stir between eight of the clock in the morning and two in the afternoon, except such cars as brought in hay for horses.

It was moved that an act might be passed against the exportation of wool, that so the manufacture of clothing might be set up and encouraged in England.

Mr. Vaughan made his report from the committee for the relief of the sheriffs of London in regard of the escapes of prisoners that were occasioned by the late fire. It was moved that treble costs should be allowed any sheriff that should be sued for such escape, but it was ordered those words of treble damage shall be left out; but if any man after this day shall sue a sheriff of London for such escapes he shall not recover any damage, and if any man had sued any of the sheriffs and had recovered against him, and upon judgment had execution against lands or goods, the sheriff complaining within ten days, if it be during the session of Parliament, he shall be discharged from the execution and shall recover his damage sustained, but without any costs.

Mr. Harbord made his report from the committee of the business between Sir John Winter and the commons concerning the Forest of Dean.[1] The report was a very long one. The freeholders and commoners had made a great complaint against Sir John Winter, that he had wasted the wood and had contracted with the King for a great deal less value than the commoners would have given him, and that he had cut down forty thousand trees, and with little profit to the King. Sir Thomas Higgins spoke much in the behalf of Sir John Winter. Mr. Vaughan made a smart speech against him and set out how unfit a man he was to have made that bargain with the King, and to have undertaken that employment, both in regard he had consumed so much of that excellent [wood] so proper for ships, and he being a Papist it might reasonably be suspected that it was a

[1] C.J. IX, 45-8. A long report.

design between him and the King of Spain for him to spoil that forest of wood and so leave us without necessary supply of timber for our shipping. It was left to the committee to consider whether Sir John Winter's contract with the King or the commoners' offers to the King were of most advantage to the King and kingdom, and to report it.

Sir John Bennet informed that a satchel of letters was brought to Cooper, one of the door-keepers; the House commanded the satchel and letters to be brought in. The letters were very many, and all subscribed with one and the same hand, and directed to several members of the House. The letters being opened, every one had a little book in verse, a foolish libel, but not anything written in the letters.[1]

FEBRUARY 13TH. This day, February 13th, a constable that had been committed by an officer of the hearth money petitioned for his liberty and the stopping of a suit commenced against him by the said officer. His case was this:

The officer commanded the constable to assist him in collecting the chimney money, and at the same time the deputy-lieutenants commanded him to collect some militia money. The constable not being able to obey both leaves his brother constable to assist the officers of the chimney money, and obeys the orders of the deputy-lieutenants, whereupon the chimney officers bring an action against the constable for his contempt. The House ordered that the constable be set at liberty and also the suit to be stopped.

The bill to empower the Bishop of Durham to elect Knights and Burgesses for the Parliament was read and committed.

The House was called and ordered that what member soever was absent and his excuse not allowed should be fined £40 and sent for up by the Serjeant, and should pay the same before he be admitted to sit in the House, and if he did not presently pay the said £40 he should be sent to the Tower until he should pay it.[2]

[1] Cf. *C.S.P.D.* 1667/8, p. 217. This libel may be *Vox et Lacrymae*, which is in verse, and of about this date.

[2] Cf. Grey, p. 70, who has only a brief speech by Vaughan, to which is added an erroneous note about payment of members. See Margoliouth, Marvell, *Letters*, notes, p. 343.

FEBRUARY 14TH. This day Sir William Juxon's bill which prayed relief against Mr. John Pory, who had been treasurer to Archbishop Juxon, who having authority to put out money of the said Archbishop in his own name hath refused to give up his accounts, and to deliver in the bonds to Sir William Juxon, whereby he may be able to pay and discharge those legacies and payments left him to pay by the will of the said Archbishop, he being his executor.

And the bill further sets out that Pory for the avoiding of the accounts and restoring the personal estate to Sir William Juxon is gone beyond the seas.

There were two libels brought into the House in two letters to the Speaker, the one directed to or signed by the Duke of Buckingham, Lord Keeper and Lord Arlington, the other by Sir John Duncombe and others; they were not suffered to be read.

Sir Robert Brooke made his report of the miscarriages in carrying on the late war;[1] the heads were these:

1. First the want of good intelligence.

2. Secondly the not fortifying Sheerness.

3. Thirdly the Duke of York his not prosecuting the victory over the Dutch.

4. Fourthly the not timely securing the river Medway.

The House only debated the first and spent all the day about it, and after many speeches made both to prove the miscarriage in the intelligence and in the counsel given to divide the Fleet, and also many speeches to excuse, it was voted that the miscarriage was in dividing the Fleet, but for the present they could not tell on whom to lay it.

The other vote, of the miscarriage in the counsel and want of intelligence, was adjourned until to-morrow morning.

It is my opinion they will make nothing of it.

---

[1] Some brief notes on this are Harl. 7170, ff. 43–5; Rawl. A, 191, f. 229, on the committee on 13 February; *ibid.* f. 233, Considerations... on discharging seamen by Ticket...dated 21 February 1667 (8), signed by Pepys and Mennes and annotated by the former as being distributed unsigned to Birch, Lowther and Joliffe; Grey, p. 70–1. See also *C.J.* IX, 49–51. Grey also reports debates on 15, 17, 18, 19 February.

FEBRUARY 15TH. This day the Lord St. John moved that a stop might be made of the waste of timber in New Forest by those that have a patent of it; it was informed that 800 trees had been sold for £300 which were worth £2000, and that one tree was sold for 46s. that had 15 ton of timber in it; the same tree was sold the next day for £16, besides the bark and top wood of it.

It was moved that the King should be humbly moved to put a stop to the felling any more, and that none that is fallen shall be carried away.

It was ordered a bill be brought in and a committee appointed to send for the wood wardens and verderers, and to examine them of the abuses, and to call for all the patents and to examine them both of the cutting down and selling timber in the New Forest and in all other the King's forests and woods.

The Lincolnshire bill was brought in by Sir Robert Carr to put off the hearing of the cause concerning Lindsey levels that should be heard on Thursday next according to the former order.

Lord Cornbury's business against Lenthall and Lady Stonehouse concerning a lease got from the Bishop of Winchester, Duppa, against the tenant-right of the old tenant ordered to be heard Monday, February 24th.

The bill for preventing judges' severity in sitting times and imprisoning jurors was ordered to be read on Monday next.

Then the House fell upon the business of the day, the examining miscarriages, and it was judged that the not timely recalling the order for dividing the Fleet upon the coming forth of the Dutch was a miscarriage in the Council.

Mr. Marvell made a most sharp speech against some of the Council, and especially hinted at the Lord Arlington as that he had got £1000 and a barony.[1]

Sir Robert Howard spoke well that the dividing the Fleet was not for want of intelligence, but proceeded rather from evil counsel.

[1] Grey (p. 70) gives Marvell's diatribe on the 14th. Pepys, on 17 February, mentions it as having taken place on Saturday, i.e. 15th. Starkey (f. 70) says: "they have been very hot upon a secretary."

After a large debate and many speeches, some against the want of due intelligence and others through the defect in the counsel, it was voted that the cause of dividing the Fleet was not for want of good intelligence, but through ill counsel.

And so it passed in the question that the not recalling that order by which the Fleet was divided was a great miscarriage.

This was debated till almost five of the clock and very many speeches made against the question, as though it should reflect too much upon the King who gave out those orders and against the Duke of York who sent them, and that it could not be fixed upon the Council, nor could it positively be said that the Council did not advise the King to stop the dividing the Fleet, and that it was unjust to condemn the Council in general for the suspicion of a few, and also that it was very unsafe to judge by the event of things; for had the Prince (with the part of the Fleet which he was ordered to take) beaten the French and come in again in due time to the Fleet, it had been a piece of good service which is now condemned for so high a miscarriage.

Those that were of the severer party argued that it was from evil counsel that the Fleet was divided, and that it did endanger the loss and ruin of the whole Fleet, and so by consequence of the whole kingdom, and that strictly to examine this did not at all reflect upon the King, but only upon his Council, or some of them, whom it was fit should be rooted out of the Council, and others put in their places to the satisfaction of the people; for, say they, if such Councillors be continued in still, the money that the people shall give, all other business will be as ill managed as formerly they have been, and the kingdom will remain still in the same poor and sad condition as now at this present it is.

After all these long and various debates it came to this question, whether the Council not advising to recall the orders upon the coming out of the Dutch fleet was not a great miscarriage.

There was great endeavours to prevent the putting this question, but at last it was put whether it should be put or not, and the House divided upon it. The noes that were against the question went out and were 100; I was one of them. The ayes that stayed in were 117.

After this the main question was put, and the ayes that went out were 123; the noes that stayed in were 99, of which I was one.[1] This vote was ordered to be resumed on Monday next.

FEBRUARY 17TH. This day many members that were absent at the call at the House were excused from their £40 fine.

The House took into consideration the orders of the House to the intent they may be more strictly kept and observed.

The bill was read concerning the judges' menacing and fining and imprisoning juries for giving (and standing to) their verdicts, and it was voted that all such menacings, fines and imprisonments of juries by justices and judges is illegal.

Sir John Winter's business was debated; it appears that he had formerly made a contract with the King for wood in the Forest of Dean, and was to pay the King such a sum of money upon that contract. It seems a good part of that money due to the King is behind and unpaid, and it appears that he owes money to other men also, and having a stock of iron and coals, these men that he owes that money to endeavour to be paid out of that stock, whereupon it was ordered that the King should be first satisfied out of the stock and then the remaining part shall be to pay creditors.

It was ordered that this day and to-morrow should be taken into debate the further enquiry into the miscarriages of the last war, and that on Wednesday the House shall take the King's speech into consideration.[2]

The dividing of the Fleet was again debated. Sir William Coventry produced three letters which were sent to recall and revoke the former orders for dividing it.

One was sent to Portsmouth and one to Weymouth and a third to Plymouth, lest any of them should miscarry and not come safe to the Prince's hands. These letters were all sent away at one of the clock in the night and came to Portsmouth the next day after noon, being May 29th.

[1] *C.J.* IX, 51-2. Meers and Seymour, Sandys and Birch: Cary and Clarges, Strickland and Reeves.

[2] Arlington in a letter to Temple (*Letters*, ed. Thos. Bebington, 1727, I, 226) on 17 February says Marvell had made some amends by moving the taking into consideration of His Majesty's speech.

Sir William Coventry gave good satisfaction to the House that he was in no fault at all in delaying the intelligence and orders.

The House then fell upon the miscarriage of the not fortifying Sheerness.

Mr. Weld was of judgment that if Sheerness had been fortified it had not prevented the Dutch from coming into the river Medway where they fired our ships.

Mr. Prynne and Mr. Henry Coventry were of the same opinion, and that a fort though fortified is not sufficient to resist the coming in of a navy, nor any thing can resist a navy from landing men but another navy to shuffle with them, and so said Sir Walter Rawleigh.

Sir Richard Temple [said] that such a fortification at Sheerness had been very necessary, and might have discouraged the Dutch from so boldly coming into the river, and said it was very fit to enquire why the officers of the ordnance did neglect it, who had a special order to see it done.

Sir Edward Massey said it was a great miscarriage and crime in any man to neglect orders given, and had those orders for the fortifying Sheerness been well and truly obeyed and executed the Dutch durst not so securely have come into the river to have fired our ships.

Sir John Duncombe affirmed that there was no neglect of orders, for there was both guns and timber and all other necessary materials and above an hundred men at work to raise and perfect that battery, who did as much as possibly men could do in so short a time; they had not time enough to perfect so great a work.

Sir Robert Brooke said that it was made to appear before the committee that there was a great want of men, and that there was not above ten men at work.

Some endeavoured to lay the neglect and fault upon Sir Valentine Pyne, who was the chief cannoneer, but he seemed to justify himself as not having anything to do with the fortification, but only to place the guns and see the workmen paid.

The King and Duke of York marked out the place for the battery.

The House spent the day upon this debate until two of the

clock, and at the last it was voted that the not fortifying Sheerness was a miscarriage.

FEBRUARY 18TH. This day Colonel Sandys brought in the petition of Sir John Carter of Worcestershire against William Milward and Robert Theswell, and to crave the relief of the House against them, they having contrary to the act of Parliament brought in some hundreds of Irish cattle, and to evade the act contracted with the churchwardens whom they had employed to seize the cattle and then to sell them to them again at a most inconsiderable value, as not above half-a-crown a beast, and so defrauding the King of his former custom of 10s. an head, and breaking the late made act. The High Constable taking notice of this abuse, and endeavouring to seize these cattle again, this Milward and Theswell with some others to help them took cattle from the High Constable by force, and beat and wounded the High Constable. This being complained to Sir John Carter and some other gentlemen, they followed the beasts and took them again from Milward and Theswell, who told Sir John Carter that if they had not been too strong for them they should not have taken the beasts from them. But Milward and Theswell have brought their action of trover and conversion against Sir John Carter, and the same is to be tried this next Worcester assizes, and Sir John Carter now prays the relief of the House to issue their order for the stopping and putting off this trial. The House thereupon ordered to send for Milward and Theswell into custody and to give the judges notice of it.

The rest of the day was spent in the debate of Sir Richard Temple's bill for a triennial Parliament, a bill condemned by all moderate men; it was for a triennial Parliament.[1] It was composed of strange and very dangerous heads to take away the

---

[1] Two speeches on the Triennial bill in Stowe 180, f. 88 (Temple) and Stowe, 404, f. 77 (Vaughan), are dated in the British Museum Catalogue February 1667/8, but the cataloguer has almost certainly erred in this matter. Both certainly concern the same matter, and are contemporaneous and in the same hand, that of a secretary of Temple's. But in Temple's speech (f. 90) reference is made to the first day of meeting of the House, and to the second day "now" before the House

King's power and prerogative of calling Parliament, as first if the King did not call a Parliament within three years, that then the Lord Keeper should issue out his writs to call one; secondly, that the Lord Keeper should take an oath to do it; thirdly, that no prorogation should be above eighteen months; fourthly, that if the Lord Keeper did not then issue out writs in his own name it should be treason in him. This bill was seconded and justified by Sir Thomas Littleton, Sir Robert Howard and Sir Robert Carr, Sir Robert Brooke and all that gang, but most generally spoken against with abhorrency in the House.

My cousin Milward spake very well against it[1] and so did Sir Launcelot Lake, who said that this bill would make the Lord Keeper a traitor if he did not obey it: "And I say", said Sir Launcelot, "he is a traitor if he do obey it." It should have been put to the question to be thrown out with a score and a mark upon it, but with too much lenity it was moved that Sir Richard should have liberty to withdraw it.

It was also voted that no bill of that nature should be brought in for the future but by leave first had from the House, and that not before ten of the clock in a full House.

In this debate Sir Thomas Littleton in justifying this bill let fall an indiscreet and indecent speech, that this bill was the only way modestly to compel the King; the saying being taken notice of, he first denied that he said so, and then afterwards unworthily and untruly said it was the modest way to compel the thing, and so most pitifully and indeed senselessly said that "King" and "thing" were so like in sound that he might be easily mistaken by those that heard him.

February 19th. This day the bill against menacing, fining and imprisoning jurors by the judges was read the second time and committed. Mr. Vaughan said that the word "menacing" ought to be left out, it being a word of too large an extent, for in

has been called, and this can obviously not refer to the meeting recorded in Milward, which took place after the calling of the House, and in the second week of the session. Both speeches obviously refer to the debates on the repeal of the Triennial Act in 1664, in which Sir Richard Temple was also prominently engaged.

[1] Cobbett, IV, 411-2, mentions Milward's speech. Cf. also Grey, p. 83, for this day's events.

some sense it might not permit a judge to tell a corrupt jury of the danger of an attaint, in a case where they shall proceed wittingly against both their oaths and duties. And that there ought also care to be taken to prevent the miscarriages of juries as well as the severity of judges.

The House then went to the business of the day, which was to take the King's speech into consideration and debate, which was also read openly.

Sir Charles Wheeler first spake to it, and began an unexpected and indeed unnecessary and generally unpleasing speech against the church government and all the abuses thereof; "And although", said he, "I cannot speak against the doctrine of the church and that the Bishops are as learned and as pious men as any are in the Christian world", yet he impertinently spoke against their courts and judicatures and against archdeacons and their courts and the exorbitances of them, and against lay chancellors and their courts, and against excommunications. Such an invective speech was not expected from [him], especially at this time, he being accounted by some good men a severe son of the Church; but it appeared to be in favour of the Presbyterians and sectaries and that party in the House, for when he was taken down in his speech, as not speaking directly to the question in hand; many of that party justified him in that speech contrary to the general sense of the House.

We had a very great and long debate about voting the King's supply; Sir Thomas Littleton and others of his judgment were earnest to know the King's debts, and whether [there] be not money in the bank of that that had been formerly given, and how all that money had been laid out, and how much it was necessary to give for this present supply. Others moved for a speedy supply, and afterwards to examine the former particulars and miscarriages in laying the money out, which hath been formerly so liberally given.

Sir Richard Temple and Mr. Seymour moved that the league made with the Dutch should be brought in read openly in the House, but it was opposed as an unreasonable motion, and the Solicitor made a very good speech against it, affirming that it was an unreasonable thing to question the league, as if foreign princes should not enter into and make a league with the King of England without the approbation and consent of the House of Commons.

These gentlemen then retracted and said they did not mean any such thing; they only desired to know how many ships the King was obliged by this league to fit out for this summer's service.

It was voted that the King's supply should be taken into further consideration on Friday.

I went to the committee of grievances to hear Colonel Vernon's cause, where Barker etc. were plaintiffs and the Colonel etc. defendants; this was the case of the Irish adventurers. Barker pretends a contract for land made with Dick and Conningham; the issue seemed to be whether Dick and Conningham did pay £7000 as adventurers, or whether they do not pretend to pay it by sea service. The cause was not heard out, because Barker's counsel wanted the testimony of one Thomson, and the House was adjourned.

FEBRUARY 20TH. This day a bill was sent down from the Lords to regulate the price of wines both with the merchants and vintners, and to prevent base mixing and adulterating their wines, and a penalty asserted; it was read a second time and committed, though much opposed by Sir John Knight, Mr. Jones and divers others in favour of the merchants.[1]

The Spanish wine was £24 a tun and so after that rate for a pipe or a butt or less vessels; sherry at £22, French wine at £23. If any man do sell any wines above this rate, or be proved to mix or adulterate any of these wines, he is to pay £100 and the wine to be poured out.

This act is to commence from January, 1667.

The penalty is £100 a tun, £50 a pipe and so proportionable to all other less vessels.

That officers be authorised to search cellars for mixed wines twice in the year.

Sir George Downing gave his reasons against this bill, first because it is a perpetual bill not limited to a time.

---

[1] Cf. Grey for this and the next days' debates.

Secondly because it was against the King's custom, and very probable to hinder the importing of wine.

Thirdly because it would be a means to hinder our exportation of our English cloth, which in Spain was exchanged and vented for their Spanish wines.

After long debate and opposition in favour of the merchants the bill was committed, but with order for amendments.

The House then fell upon the debate of the miscarriages of the last war, which was the business of that day.

The first thing that was voted a miscarriage was not prosecuting the victory against the Dutch according to the orders of His Royal Highness.

Then it was debated where and on whom to fix the miscarriage.

First they name and question Sir John Harman, a very gallant and deserving man, and is now in the West Indies.

Sir Robert Carr and Sir Robert Brooke are ordered to go to His Royal Highness, to desire him to give order to his secretary, Mr. Wren, to write to Sir John Harman, so soon as it shall be known that he is certainly returned and come into the Downs, to come and make his appearance before the House of Commons and give his testimony of the truth of this matter.

Captain Elliott was produced to witness that he being in command under Sir John Harman and being appointed by him to command such ships, Sir John Harman being then very sick and in great danger of death said these words unto him, "I am now to take my leave of you and all the world; and I hear that some speeches are given out that [I] gave orders which hindered the prosecution of that victory contrary to the orders given by the Duke of York to Captain Cock, and I desire you when I am in my grave to vindicate my memory, and to declare from me that I do believe that if the victory had been prosecuted it had destroyed a great part of the Dutch fleet, but I had orders for what I did, and such as I could not withstand, and I do believe the Duke of York was not acquainted with them."

The next miscarriage was charged upon the Earl of Sandwich for calling home the Fleet, the Dutch lying still upon our coasts and doing us continually much damage, we having no fleet out to encounter or oppose them. But the Earl of Sandwich being now Ambassador in Spain the further enquiry into this was adjourned until his return into England, but it was voted a great miscarriage.

FEBRUARY 21ST. This day Sir William Juxon's bill against Pory was read the second time and committed, but it appears that it will be spoken against at the committee.

Sir Robert Brooke made his report from the Duke of York that he did not understand that Sir John Harman was in the Downs (though it was so reported), but so soon as he did know certainly that he was in the Downs he would send his own orders to him to attend the House of Commons.

Mr. Coleman made his report from the committee appointed to hear the business between the Lord Gerrard and Carr, that Mr. John Lewen did call Stephen Carr[1] (the brother to the plaintiff, William Carr) rogue and beggar, Stephen Carr being come to attend the committee as a witness for his brother against Lord Gerrard, and that Lewen gave him threatening speeches in the lobby; whereupon it was ordered to send for Lewen into the [Serjeant's] custody and to answer the abuse.

William Carr presented a petition by Sir Nicholas Cary against Lord Gerrard for his imprisonment, fining and standing on the pillory; it was read and referred to the same committee.

The House went into a Grand Committee of the whole House; the Speaker left the Chair and Mr. Seymour was called to the Chair.

The first thing taken into consideration was to know how much the last poll bill did amount to. The sum given in was £237,000,[2] out of which Sir Robert Long said that by bills there had been disbursed £337,000, and also that so much of the eleven months' tax had been likewise laid out for the late war, from Michaelmas, 1666, to Michaelmas, 1667, and for what it had been laid out and at what times.

It was informed that a considerable part of the poll bill was unpaid and not as yet brought into the Exchequer; it was ordered that it should be examined and an account given of all

---

[1] The writing in the MS. changes here, becoming bolder.
[2] Cf. Grey p. 89: the sum should be £1,600,000.

such sums as are behind, and what counties have paid all that was charged upon them, and what counties have not paid, and what money is behind of any county and in whose hand it is; this being done that we may know whether the King have any money in his treasury or bank and how much it is necessary to raise for his present supply for setting out the summer's fleet.

A committee is appointed to inspect these things and to give an account of them to the House on Monday next, and to enquire whether the money of the poll and the eleven months' tax now said to be laid out have been employed for the carrying on the last summer's war, and for no other use.

It was ordered that the House should take into debate and proceed one day upon grievances, and the King's supply another day, and alternately until they be perfected.

FEBRUARY 22ND. This day[1] Mr. Coleman made his report from the committee appointed to hear the business between Mr. Fitton and Lord Gerrard. In the first place Lord Gerrard's petition was read, which he preferred to the Lords against Mr. Fitton, to have justice against a libel which was sent abroad by Mr. Fitton and Granger.

Secondly the Lords' sentence against Mr. Fitton was likewise reported, which was that Mr. Fitton should be fined £500 to the King, to be sent prisoner to the King's Bench and there kept close prisoner, and to be bound to the good behaviour during his life.

Thirdly Granger's narrative was read, which consisted of many heads, and contained many horrid miscarriages of Lord Gerrard, if they be true; but in regard Granger is so notorious a villain and Carr (who is no better) is the chief agent and solicitor for Mr. Fitton in this business, I am persuaded that Mr. Fitton will not do himself much good or advantage, especially since I heard in the House (openly) the declaration of Sir George Carteret, who laying open many villainous acts done by this Granger and owned and confessed by him, and that he came with Lord Gerrard to Granger to the gate house where

_____

[1] *C.J.* IX, 55. Milward omits the date. Grey (pp. 90ff.) deals only with Fitton. See also for this day S.P.D. 29, CCXXXV, no. 42.

Granger was a prisoner, and where Sir George had formerly been with him; Sir George said that Granger at first sight did not know Lord Gerrard, and so went on with some discourses of his threat[en]ing and counterfeiting men's hands (at which it appears he is exquisitely notorious), but at last when he perceived that Lord Gerrard was there he fell down on his knees and begged his pardon, and with tears did confess that he had done his honour most abominable wrong in forging the deed by which Mr. Fitton did claim a right to Sir Edward Fitton's estate at Gosworth.

Then the House fell upon the business of the day, which was the consideration of the miscarriages of the late war.

The first that we fell upon was the damage that the Dutch did us the last summer.

It was then affirmed that whereas the King had 8000 in pay on shipboard there was not in readiness men and ships to be drawn forth in any reasonable sufficiency to defend the river Medway and Thames and this (as was most just) was voted a very great miscarriage.

In the next place, the payment of men and ships by tickets was also voted a miscarriage and charged upon Lord Brouncker. Sir Fretchville Holles said much in his defence. Sir John Northcote said as much against him, in that when there was ready money to pay the seamen Lord Brouncker gave order not to pay any more with ready money but with tickets.

Sir Thomas Meers said that although it might be lawful for Lord Brouncker to pay one particular ship with tickets by verbal order (as was said he had such order) from the Duke of York, yet it cannot excuse the general payment by tickets from being a miscarriage.

Sir William Penn moved in behalf of himself and other of the officers of the Navy that they might be heard at the Bar in their own defence and justification, and to make it appear that it was no fault or miscarriage to pay by tickets, for many seamen did desire it, but the fault that was was that those tickets were not discharged with ready money in due time.

Sir George Carteret declared it openly that it was ever against his judgment and advice to pay seamen by tickets, and that he ever held it a very dangerous thing, and further said that Cromwell would never pay by tickets, but made the seamen and soldiers stay until ready money came in to pay them.

Prince Rupert and the Duke of Albemarle did justify Sir George Carteret under their hands, that he ever did dislike paying by tickets.

Sir William Penn also saith that he had their hands to testify that he was ever against paying by tickets.

Sir John Birkenhead affirmed that Sir William Batten said to him that when there was not present money tickets might do well, but when there was ready money, then tickets were no good payment.

Mr. Marvell said that although the officers upon hearing may clear themselves, yet it was requisite that they should be desired to inform the House where the fault was, for there is no question but that they are able to do it.[1]

In conclusion it was voted that to pay ships and seamen by tickets was a great miscarriage.

FEBRUARY 24TH. This day Mr. Jones made his report from the committee that were appointed to inspect the abuses of importing Irish cattle, and brought in this amendment, that where any Irish cattle are seized and fraudulently bought again, as it was usual practice for the importers to buy them at a small value, as half-a-crown a head or the like, that the same cattle may be seized again at the next parish, and so at every other parish where they shall be found.

Mr. Lewen that was in the Serjeant's custody for calling Stephen Carr a rogue in the lobby was brought to the Bar and upon his knees was discharged.

Sir Robert Brooke brought in a paper without a name, charging some person or persons for selling offices. His aim was at Sir William Coventry, as was thought, but in regard there was no name to it it was not permitted to be read.

FEBRUARY 26TH. This day Mr. Weld reported Lord Cleveland's bill for selling land to pay his debts.

---

[1] The dating of the MS. p. 195 above corrects the information given by M. Pierre Legouis (*Marvell*, Oxford (1928), p. 264, n. 153).

Colonel Birch brought in a bill for settling a free trade of the silk throwsters, who were formerly tied to a certain number of forty or thereabouts; and also for the severe punishing of any that shall steal or embezzle any of their silks.

The man that was in custody for commencing a suit against young Felton was discharged; it seemed that man had distrained some cattle of young Felton's for rent, and Felton taking the cattle from him, the man brings his action against him. Sir Francis Felton, the father, being a member of Parliament, and it being pretended that the cattle was his, upon that pretence the man was sent for and committed, but upon examination of the matter it was made to appear that the cattle were young Felton's, and so no breach of privilege of Parliament, and thereupon the man was discharged.

The report of the former poll bill was brought in, that the Lords had paid in all but £6000; that divers counties were either in part or in the whole behind of their poll money.

Then the House fell upon the business of the day, which was the King's supply. The House had a long debate about it until seven o'clock at night; some were for raising no supply at all, supposing that there was sufficient money in arrear (of that that had been formerly given) to supply the present occasion, and therefore it was not necessary to raise more; and this party seemed prevailing a great while, and the House being thin at one time, if it had been then put to the vote would have gone near to have carried it, but the House filling and members that were gone out coming in again, the royal party prevailed, and it was voted that a supply should be raised not exceeding £300,000, and that no part of it should be raised by a land tax or home excise.[1]

FEBRUARY 27TH. This day a report was made of the Forest of Dean, and brought in in the nature of a bill, but to this effect, that the Forest of Dean did consist of two and twenty thousand acres, of which the King was to have eleven thousand acres to

---

[1] Cf. Grey, pp. 93–7, who reports Birch, Littleton, Seymour, etc., in debates on supply on 26, 27 February, and has other figures. Holland's speech in Appendix I might have been given either day.

himself to enclose and to be settled on the Crown for ever, and to be kept enclosed for the growths of timber, and that no taxes or payments be laid upon it, but to be freed from all taxes whatsoever, but only the keepers' fees when there fall any deer. And that the cord wood of birch, beech, hollies, hazel and elders of the other eleven thousand acres shall be allowed for enclosing and maintaining the fence of the King's park, and that no man shall presume to beg or take a grant of the whole or any part of the King's eleven thousand acres, but he shall be liable to a fine for the first offence, and the second offence shall be felony.

That no pannage (that is, gathering of acorns) shall be had or granted for the first sixteen years.

It was moved by Sir William Coventry that all treasurers that have received the King's money and have not paid it in shall be called to an account, and for the time that they have kept this money above the time that was appointed for the payment of it into the Exchequer they shall pay double damages, or the double principal.

There was a report made of the abuses done the people by the officers employed in collecting chimney money. It was moved that no stoves nor earthen places to keep meat hot, nor stills, nor ovens, cauldrons or furnaces, nor hearths only to avoid smoke or take ashes from ovens, or smiths' forges or blowing houses, nor cottages that have three chimneys, nor such houses as do not pay to the King and Church and poor, should not be liable to pay according to the act; and the ministers and churchwardens shall have power to condemn or acquit any person called in question by the officers of chimney money as they shall see just cause.

That no chimney that is truly and really sealed up shall pay.

If any man that shall be complained of for not paying his due chimney money do stand out against the judgment of the minister and churchwardens, he may [be] committed by them to the gaol for ten days, and must put in sureties for his appearance at the next assizes or sessions.

The House then fell upon the business of the day: raising the King's supply.

Sir John Cotton moved to raise the £300,000 upon the luxury

of eating and drinking; he said it was ill with Rome when for delicacy and luxury a fish was of more value than an ox.

He was for laying this tax upon wine and excess of apparel.

Sir Fretchville Holles moved to lay this tax and collect it by subsidies.

Sir Thomas Meers was to lay it upon foreign goods at the custom house, but yet for this time only.

Mr. Prynne to lay it on French commodities.

Mr. Sprag to lay it upon wine to prevent excessive drinking, but not upon anything to hinder good hospitality.

Colonel Sandys to lay it upon wines, and to raise the price of them a third part.

Sir John Knight[1] in favour of the merchants moved to raise it by a poll bill.

Colonel Birch to lay it upon wine and to raise the price of French wine fourpence a quart would advance to £80,000 a year.

Mr. Vaughan moved to raise the money not simply on the wine but on the abuses of the vintner, both in the measure and mixing it.

Sir John Arnly to lay £4 a tun on the merchant, and he to raise it to the vintner and the vintner to raise it by the quart, and he to pay it that drinketh the wine.

After this the House took foreign linen into debate, but in the end they adjourned the debate until Saturday.

FEBRUARY 28TH. This day Sir Thomas Heblethwaite's bill was read: the bill did pray that he might be empowered to sell his lands in Weaverthorpe[2] to raise money for his daughter's portion, he having improved his manor at Norton to as much and more as Norton and Weaverthorpe were worth when he made his settlement in the time of rebellion.

The bill concerning the Forest of Dean was read the second time.

---

[1] Knight is inserted in the MS. here in what looks like Milward's own handwriting.

[2] Weaverthorpe is in the East Riding of Yorkshire, between Malton and Bridlington, but nearer the former. Norton now seems to be a part of Malton, and is thus in both the North and the East Ridings.

Then the House fell upon the business of the day, the debate upon the payment of ships and seamen by tickets, which had been voted a miscarriage.

Sir John Maynard made a very good and severe speech against payment by tickets, and that to defraud by that and the like deceits was no less than traitorous; and those that are guilty of such deceits deserve to suffer accordingly.

Sir Courtney Poole seconded it, and moved that those that were found guilty should be forced to refund or to be hanged.

It was informed that there was an order made by the officers of the Navy for the payment of seamen in this order:

First the tickets of dead men and those that were killed in the service should be first paid and discharged.

Secondly the tickets of those men that were wounded.

Thirdly that those that had been longest in the service should be paid first.

This order and rule was observed only one week and no more.

It was ordered that on Thursday next the commissioners of the Navy and the officers of it should give an account to the House why the former order and rule for paying seamen was not continued, but why again they paid by tickets.

John Lund petitioned the House against Sir Thomas Hampson.

We had a stout debate upon several complaints against the insolence of sectaries in several counties, of which the House was informed by several members, viz: Sir James Thynne, Randall Egerton, Mr. Coke, Sir Thomas Meers; this ordered to be considered and debated on Wednesday next.[1]

FEBRUARY 29TH. This day the bill was read for regulating the abuse of the chimney officers.[2]

Sir John Morton complained of one Constantine, that lived in the town for which he served, to be a seditious person. Sir John produced a letter that had some dangerous and dark expressions in it. It was put to the question whether Constantine

[1] Again corrections in the MS. seem to be by Milward.

[2] Cf. Grey and Marvell, whose letters of 29 February and 7 March are illuminating (*Letters*, pp. 66–7). *C.J.* IX, 58 on division below: 78–96, Carr and Trelawney, Cary and Weld.

should be sent for into custody; it was carried in the negative 16 voices; I was for the affirmative, but we lost it.

The House then went to the business of the day, which was the raising the King's supply.

Sir Robert Howard moved to lay it upon wine, that the vintners shall be charged with the £300,000 and that they shall raise the price of every pint of wine.

Sir Heneage Finch and Sir Robert Atkins proposed to raise it upon wines and to lay it upon the vintner.

Sir Richard Temple moved to lay it upon wines at the custom house, and not upon the vintner and retailer; his reason was the charge of collecting it that way, which could not be done but by a multitude of officers.

Lord Gorges was for laying it on the retailer and not at the custom house.

Mr. Solicitor was for laying it on the retailer and not on the custom house; his reason was because commodities were subject to be stolen and concealed from the customers, and that the vintners may best bear the tax.

And whereas the importing foreign linen is much complained of, if this tax may some part of it be laid upon it it may be a very good means to discourage the importing that commodity and set up and advance our own manufacture of linen.

Sir George Downing moved to lay it upon wine, brandy and linen at the custom house, especially if we would discourage the importing and trade of those commodities.

Upon a long debate upon this subject, and the House growing thin, it was put to the question whether this supply in part should be laid upon foreign commodities and whether these words, "upon the cast commodities" should be added. The committee divided upon it; the ayes were seventy odd, the noes were 50 odd, of which I was one.

It was next put to the question whether the supply to be raised upon foreign commodities should be by an excise. The House was divided upon it and the noes carried it, and thereby that party did suppose they had obtained their ends, supposing that it would never be raised on foreign commodities at the custom house, and in the end to cast it upon the land, which would discontent the people of the nation generally and dissolve the Parliament.

I do not remember that that party ever carried a question down in the House as they did this day, which they only did now by taking advantage of a thin House, which in a full House they could not have done.

MARCH 2ND.[1] This day the addition of the Irish act against the importing of Irish cattle was brought in engrossed and read; it did indemnify all such as should seize such cattle so imported, and that all such cattle and ships after the second of February, 1667, shall be lawfully seized on, and one half of them for the benefit of the poor of the parish where they shall be so seized and the other half to themselves that do seize them; and if they shall be fraudulently sold again to them that brought them over at a low value, to defraud and avoid the act, it shall be lawful to seize them again in every market or parish, and so *toties quoties*; and if any persons that so seize them shall be sued at law they shall plead the general issue not guilty, and shall have treble costs.

The title of this act is, "An additional Act to prevent the Importation of Irish Cattle". It was ordered to be sent up by Sir Robert Carr.

The rest of the day was spent in hearing the case between Mr. Lenthall and Lord Cornbury, in which cause the testimonies of Mr. Lenthall and his wife were not admitted, which proved much to his prejudice.

It was expected the Duchess of Albemarle would have been at the hearing to have witnessed the bargain for the lease between Mr. Lenthall and the last Bishop of Winchester, Duppa, but it was said she was sick and in her bed. It was therefore agreed by consent and so ordered by the House that one counsellor of either party and Sir Robert Howard and Mr. Harry Coventry do attend the Duchess and to receive her testimony.

The Duke of Albemarle sent in a certificate of Mr. Lenthall's good service in the King's restoration.

MARCH 3RD. This day Sir Thomas Heblethwaite's bill was read the second time, but spoken against by Sir Robert Atkins

[1] Grey omits this but reports the next day.

and Sir Courtney Poole, justified by Sir Thomas Gower and Lord
Richardson, and was committed.

The bill for indemnifying the sheriffs of London for escapes
of prisoners in the late dreadful fire was brought in, engrossed
and read, and sent up by Sir Clifford Clifton.

Then the House went to business of the day with the debate
of Fitton's imprisonment by the Lords, upon the suggestion of a
scandalous paper published by Mr. Fitton. The debate was
whether the Lords did not commit him to prison illegally by
their own power upon Lord Gerrard's petition.

The sentence passed by the Lords upon Mr. Fitton was this:
that for publishing a scandalous libel against Lord Gerrard he
was fined to the King £500; to be imprisoned during the King's
pleasure and to put in sureties for the good behaviour during his
life.

The question is first whether this business simply taken be
legal in the Lords thus to proceed.

And secondly, supposing this paper to be a libel against Lord
Gerrard, whether the Lords have power legally to give such
judgment and inflict such punishment against a commoner of
England.

And thirdly, whether a crime committed against a particular
Lord and not reflecting upon the House of Peers may legally be
punished by the Lords, or whether it doth not more properly
belong to the courts in Westminster Hall to be tried there.

First because the commoner prosecuted hath not that free
admittance to make his defence and address to the House of
Lords as he may have in the inferior courts.

Secondly several precedents were produced where the Parliament hath referred divers such causes to be tried by the common
law; and so also Lord Gerrard might have had his remedy
against this libel, if it be one, at the common law.

There was a libel against Judge Coke, aspersing him for
giving an unjust judgment; it brought it to a trial and the Bar
in Westminster Hall and recovered damages against the party
and a severe punishment also against him.

To proceed in this case by a petition to the Lords is to flee to
an arbitrary power, by which the subject loses his liberty and

the benefit of the law, and being sentenced by the Lords, is deprived both of the trial by his peers and by a legal jury upon their oaths.

The calling thus before the House of Peers by a petition is neither a trial by our presentment nor by a due process by twelve honest men. If the Lords may thus proceed against any man, then there is no need of counsel to plead his defence, for if Lords in this way of proceeding will be both accusers and judges, and so deprives a commoner both of his try of his neighbourhood and also deprives him of all exceptions against his tryers, and bars him against all privileges of exceptions of errors in judgment and appeals.

If a man be tried in a legal way he ought to be tried by his peers, by a jury of twelve honest men upon their oaths; and if it be an equitable cause it ought to be tried in a court below.

In all courts below there is either relief to be had or there is not; and if there be relief then it is most proper for those courts; but if those courts cannot relieve, it is most certain the Lords cannot create a relief.

There is no precedent that the Lords have power to punish a libel in this case, and where no precedent hath been or can be produced it is a good plea against judgment of this nature.

In the time of Richard II Cavendish, a fishmonger, complained of and against Michael de la Pole for money that was owing to him for fish that he had furnished him with; Cavendish, not being well satisfied with the proceedings, complained against the Chancellor as being, as he said, corrupt in his judgment. Cavendish thereupon was impeached before the Lords for libelling the Chancellor; the Lords would not meddle with the cause, though it was in the case of a Peer, but referred it to an inferior court, where it was tried and Cavendish was fined for the libel. Note that there is difference between a slander[1] and a libel in time of Parliament, which ought there to be tried if it concern a member, and a libel out of doors, the Parliament not sitting, that ought to be tried in Westminster Hall by a jury. But it is said that this libel was against a Peer in the time of Parliament, and therefore was a contempt of their privilege and

---

[1] MS. reads Fraudell here (for Slander?).

authority. Suppose it were a contempt and therefore punishable by the House of Peers, and that the party offending should be imprisoned by them, yet the sentence of imprisonment beyond the time of session was unjust, and therefore Fitton ought not to be continued in prison after the prorogation of that session.

MARCH 4TH. This day the bill for the Lincolnshire fens was read the first time.

Then the Lord Cleveland's bill to enable him to sell his land for the payment of debts.

A bill was read concerning writs of errors that were passed in the Exchequer Chamber. It was the rule of that court formerly that a writ of error should not pass unless the Chancellor or Lord Treasurer were present; now by this bill it is provided that there being no Lord Treasurer, but four commoners of the Exchequer, if those commoners be present it is sufficient to pass a writ of error.

Then the House fell upon the business of the day,[1] which was to receive the reports of abuses committed by sectaries and non-conformists, and unlawful meetings at conventicles. Sir Hugh Windham informed the House of one of his own parish that formerly had been one of Cromwell's captains, keeps a conventicle and opposeth a very worthy minister that serves there, and draws many of his auditors from his church to that conventicle.

Many other complaints of the same nature were made, but the further debate of them was adjourned until Wednesday next.

We had a debate that lasted almost five hours about sending an address unto the King to issue out his proclamation to put the penal laws in execution against nonconformists and conventicles and unlawful meetings of Papists, Quakers and sectaries; this was mainly opposed by the undertakers, but in the end it [was] voted that His Majesty should be desired to send out his proclamation to that purpose.

We carried up the bill against Irish cattle; Sir Robert Carr carried it up.

---

[1] Cf. Grey, pp. 103–4; Starkey, f. 80, etc.

MARCH 5TH. This day[1] Colonel Sandys his bill for his proportion of lands in Bedford levels was read, for the regulating the assessments among them. It was passed and ordered to be sent up to the Lords.

The Lord Fitzharding carried up the humble desires of the House to the King, that he would please to appoint them a time that they might attend His Majesty, and brought the King's answer that he would meet the House this day in the Banqueting House at three of the clock.

Then the House went upon the business of the day, to hear the defence of the commissioners and officers of the Navy in the paying of seamen by tickets. They came to the Bar, and one Pepys undertook the whole business for all the rest. He made a narrative of almost three hours long in answer to these particulars:

First, that it was Lord Brouncker that paid seamen at Chatham by tickets.

Secondly, my Lord being asked why he did so, made this answer, "I know what I have to do".

Thirdly, that in paying by tickets they did it irregularly, as that they paid tickets that were bought before those that brought their own tickets and had done the service.

Fourthly, there being an order made for the regular paying of the seamen and soldiers, yet they kept not that order.

Pepys divided his narrative into these three heads:

First, he showed the usefulness and necessity of tickets.

Secondly, concerning the charge of irregular paying by tickets.

Thirdly, concerning the paying of seamen and ships by tickets.

For the first, that tickets were useful and necessary:

First, in regard of men that are dead, to whose widows and executors they give tickets, by which they may receive the pay of those that are dead.

And upon the death of a commander of one ship, and a new

---

[1] Grey omits 5 March. Pepys's speech, though unnoticed by his biographers, was printed by E. S. de Beer in *The Mariner's Mirror*, January, 1928 from this Diary.

commander placed in his room, it may be he may bring with him 20 or 40 soldiers or seamen, and so it is necessary to give them tickets.

Secondly, tickets are necessary upon the change of men, as if they put out unserviceable and take in more serviceable men.

Thirdly, tickets are necessary where there is not ready money.

He said that no tickets were granted but such as were signed by the commander of the ship.

Tickets may be extremely abused if not well looked to, both in counterfeiting tickets, and some may by threatening get double tickets, but it is not in the power of the commissioners of the Navy to increase or diminish the number of tickets.

It is ordinary for a ship that is well manned with 700 men to have 1500 or 2000 names in the muster book, because of the several ways of altering and changing men, as by the death of some, the removing of others and cashiering of others and taking new men into all their places.

Of 55 ships there was not in two years' war above 5000 men paid by tickets by the officers of the Navy, whereas treble that number have been paid by the admirals.

It may be there hath been some irregularity in paying with tickets, and some that have been paid before others that were in due order to be paid not so soon.

It was judged necessary by His Royal Highness and so judged by him, being our High Admiral, that payment should not be bound up to time and order, but that upon some great necessity some may be paid now, that in due order ought to stay until some others should be first paid. And that this should be left to the discretion of the officers of the Navy; nor can that be called irregular that never was regular; and therefore those officers are not to be condemned if the pitiful necessity of some have been relieved before others out of the strict order.

Whereas it was objected against these officers that they had made an order for the due payment of seamen, but did not keep and observe that order above one week, Mr. Pepys said that such an order was only spoke of and designed, but was never ratified nor signed; nor were any future orders (though some were made) strictly obliging, nor the regularity of them strictly kept.

These commissioners do altogether justify themselves from any indirect or partial paying by tickets, but only where mere necessity did compel them.

The third charge was their discharging men and ships by tickets, to which he answered that they were so far from doing it to the disadvantage of the men that because they had not ready money to pay them (which they say was the only reason why they paid by tickets) they victualled some ships that were to be laid up only to keep the men in pay until they were in capacity to pay them.

At three of the clock we attended the King, who assured the House that he would send out his proclamation as we desired, and he hoped we would take the second part of his speech into consideration as we had voted. Thence we came back to the House and adjourned until the next day.

MARCH 6TH. This day [a] bill was read the first time for settling the churches in Southampton; there are five churches in the town and very small maintenance for them. The bill prays that they may be thus divided: two to be laid together and the other three to be laid so also, and that there may be but two only; and the maintenance of the five to be laid and appointed for the two thus disposed. The bill was not opposed, but it was only moved that those churches that stood void upon this alteration should neither be converted to any profane use or common employment, nor should be made use of by fanatics or nonconformists to have conventicles and unlawful meetings in them.

A bill was read for the naturalising several persons.

A bill was read that concerned Mr. Davies Weymondsold[1] and Mr. Dowdeswell, whose son married Mr. Weymondsold's sister; it was passed and ordered to be sent up to the Lords.

There was a bill this day to be read the third time, engrossed and to be sent up to the Lords for the indemnifying the sheriffs of London for the escape of prisoners in the lamentable fire,

---

[1] *C.J.* IX, 61. Milward appears to have confused the name of this gentleman, Davies Weymondsold, with that of his property at Wimbledon [f. 66].

but Mr. Vaughan made a just exception against it, because the
Warden of the Fleet was left out in [the] engrossed bill, and was
in the paper bill when it was read, and therefore, saith Mr.
Vaughan, it is an imperfect bill and not the same bill that was
ordered to be engrossed. The truth of the business is this: the
Warden of the Fleet refused to pay his fees for the bill, and so
the clerk left out that proviso that concerned him, and it is said
that he refused to be joined with the sheriffs in that bill, but
would have a particular bill to himself. But I believe now they
are agreed, and the bill will be now engrossed and then read and
passed and sent up to the Lords.

It is affirmed that [if] a bill be passed and several persons and
their several interests be concerned in it, every several person
and interest are to pay for it as if every one had a several bill.

Colonel Kirby moved that leave may be given to bring in a
bill for regulating the exorbitant fees of the six clerks in the
Chancery.

The King sent his letter by Secretary Morice to hasten his
supply, and to acquaint us that he had caused fortifications to
[be] made at Sheerness and other places which would require
much money; and that when we had raised the money for the
supply we may put it into such hands as we best liked.

The House sent Sir Robert Carr and others to the commissioners of accounts to desire them to give the House a particular
account of their proceedings, but the commissioners said they
could [not] as yet do it.

Sir Thomas Meers made his report from the committee of
those commodities that may be charged at the custom house, as
namely wine, linen, brandy and tobacco; and he said it is probable
those may raise £300,000 in one year. He gave particular
accounts of the sums and quantities brought in, which I could
not exactly set down.

Then was proposed to lay so much upon every ton of goods
that is brought in, one part to be paid by the owner of the ships
and two parts by the owners of the goods, with a regard of the
value and quantity of the goods.

This proposal was well approved by many, but spoken against
by Mr. Jones, Mr. Swinsen and the Solicitor; but approved by

Sir Richard Ford. I went to dinner with Sir Robert Carr and stayed not out the debate.

MARCH 7TH. This day the bill to prevent robbing was brought in and reported by Sir Thomas Clarges; it consisted of many heads and amendments. One was that if the thief and robbery was not complained of within 18 days the money should not be recovered of the county. Secondly, by that no carrier and waggoner that carried goods, plate, ready money or jewels should pay for it if he was really robbed of it, unless he travelled on the Sunday and was then robbed of it. Thirdly, that the county shall not pay above half the money that is taken from any man.

Many spoke against the bill and therefore the further debate of it was adjourned until Monday in a full House.

Then they went to the business of the day, to raise the King's supply.

The House began first with tunning; many exceptions were made to it, as whether parks and tubs and small vessels should be comprehended within tunning; also to consider the quality of the goods and the countries from whence they came; this was much insisted on by Mr. Spry.

Sir John Morton moved that this £300,000 should be laid on rich men both in country and corporations.

Sir John Goodrick was proposing another way to raise the supply, but before he opened it I was sent for out to my son Jennens, who came to acquaint me that my daughter Anne was extreme ill. I was constrained to go away and leave this day's debate.

MARCH 9TH. This day the bill of silk throwsters was read the second time and was opposed by a petition of the warden and patentees of that trade set up by an act of Parliament.

The House then went to the business of the day, the further consideration of raising the King's supply.

There were four foreign commodities named on which to raise the £300,000, viz: wine, linen, brandy and tobacco.

Sir Anthony Irby said that raising the price of wine one penny in the quart would raise £60,000.

Others added two more commodities to the former four,

14-2

cordage and currants. Foreign iron was also proposed, excepting Spanish iron, and it was said that foreign iron might bear an excise of 12s. 6d. the ton.

Sir Thomas Lee proposed subsidies for raising the supply.

Mr. Vaughan said that subsidy was a land tax and the most ancient land tax, and that all taxes differ only in name, for they are all an excise or a tax, be they of what nature they will.

If it be raised by subsidy the landlord pays it; if by a land or monthly tax the tenant pays it.

The land tax having been so long continued hath made both landlord and tenant unable almost to pay any more, and if it shall now be laid on the land it cannot be raised, and so the King will be disappointed of his supply.

MARCH 10TH. This day the Lord Ailsbury's bill was read for draining Deeping fens. It was moved in the bill to have an enlargement for three years more (than was allowed in the former bill) to perfect it; and it was also prayed to have liberty to dig earth from the banks six score yards. And that if any person shall make any breach in the banks, he shall be liable to make satisfaction according to the damage; and that all persons that are concerned in this damage shall be compelled to pay their proportion. Lord Castleton spoke against the bill, but yet did not oppose the committing of it, because (he said) he did believe the charge would be so great and the profit so little that the bill would fall of itself. The bill was committed, and I am one of that committee.

The amendment of the bill for the preventing high-way robbery was brought in; it was moved that whereas by the present statute 40 days are allowed for the apprehending of a thief that hath committed a robbery, that the time may be enlarged to 80 days, in which time if the robber be taken that then the county shall not be liable to pay the money taken by the robber.

There was a great debate upon this in the House, whether 80 or 40 days should be allowed, and the House was divided upon it. The ayes that were for the 80 days were 36, of which I was one; the noes 72; and so it was 40 days.[1]

---

[1] C.J. IX, 64, 36–72, Lake and Allen, Arnley and Harbord.

That money taken from carrier or waggoner shall not be made good by him unless it be taken from them carrying on the Sunday.

That the county shall not be liable to pay above half the money taken by thieves from any man upon the high-way.

That any two or more of the next justices of peace to the place where the robbery is committed shall be empowered to compound for the county with the party robbed, and shall cause the money so compounded to be levied upon the towns and hundreds where such robbery is committed, and where such money is not paid they shall have power to distrain for it, and to sell the distress.

Then the House proceed[ed] to the business of the day, which was about the supply, but the day was almost wholly spent to two of the clock about nulling the former vote, that foreign commodities should not be taxed by an excise; their vote being now recalled, the £300,000 may be raised upon the merchant and vintner.

And other foreign commodities likewise may be brought in if occasion be.

It was moved that some part of the £300,000 should be raised by a subsidy. And at the same time it was urged by others to raise supply by a poll bill; but neither proposal would be accepted.

It was ordered to take the later part of the King's speech into consideration to-morrow, and the next day to resume the debate of raising the King's supply.

MARCH 11TH.   This day the bill for indemnifying the sheriffs of London was passed and sent up to the Lords by Mr. Vaughan.

Dr. Wharton's bill was likewise passed and sent up to the Lords by Colonel Kirby.

Mr. Lawrence Rooke's bill[1] was read to enable him to sell some lands to raise portions for seven children, but was opposed by Sir William Lewis, Sir Thomas Lee, Sir Courtney Poole and

[1] *C.J.* IX, 64, gives here Laurence Rooke, not Brooke as in MS., with the division, 44–66, Thurland and Head, Poole and Weld. Cobbett appears to have taken Grey's account of the debates on this date and on 8 April (IV, 413–17).

Mr. Weld. The House was divided upon it, but the noes carried it, and so the bill was cast out; I was for the bill.

The bill was read for the providing for the children of those that die intestate where administration is granted to another: that the wife and children shall have their due proportion out of it.

Then we took into consideration the later part of the King's speech, which was read.

Colonel Kirby moved that the reasons upon the King's declaration at his restoration and coming in should be likewise read.

Sir William Lewis was against the reading of the reasons.

Sir John Birkenhead said they ought to be read in order to the debate of the King's speech, because the reasons come immediately from the King.

Sir John Goodrick moved to lay aside this debate, and to refer it to the Convocation.

Sir Thomas Meers was for reading the reasons, and so was Sir Philip Musgrave.

Mr. Swinsen moved that the declaration upon which the reasons were grounded might be read also.

That was moved that no indulgence should be granted to the dissenters to the present established government.

It was mainly urged by some that the King had sent a message from Breda for some liberty and indulgence to tender consciences; to this it was answered that that message was not binding, because a toleration against an act of Parliament cannot be granted but by repealing that act and passing another.

Secondly to grant an indulgence in this kind is to establish a schism by law, against a former act.

Thirdly it will create an infinite and daily trouble to the King by way of petition; if a toleration be granted to those dissenters it may probably end in Popery.

It is also without precedent, and will bring great disturbance to the present established peace.

Colonel Kirby moved that the laws that were made in '62 and '63 might be put into execution against nonconformists and disturbers of the peace. He also affirmed that the King now lately setting out his proclamation had done much good, for where Mr. Manton had a constant conventicle in King's Street, and where they publicly met, since the proclamation it is held more privately and is more restrained.

Sir Hugh Windham affirmed that in Queen Elizabeth's time the nonconformists petitioned for a toleration; the Queen bade them present a new form, which they did, and put the same into Lord Burleigh's hands; but that was laid aside also. They afterwards petitioned for another indulgence, and that they might bring in a better form; this was likewise granted. Then they brought in the former, and comparing them together they found they very much differed. The Queen bade them go home and when they reconciled these two she would give them an answer.

Sir Robert Holt moved that the dissenters would declare what they would desire, and in what they would acquiesce.

Sir Thomas Littleton moved to read the King's declaration that he sent from Breda, which declaration he there had ready to produce; it was of '62. It said that no man should be punished if he did not disturb the peace and government. In this declaration the Papist may challenge full as much of an indulgence as the Presbyterian or any other dissenter.

Colonel Sandys said that where toleration was granted point of religion it was necessary that a standing army be established to keep the several opinions in order; and he also moved that those men would declare what they would desire.

Sir Humphrey Winch was altogether against a toleration, but he was [for] a bill of comprehension, to take in more persons into the Church. Also he moved against the fraudulous [scandalous?] practices of officers in the ecclesiastical courts.

He also spoke how much the outward piety and good behaviour of the nonconformists won upon the people, and how great offence those that did conform gave to the common people by their looseness of living and other miscarriages.

Sir John Arnly said that many took offence at the errors of the government, but not at the government itself.

Sir William Hickman spake against the miscarriages and corruptions of the Chancellor's courts, and therefore moved the reformation of them, to take away the exceptions of the dissenters.

Sir Robert Holt moved that the dissenters would declare wherefore they did so earnest press the reading of the King's declaration.

Sir Thomas Littleton answered that it was very proper that it should be read, it being relative to the Parliament's reasons that were read, and that in regard of the declaration and contents of it, the reasons were out of doors as to this business, further than they looked at an indulgence and a toleration. He made a very long and impertinent speech, and indeed such a one as I never heard him speak; he extravagantly ran into foreign nations and heretical opinions tolerated in Poland, and concluded with this, that the restraint of conscience in England was the occasion of the late war.

Sir Thomas Meers on the contrary and more truly said that the reasons were a perfect bar and stop to toleration, and made the Declaration of Breda to cease and be of no effect; and that being so, what would they have, for the King in that declaration saith expressly that they shall assent to and receive the discipline and ceremonies now established in the Church of England.

Sir William Thompson moved for a toleration and liberty of conscience, because those that desired it were true worshippers of God, and that a restraint would prove destructive to trade, by driving many of them into foreign countries, and so take the trade with them, and experience (saith he) shows that where a restraint hath been put upon tender consciences those countries have decayed and become low: witness Spain, which at this time by reason of the Inquisition is very weak and low, and Holland and France, where there is a toleration, are rich and potent.

Sir John Denham said it is true, Holland and France did tolerate several religions amongst them, but it is as true that they keep a standing army in pay to keep them under and in obedience to their government. He also said that this conscience so much pretend[ed] to was nothing less than spiritual pride, that this conscience showed itself in the rebellion, and their disturbing the peace and breaking the laws established.

It was again moved by Sir Robert Carr that they would declare what they would have and what would satisfy them.

Colonel Birch, though he was much for them, yet did say

that until they did declare what it was they did desire there could be no way of proceeding to their satisfaction. He moved that the eight heads of the declaration may be read.

Mr. Chune made a long formal speech in which he told them that they were all born within the Church; had received their rights and dues from the Church; what then should cause them to dissent and separate from their mother? It was the devil that first moved them to dissent, and then a rebellious Parliament that did countenance and justify them in that rebellion, to the spilling of the blood of His sacred Majesty. It was this pretended conscience that murdered that King, dissolved the Parliament and enslaved the liberty of the nation, and that did tyrannise over the orthodox clergy.

Mr. Swinsen urged that by reason of the late wars there hath been a long and great separation from the Church, in which time many have been brought up in a form of worship, and knowing no other, it will be hard and not easy upon the sudden to reduce their consciences to that discipline they were never acquainted with. He moved to put it to the question whether some condescension may be yielded to in order to a union and composure, but it would not be granted.

Sir Philip Warwick said that the word of God and government were the greatest ties of conscience, and if authority can truly show the legality of a thing enjoined it ought then to be assented to out of a good conscience, and where a thing that is simply indifferent, that is neither commanded nor forbidden by the word of God, the thing (that is so) being enjoined by a lawful authority is then more than indifferent to those that are subject to that command, and ought to be obeyed by them for conscience sake.

Sir Philip Musgrave said that the dregs of schism are so deeply settled in men that indulgence will never purge them out. It is to be wished that all profaneness and debauchery were restrained and duly punished to avoid the scandal and objections of the dissenters.

Lord Gorges said that the government established ought not to be dispensed with nor any toleration to be granted against it.

Mr. Ratcliff moved that the act of uniformity might be

reviewed and to be taken into consideration where it is too severe against non-subscription or in the point of subscription, and the covenant and assent and consent; and a conference of divines be admitted of both persuasions, and to purge out the scandals both of civil and ecclesiastical courts and jurisdictions.

Sir Walker Young spoke much for an indulgence but very impertinently and very little to the purpose.

Sir Charles Wheeler moved for an application to the Convocation, but in favour of the Presbyterian (as he professed) he desired an indulgence.

Sir Thomas Littleton said it was an unreasonable thing that was desired from the dissenters, or that they should declare the particulars of what they desired or would acquiesce in; neither that a standing army was necessary if a toleration should be granted them. He also instanced in Poland, where there was a general toleration and yet no standing army; he also asserted the Calvinistical government allowed (as he said) in King James his time. And no alteration was pressed till after the death of Archbishop George Abbott.

The main drift of his discourse was to prove that in this government now in force there are many innovations, as the removing the communion table from the body of the church to the place where it now stands altarwise, and bowing to the altar and many other ceremonies. And although (saith he) bowing to the altar be not strictly enjoined to all, yet those that did bow to it were the only men that were preferred. And he concluded that the strictness and restraint that was put upon tender consciences was the occasion of the late war.

Sir John Cotton said that the occasion and stirring up people to the war and late rebellion were these and such like rebellious principles and assertions:

First that the King is *major singulis*, but *universo minor*.

Secondly that the King is a minister and is only to command as he is good. *Dominium in gratia.*

Thirdly the principle of self-preservation, and that where that was invaded it was lawful to take up arms.

Sir John Birkenhead made a long and most excellent speech and discourse to the point in hand; he showed that although

there was not strictly a standing army in Poland, yet there was
so well a formed militia that it was sufficient to defend them
[from] foreign invasion and to keep the government established
in safety.

That the Emperors Theodosius and Honorius established a
government and enjoined a conformity to it, that they would
not suffer any man to make a will and to dispose by it that did
not conform to the government.

That the toleration in Poland was the rise of all sorts of
heresies and villainous opinions, as the blasphemous denying
the divinity of Christ by Arius, of denying His humanity by
another, of denying the possession of the Holy Ghost by a third,
of denying the omniscience of God and so freeing it from con-
tingencies; but notwithstanding these damnable heresies grown
by that toleration, yet the militia was so well formed that it kept
the government entire and in peace.

Although the army in Holland was not raised principally to
keep sectaries in order and obedience to the government, yet
had it not been for that army those many and several opinions
had not been kept in that good order and obedience as the army
kept them.

Archbishop Cranmer and the Convocation brought in articles
in Edward VI his time to establish the government then set up;
and in Queen Elizabeth's time Lord Burleigh and the Lords
desired her that she would continue the liturgy of Edward VI,
which accordingly with very small amendments was retained,
and she was a most strict prince for conformity.

King James in all his acts of oblivion evermore excepted
nonconformists, and at his coming to the Crown of England
was hardly persuaded to admit of a disputation, but after that
disputation was had and performed by Dr. Reinold, a most
learned man and worthy divine, and others in behalf of the
nonconformists he would not give them a toleration, no, not
so much as for an hour, and afterwards they conformed.

They complain (saith Sir John) of Arminians, and yet he
was a Puritan and differed from them only in the point of free
will.

Look through all the government of Jew, Pagan, Turk and

Christians, and it will be found that they never tolerated any in point of ceremony and worship.

It is true that the King may establish one liturgy in England and another different from that in Ireland and a third different from both in Scotland, but he never did admit of any difference in ceremonies or worship or liturgy in the same church.

If (saith he) we look upon the covenant, how they took it with hands lifted up to heaven to extirpate prelacy and the government established in the Church of England, and that they would not admit any into the ministry or to spiritual living, nor so much as to teach a school, although it were but in a private family, unless he would first take the covenant.

When Cromwell was petitioned by one of his own name and his very family to spare the King's life he told them he would gladly do it, but he could not do it for conscience sake.

When we remember the villainies that those men committed under pretence of conscience, the younger sort of them unlearned and ignorant, and that no oath (of which they had taken many) would bind or hold the older, we may well be cautious that we be not again cheated and destroyed by indulging their conscience into a new rebellion.

And whereas it is moved by some in favour of those tender consciences to recommend this debate to the King and to cast in his resolution, it can by no means be judged fit to trouble His Majesty with it, but rather to desire the Convocation to draw up something that may settle the difference. So far Sir John Birkenhead.

Sir Edward Massey made a slight objection to Sir John Birkenhead's discourse of the militia and toleration in Poland, but it was of no weight, nor worth taking notice of it; he was [for] referring this debate to the King.

Mr. Harry Coventry said that a union was good and to be wished, but not such a union as would destroy the church. He was against the recommending this difference to the King, for, saith he, it is unreasonable, the King having committed it to us and commanded us to advise what is to be done, that we should return it to him again and pray him to advise and determine it. It is rather fit (saith he) to revive the committee of religion, and that the committee hear the parties on all sides. This [was] much disliked by the dissenting parties, though in my judgment it was very properly moved.

Mr. Boscawen and the dissenters earnestly pressed the sending it to the King.

Sir Thomas Strickland was as much against sending it to the King, because it was difficult business, and so fitter for the advice of his Great Council, but matters of an easier nature His Majesty may dispose of and determine of them as he pleaseth.

Mr. Seymour was against the bill of comprehension, for (saith he) three Presbyterians did endeavour to be three bishops; he was also against referring this debate to the Convocation, nor was he for rending a seamless coat by schism, but he would have every man to wear his coat after his own fancy; if one would wear a plain coat let him so wear it, and if another will wear a fringed coat let him please himself, without any restraint put upon him; but because this strict government of the Church hath not wrought the peaceable effect that was expected, therefore he moved that we should try a more easy way, by taking the restraint off tender consciences and using lenity and giving them some indulgence; for acts of severity never gain love, and where there is not love to a government it will never be truly and cordially obeyed. In his discourse he drives at an interest more than at religion; and so concludes that we should move the King to have a respect to tender consciences lest they decay the trade of the nation.

Lord Fanshawe said that if these tender consciences were so good as is pretended to then they should live without offence to God and man, but what villainies did these men commit when they had the power in their hands is most notorious; let us not (said he) stand in fear of their number, of which there is so much noise, but let the laws be put in execution against them, and they will soon be brought under, as he had the experience of some persons in Herefordshire who frequented unlawful meetings, and upon the execution of the laws they have conformed and come in good order to the church.

Sir Robert Atkins spoke, but to as little purpose as any man; he spoke against atheism and vice, but nothing that did concern government; he said that the people of England were much addicted to religion, and therefore they ought to be indulged; he insisted upon the reforming the exorbitances of the ecclesiastical courts, and no man should be punished for his conscience, but for blasphemy, idolatry and disturbing the peace and government.

Sir Robert Carr was against that the King should take this difference into his consideration, and did believe that some persons had suggested to the King that the Parliament was for a toleration, and to the Parliament that the King was for same.

Mr. Prynne said he was for taking away the causes of separation, and the vacancy of many churches was a main cause, for some churches not having any ministers, the people took a liberty to go where they had a fancy, and therefore moved that painful ministers might be put into such churches.

Secondly he moved against pluralities, and by confining ministers to one living he would be more constant to that cure, and be continually resident there, and by that means the people and minister would be better acquainted, and so better affected to each other.

Secretary Morice moved to adjourn the debate, which accordingly the House did, until that day month. And the House passed another vote, that the House should be called the Monday before this debate should be resumed.

It was voted that an £100,000 should be raised on brandy and wines and that the vote that no excise be laid on foreign commodities should be recalled and the commodities set at liberty.[1]

MARCH 12TH. This day the debate of Bedford levels was taken up, and it was moved that assessments should be equally laid and gathered by distress where they were not paid; and that all men that are concerned shall pay to the repairing of such damages and reparation of lands as have been damnified by the draining, and in case of refusing to be distrained on.

Lord Gorges was against this motion, in regard that the drainers have sustained no damage.

[1] Cf. Marvell, *Letters*, pp. 68, 69 and Grey, p. 115.

Colonel Sandys in respect of Sir John Cutts moved that he might be heard at the Bar, and also he does believe that he is not at all damnified by [the] levels, and therefore moved that nothing in this House might pass against the drainers before they be heard, and if there be procured any order or judgment against them, that they may have liberty to appeal to the courts in Westminster.

Mr. Crouch affirmed that Sir John Cutts was damnified by the draining £200 per annum, and divers more were likewise hurt by it.

Then we fell upon the business of the day, the raising of the King's supply.

Colonel Sandys moved that an act might be passed for to send out privy seals, and that none should be above £500 nor any under £50, and only to raise an £100,000 ready money to lend it to the King for six months gratis, and to be secured to be paid out of the first money raised of the £300,000.

Sir Jonathan Trelawney moved to send to the city of London to borrow an £100,000 upon the security of the £300,000.

Sir Launcelot Lake seconded that motion, and alleged Cromwell's precedent.

Sir John Arnly liked the way of borrowing it of the city, but moved that the Parliament would fix upon some commodity or way of raising the £300,000 which might be a foundation for that security.

Sir Nicholas Cary said there was a probability of a discovery to be made of those that have cheated the King, and that the tax may be laid upon them.

Sir Anthony Irby moved the Speaker to leave the Chair and that the committee of the whole House do consider of a way how [to] raise the same, but it was opposed and the Speaker did not leave the Chair.

Sir John Knight moved for privy seals.

Sir Hugh Windham to lay a fund of credit upon wine.

Colonel Birch moved to raise French wine 4d. and Spanish 6d. a quart till £80,000 was received.

Sir Thomas Lee was against naming or agreeing upon any sum until some way was resolved on how to raise it.

Colonel Sandys was for laying it wholly upon wine and brandy.

During this debate of laying this supply upon wine and brandy Sir Thomas Littleton put in an exception against an excise.

Sir Nicholas Cary moved that no member of this House should have any hand in any excise.

Sir Robert Carr seconded that motion that no member should have any share in forming any excise.

Sir John Birkenhead moved that no member should have anything to do in collecting this tax upon wines and brandy, but he was against the making void all grants made to those that are farmers of the excise already settled.

Lord George moved that all those that have anything to do as officers of the excise should be expelled this House.

Colonel Birch was for an excise on wine and brandy, and that commissioners be appointed to impose it, and order the collecting of it, and give an account of it quarterly.

Sir William Thompson was against the laying an excise on wine and brandy in London, and bills of mortality, but to lay it on all other places of the kingdom.

Sir Thomas Lee was against laying it upon wines all England over, but to lay it only on London, and bills of mortality and port towns.

Sir Robert Holt against laying it on inland country vintners, because it may cause many of them to throw up their livings, which will prejudice the Duke of York.[1]

Mr. Waller moved that this tax be only laid on the unlicensed vintners, and then it will neither prejudice the Duke of York's revenues nor be hurtful to landlord or tenant.

At last the House resolved to raise an £100,000 on wine, and to sit again to-morrow further to consider the manner of raising it and the rest of the supply.

MARCH 13TH. This day Sir Thomas Felton's bill[2] was read, committed, but it was moved that the bailiff that had been in

[1] *Statutes of the Realm*, v, 15 Car. II, c. 14, for the Duke of York's revenue from license, etc. Bills of Mortality here imply the area in and round London for which they were issued.

[2] *C.J.* IX, 66, gives Henry for Thomas Felton. For this day see also Cobbett, IV, 417; Grey, pp. 115–16.

custody for distraining his beasts ever since the last adjournment should be considered in his fees, because he could not be heard by reason of the adjournment.

The motion to renew the act against conventicles held a debate of two hours. Many spoke effectually for it, as Colonel Sandys, Colonel Strangways excellently, cousin Milward, Sir John Denham, Sir Thomas Meers, Sir Robert Holt and others. Against it there spake Sir Thomas Littleton, Mr. Swinsen, Mr. Marvell, Sir Robert Carr, Mr. Jones and others, but to little purpose, for it was carried with a multitude of voices in the affirmative, of which I was one.

I went that day to Lambeth, and the House voted afterwards to lay 4d. a quart on French wines, 6d. on Spanish wines and 1s. on brandy, and to take up the supply again to-morrow.

MARCH 14TH. This day Mr. Crouch made his report from the committee concerning Humphreys and his sub-farmer of the chimney money in the North Riding of Yorkshire, and their four agents or servants. A complaint had been made by a constable and some others of that Riding that this Humphreys and his agents had collected hearth money in a violent way, with foot soldiers and their muskets, and because the constable did not do what they commanded him they abused him and caused him to be imprisoned to his damage of £40. Upon complaint Humphreys and his four men were sent for up into custody; they moved the House now for their liberty, and the committee also moved for it. The House generally consented to the release of the four servants, but in regard that Humphreys had been and was a notorious knave, denying his hand to divers warrants that he had issued out and, as his men confessed, had ordered to be signed with his hand and sent out, and also because of the great damage that the constable had sustained by his imprisonment and ill usages, the House ordered that he should likewise have his liberty, but withal that he should make reparation to the constable as the justices of peace of that Riding should appoint.

The House then took up the business of the day, concerning the King's supply, but before we proceeded Sir Thomas Meers

informed the House that some of the commissioners of accounts
were at the door and desired to give the House an account how
far they had proceeded; whereupon it was ordered to call them
in, but before they were called in we had a great debate whether
they should have chairs set [for] them or not, but in regard Lord
Viscount Halifax was not there it was said no Peer was there,
for Lord Brereton was not a Peer of England, and therefore they
had no chairs, but the seats only at the Bar was prepared for
them; the Bar was not let down, and Lord Brereton and five
more of the commissioners came in.

Sir William Turner (who is pricked for next Lord Mayor) was
speaker for all the rest; he presented to the Speaker a book of
seven sheets of paper written close on both sides. There was a
debate whether it should be then read or not; it was ordered to
be read, and it was a very exact form and method of their
proceedings. It did inform that some persons did abscond and
would not be brought in to make their accounts to what they
were able to charge upon them; they also informed of the great
abuse of buying tickets at 7s. per pound and some at 5s. the
pound, and also of the irregular paying of such tickets; but they
gave us no account as yet of the disposing of any moneys. When
the book was read the commissioners were called in and the
House gave them their hearty thanks for their excellent method
and great care in their proceedings, and prayed them to continue
the same, and that this House will at all times and upon all
occasions be ready to assist them.

Sir Thomas Meers from a private committee reported to the
House that there is in one whole year brought into England
15,000 tun of wine, which at 4d. a quart French and 6d. a quart
Spanish cometh in one year to £300,000, out of which abate for
wine in private cellars £40,000 and for leakings and lees of
French £30,000 and of Spanish £30,000 and there remains to
be rated £200,000. And of brandy brought in in one year,
750 tun, which at 1s. a quart will yield £88,000, by which it
appears that of wine and brandy in one year two hundred and
eighteen thousand pounds; to which if the excise of tobacco may
be added, it will make up the whole sum of £300,000 in one
year. He moved that this imposition upon brandy may be

continued eighteen months if the sum of £300,000 be not raised in one year.

MARCH 16TH. This day Sir Thomas Heblethwaite's bill was read, passed and sent up to the Lords by Sir Thomas Gower.

Two more bills of the like nature were read and committed.

Then was read the petition of the Irish adventurers; it was long debated. Mr. Harry Coventry spoke against it, and alleged that those adventurers could not as yet duly make their claim, because their adventures were conditional, that is, that they should have the rebels' land for their adventures when the rebels were conquered; but the rebels were never conquered until Cromwell's rebellion in Ireland, when he destroyed the King's party and interest there and made them the rebels, and shared the Duke of Ormond's estate, and many other loyal Irish gentlemen's and others that joined with the Duke to maintain the King's interest. Mr. Coventry was irregularly taken down in his speech by Sir Edward Windham, the King's Marshall.

The House then fell upon two debates, first that the Irish petition should be read this day month; secondly that it should be taken into consideration this day fortnight the first business of the day.

After a very long debate it was put to the question whether that question of taking it into debate on Monday fortnight should be put or not; the ayes were 96, of which I was one; the noes were 128.[1]

Then it was put to the question whether it should be heard at the Bar this day month, and it was carried in the affirmative.

Then certain qualifications were added to the question, of saving the possessions and present interest of adventure purchasers by patent soldiers and '49 officers and the Duke of York's interest; so that the adventurers may gain little by it.

It was voted to take the King's supply into consideration to-morrow at nine of the clock, and to meddle with no other business but how to raise that money.

Secretary Morice acquainted the House that the King had a

[1] C.J. ix, 68, 96–124, Angier and Massey, Wheeler and Seymour.

desire that they should adjourn for a short time, and that we speedily meet again after the holy days.

It was ordered that we should adjourn on Wednesday to Thursday in Easter Week.

MARCH 17TH. This day a bill was read the first time to enforce the payment in of the arrears of the last poll money and all other moneys of the King's, whether unpaid by those places that it was charged upon, or whether it be in the hands of collectors, or receivers, or any other person. And that whosoever after a blank day in May, 1668, shall not have paid in all his assessments, or whatsoever receiver or other person shall have any of the King's money or assessments in his hands, and does not pay it in by the blank day in May, he shall pay full interest for it and be liable to a further punishment.

The House then went upon the business of the day, the raising the supply. Sir John Knight began and spake against the excise of tobacco; and his reason was for that it being managed in the plantations by our English natives, it was in a manner a home commodity, and that it was the only way to destroy that plantation by laying too heavy a tax upon it, and by that means to transplant that trade into Holland, by venting there at a less custom and by encouraging the Dutch to plant it in their plantations, it being so vendible a commodity.

Mr. Weld spoke against laying it on the retailers of tobacco, but lay it at the custom house, and likewise to lay a charge upon foreign linen at the custom house.

Sir William Coventry spoke against laying it at the custom house, because it would endanger trade and endanger the King's custom already settled, and hinder the carrying out of our old shoes and hose, clothes and other mean commodities.

Sir Thomas Lee against paying the excise of tobacco upon the retailer, but to lay it at the custom house.

Colonel Birch for laying the excise upon the retailer, but withal he moved to put it to the question whether tobacco should be charged at all in raising this £300,000.

Sir Thomas Clifford was against laying it on the merchant at the custom house, because it might cause the merchant to abate the trade of tobacco, and by that means our old shoes and clothes and such like mean commodities for it.

Mr. Waller said since it is not convenient to lay it at the custom house we should have recourse to the House to set us at liberty from a former vote, that we might lay it upon the retailer.

Sir Edward Turner moved that whereas we had voted to lay £100,000 upon the retailers of wine for eighteen months, to lay the other £200,000 upon the merchant the next year and so charge wine with the whole £300,000.

Mr. Vaughan made a distinction between laying the tax at the custom house and to lay it upon the custom house; to lay it upon the custom house, he said, was to charge the merchant and might prejudice the King's custom already laid upon the commodity, but to lay it at the custom house was only to lay it on the retailer.

Sir Thomas Littleton was for laying on tunning, upon all ships that bring in wines, except such as bring in Malagas, because they bring in other commodities with these wines.

One of the chief arguments against laying at the custom house is this: when the custom is heightened and raised it will tempt them to steal the commodity and to conceal it, and so the King will lose both the present tax and his custom also.

The House rose to dinner and adjourned till three of the clock; I came not into the House again until six of the clock, and then it was put to the question whether the tax upon wines at the custom house should be added to the tax upon retailers towards the raising of an £100,000. The House was divided; the noes that went out were 57, of whom was my cousin Milward and Sir Job Charlton; the ayes were 68, of whom I was one.

MARCH 18TH.   This day a private bill was read,[1] and then the House took up the business of the day, which was the last day's vote, that the tax upon wines and brandy at the custom house should be added to the tax upon retailers for raising an £100,000.

The Lords sent us down the explanatory bill for keeping out Irish cattle, which they had passed with some amendments.

[1] *C.J.* IX, 68. The private bill was Beckham's. For this and previous days see Grey, pp. 116–20. Tellers for the division above, Frederick and Knight, Carr and Musgrave.

They also sent us a message that they had adjourned until Thursday sevennight.

Many speeches were made this day by divers members against laying an imposition upon wines, some against laying it upon vintners and many against laying it at the custom house.

Sir John Knight made a long impertinent speech, and so did Sir Charles Harbord, against it, and so did divers others also, both in regard of the uncertainty of how much it would raise and against the time, which was eighteen months, designed to raise it in, which was said would gain no credit to borrow present money, and also that it [would] be destructive to trade.

Sir William Hickman moved to lay it upon stocks of trade, but not upon stocks of cattle upon grounds, and upon money at interest.

The House upon other motions inclined very much to a moderate poll bill, and in it to bring in dignities, both of clergy and laities, and all other persons that are not worth twenty pounds, and all money and stocks of trade.

This motion took very much in the House, especially with the nonconformists and courtiers, but there was a great debate about taxing the clergy.

Mr. Prynne moved that all delinquents, especially such as fight duels, and chiefly those that fight them now in Parliament time, an act now being prepared against duels, that they should forfeit their whole estate for the public service; he instanced the late unfortunate and unwarranted duel wherein two were slain; and also that they should be highly taxed that have got estates by cheating the King and kingdom.

To this Sir Thomas Littleton replied in excuse of the Duke of Buckingham and the duellists,[1] and said that it could not be denied but that there happened a great and sad miscarriage; but since it received a pardon under the Great Seal he hoped the House would not vacate the King's pardon. He then fell foully and unmannerly upon the bishops, and moved that they

---

[1] Buckingham fought Charles Talbot, Earl of Shrewsbury, on 16 January, at Barn Elm, his seconds being Robert Howard and William Jenkins. Charles pardoned both contestants shortly before Shrewsbury's death two months later.

should now pay the two subsidies which the King had formerly remitted.

Many were offended at his speech endeavouring to excuse a vicious and notorious murder, and so much to inveigh against the reverend clergy.

Many spoke against the bishops as having raised great sums of money and were wanting in charitable works; and some Yorkshiremen no favourers of them.

Many replied in their defence, and the Solicitor made a most worthy and excellent speech in justification of bishops, and their charitable and pious acts; he with a noble and pious expression remembered and quoted a saying of Bishop Andrews, who said that he would make it good against the gainsayers of all [the] world that the clergy of England since the first reformation had done more works of piety and charity in the first century since the reformation than had been done in any part of Christendom, and that the now present bishops had given thirty thousand pounds to relieve the captives in Algiers; that they have given to the King a great benevolence; that the present Archbishop of Canterbury had built a public structure in Oxford[1] for the public service of the University which would cost him £15,000.

Much more was said in their justification.

In conclusion the bishops are not particularly rated in the poll (though they are not altogether excepted out of it), but are left to the Convocation to see what (of themselves) they will advance towards the raising the £300,000.

It came at last to this vote, that an £100,000 should be raised on the vintners and £200,000 by a poll, and what the poll did not make good and raise of the £200,000 should be raised on wines at the custom house; and so we adjourned until Thursday sevennight.

MARCH 26TH. This day the Speaker was moved to grant out a writ to elect a member in the place of Sir Edward Walpole, who is dead.

Sir Peter Chamberlayne's bill was read to have an act passed to confirm to him and his heirs for ever the privilege of making

---

[1] The Sheldonian.

all such vessels as he shall invent to sail against all winds in a straight line.

The engrossed bill for enabling the County Palatine of Durham to send two knights and two burgesses to Parliament; that the King shall send down the writs and the Bishop see the execution of them, without any prejudice to the county, or against its privilege.[1]

Sir Gilbert Gerrard spake against the bill, he having formerly married the Bishop's daughter; this bill seems to break in upon the power and prerogative of the Bishop.

It was urged that the Palatinate of Durham should have the same privilege of sending up members, as well as the Palatinate of Chester. It was answered by Sir Gilbert that Chester was not empowered to do it upon the same ground. He also affirmed that most of the county were against this bill, and that the county never having this power never suffered any prejudice by it.

Dr. Burwell said that if this bill should pass all the Bishop's tenants (which were a great part of the county) would be excluded from having voices, they being copyholders, and so the freeholders, which are not a tenth part of the county, should only be the electors. He also affirmed that the election hath been in the same state that now it is time out of mind, and that this motion now brought in by this bill had formerly been rejected.

Sir Philip Musgrave moved that though this House did not pass this bill, yet that they would not cast it out, but leave it to the Lords, and let the Bishop, being a member of that House, manage his own business there.

Sir Thomas Gower spoke not against the bill, but brought in a proviso that the manor of Creak [Craik], being a member of the Palatinate but lying in the North Riding of Yorkshire, should pay all taxes and assessments in the North Riding, as formerly it had done continually.

Dr. Burwell affirmed that Craik had ever paid taxes with Durham, which Sir Thomas Gower denied.

Mr. Vaughan spake against the bill, in respect that it was not necessary to increase the numbers of members, the House not having room sufficient to contain those members that were already elected, and that multitude of members retarded business.

[1] Cf. Grey, pp. 120–21.

Sir Thomas Strickland spoke for the bill.

It came at last to a question whether the bill should pass or not; the ayes that went out were 50; the noes were 65, of which I was one.

Sir Jonathan Trelawney brought in privately a particular of the bishops' bounty (in abatement of their fines) and giving money to the King and other pious and charitable works to the value of four hundred thirteen thousand and eight hundred pounds.

It was moved that Sir Allen Broderick and Sir Vincent Churchill, two commissioners for selling the lands in Ireland, should have liberty to go into Ireland, being so appointed by the King, to assist the committee there in selling lands not yet disposed of.

This was obstructed by Colonel Sandys and Mr. Jones.

The Solicitor was for it, because (said he) if they do not go the whole business in Ireland may be obstructed, there being without them but three of the quorum, and if any of them should by chance fall sick the other two cannot proceed.

It was urged that in regard the business of the adventurers was to be heard here at the Bar on Monday fortnight, that they should stay their going until that time, and then they may go when that hearing is past, which might be time enough to perfect the business in Ireland. To this Sir Vincent Churchill replied that [the] King could not enlarge their time one day without an act of Parliament, they being limited by a former act of Parliament to a certain day, viz: the 4th of May, beyond which they could not proceed; and that there was 6000 acres to be distributed amongst them, and therefore the King thought it convenient to send them away.

Sir Anthony Irby spake against it and said that if their going had been moved before the adventurers' case had been appointed a day of hearing, he should not have been against their going, but since the day was appointed on Monday fortnight he thought they ought not to go before, but to stay and give the House satisfaction in the business.

Mr. Marvell was for adjourning their going until the adventurers' case was heard at the Bar.

Sir Vincent Churchill said that there can be no longer time

given to the committee in Ireland for the settlement of that business beyond the 4th of May, and that it was unreasonable that the adventurers that had already two parts settled upon them, and others that deserve as well as they, for whom this third part was reserved, should be kept from it, being in great want and ready to starve without it.

It was put to the vote whether they should be permitted to go or not and it was carried in the affirmative.

It was ordered that the report of the miscarriages of the officers of the chimney shall be made to the House to-morrow.

Sir Robert Carr moved that the committee appointed to look into miscarriages be renewed, that they may enquire what officers of the Navy have been guilty of miscarriages, that being found out they may be laid aside and others put in their places.

Colonel Sandys moved that the same committee may enquire of the cause why Sir John Harman is not come home, it being supposed that he is ordered to keep away.

Mr. Wren, the Duke of York's secretary, informed the House that he had a letter from Sir John Harman on 8th of January; that he only stayed for provision and victuals for such ships as he was to leave beyond the West Indies and as soon as that provision did come to them he would come away for England.

The House being in a Grand Committee it was debated whether the House of Commons had power to set a poll upon the Lords.

Sir Edward Turner said the House of Commons had power and had assessed the Lords, but the Lords had ever made choice of their own commissioners to collect.

Mr. Vaughan moved that the nobility and gentry should stand in the poll as they did the last time, but that the poor should be eased.

It was voted that the laity should be rated at half of that they were rated at the last poll.

No man not worth £20 should pay for his children, nor any child under the age of six or not worth £50 to be polled, but this was adjourned.

MARCH 27TH. This day Colonel Wanklin, who had married the Lady Marlborough, petitioned against Mr. Ash, the son of John Ash, of Goldsmiths' Hall, who brought in an injunction to stop the Colonel from committing waste upon the lady's jointure, served the injunction upon five of the Colonel's servants and imprisoned them, which he affirmed was a breach of his privilege, being a member of the House of Commons; and therefore moved that his men may be set at liberty, and that Mr Ash may be sent for into custody. It was debated whether to serve an injunction on a member in Parliament time be a breach of privilege; some were clear of opinion that it is a breach of privilege, others were of opinion that it was not.

It was ordered to send for Mr. Ash into custody, but not to set the Colonel's servants at liberty.

Sir John Maynard said in some cases it was a breach of privilege and in some cases not, as for example a member of Parliament sues another man that is not a member: he that is sued cannot have due proceedings against him in law, by reason that he is a member and in Parliament time, and so is without all manner of defence; in this case if he sue the member with an injunction to stay the suit, this is no breach of privilege of Parliament.

Sir John Maynard moved to have liberty to bring in a bill to direct a way how to serve a process with less damage to persons and with less trouble and charge.

It was ordered that the bill concerning the granting of letters of administration of goods intestate to prevent the unequal distributing of such goods be committed.[1]

Mr. Crouch made his report from the committee for the better regulating the officers for collecting chimney money. That if any person procure a certificate from two justices of the peace in his own behalf, if the certificate prove false he shall be fined in a sum not exceeding a treble nor less than a double of the King's money that was due for him to pay to the King, from which he endeavoured by this false certificate to free himself. In case of certificates justices of peace are empowered to administer

[1] Grey (p. 121) gives a speech by a Milward, presumably Robert, on the share of infant children.

an oath. The fine upon a false certificate is to be paid to the
officers of the chimney money, and to be levied by distress (in
case it be denied) by warrant under the hands and seals of two
justices of peace. This distress is to be levied within five months
after it is due.

If a man leave his house and a half-year's rent for his
chimneys be behind, if it be demanded within five months, he
that comes into that house as a new tenant or occupier of it shall
pay that half-year's rent, and therefore he ought to foresee that
all the rent for chimneys be paid before he enter.

But if it be not demanded within five months after he is
entered the house then he shall not be liable to pay it.

MARCH 28TH.   This day it was moved to set at liberty Colonel
Wanklin's servants imprisoned by Mr. Ash. After some debate
it was resolved that his bailiff and another servant should be set
at liberty, because they were his menial servants, and so were
within privileges, but the other three that hired to work for
wages ought not to be set at liberty, by order of the House,
because they are not privileged by Parliament, for the privilege of
Parliament extends to his own person and goods and his menial
servants, but not to protect others that are not his menial servants.

This day it was moved by Sir Edward Massey and Sir Hugh
Windham against Sir Peter Pindar for exacting undue fees at
the custom house; he was much defended by Sir Thomas
Smith, Colonel Birch and others. It was ordered that it should
be referred to a committee, and he be sent for but [not?] into
custody to answer their charge against him.

Sir George Downing brought in a bill for exporting corn,
beef, pork, mutton, swine, beasts, horses, mares, sheep and
foals that are carried into foreign parts in English ships. It was
read and ordered a second reading.

Sir Heneage Finch brought in his bill raising £100,000 upon the
retailers of wines and brandy, French wines to pay 4d., Spanish
6d. and brandy 1s. a quart; and the retailer to sell French wines
at 1s., Spanish wines at 2s. and brandy at [10s.] a quart.[1]

[1] The Act does not specify the price of brandy retail, though it con-
firms Milward's figures on French and Spanish wines (*Statutes of the
Realm*, v, 631), but see below, p. 241.

If any English strong waters be mixed with brandy, they shall pay as if they were brandy.

It is moved that the King appoint commissioners and that they have power to enter into cellars, but yet with the consent of the retailers first required, that likewise to be done between sun rising and sun setting. If any retailer refuse to suffer the commissioners or their agents to enter and examine their cellars, being duly required, he shall be liable to a fine.

If a retailer be oppressed by the commissioners or their agents, upon his just complaint he shall be relieved.

If a retailer make his composition and do not pay his money in due time he is to be distrained and the distress is to be sold.

If a retailer refuse to suffer his cellars and stores to be viewed, the commissioners may break into such cellars.

The commissioners have power to compound with the retailers for so much, and for such a time, until the hundred thousand pounds be raised and interest for the credit of it.

The sum to be compounded must thus be paid, a third part in hand and the other two parts at such times as shall be agreed on.

The commissioners and their agents are to take an oath to do justly.

The rate of wine shall begin May 1st, 1668, and end November 1st, 1669.

No merchant importer shall sell any wine but to the retailer, unless he first pay the same proportion as is charged upon the retailer and upon forfeiture of the double value.

No man is to retail wine but by licence.

The commissioners are to pay in all such moneys as they shall receive within so many weeks.

The commissioners are to make duplicates and to return them by such a time in to the Exchequer, that so it may be known when the £100,000 is raised, and when the £100,000 is raised, then the wines are to be sold again at the same price as now they are sold at.

If a retailer take above the price now allowed he is to forfeit so much.

This bill was read, and spoken against by Sir John Knight and Sir Thomas Meers, but ordered to be read the second time on Tuesday next.

Sir William Killigrew and divers others with him moved the House to reverse an order made yesterday at three of the clock in a very thin House, when there was but 50 members present, for in passing that order by a question the House was divided: 25 were for it and 25 against passing it; the Speaker's voice carried it in the affirmative. The business was this: the case of Lindsey levels was formerly ordered to be heard at the Bar on Tuesday next; by this last vote it was put off until Friday sevennight. Sir William Killigrew now moved to reverse that order so gotten at an undue time and in so thin a House, and that it may be heard according to the first order on Tuesday next. There was a great stir and stiff debate about it, but at last it was ordered to be heard on Tuesday sevennight.

The House made an order that no new business or new motion shall be received after twelve of the clock.

MARCH 30TH.   This day the bill was brought in for continuing the act against conventicles; it was opposed by Mr. Marvell, but it was ordered to be read to-morrow.

It was moved in the House that the justices of peace shall be looked into, and where any have neglected to do their duty that they shall be put out of their commission.

It was ordered that the Knights of the Shire attend the Lord Keeper to see the catalogue of the justices and to inform him of their miscarriages. I told them that I would not be informer of the miscarriages, but I would inform them who had been committee men and decimators, if they would put them out.

The Lords sent down two provisoes with the Irish bill; one was that where any town, parish or constabulary shall connive at any Irish beasts that shall pass through them and not be seized on, that town or parish shall be fined £100, the same to be employed for a stock for the poor at the house of correction.

This was said to be somewhat too severe, but at last it was restrained to those towns or places where such cattle are first landed or imported and that such town takes a composition, and so takes no notice of their landing and passing away.

Secondly if any person shall enter into a conspiracy against this act and the same shall be discovered within one year, it shall be *praemunire*.

The bill against transporting wool out of this kingdom was read and a prohibition of wool houses to be made use of near the sea-coast. Sir Robert Carr and some others moved that the wool houses at Romney Marsh and some other marshes that are far from the habitations of those that own the sheep there may be allowed, although it be near the sea-coast, so that they give assurance not to transport their wool into foreign countries.

It was also moved that the same prohibition may be upon Ireland.

It was moved that the law that made transporting of wool to be treason should be repealed, and another penalty put on it.

Another bill was brought in and read the second time for the exporting of corn, beef, bacon, pork, cattle, horses and mares, at such an impost.

The House went upon the business of the day, which was upon the poll bill. It was voted that every single person not excepted in the bill shall pay his twelve pence; that the children of householders not above sixteen years old shall be excepted.

That aliens in all capacities shall pay double, and the Jews more.

Secretary Morice acquainted us that the King commanded our attendance in the Banqueting House at three of the clock, where he would communicate something to us.

I went to Lambeth to dinner, and thence came to Whitehall, where the King told us that he desired and conjured us to hasten his supply, that he might make his engagement good with his neighbours and allies, and that he might, as he is engaged, set out his fleet; and that we would despatch all other business that we might go home at Whitsuntide.

We came back to the House and the Speaker reported the King's speech.

It was then ordered that the House at ten of the clock should every day fall upon the King's supply until it was perfected.

Sir Robert Brooke and others of that gang endeavoured to obstruct that vote but they could not.

It was moved by Colonel Birch that the two great miscarriages

—the first was the mis-spending the great sums of money that have been raised, the other the not securing the river Medway—should be looked into and examined.

MARCH 31ST. This day a complaint was of the great decay of churches, and that they were very much out of repair, and that the ecclesiastical courts had no other power to force their repair, but only excommunication, which was of no force at all with some men, especially those that did willingly absent themselves from the church.

Mr. Speaker said it did not belong to the ecclesiastical court to appoint the raising and levying money for such repairs; that did belong to the constables and churchwardens to do it by a general assessment amongst the parishioners and inhabitants, and if any man did refuse to pay his assessment the civil magistrate was to enforce the payment; the ecclesiastical court had only power to enforce the repair, but not to raise any money.

It was ordered that a bill be brought in for the repair of churches.

The bill for preventing high-way robbing with the amendments was brought in; all the amendments upon reading were rejected and it was referred to the old statutes.

The House then took the business of the day, the King's supply.

The bill for raising the £100,000 upon retailers of wine was read, and very much opposed by the dissenters.

It was moved that the bill should extend no further than the times of communication and bills of mortality, and that it shall not concern the country vintners because of the great rent that they pay to the Duke of York for their wine licences.

The vintners, I perceive, are fallen in with the Presbyterian party to avoid the present payment and indeed to throw out the bill and so to obstruct the raising this money.

APRIL 1ST. This day was received the bill of Sir Gervase Clifton and Mr. Clarkton concerning the enclosure of a common at Wakefield. Sir John Northcote and Mr. Weld opposed the bill; Sir Philip Musgrave and Lord Richardson spake for it. It was put to the question whether the bill should be cast out or committed; the House was divided upon it: the ayes that were for passing the bill went out and were 30; I was one; the noes were 29, and so we carried it.[1]

Then the bill for redressing abuses in collecting chimney money was read and passed.

Sir Robert Holt moved that the forges of smiths and nailers should be excepted and not paid for as chimneys.

If the officers of the chimney money come to the constable and require his aid he is to assist them in demanding the rent due, and is to have sixpence a time, and if the rent due be unpaid and a distress taken, then he is to have 1s. for every distress that is taken.

That no member or other person that is a farmer or officer of chimney money shall be a judge or justice to give judgment in that case.

It was this day debated whether the £300,000 should be wholly raised in wines or not. After a long debate it was voted that the £300,000 should be laid upon wines and brandy, and that the retailers should be charged with it, and that they should sell their French wines at 1s. and their Spanish at 2s. a quart, and brandy at 10s. a quart, and this to continue from the first of May, 1668, to the first of November, 1670; and in case this sum of £300,000 be not raised in this two years, that the remainder shall be raised at the custom house in one year.

APRIL 2ND. This day[2] Mr. Harbord made his report from the committee concerning the reforesting of the Forest of Dean, and the enclosing of eleven thousand acres for the increase of timber.

It was committed again to the same committee to perfect one amendment and ordered to be brought to-morrow in again.

Then the House went to the business of the day, to perfect the supply.

A question was started whether the tax upon wine should be laid on the first or last retailer, and how to prevent the often retailing and paying the excise of the same wine more than once.

[1] C.J. IX, 72, 30–29, Richardson and Gower, Northcote and Weld.
[2] C.J. IX, 73–4. MS. omits dates of 2 and 3 April.

This debate perplexed the House more than a little, and held at least two or three hours, nor could it be resolved how to prevent it, if the words of the bill "all and every retailers" be taken in a liter[al] sense.

It was voted as the sense of the House that no wine should be twice charged with this payment.

It was then voted to recommit it, and that the committee do bring in a clause to-morrow to comprehend the sense of the House, that the same wine be not twice taxed.

The House then adjourned until three of the clock, and then the Lord Cornbury's and Mr. Lenthall's cause was heard at the Bar.

Mr. Lenthall was plaintiff, and sought to be relieved against Lord Clarendon, because, as he alleged, Lord Clarendon had wrongfully thrust him out of a lease which he held of the Bishop of Winchester; and to obtain that lease from him he used many indirect ways, as imprisonment of his person, threatening to hang him for treason and such like. Counsel was heard on both sides and all that could be said for them both.

The business was to me very dubious, and I being unwilling to wrong either party with my vote came away at seven of the clock at night; yet in the strictness of law and right I do believe Lord Cornbury hath the better of it.

When the House had fully heard the cause and the counsel was withdrawn the House took the merit into consideration, and without any long debate or less opposition the House voted to throw out Mr. Lenthall's petition, and ordered that a bill be brought in to compel Mr. Lenthall to provide portions for the young gentlewomen out of his estate, he having had a great estate of land by their mother, which he caused her to settle upon him, and in lieu of that disposed of his lease to raise them portions, which they should [have] had out of their mother's estate of land, and so hath left the poor young gentlewomen destitute of portions unless the House of Commons relieve them.

APRIL 3RD. This day Francis Hollingshead's bill was read the first time, and was ordered a second reading on Monday next.

A petition was read in the behalf of the indigent officers,

signed by four or five of them in the name of all the rest. The petition was spoken against in regard that those persons pretended a deputation from the rest of the indigent officers, when it is believed that those formerly had taken the money to themselves, and not suffered the other to have any share with them, and it is suspected that they will do the same again.

My cousin Milward is ordered to bring in a bill to call the treasurers of that money and all other persons that have any of that money in their hands to give an account of it, that those [that] are in need and are truly indigent, and have not had any part of it as yet, may be relieved and have their shares also, and then if there be any surplusage, that may be divided amongst them all.

The Lords sent us a message that there were some faults escaped in the act for Bedford levels through fault in the clerks in the engrossing it, and that they desired a conference for the rectifying and amending it. This was Colonel Sandys's bill for the regulating the taxes and assessments of Bedford levels.

A complaint was brought in against Judge Tyrrell forcing a jury to go out again upon a prisoner after he had been tried before Chief Justice Keeling, and had been acquit by the jury, and had upon his knees prayed for the King, Judge Tyrrell being present at his trial.

This complaint was brought in by Sir Robert Carr and Colonel Slanning, whereupon a bill was ordered to be brought in by Sir Thomas Gower against the miscarriages of the judges in general, as there had been against Chief Justice Keeling.

The act of the militia was taken into debate and referred to a committee to consider of the defects of it, to prevent the illegal imprisoning of men by the Provost-marshal. This was pressed very much by Sir Thomas Littleton, upon Mr. Lenthall's imprisonment under the Provost-marshal both in Oxford and London.

It was moved that all the members that were deputy-lieutenants should be of the committee, but it was carried in the negative, and, as was said, the justices of peace that were not deputy-lieutenants opposed that motion.

I went this day to dinner to Sir George Carteret's, and afterwards went to the House again to the committee, to hear the debate of granting letters of administration *de rationabile parte bonorum*, where the party dies intestate. It was moved that that power of granting letters of administration in that kind may be taken away from the ecclesiastical court and be placed in the courts of the common law. This motion was debated by Sir Robert Wiseman and Sir Walter Walker, who both spake and argued most learnedly and excellently in the right of the ecclesiastical courts and jurisdiction.

The committee adjourned the debate until Thursday next.

APRIL 4TH. This day Sir Trevor Williams brought in a petition from the vintners and merchants that if the Parliament would accept of it, the vintners would advance an £100,000 present money, and the merchants would secure the other £200,000, but because there was neither merchants' nor vintners' hand to the proposal the House denied the reading of it.

It was said that it was only a design to put off the King's business and to retard the raising of the money, and no reality at all in the business.

Colonel Birch brought in a clause to prevent the double payment of the excise of wine by the retailer. It was opposed, though weakly, yet with much confidence, by Sir John Knight, as a thing hurtful to the King's revenue, and that notwithstanding all fair pretences the retailer would be forced to pay the excise twice over for it.

Colonel Birch made a good reply that the excise may be well discharged by a certificate which would discharge and satisfy all interests.

The strong waters imported that were to be excised were called brandy, ruske, rum.[1]

We spent three hours in debate about words, what to call the strong liquors that should be taxed.

There is a suit depending between the farmers of the excise

---

[1] Cf. Marvell, *Letters*, p. 70: "We have bin day by day upon the King's supply, we have not made any considerable progress." Ruske is probably an error for Rack or Arack, brandy. No Russian liquor is known in that period by such a name.

of strong waters and the merchants, whether brandy was within the nature of such strong waters as are to be excised, and upon this there was a great and unnecessary dispute in the House, and it did not in any case determine the suit depending between the merchants and farmers, but this was started on purpose to hinder the raising the King's supply. At last it was resolved that all brandy and spirits and also all strong waters whatsoever that were imported shall pay 1s. a quart by the first retailer.

All committees were adjourned, and so the House adjourned also till Monday.

APRIL 6TH. This day a bill was presented that whereas Mr. Lenthall had married a lady that had £400 per annum of land of inheritance, and had persuaded her to settle this estate upon him in fee, and in lieu of it had settled an estate upon her (that was the King's) for the preferment of her children, which when the King was happily returned was taken from them, and so proved an unwarrantable estate, it was prayed by the bill that the sum of £6000 should be raised out of Mr. Lenthall's estate for the portions of one son and two daughters, in full recompence of the estate which upon the marriage came by the mother and did belong to them.

A proviso was brought in for the Forest of Dean, that the King may have power to set leases of the underwoods and mines for 50 years; some moved that the King may have power to set leases for a longer time, others that he may have power to set mines out of the 11,000 acres that are to be enclosed for timber; but not within them, because by those mines and the people that come in with horses and carriages to get and fetch away the mines the young trees as they grow up may be spoiled.

Mr. Goring, a member of the House, complained that during his attendance his horse was distrained and sold for an assessment for the poor. It was debated whether this was a breach of his privilege; some said it was a breach of privilege, and that goods were privileged as well as person; others that the privilege extends to the person but not to goods; but in the end it was resolved that the privilege extends to goods, and therefore it was ordered that the man that distrained the horse should be sent for to give an account of it to the committee for so doing.

APRIL 7TH. This day[1] the bill was read the second time in the behalf of the Lady Stonehouse's children, that Mr. Lenthall shall set out land to secure £6000 for their portions, in regard that Witney, that was settled upon them in lieu of the land their mother passed away, was recovered from them. The bill was opposed by Mr. Seymour and others, but was at last committed.

A bill was read to enforce all receivers and other officers (sheriffs excepted) to bring all such moneys of the King's that is in their hands and not brought in and accounted for, or neglected to be collected by them.

The House was called yesterday.

This day the great business of Lindsey levels between Sir William Killigrew and Sir Robert Carr was heard at the Bar.

APRIL 8TH. This day the bill concerning Mr. Lucien Fowler was brought in by my cousin Milward and moved [by] Mr. Chetwind; it informed that whereas Mr. Fowler the grandfather by his wife had appointed that Mr. Cholmondeleigh should be guardian to his son, Lucien Fowler, being an infant, and the said Mr. Cholmondeleigh appointed Mr. Fowler, grandfather to the infant, to gather the rents of his estate, and being desirous to be eased of the trust and to transfer it to Mr. Fowler the grandfather: it was moved by the bill the said Mr. Cholmondeleigh may be discharged by an act of Parliament and confer it upon Mr. Fowler the grandfather, all parties consenting to the bill.

It was very much opposed by Mr. Seymour, as that it was a wrong to the infant, as if Mr. Cholmondeleigh was liable to an account, which Mr. Fowler the grandfather (concerned in this bill) will not be for the profits of the land.

But upon my cousin Milward's opening the case and showing the mistake the bill was committed.

Sir Thomas Gower also opposed the bill, pretending that his son and Sir Richard Temple had a right to that estate and inheritance, and so ought not to be barred by an act, nor the estate by a side wind settled on the infant.

[1] Grey omits the 7th, but is interesting on the 8th (pp. 126–32).

The bill for trial of Peers was read; it was sent down engrossed from the Lords. The bill did inform that the High Steward should give summons to all the Peers of the Realm to be present at such trial, but if upon the summons they do not all appear, yet there shall be to the full number of twenty-five, and all of them of full age of one and twenty years.

Also that any she Peer shall be likewise tried after the same manner.

Lord Richardson spake against the bill and said it broke in upon the King's prerogative for the Steward to appoint the number of Peers for the trial of any individual Peer.

Mr. Vaughan also said that some things in the bill were not just, that it took away all exceptions of the Peer that was to be tried, that he might justly take against any Peer that was to be his trier; and that it did encroach upon the King's prerogative.

But after some debate it was ordered a second reading.

Sir Thomas Dawes his executor brought in a petition to be relieved against the farmers of the customs for a debt of £30,000, they having received £250,000 for which they have made no true account.

It was ordered that his petition should be referred to a committee.

It was reported from the committee of grievances that the patent from the lighthouse at Milford Haven was a grievance and therefore ought to be called in, because the patentees had illegally raised money on the country which neither they nor any patentees or others whatsoever can legally do without an act of Parliament; also that those three men that were appointed to collect the money be sent for up to answer it.

Sir Jonathan Trelawney spoke in behalf of the lighthouse as a thing most necessary to seamen that came near that coast.

Sir John Northcote spoke against the lighthouse, and that the raising money for it without an act of Parliament was a grievance and illegal.

Sir Fretchville Holles said the lighthouse was a thing of great use, for although it be true that Milford Haven is a very good and safe harbour, yet there is a rock in the very middle of the harbour that at a low water is not above seven foot water, and although the harbour be good on both sides yet in a dark night without the directions of that lighthouse it may be very dangerous for ships to come in.

Mr. Waller said that a patent with the Great Seal is warrantable until it be proved a grievance and illegally granted, and therefore the persons that act by it are not in fault, and therefore he believed that the three persons that were collectors ought not to be punished.

The House then went to the business of the day, to consider of the later part of the King's speech.

Sir Fretchville Holles made a very long and impertinent speech in order to a toleration to all dissenters from the Church, and in conclusion moved to make an address to the King to take the business into [his] hands, and to call some principal persons of all the dissenters, and to receive proposals from them.

Mr. Coke very honestly moved that we should not trouble the King with it, but that dissenters should bring in their proposals to the House and show their reasons why they do dissent from the government established.

Colonel Birch made a long impertinent speech, that to grant a toleration was for the King's interest; it would unite the hearts of his subjects to him; it would prove for the interest of the nation, the advantage of trade and for the interest of religion to comprehend some that were now dissenters and to bring by that means some of them to the Church, and so to leave out fewer to oppose the government. It would be the decay of Popery, which was greatly increased by our divisions. He also moved that this particular of assent and consent should not be imposed nor none of the new oaths.

Mr. Steward spake well and said that to yield to a toleration or to indulge liberty without proposals from the parties that desired it is to arraign the present government established, which is both illegal and prejudicial to the peace of the Church, it being formed and established by a legal authority and without any exception at that time by the now dissenting party, and now to satisfy them by a toleration is in a manner to justify the dissenters in their schisms and separation.

Mr. Waller said it was not reasonable that the dissenters

should bring in their proposals, but he argued it very poorly; he was also against the referring it to the Convocation, because, said he, they have no power to make civil laws, for that power only belongs to the Parliament.

Mr. Vaughan was altogether against referring it to the King, for it is unmannerly, (said he), to cast aspersions upon the King, which will unavoidably fall out from the dissenting party if they be denied their desires, though they do it without all loyalty or justice.

Mr. Swinsen said it was very just to refer it to the King, because of his declaration from Breda, whereby he stands obliged to have regard to their tender consciences and to give them indulgence; and if he please to undertake it, it may be an especial means to bring the bishops to a condescension also.

After a debate of three or four hours it came to a question who then we should send to the King to desire him to take the business into his own consideration and judgment, and that he will be pleased to call before him some of the head and chief men of all persuasions and to receive their proposals in order to a union. The House was divided upon the question; the ayes that were for it went out and were 70; the noes that were against sending it to the King were 167 [sic], of which I was one.[1]

It was afterwards moved that we should propose some particulars.

Sir Thomas Lee moved that all new oaths should be taken away and not be imposed.

Sir Thomas Meers moved that before we came to particulars that it should be voted and resolved that this bill of comprehension should not extend to a toleration.

Very much was said about it.

Mr. Vaughan spoke excellently to the question; for, says he, if this bill of comprehension be brought in and this tender conscience be pretended to in hypocrisy, then the pretence is only to subvert the present government, and to base ends, to raise new troubles by destroying the laws. If it be sincere and out of conscience, then toleration is of so large an extent that it may concern the grossest heretics and all other gross opinions as those that move for it, for neither those that deny the humanity

[1] *C.J.* IX, 77, 70–176, Henly and Owen, Holt and Cope.

of Christ nor his divinity, nor the possession of the Holy Ghost, or that hold other damnable heresies, as Arius, Eutiches, Macedonius and others, nor the Papists, but they maintained those heresies and opinions out of conscience, or at least so pretended, as much as any of these now do that separate from the Church, and may as well claim an indulgence in respect of conscience as any of these can do.

He moved it, and it was seconded, that the debate should be adjourned, and in the meantime it shall be lawful for any members within the House to bring in a bill, or any others out of the House to bring in a petition with the particulars of their desires and wherein they will acquiesce.

It was ordered to adjourn the debate for one whole week, and to take it again into consideration on Wednesday next.

The three declarations of *I, A.B.*[1] in the act of uniformity were read, and Colonel Birch most shamefully moved that they might be abolished as new things, and then the dissenters (said he) will acquiesce and submit to the government.

APRIL 9TH. This day Mr. Taylor's bill was read (who was a member of Parliament and is dead) to enable his executors to sell 260 acres of land, it being by a gross mistake in the fine expressed but 60 acres of land and 260 acres of wood, whereas there should have been expressed 60 acres of wood and 260 acres of land; the bill was ordered to be read.

Colonel Sandys moved that a bill may be brought in to recall all grants in remainder made by the King of offices and places; it is consented to.

It was moved that a bill should be brought in for the repair of Corre bridge[2] in Yorkshire, but it was opposed by Mr. Scawen.

Colonel Birch made his report from the committee of the silk throwsters' bill with this amendment, that they shall not be stinted to take any number of prentices, for it seems they were

---

[1] Statutes of the Realm, v, 365. "Form of Assent."

[2] *C.J.* IX, 77, does not mention Corrie Bridge, and I have not been able to trace such a place in Yorkshire, although there is one in Scotland. Possibly Scoreby, near Stamford Bridge. Grey omits the 9th, gives an account of the 10th, omits 11 and 13 April.

formerly stinted not to take above the number of three. The bill was ordered to be engrossed.

Then the House fell upon the business of the day, the King's supply.

The committee debated the paragraph of strong waters.

Sir John Knight spoke against the imposing 1s. a quart upon strong waters made in England of foreign ingredients, as lees of wine and sour wine, because, said he, these two commodities, lees and sour wine, have already paid custom and excise; and secondly because strong waters and brandy are made up of English commodities as well as of the other two.

Colonel Birch spoke for the paragraph and for the taxing of all strong waters imported or extracted over again in England, or else the King's supply will lose a considerable part that may be raised by strong waters, and it is fit to lay a good tax upon these imported strong waters and brandy to discourage the bringing them in, they being most harmful and destructive to the health of our Englishmen's bodies.

These imported strong waters are called brandy, ruske, rum.

It was moved that all strong waters imported should pay 1s. a quart and all strong waters extracted in England out of foreign commodities shall pay 8d. a quart.

After a very long debate it was put to the question whether the paragraph should be part of the bill; the committee was divided to the right and left hand; it was carried in the affirmative; I was one.

The Duke of York sent a message to the House to let them know that according to their desires he had sent to Sir John Harman to hasten his return, and that he was now come to the buoy in the Nore, and that he would send to him to attend the House as soon as he had disposed of the ships in the buoy of the Nore.

APRIL 10TH.   This day Mr. Taylor's bill was read the second time and committed.

The House ordered to return the humble thanks of the House to His Highness the Duke of York for his care in sending to Sir John Harman.

The bill for the six clerks of Chancery was read; it was alleged that the complaints of the under-clerks (who would share with the principal clerks in the fees of the court) was not warrantable, but so far only as it tended to regulating the fees. And also that everyone that shall be admitted a clerk or an attorney in the court shall take the oaths of supremacy and allegiance and the oath of the court, and shall take but ten groats fee for a cause, and but 4*d*. for a sheet of paper written by them. The bill was ordered to be committed.

Mr. Harry Coventry moved that it was unreasonable that the under-clerks, which were but as servants to the six clerks, should be admitted to be equal sharers with them and by that means increase [the] number of clerks, which was the only way to multiply suits; but he said it was just to regulate the exacting of fees.

It appears that a member of the House of Commons is one of the six clerks, and therefore if he will he may have the cause heard at the Bar of the House.

Sir Fretchville Holles complained that he was served with a *sub poena* out of the Chancery, which was voted a breach of privilege.

The bill for enlarging the time for the act against conventicles was read. Sir Adam Brown moved that this amendment may be added to the bill: that whereas by the former act a fine was laid upon them (not exceeding £5) by the justice of peace, and where any refuse to pay that fine to commit them to prison, that now this imprisonment shall be spared as most inconvenient, and instead thereof to levy the fine by distress and the money to be disposed of for the benefit of the poor of the parish; by this the poor for their own benefit and relief will be the more ready to discover all such conventicles and unlawful meetings within them which otherwise may escape undiscovered.

Then the House proceeded to the business of the day, the King's supply.

There was a very great and long debate about these words, "every retailer", that they might be left out, and this was earnestly pressed by those that favoured not the bill, and it was on purpose to make the bill ineffectual, and to take it off the retailer, and to put it upon the merchant, on whom it was not possible to raise money, especially this year, and so at last to lay it upon land, or to bring in a poll bill.

It came to the question whether these words "every retailer" should be kept in the paragraph; the committee was divided, and carried it in the affirmative almost by a double number; I was one.

The Lords sent us down a message that they have agreed to our bill for the indemnifying the sheriffs of London and Warden of the Fleet concerning the escape of prisoners in the late dreadful fire.

Also they sent us down two bills, the one concerning administration of goods intestate; the other was Sir Thomas Heblethwaite's bill, which was to enable him to sell land to pay debts and to raise portions for his children.

Lord St. John moved to have leave to bring in a bill to prevent the denying *habeas corpus*.

APRIL 11TH. This day Francis Hollingshead's bill was read a second time and committed.[1]

Sir Henry Vaughan's election that was questioned, because he was said to be outlawed (before the election) after judgment, was voted legal, because he was but a surety and not principal in the action, and besides there was proved to be very indirect dealing used by Jervas the attorney.

Sir Charles Hungerford moved to have leave to bring in a bill for the retrenching interest money from six per centum to £4 per centum. It was seconded by several persons, as Sir Thomas Lee, Mr. Boscawen and others. Sir William Thompson spoke against it, unless (said he) a register book was first set up to enter the debts and mortgages of every man, that so it may be evident to every lender what security he may have.

Colonel Birch was against the falling interest money so much at one jump (for so he termed it), that it should not be less than £5 per centum. Many said the inconvenience may be as great or greater (in the abatement of interest) as the convenience or advantage could be, so the motion was laid aside for the present, because it was impossible that the bill could pass in this short time we were to sit.

[1] *C.J.* IX, 79. Milward one of Leigh's committee.

Sir Thomas Lee and Colonel Kirby according to order attended the Duke of York with the humble thanks of the House for his great favour in sending to Sir John Harman and hastening his return. The Duke sent the House word by them that he had now sent to him to the buoy in the Nore to come away as soon as he had disposed of the ships there, and the wind being now southward he hoped Sir John would be here within two or three days, and as soon as he comes he shall attend the House.

It is said Sir John Harman hath brought in with him the Smyrna fleet, the West Indies, the Straits and some East India ships, in all to the number of 60 sail, very rich, some say almost to the value of two millions, and that one ship hath brought in 400,000 pieces of eight.

The narrative sent from the commissioners of account was read, in which they have discovered a great deal of miscarriage, both in my Lord Sandwich and his officers at sea, in breaking bulk and embezzling and converting to their own use a vast sum of silk, spices and other rich commodities taken prizes from the Dutch in two East Indian ships, the one called the *Golden Phoenix* and the other the *Slaughteny*. And that after they had thus unjustly and contrary to an express act of Parliament broken bulk and shared these goods the Earl of Sandwich then procured the King's hand to warrant this their misdoing and distribution.

It is ordered[1] that this narrative be taken into consideration and thoroughly debated on Tuesday next, and in the meantime that the thanks of the House be given to the commissioners, and that they be desired that if they have made any new discoveries, that they will impart them to the House, and that if they want any power to enable them further and more effectually to proceed that the House is ready and willing to enlarge their power as far as they are able.

Sir William Killigrew's business concerning Lindsey levels that should have been heard at the Bar is on Monday morning next ordered before all other business to be then heard.

APRIL 13TH. This day the business of Lindsey levels was heard at the Bar. Sir Robert Carr's counsel opened the cause, and that

[1] Cf. Harl. 7170, f. 73 ff.

the Earl of Lindsey was named the chief undertaker and trustee for the rest of the undertakers.

Whilst this was in hearing at the Bar, the Lord Fitzharding acquainted the House that [he] had a message to deliver them from the King, whereupon the counsel of both parties were ordered to withdraw, and then the Lord Fitzharding gave the Speaker a paper which did inform the House that the King did intend to put an end to this session on May the fourth, and therefore did desire them to hasten the supply and to perfect all other business that did concern the public good of the nation.

It was moved (hereupon) by some to lay aside all other business and to fall upon the King's supply, and to take up no other business, and if any man should offer any other business to the House before the King's supply should be raised and settled he should be called to the Bar to answer it.

This motion was opposed by Sir Thomas Lee and Sir Robert Howard; they moved that the grievances of the nation should go hand in hand with the supply; and that order made for the further examination and debate of the embezzling and plundering of the prize ships, according to the narrative sent from the commissioners of the accounts should be observed to-morrow, and that the King's supply should be taken in hand on Wednesday and so on every other day until it was completed.

This after some debate was voted and ordered.

Then they took up the debate of Lindsey levels, and it was moved to send for the counsel again, but there was some offers of a treaty and that it should be referred to some members to hear and conclude a peace if it may be, or else to report their judgments of the cause; but this motion not taking effect, the counsel was called, and so they proceeded, but to no considerable purpose, for the counsel went on with their proofs and the House sat some hours to hear them, and in the end did order the counsel on both sides to sum up all their evidence on Friday next.

APRIL 14TH. This day Sir John Morton[1] and Sir John Fitzjames, burgesses for the town of Poole, complained against

[1] MS. reads Moiton. Grey omits the dispute about timber.

Constantine, a man of the Long Robe, who did (as they say) stir up a factious party, and spake ill words against them as being members and against the House of Commons and their proceedings.

Mr. Whorwood moved to have leave to bring in a bill to be relieved against a decree that had passed to enforce him to give alimony to his wife, and that the House would reverse the decree.

A new bill was read for another rule and order for the rebuilding of the city of London, and first to consider of such streets as are to be enlarged.

Secondly, to consider of such market-places as are necessary to be erected.

Thirdly, to make recompense to those that lose their ground in making the streets uniform.

Fourthly, where there are two or three or more concerned in building, if some will build and others refuse, he or they that will build shall go on with it, and when they have finished the work they shall enjoy it all until those that refused shall pay their just proportions.

Fifthly, the surveyors shall regulate the alterations of grounds for uniformity of the building.

Sixthly, all wharfs shall be set out as they are now bounded.

Seventhly, Cheapside shall be built as it is now set out for the breadth of the street.

Eighthly, every foundation shall pay to the Chamberlain six shillings for every foundation laid.

Ninthly, that it shall be lawful to take up any ground within five miles of London to lay in timber and materials for the building of London, paying for the same ground.

Tenthly, that it shall be felony to carry away and embezzle any iron or lead out of any of the cellars in the ruins.

Eleventhly, whereas by a former act it was granted that they should have three years to rebuild, now it is ordered that four years shall be allowed.

Twelfthly, that one shilling a chauldron shall be laid upon coals towards the discharge of building.

Thirteenthly, that 49 churches shall be rebuilt, and a due consideration had what parishes shall be laid to every church.

Fourteenthly, that no building be made within forty foot of those streets that shall be appointed for the wharfs.

This bill was almost two hours in reading, and some exceptions made to it, but appointed to be read again on Thursday next, and it is believed it will be much spoken against.

The House then went to the business of the day, to examine upon the narrative of the commissioners of accounts about the embezzling prize goods; and first they began with Sir William Penn. They charged him that he came with Sir William Barclay to break bulk contrary to an act of Parliament, and that he did distribute several great parcels of rich goods, and gave warrant for the sale of them, and that he had £2500 for goods sold to the merchants and tradesmen above what the King allowed to be sold or gave them. He acknowledged that he had some of the goods, and that what he did was in obedience to the orders of Lord Sandwich, who was his general. He desired to have the particulars of his charge, and to have leave to give in his answer on Thursday next.

This desire was opposed by some, but in the end the House consented to it.

There are great reflections on Lord Sandwich both for cowardice and giving away and distributing of the goods and afterwards gaining the King's hand and seal to confirm and justify the disposing of them.

It was an earnest debate whether Sir William Penn should be heard by the House or by the commissioners.

It was thus resolved that the commissioners had power granted them to hear and determine, and where they found that any man had embezzled the King's goods, that they might return it as the King's debt into the Exchequer, and also inflict such further punishment upon the offenders as the offence may deserve; but if he was a member of the House that shall be guilty of an offence, they must first have the orders of the House to punish him.

In conclusion it was ordered that Sir William Penn should have time until Thursday next to put in his answer, and that Tiddman and two others should be sent for likewise to answer to their charge.

APRIL 15TH.   This day Mr. Whorwood brought in his bill for
the reversing a decree which his wife had got against him for
alimony; it was read and ordered a second reading to-morrow
morning.

The bill for silk throwsters engrossed was read; it did make
void any former law which did prohibit any of that trade to take
above three prentices at one time.

The bill to prevent high-way robbing was engrossed and read
and passed.

The Lords sent us two bills which they had passed.

One was for the improvement of the Forest of Ashdown.

The other [about allnage].[1]

The House then proceeded to the business of the day, the
consideration of the security to be given by the vintners. The
debate of this held four hours: whether they should give any
security for the payment of the excise laid on wine and brandy
and other imported strong waters. At last it was resolved that
the retailer should give his own bond for the excise for twelve
months, to be paid at four quarterly payments.

In the afternoon I was at the committee for the bill to continue the act against conventicles. It was ordered that two or
more members should consult the original act in the Lords'
House and examine that printed act by that original, that so they
may perfect this bill, both in regard of title as also in respect of
the subject matter according to that original.

It was voted at the committee to fill up the blank with these
words, "to continue for seven years and thence to the end of the
first session of the next Parliament".

APRIL 16TH.   This day Mr. Whorwood's bill was read the
second time and committed.

The bill for the Forest of Dean was read, engrossed and
passed and sent up to the Lords.

It contained that no timber trees should be cut down without
order from the Lord Treasurer and others in authority, and that

---

[1] *C.J.* IX, 81. The other Act was for ascertaining the duties of subsidy and allnage, which had passed the Lords, and was to be debated
and, possibly because of Holland's speech given in Appendix I, rejected
by the Commons on 20 April.

there shall be 11,000 acres enclosed for the growth of timber, and that it shall be reforested and deer kept there not exceeding 800.

Sir Thomas Gower tendered a proviso that no deer should be put in until one and thirty years after it was enclosed, that the wood might be the better preserved.

Sir Denham Throckmorton was against the proviso that no deer should be put in, for (said he) it is already voted that it shall be reforested, and vert and deer are essentials to a forest, and to call it a forest and not to have deer in it is a contradiction; and therefore he moved that it may be left to the King's pleasure whether there shall be deer or no. The proviso did not pass.

Mr. Vaughan was [sure] that there should be deer therein, because of the clause "reforesting it", for (said he) it hath relation to vert and venison.

This debate whether deer or not was put to the vote, and it was carried that it should be left to the King and his officers whether there should be deer or not. Afterward it was carried upon the question in the affirmative that there should be deer; I was one.

A proviso was tendered to prevent firing of copses, that if anyone was proved to have fired any copse within the 11,000 acres before one or two justices of peace by one credible witness, he shall for his first offence be whipped publicly on a market day and in market time; and for the second offence to be guilty of felony and so proceeded against.

For his first offence after his whipping he shall be sent to the house of correction and remain there, but not exceeding one year.

The House then went to the business of the day, the business of the miscarriages of the Flag officers breaking bulk and embezzling the goods.

Sir William Penn was the only man at present that was prosecuted. Many spoke for him and many against him; he pleaded the Lord Sandwich his orders for what he did.

It appears that my Lord Sandwich had the greatest share in the good[s] and was most in fault.

Sir Robert Atkins argued the case notably against Penn: both

that he ought not to have a vote in this case, being a member and
so concerned in the crime, and that it was a double crime in him
that being a member and a soldier too he could not plead ignor-
ance, but must well know the law.

It was voted that an impeachment should be drawn up
against him.

APRIL 17TH. This day[1] Mr. Taylor's bill was brought in
engrossed; it was read and sent up to the Lords. The lands to be
sold are in Clapham.

Sir Robert Brooke in a petition from the company of the East
India merchants who had been complained of to the House of
Peers by one Skinner, an East India merchant, upon which
complaint the Lords proceeded to judgment against the merchants and gave Skinner £6000 damage against the East India
Company, whereupon they have desired Sir Robert Brooke to
move the House of Commons to read their petition and to take
their cause into due consideration.[2]

The petitioners were called in and owned their petition, and
the House took it into consideration in the behalf of the commoners of England.

The House proceeded to the business of the day, the King's
supply.

The first thing that was moved was that the House should
move the King to nominate his commissioners for the gathering
this £300,000.

Sir Thomas Lee moved to postpone this paragraph until we
agreed of the power that the commissioners should have before
they were named.

Sir Edward Windham was for naming the commissioners first
and then to consider of their power.

Lord George moved that the King would be pleased to name
the commissioners, but that they should be no members of the
House.

---

[1] *C.J.* IX, 82. MS. omits the date. See Grey, p. 136.
[2] See bibliographical notes for debates on the Skinner controversy. Particularly interesting are Add. MSS. 25116, Sloane, 3956.

Sir John Duncombe moved that the House would name the commissioners, and not refer them to the King. In the end this clause was suspended for the present.

The House went on very orderly and readily to the perfecting of the bill, and I believe would have gone through a good part of it, but that Sir John Harman came to the door, which put a stop to the business, and the House took up his examination, which took up all the rest of the day.

Sir John Harman was called in, and the Speaker told him that it was reported to the House that the Duke of York in 1665, having obtained so great a victory over the Dutch and slain their admiral, and in full pursuit of their fleet, and in all probability had destroyed their whole fleet, he going to take a little rest gave Captain Cock orders to keep the sails full, and to lie as near as he could to them, that so he might fall upon them again as soon as it was light; but Mr. Brouncker came in to Captain Cock and advised him to lower the sails. Captain Cock answered that he would not do it because the Duke had given him orders to keep the sails full, whereupon Mr. Brouncker went to Sir John Harman and told him that he came from the Duke, and that he should lower the sails, whereupon Sir John Harman commanded Captain Cock to do it, and by that means the Dutch got away from us, which when the Duke perceived in the morning he was much displeased at it.

To this Sir John Harman answered that he doth confess that he gave Captain Cock orders to lower the sails, for, saith he, the Duke's ship, which was the prime flagship, lay so near the enemy's whole fleet, and all or most part of our own ships so far behind us, that if we had not lowered the sails the Duke's ship might have probably fallen into the midst of the enemy's ships, and so had been in great danger to be lost.

There was a waterman did certify (who was present) that Mr. Brouncker told Sir John Harman that the Duke gave orders to slacken the sails, and that Sir John Harman replied that it was strange that the Duke, having given former orders to keep up the sails that they might attack the Dutch as soon as it was light, should now command to slacken them; whereupon Mr. Brouncker goes into the ship and presently returns and said that the Duke sent orders by him to slacken the sails, and so it was done accordingly.

Sir John Harman saith he doth not remember this, but saith when he went to his cabin to rest for one hour he gave orders to waken him at the hour's end, but they let him sleep until fair light day, and then the Dutch were got almost out of sight; but still affirms that it had not been prudence to keep the sails full, for by that means the Duke of York might have fallen into the Dutch fleet and so have been in danger to be lost.

Sir Fretchville Holles said it was fit Sir John Harman should be taken into examination, and to see how he can clear himself, for he being the chief officer under the Duke should have seen the Duke's orders obeyed, and not to have given contrary orders at any man's importunity.

Sir John Denham said that the waterman's testimony was false, for Mr. Brouncker never went off the decks to bring any orders from the Duke.

Robert Trump, Sir John Harman's servant, affirmed that Mr. Brouncker said that he came from the Duke with orders to slacken the sails, and that Sir John Harman was angry at the message, but said, "If it must be so I cannot help it, if the Duke's orders be such," and so he gave Cock orders to slacken the sails.

Sir John Harman doubtless hath brought himself into danger by taking too much upon himself and not speaking the truth and plainly of Brouncker. It is too manifest that he doth dissemble, for Captain Elliott said that he being with Sir John Harman at Gotenburg, Sir John was very sick and so very ill and near unto death as both himself and others did believe he could not live an hour; he then called Captain Elliott to him and said this: "I am now a dying man, and know I shall be aspersed when I am dead, and it will [be] laid to my charge that I gave orders to slacken the sails, which was the cause that the Dutch fleet did escape us. I pray you when I am gone vindicate my honour to the world and let it be known that what I then did I had orders to do, and did it by command, but I had no orders from the Duke of York." Sir John being asked what he said to this replied that he did not remember any such thing, but it might be he was in some high distemper if he said it, and so might not well remember what he said.

It was a great debate whether Sir John Harman should be committed or not, but at last it was voted that he should be committed to the Serjeant to be brought in on Tuesday to a further examination. I was against his commitment, and would have taken his word to come in that day.

Mr. Brouncker is not secured, but is to be further examined on Tuesday next.

We sat this day until seven of the clock at night.

APRIL 18TH. This day Mr. Fowler's bill was read the second time and committed, but the committee was ordered to have respect to the interest of Sir Thomas Gower and Sir Richard Temple, for if this young Fowler die, their sons are heirs at law to this estate.

The Duke of Richmond's bill for allnage,[1] that is, for making cloth, was carried for him.

The London bill was read the second time.

APRIL 20TH. This day Sir Thomas Doleman complained that the Heralds sent down to pull down and deface the scutcheons and banners of Thomas Clement[2] [blank in MS.] that were set up by a herald painter, which Sir Thomas understanding caused them to be taken down by his own servant, yet notwithstanding the Heralds' agents threatened to come into his house and to break open his trunks for them, and to take them away; but in regard that they had not done any such violence the House could not do anything against them.

Sir John Bennet complained that his cook-maid was arrested in his own house, which was the post-office, which he said was a breach of privilege, and as Mr. Harry Coventry said, was a breach of the King's privilege, for the post-office where the arrest was made was the King's.

It was said and so resolved that it was no breach of privilege

---

[1] See p. 258, n. 1 above, and Appendix I, *C.J.* IX, 84, and below, p. 264.
[2] *C.J.* IX, 83. St Clement's is meant here. A blank in the MS. shows the copyist's indecision. Mowbray was the name of Sir John Bennet's servant mentioned below.

to arrest the servant of a member of Parliament, but after the servant was arrested, if he was sent to release him and certified that he was a servant of a member, and then he refused so to do, this was a breach of privilege and the party ought to be sent for into custody.

The bill for the Duke of Richmond's allnage was to be read; this allnage it seems is a certain excise for examining and setting certain lead marks upon woollen cloth, to make them more saleable and allowable both in regard of their breadth and length. The bill was much debated and opposed. It came to a question whether it should be read or not, and the House was divided upon it. The ayes that were for it went out and were 73, of which I was one; the noes against the reading it were 70.

But after the reading of the bill, upon debate it was proved a grievance, because they extended their commission or patent beyond its due limits, and exacted fees upon stuffs, which was a new grievance, and so the bill was cast out.

The House took up the business of the day, the case of the Irish adventurers, who laid out their moneys upon Irish rebels' lands when the rebellion was suppressed.

The counsel of the adventurers opened their case at the Bar.

Mr. Howard of Escrick, a well-spoken young man (but indeed too fine and affected), was full two hours in opening the case. He branded the commissioners with many heinous miscarriages; especially he highly charged Baron Rainsford with horrid injustice, and also Sir Thomas Beverley and Sir Allen Broderick. That they denied the King's interest, that they favoured the rebels, that they made many innocents that were notorious nocents, that they denied the testimony of the officers of '49, though these officers were not concerned in the adventurers' claims. And that they would not admit the testimonies of their tenants, although they were but tenants at will. That they admitted of negative proofs, as where it was proved by witness that such a man was at such a place and at such a time, and assisted the rebels in storming such a fort and killed such a particular man, yet the commissioners did admit of a testimony that he was not there, but was a youth and at school, and an hundred miles off. That they discouraged such witnesses as gave in evidence against the Irish by cross interrogatories, and countenanced those that gave evidence for them. That they denied the usual trial by juries, and made themselves judges of facts, and when some were complained of, that they had such proportions as was not due to them, they would extenuate it and say it was a small matter: what was an hundred acres of such land? There were amongst many others three most notorious persons, viz: Allen, Howard and the Marquess of Antrim. Allen was the head of the rebels and the other two had ruined four hundred families, and yet Baron Rainsford did acquit these three as innocent persons.

They also complain of an act of Parliament which passed in the Parliament of Ireland, which did acquit Lord Antrim, which did acquit him and made him innocent.

That these commissioners, having power by their commission to sit but eleven months, they not having sufficiently wronged the adventurers in that time enlarged their time at their own pleasure, and without commission, and sat seven weeks longer in whole days, and in these seven weeks gave away many hundred acres to very nocent persons. They also took away a third part of the adventurers' dividends and disposed it to Papists that had been in arms.

They affirm that the aforesaid act of Parliament was obtained by a very corrupt party, and it was justified and approved by the commissioners and they made it a colour for their unjust proceedings.

They say that that act did invalidate a former act of the English Parliament, which had voted Lord Antrim and divers others to be rebels.

The adventurers say that the decrees that are made for the Duke of York's lands and for all such other land and rents that are for the King ought to stand and be made good, but the decrees made by the commissioners for the rebels' portions of lands are, and ought to be, void.

Also they say that all grants and patents made by the King are to be confirmed.

The last witness that they produced was Mr. Poole, who was

one of the officers of the year '49, and upon that account was excepted against by the counsel of the commissioners.

It was moved that it should be put to the question whether he should be admitted a witness or not.

It was then moved that the House should adjourn for an hour, which was put to the question, and the ayes carried it. I was one of the noes.

At three of the clock we came to the House again, and then it was put to the question whether Poole should be admitted a witness or not. The House after some debate was divided upon it; the noes went out and were 77, of which I was one; the ayes were 79, and so they carried it [by] two voices.[1] And had not the Cavaliers foolishly neglected their coming to the House, both he and all the officers of '49 had been excepted against and their testimonies not been taken as evidence, which had without dispute carried the cause against the adventurers, which now will prove more dangerous to the commissioners.

Poole gave in evidence that the commissioners did declare men innocent (most irregularly) that [were] notoriously nocent, as Lord Antrim, Allen and divers others. Mr. Thelfe, a clerk, also gave in evidence that Lord Antrim being accused of nine several crimes, and he being a clerk and appointed to take notes, was forbidden to take any notes or set down any passages of the courts, and the commissioners at that time did acquit Lord Antrim of all those crimes.

Mr. Poole affirmed that until the Lord of Ormond came into Ireland in 1646 the Irish could not nor durst not go publicly up and down in safety, but were in danger of killing; but after he came they had more liberty and went up and down more securely.

He also saith that the commissioners admitted negative witnesses to justify nocent persons, and particularly Allen, who was proved to be in the head of the rebels, yet by the testimony of other rebels and the people that were in the same condition of nocency both Allen and divers others were acquitted, for it seemed there was another Allen, who being absent and out of danger they made use of, and laid the crime upon him to justify this Allen, which when it was so made appear to the commissioners they made a jest of it to acquit the nocent Allen. And

[1] *C.J.* IX, 84. Weld and Whorwood, Clarke and Pleydall.

although the commissioners knew very well that those witnesses had been rebels yet they took their evidence in the behalf of Allen and others.

He also affirmed that the commissioners denied the testimonies of others and their tenants against those that were accused to have been in rebellion.

The adventurers' counsel alleged that the commissioners by their commission had power to sit but for eleven months, but that they of their own accord and by their own power sat seven weeks longer that they had no commission so to do, and in that time made several decrees to acquit very many notorious nocent persons: and that in those seven weeks they did not give sufficient warning to the adventurers and their counsel to defend and make good their claims against their decrees, but gave from them 500,000 acres of land to most notorious rebels; and also in those seven weeks they acquit three hundred nocent persons, and yet never gave any reason for such their judgment.

The Marquess of Ormond's acreage came to eleven hundred and sixty pounds when he was innocent, and when he was nocent he received the same £1160.

That the commissioners allowed forged deeds in favour of nocents, deeds that did bear date above thirty years, with new seals not seven days old, on purpose to destroy the title of the English adventurers.

They also affirmed that the Speaker of the House of Commons in the Parliament of Ireland did inform [the] House against the proceedings of the commissioners and the speech is entered into the Journal.

To this Sir William Scroggs replied that three parts of that Parliament were adventurers, soldiers and persons claiming under them, and that the Speaker was one of them.

Colonel Vernon was called in to prove this, but he failed in it and did hurt to the cause.

APRIL 21ST.   This day was read the bill for the indigent officers, whereas the King had formerly given them £60,000 and that some part of that was not yet paid and some offices not yet taxed for raising this money for them, the bill did pray that Sir John Bennet, who was treasurer for that money, and Mr. John

Cooper, who was receiver for some part of it, should give in their accounts what they had received and what was in their hands, and to pay it speedily in, and where any money was in arrear in the hands of any person, and what offices they know that were not taxed, to give notice of it, and to cause the same to be taxed and collected; and if any person in whose hands such money or any part of it is remaining do not forthwith bring it in and pay it, it shall be lawful for these commissioners of accounts to punish them according to the bill.

Sir Robert Howard reported the articles of impeachment against Sir William Penn.[1]

First that the Lord Sandwich, being Admiral of the Fleet, having taken prize the two East India Dutch ships, the *Golden Phoenix* and the *Slaughteny*, very richly laden, Sir William Penn, contrary to an act of Parliament, and conspiring with several other persons, did break bulk and took out several goods out of the ships, to the value of one hundred and fifteen thousand pounds, besides jewels and other rich commodities, and divided the same, being the King's goods, amongst themselves.

Secondly, the said Sir William Penn, being Vice-Admiral, went with Sir William Barclay into the *Slaughteny* and gave orders to all the officers in that ship to give obedience to Sir William Barclay in whatsoever he did, because he had Lord Sandwich his orders.

Thirdly that indirectly they got the King's privy seal to allow of this division of goods, although they had done their work and made their distribution of the goods long before.

Fourthly that Sir William Penn, after this dividing of the goods, got a great proportion of the other parts of the goods and sold them at a very great value for his own use.

It [was] moved in the House by way of question whether Sir William Penn, being a member of the House, could be called in question or sentenced in the House before he had received his sentence and doom from the Lords, who were a court of judicature.

It was answered that Sir Giles,[2] being a member of the House in Edward III's time, for exacting some illegal fees of ale-houses

---

[1] *C.J.* IX, 85–6. Articles against Penn and Brouncker.
[2] Sir Giles Mompesson and Richard Lyons are confused here.

and victualling houses was called to the Bar in the House of Commons, and was committed to the Serjeant to be kept in custody.

This impeachment of Sir William Penn was brought in for a conspiracy between him and Lord Sandwich for breaking bulk and dividing and embezzling the goods of those two ships.

Mr. Vaughan spoke against naming Lord Sandwich in regard he was absent and now in Spain as an ambassador, and so could not make his defence.

Sir John Birkenhead said it was not fit that the Lord Sandwich should be impeached, because it might lessen his esteem in Spain, being now an ambassador there.

It was resolved that precedents should be sought and consulted in the case, but in the meantime the House ordered that the impeachment should be engrossed.

It was then debated that since Sir William Penn was now impeached whether he should not be ejected out of the House, or suspended for the present. It was resolved only to suspend him, for to eject him was to pass a sentence against him before he had received his trial in the court that was proper to give judgment against him.

The House proceeded then to the business of the day, to receive the answers of Sir John Harman and Mr. Brouncker.

The Serjeant was sent to enquire and summon Mr. Brouncker, but he was not to be found, whereupon he was voted ejected out of the House as no member, and a writ sent out by the Speaker for a new election.

Sir John Harman was then sent for in to the Bar; he desired that he might give in his answer in writing, which was consented to, in which he told the House that Mr. Brouncker came to him to persuade him to give orders to lower the sails, which he denied to do; "for", said he, "the Duke hath given express orders to the contrary, and to lie as near the enemy as may be with full sails in order to attack him as soon as it shall be light." Whereupon Mr. Brouncker said that he would go to the Duke and bring him his orders, and went from Sir John Harman, and presently returned and told him that the Duke did send orders by him that the sails should be slackened, and not to run into any present danger.

Many questions were asked Sir John Harman, which at the time I could not stay to hear his answers to, for my daughter Anne being extreme ill I went to her.

I must confess I was very [much] for Sir John Harman, who is a very gallant man, and very humble and modest, and many of the House seemed very severe against him; but when I came into the House again I found the House in a better temper to Sir John than I expected, for they did release him from his imprisonment from the Serjeant. And although in truth he cannot be excused wholly from disobeying the Admiral's orders, yet it was well urged that it was no part of his own inclination, but seduced and wrought upon by Mr. Brouncker's importunity.

The further debate of it was suspended, and the Duke's pleasure to be known as to the further proceeding in this business, and I hope it will come off well.

APRIL 22ND.   This day the bill for falling interest was read the first time; it was hastened on by Colonel Williams and Sir Robert Brooke, but opposed by Mr. Waller, who said that it might prove very dangerous to the unsettling of the trade of the nation; that it was not the way to make money plentiful, nor land at a better rate, for it is scarcity of money that makes land at so low a rate and not the height of interest that makes it, nor is it the falling of interest that will make money plentiful, for it [is] with money as it is with other commodities, when they are most plentiful then they are the cheapest, so make money plentiful and the interest will be low.

And although the lowness of interest after two or three years may make land sell something better and dearer, yet it will hardly ever raise the rents of lands.

Mr. Love also spoke against the falling of interest, because it would be a means to obstruct the bringing in of silver, for whereas other commodities yield ten in the hundred bullion and silver will not yield above four, which will take away the chiefest means to make money plentiful. He said in Turkey money was generally at ten in the hundred, sometimes at forty in the hundred, and in Turkey there was as great store (if not greater) as in any other country whatsoever. He also said that whereas it was alleged that money was so plentiful in Turkey because interest was low, it was clear contrary, for the interest there was low because money was plentiful.

After a little further debate it was ordered that this debate should be adjourned till Monday.

The House then went to the business of the day, the King's supply, and debated all the rest of the paragraphs of the bill and passed them, and ordered to report them to the House to-morrow morning.

In the afternoon I went to the committee for Francis Hollingshead's bill, and it was ordered to be reported to the House to-morrow morning.

My Lord Gerrard's cause was examined at the committee, and as long as I stayed Carr lost ground, for he did not make anything good against the Lord as a wrong done to himself by Lord Gerrard, but endeavoured to prove miscarriages in him which had no relation at all to Carr, neither did he prove the miscarriages sufficiently so long as I stayed.

APRIL 23RD. This day the bill for *Habeas Corpora* was read; it informed that if a man be committed to the gaol (so that it be not after judgment) or refuse to give bail, he shall not be continued in prison above nine calendar months, but upon his *habeas corpus* shall be set at liberty; but upon new proceedings he shall be remanded again to prison.

It is ordered a second reading to-morrow.

Sir Allen Apsly's bill was read, which informed that his father had laid down for and lent the King Charles II great sums of money for the victualling the Navy. The King had passed certain lands to trustees, Mr. Austen and others, for paying of this debt; Austen instead of paying the debt hath passed away the land from one man to another and the debt is still unsatisfied. This bill prays that the land may be restored to the King again.

A bill was sent down from the Lords and was read which sets out that where a man dies intestate and the ordinance grants letters of administration, all the personal estate, the debt being paid, shall be thus divided: the widow shall have a third part, and every [one] of the younger children, or grandchildren if there be no children of the intestate, shall have equal shares of the rest. And if any son that is not heir shall have a real estate to the full value of the personal estate, he shall have no part of that personal estate. This bill is and will be spoken against.

The bill for indigent officers was read. Sir Thomas Clarges spoke to the amendments of the bill, it being in some things very defective, as where only the treasurer and collector are to be called to an account, that the receivers in whose hands a good part of the money is shall likewise be called to an account, and the money required of them; and those offices to be taxed that have not been taxed as yet.

Sir George Carteret is ordered to bring in his perfect accounts to the commissioners of accounts.

The Lords sent us a message that they had sent to the King for wearing of cloths of our English manufactures, and that the King commanded both Houses to attend him at Whitehall at three of the clock to-morrow.

Dr. Chamberlayne's bill for sailing in a straight line against any wind was brought. It was to this effect: that if he did bring this to perfection before the year 1671 then to have a patent for those vessels to him and his heirs for ever; and that no man shall make any of those vessels but himself.

The House then went to the business of the day, the further hearing the cause of the adventurers and commissioners of Ireland. The adventurers' counsel went on with their evidence and offered to the House an instrument with a broad seal, but being asked whether they would have it read as evidence, they answered, "No, but only to inform the House of matter of fact", whereupon the counsel were ordered to withdraw and the motion was debated. In the end it came to a question whether it should be read or not, and the House was divided upon it; the ayes that were for the adventurers went out and were 50; the noes that were against the reading of it were 97, of which I was one.[1]

The adventurers' counsel endeavoured to make void an act of Parliament of Ireland, and to insist on the act made in England in the 17th and 18th of the late King. By this late

[1] *C.J.* IX, 87, 75–98. Seymour and Cary, Brampston and Birkenhead.

act of Ireland the commissioners act and make decrees of which
the adventurers complain, and say that by the act of 17 and 18
of the late King the King gave two millions and half of acres
to the adventurers, and now by this late act of Ireland they are
to have but two-third parts. Also they say that there are
patentees that have got another large proportion of acres from
the adventurers, before they had that that was granted them by
the former act. And so there is not left to the adventurers above
400,000 acres of land for their shares, and that land that is left
them is of a very mean quality, not worth above £180,000 [in]
all they had disbursed above. And that the commissioners have
given the residue of the two millions and half of acres to notorious
nocent Papists.

Mr. Howard again began a most impudent and reproachful
speech against the commissioners and was reproved by Mr.
Harry Coventry, and the counsel thereupon was commanded to
withdraw. After some debate it was moved that Howard be
called to the Bar to answer his miscarriage upon his knees. But
at last the counsel was called in and he received a sharp repri-
mand from the Speaker.

Then the counsel proceeded and mainly endeavoured to make
the decrees that the commissioners had made by virtue of the
Irish act to be void, and they say further that there is given
away so much of the adventurers' land (that was given them by
the King) to patentees and nocent Papists that the King hath
not so much land left him in Ireland as will give him just
satisfaction.

And so far the adventurers' counsel proceeded.

And then began the counsel for the commissioners.

And Sir William Scroggs did open their cause, and he began
most excellently in taking notice of Howard's unmannerly
speech, and gave him a most handsome and sharp rebuke, and
so went on learnedly and excellently in opening and stating
truly the case.

And first he began with the adventurers' pretending to have
laid sums in suppressing the rebellion: he said they pretend to
have laid out greater sums than ever they can make appear that
they have done, and that many of them that say that they have

adventured and disbursed great sums and do claim the benefit of the act of 17th and 18th of the late King were rebels against the King, and joined with Cromwell against the King and his loyal subjects, and to whom Cromwell gave the estates of the King's loyal and faithful subjects, as rebels. And yet notwithstanding this horrid rebellion of theirs the King set out a gracious declaration for the relief of his good Protestant subjects and innocent Papists and also for the adventurers, but not to allow and make good Cromwell's doubling ordinance, for Cromwell gave to them that fell to him in his rebellion a double proportion and larger measure of acres. Upon this followed the two acts of Parliament made in Ireland.

The first act, called an Act of Settlement.

The other an explanatory act.

And he sent seven commissioners[1] into Ireland with commission to proceed upon those two acts. The commissioners spent some considerable time in preparing this business, and settled rules to guide and direct persons in making their claims regularly. Mr. Harry Coventry was a commissioner among them from January to February, and then was commanded away, and so there were but six commissioners from February to May, and so in all controverted cases they were three to three.

There was eight hundred and twenty persons that put in their claims, of whom three hundred of them were Protestants; two hundred were nocent Papists and all the rest innocent Papists.

There was a thousand more that pretended to be innocent that could not be heard in respect there wanted time.

When the explanatory act was passed Baron Rainsford and Sir Thomas Beverley were sent for out of Ireland, and had no hand in any future actings, and were justified in England at the Council Board for what they had done.

By this explanatory act so much complained of by the adventurers they had two parts of three of the acres set out for satisfying all their interests, and those two parts freed from all quit rents and payments and clear to themselves.

But if these adventurers should be strictly examined, not-

---

[1] There were seven commissioners under the Act of 1662. See *C.S.P. Ireland*, 1660/2, p. 577, for list.

withstanding all their specious complaints they will be found in a condition to forfeit the most part of those two parts.

It was affirmed and proved that the commissioners were so far from justifying nocent persons (of which they were accused) that those claimants after all the charge and opposition that could be made against [them] were not found guilty, yet the commissioners put them upon it to prove their own innocency before they would acquit them, which was very hard measure. Whereas it [was] charged upon the commissioners that they admitted negative proofs, it was very just for them so to do in some such manifest cases as came before them.

For in the case before alleged: such a man was accused for a nocent, he being in arms at such place and at such a time amongst the rebels; the man so accused brings sufficient proofs that he was not there, but at the same time in another place so many miles off. This being sufficiently proved was judged by the court to be a good justification, and this is that that the commissioners are complained of for admitting negative proofs.

And if such proof shall be called negative proofs and not admitted, there is no man how innocent soever but he may be unjustly accused and suffer, if he may not be suffered to clear himself by such negative proofs.

The commissioners were so far from discharging the nocent that where any man did make his claim and was opposed in it as being said to be a nocent, although they that accused him did not bring any direct claim against him, yet if he did [not] by some one act or particular make his innocency appear, the commissioners would not acquit him nor admit his claim.

And the commissioners were so far from denying to hear witnesses and to receive their testimonies that they admitted of affidavits taken before a justice of the peace, though the party that made the affidavit and had taken the oath could not be found.

And one man that had no other witness against him but the single testimony of a soldier of '49 and who also had an interest, yet by that testimony was made a delinquent.

It was also said against the commissioners that they did not try the nocents by a jury of twelve men, but did make themselves absolute judges of all crimes and causes.

18-2

To this Sir William Scroggs answered that the act that did empower them to sit as commissioners did not give them power or direction to make use of juries.

As to their sitting seven weeks beyond that time given them by their commission, and that in that seven weeks they did act and pass more decrees than they had done in many months before against the interest of the adventurers and in favour of the nocents, they make this reply, that a great part of the time allowed them to sit by their commission was spent before they came into Ireland and began to sit, and therefore their time of sitting was several times enlarged, as one time from the 22nd of September for twelve months, following which the commissioners in right of time might have extended to the 22nd of September following, but they only made use of twelve calendar months, 28 days to the month.

The commissioners are likewise charged to acquit one Allen, who was a chief man in the rebellion, and also say that divers Irish witnesses were produced against him; to this they say that there were witnesses against Allen, a rebel, but when it came to the due proof this was not that Allen, but did differ from him in stature and hair, for that Allen was of low stature and of a red hair, and this a tall man and of a sad and dark coloured hair; and to show himself not to be the man accused he put off his periwig in the court.

Another charge against the commissioners was that they acquit one Hoare, a rebel. To this they say that this Hoare was an infant and but four years of age, whom the adventurers would make a nocent because his ancestor (I think his grandfather) had been in arms in rebellion.

They were also charged with acquitting Bellingham, [a] person indicted and outlawed, and yet they could never prove nor produce the outlawry.

The next charge against the commissioners was that they allowed illegal deeds and deeds that were forged, and one in particular that had a date of thirty years' standing and a new seal put to it not [se]ven days old.

Lastly the commissioners were charged for favouring the Lord Antrim. For this they produced the King's letter and caused it to be read, which said that what the Lord Antrim had done was acknowledged to be good service by the late King, and to be done in service to him, and therefore he should not be made a nocent.

The commissioners say that this deed now questioned was such a deed as was afterwards produced at the Bar and was justified by a jury of twelve men to be a good deed.

The counsel said that it was a very hard thing and unreasonable to be expected that the commissioners should be able to answer to every single and particular case that they might pick out of so many hundreds after so many years passed, and that they should remember them all with their circumstances which no judge whatsoever was able to do.

These '49 officers or soldiers so much spoken of are of two kinds:

First, those that in the year '49 fell off from the rebels and Cromwell and came in to the King.

Secondly, the '49 postponed that continued under Cromwell to the last.

These last '49 are not to have any divisions until the first '49 be satisfied, and then they are to have their shares in the overplus and reversion.

The counsel said that the truth was this, that if the commissioners would have been biassed by the adventurers all the loyal party that had stood and hazarded themselves for the King and his interest would have been made nocent as well as rebels indeed.

APRIL 24TH. This day Mr. Crouch made his report from the committee of the amendments of the bill for the enlarging the time against conventicles, that it should continue and be in force for seven years, and from thence to the end of the first session of the next Parliament.

Sir Adam Brown brought in a proviso to enable the magistrate where any persons were taken at any conventicle either to imprison them or to lay a fine upon them not exceeding £5, and to levy the same by distress; for, saith he, this pecuniary mulct may be of a better effect than the punishment of imprisonment.

That it may be lawful for a magistrate of a corporation or two justices of the peace to impose this fine and then grant their warrant to distrain for it; and if the officer after he hath received the warrant do refuse to distrain he shall pay for every such offence ten shillings.

That the officer (where such fine is refused to be paid) may in due time between sun and sun break open the doors of any such house where the parties refuse to let him in, between sun rising and sun setting, and take the distress; and when the fine is satisfied, then no other punishment is to be inflicted on the offender.

This proviso caused a long debate, whether it should be added to the bill or referred to a committee. It came at last to a question and the House was divided upon it. The ayes that were for committing it were 50; the noes were 120.[1]

Secretary Morice brought a message in writing from the King, which said that in regard there was business upon our hands and not likely to be perfected in a short time, therefore he desired that [we] would pass the bill for his supply, and such others as are most necessary to be passed at the present, that so the House the 4th of May may rise, at what time he would not prorogue the Parliament, but only adjourn it for three months, that so if occasion be he may more speedily call us together again.

The bill of *habeas corpus* was read the second time. It directed that no man should be kept in prison above six months, but should be brought to his trial, and if then he was not legally proceeded against within six months he should have his *habeas corpus* upon the first moving for it.

The articles of Sir William Penn's impeachment were read:

First that he did conspire with divers other persons to break up the holds in the *Golden Phoenix* and *Slaughteny*, and contrary to the law did take away and embezzle very many rich goods to the value of £115,000, besides jewels and other precious stones.

---

[1] *C.J.* IX, 87. Milward's figures must refer to an earlier vote not given in the *Journals*, which gives a division here, 124–58, Trelawney and Williams, Mallet and Street, for making the Proviso part of the Bill.

Secondly that he did go with Sir William Barclay to the *Slaughteny*, and there commanded Sir Joseph Jordan to yield obedience to Sir William Barclay in whatsoever he did desire; and also that he brought with him divers soldiers which did assist Sir William Barclay in breaking bulk and in carrying away very much goods.

Thirdly that Sir William Penn did sell many of those goods and gave warranty to uphold them.

Fourthly, after he had done this he was instrumental to procure the King's privy seal to warrant and justify his embezzlement and illegal taking away those goods.

Fifthly that the said Sir William Penn, after they had got the King's privy seal, did take away and sell more goods to the value of £2000.

Mr. Scawen was against sending up the impeachment until he was first dismembered and put out of the House.

Mr. Harry Coventry was against expelling him out of the House before something was proved against him.

There was a long debate whether a member of the House, so long as he is so, can be taxed by the Lords without breach of privilege, which if we now should give way to might give the Lords too much advantage to break in upon our privileges.

Mr. Waller said that the House of Commons hath no power to punish any commoner of England but in case of breach of privilege of Parliament, and therefore we cannot expel Sir William Penn if he have not broken the privilege of Parliament.

Mr. Speaker said that an impeachment is in the names of Lords and Commons of England, and that Sir William Penn being a member, how can he be impeached unless a man may be impeached by himself and in his own name? And he cannot himself waive his privilege of Parliament by submitting to the jurisdiction of any other inferior court.

This is a difficult case, for to expel him upon a bare accusation without proofs seems very unjust; and on the other side, unless he be first expelled and made no member, it seems as illegal and irregular to send up an impeachment against him.

Colonel Sandys said that he might be impeached although he was a member and not expelled, for if a man commit murder or felony he must be tried by a jury of another's Bar, and needs not to be expelled, and yet this is no breach of privilege. And if he be acquit the House receives him again as a member. And so it is in this case, if [he] be impeached and come fairly off the House receives him again as a member, which they cannot do if [he] be expelled without a new election.

Mr. Vaughan said the privilege of the House was grounded upon the attendance of the House, for wherefore is the person of a member not to be arrested but because he may attend the service of the King and country in Parliament. In the time of prorogation a member's privilege is suspended, and he may be arrested and proceeded against in any court of justice.

Sir William Penn being now suspended from attending the House may be impeached without further expulsion, and if he be acquit he may give his attendance again in the House as freely as ever he formerly had done.

It was then resolved that he being suspended may be impeached.

A question then was put whether the impeachment should be sent up to the Lords' Bar and delivered to the Lords at a conference. It was resolved that it must be delivered at a conference, and accordingly it was presented to the Lords by Sir Robert Howard at a conference.

Sir Robert Atkins made his report of Skinner's petition against the governor and merchants of the East India Company for taking his goods, assaulting his person and taking an island from him.

The judges in Westminster Hall gave their opinion that he might be relieved in the courts of Westminster Hall for assaulting his person and taking away his goods in the East India, but not for his island.

Sir Robert said that it was illegal and against the liberty of a subject for the Lords to judge a cause that might be legally tried and determined in the courts in Westminster between party and party.

That the Lords' taking this cause into determination, Sir William Thompson being a party and a member of the House of Commons, it was a clear breach of privilege in them.[1]

[1] Cf. Add. MSS. 25116, f. 116.

APRIL 25TH. This day[1], although it was St. Mark's Day, the House sat, and Mr. Steward made report of the bill for the supply. The House spent their whole time on amendments, whether brandy as it is first brought in be strong water before it be dulcified and refined.

This was not then determined, because it did concern [a] suit depending between the farmers of excise and the merchants importers.

APRIL 27TH. This day Sir Robert Howard's lady's petition was brought in by Colonel Randall Egerton; it contained a pitiful complaint of his ill usage towards her; she being a match to him worth £40,000, she saith that he refuseth to cohabit with her for this twelve month, that he imprisoned her in his house, forbade all tradesmen to give her credit; and whereas he had formerly allowed £6 a week to maintain her one servant (it being a small allowance for her desert and quality) he hath taken the same from her, and leaves her in a condition ready to famish and starve.

Sir Robert moved that this petition of his wife's may be read to-morrow morning, and accordingly it was so ordered.

The printed paper of indigent officers (which was delivered to divers members and I had one) was debated in the House and much disliked, it being too bold with the committee and some members. It was recommitted to be retracted and amended, and it was resolved to relieve them.

Then the House took up the business of the day, to go through the rest of the amendments of the bill for the King's supply. The House perfected all the amendments except three or four which are to be taken into debate and consideration to-morrow.

APRIL 28TH. This day the bill against transportation of wool and for allowing two wool houses near Romney Marsh was read the second time and committed.

Mr. Whorwood's bill against his wife read the second time and committed to be engrossed.

Sir Richard Lucie, whose grandchild or son (I am not certain whether) being under the age of 21 and presently to be married

[1] *C.J.* IX, 88, a much fuller report.

to the [Lord] Berkeley's daughter, and by reason of his nonage not being able to settle a jointure, hath got leave of the House to bring in a bill to enable him to make a jointure of certain lands, and that all other lands may remain as they were settled at the first.

The bill was read, and Colonel Sandys did not speak against the bill, nor against the committing of it; he only moved that the committee, when the bill is brought before them, may take notice of the claim of the Lord Sandys, he having title to certain lands that had been Mr. Read's which lay mixed with Sir Richard Lucie's estate.

Sir Charles Harbord made his report for the calling in certain sums of money that belong to the King which are kept back and unsatisfied by some receivers and others, that they be ordered to bring the money in by the first of July next, or else to pay interest for it not exceeding £12 per centum; and that no man shall receive any sums of money for the King to keep it in their hands above two months after they have received it.

The bill for continuing the act against conventicles[1] being engrossed was read; many impertinent speeches were made against [it] by the sectaries and those that affect the Presbyterians, and several provisoes were tendered to be added on purpose to clog the bill that it might not pass in the House of Lords.

Very many good speeches were made for the passing the bill as it now was penned, both by Mr. Vaughan and others, that the former act may be continued for seven years, and from that time to the first session of the next Parliament; and that instead of imprisoning those that are taken at those unlawful meetings, that they be fined by the chief magistrate of the corporation, or two justices of the peace, the fine not exceeding £5, and the same to be levied by distress in case of non-payment, and the distress to be for the relief of the poor; and that it may be lawful for the constable or other officer by warrant under the hand and seal of the chief magistrate of the corporation, or two justices of the peace, to break open the doors of any such house (where entrance is denied them) to take such distress, so that it be done in the day time and between sun and sun.

---

[1] Grey omits 25 and 27 April. Marvell (*Letters*, p. 713) believes the conventicle bill will pass. Cf. Cobbett, IV, 421, 28 April; Grey, pp. 146–7 on this debate.

Sir Robert Brooke brought in a proviso to make this act to reach the Papists as well as the sectaries.

This proviso (though not so intended by him or any of that party) was a very great favour to the Papist, and a mitigation of a severer law that is in force against them, which is that if they be taken at any mass or private meetings of that nature the penalty is an hundred marks; and by this proviso if they be taken at any of their private meetings or conventicles the fine is not above £5.

The House was divided upon the question whether Sir Robert Brooke's proviso should be read or not. The ayes went out and were 69; the noes were 84, of which I was one.

Sir Trevor Williams brought in another proviso to be added to the bill; it was for putting in execution the penal laws against recusants, and the House was divided upon it whether it should be read or not. The ayes were 92, the noes 100, of which I was one, because this proviso was brought in on purpose to clog the bill, the statutes against recusants being already as much in force as this proviso can make them.

After three or four hours' debate it was put to the question whether the bill should pass as it was now engrossed. The ayes went out and were 144, of which I was one; the noes were 88.[1]

It was debated whether Sir Robert Howard's lady's petition should be read or not. Sir Robert had leave to open the case, and made it very ill against her, and did seem to offer and desire a reconciliation, and produced the testimony of Lord [St John] to purge himself; but the case was not determined, and so the House adjourned.

APRIL 29TH. This day Sir Richard Lucie's bill was brought in engrossed, read and passed.

Sir John Fagg brought in a bill for such a forest,[2] which was ordered to be read the first Tuesday sevennight after the House shall next meet again.

The House then went to the business of the day, the amendments remaining of the bill for King's supply.

[1] *C.J.* IX, 90, 69–84, Brooke and Doleman, Trelawney and Clifton; 144–78, Fanshawe and Crouch, Henly and Radcliffe.
[2] *C.J.* IX, 90. Ashdowne Forest. MS. has Ffragg—Fagg.

The first amendment was the inserting of the word "paid or secured".

The second that if a man take a false oath in certifying or concerning the bill he shall be proceeded against as in case of perjury.

Thirdly that all cellars, warehouses and other places in the retailer's occupation where he hath any wine may be searched.

This amendment endured a long debate, and especially concerning the cellars of other men, where it may be supposed that the retailers may lay in their wine, whether they should be searched without the consent of the owners first required. Because there might be a double inconvenience in it:

First, if such cellars may not be searched, the King by concealment of wines may be hindered of a great part of the tax.

Secondly, if they may be searched, it may be a very great prejudice to every man to have his cellars and rooms searched and looked into upon that pretence, although there was never any wines there.

This amendment was postponed for the present.

The fourth amendment was concerning what punishment shall be inflicted upon transgressors of the act.

The fifth amendment was to prevent the raising of more money than the £300,000.

That the commissioners make their accounts quarterly to the commissioners of accounts upon oath of all moneys received and secured to be paid, and the commissioners of accounts to certify the same to the King and the two Houses, if they be sitting, or to the Lord Treasurer or commissioners of the Treasury what is paid or secured to be paid, and how much is unpaid, and also what penalties and how much is due upon the penalties, as in the excise; and this to be constantly done within 16 days after every quarter.

And after the commissioners of accounts have received an account of the £300,000 with interest, and £10,000 for charges of collecting is paid and received, that then they shall certify so much to the King and the two Houses, if they be sitting, or to the Lord Treasurer or to the commissioners of Treasury. And after ten days that such certificate is made, that this present act shall cease.

MAY 1ST. This day the amendments of Mr. Fowler's bill were
reported. Sir Richard Temple's claim was reported to the House
by the Speaker by Mr. Seymour and Sir Thomas Lee. It was
ordered that the bill should not pass until Sir Richard Temple
and his counsel should be heard at the Bar, whereupon it was
further ordered at the Bar on Monday next.

Mr. Vaughan reported a clause that concerned the paying in
of the £300,000 into the Exchequer, and from thence the same
shall be paid for the payment of officers, soldiers and seamen
for the present fleet now set out and to no other use. And the
same £300,000 to be kept apart and distinct from all other the
King's moneys paid into the Exchequer. And that the £10,000
allowed for the charges of collecting the £300,000 and interest
money at the rate of £6 per centum be paid out of the Exchequer
out of the same money.

It was also moved that a clause be added that no fees other
[than] for paying in the money or paying out or receiving it or
any part of it by the security that had lent money upon it, or
by any officer, seaman or soldier, be exacted by or paid to the
officers of the Exchequer.

It was moved that these words, "summer guard", may be
left out, because the King hath the customs granted to him to
maintain guards for the narrow seas, and it is not intended that
this money raised is to pay that guard, but for this payment and
setting forth this extraordinary fleet this year, 1668.

There was a proviso brought in for ascertaining some part of
the revenue of the customs only for the use of the Navy for a
constant yearly guard, and it should not be anticipated, borrowing money upon any security of it, as it is used at this present
time, but that it shall be as a bank and store at all times to supply
that occasion.

There was a long debate about it and many good arguments
used for the reasonableness of the proviso, in order to prevent
the misspending it any other way, that so there may be a constant
supply of the Fleet.

There were also used very good arguments against the proviso, as that it did seem to put a distrust in the King, who had
always been extremely careful of the Navy, and had to his great

expense made a good addition of ships since his restoration. And that it was very unseasonable to bring in such a proviso at this time, the bill being ready for the engrossing.[1]

In the end it came to a question whether the proviso should be read a second time or not. The House was divided upon it. The ayes that were for the reading went out and were 93; the noes were 134, of which I was one, because it was unseasonably brought in to obstruct the former bill, otherwise I wished it were done.

Colonel Birch made a very good speech against reading it now a second time, alleging the unnecessariness of it, or distrust of the King, since the King had in the four first years that he came in laid out of his own money for the repairs and increase of the Navy and stores between six and seven hundred thousand pounds.

At last the bill for the supply was ordered to be engrossed.

Mr. Vaughan reported and opened the petition of the East India merchants, who upon the complaint of one Mr. Skinner, a merchant, to the House of Lords, were judged by the Lords to pay to the said Skinner £5000: one thousand pounds this day, two thousand pounds at the end of the next six months, and the other two thousand pounds at the end of the next six months after that. This he affirmed was a breach of the privilege of the Commons of England, and an especial breach of the privilege of the House of Commons, there being nine persons of this East India Company members of the House of Commons, which contrary to their privilege are made liable to this judgment.

It was desired that these privileges may be debated between the Lords and Commons at a conference.

In the meantime it was voted and ordered to send for Skinner into custody. It was also moved to send for Skinner's counsel that pleaded for him at the Lords' Bar into custody, but it did not pass.

It was ordered to take up this debate again to-morrow morning.

MAY 2ND. This day upon Sir William Killigrew's motion for the hearing of his cause concerning Lindsey levels it was ordered

[1] Cf. Grey, pp. 148-9, who assigns these speeches to Howard and [R.] Milward.

to be heard peremptorily the first Tuesday at the next meeting of the House.[1]

The bill for naturalising several persons being engrossed was read and passed, although Colonel Birch did inform the House that he had a paper put into his hands which did give him to understand that one Simon Faucis, who was named in the bill to be naturalised, was a Jew; he therefore moved that for the future none may be naturalised unless they (after the ancient rules of Parliament) be brought up by the Mace to the table after prayers, and there be examined.

Sir Humphrey Winch upon this oration told a story of one naturalised at Oxford since the King's restoration, who two or three days after he had been naturalised told Sir Humphrey Winch that he would willingly take the oaths of allegiance and supremacy, but would be pulled in pieces with wild horses before he would receive the sacrament of the Lord's Supper, and that the same man is a Papist at this day.

It was moved that the bill for the city of London should be read; the bill was spoken against by Colonel Sandys, Sir Launcelot Lake, Sir Humphrey Winch, for taking away their land and inheritance and leaving them without assurance of recompense or admitting them to be heard in their own defence of their right.

The House proceeded to the business of the day, concerning the privileges of the Lords.

The petition of the East India Company was read, upon which the reporter, Mr. Vaughan, did open the petition, that it did complain that the Lords had passed judgment upon them and given damage of £5000 to the complaint of Thomas Skinner.

Sir Robert Atkins said that he could not be well satisfied that the Lords had broken the privilege of the House of Commons, for although some of our members were concerned in the £5000 damage, yet it ought to be considered whether there were not a common stock that belonged to that Company, or whether every merchant had his own proper stock; if there was common stock, then the Lords' giving judgment against the company in general

[1] Cf. Grey, p. 150; Marvell, *Letters*, p. 73.

was not a breach of privilege, for it may be they did not know
that any members were concerned in that action, nor was there
any person that claimed that privilege for them, and therefore
it cannot be breach of privilege in the Lords, but in Skinner
only.

Mr. Prynne said it was no breach of privilege in the Lords,
because the East India merchants did not assert their privilege,
and therefore it was no breach of privilege in Skinner neither.

Sir John Maynard[1] said that to sue a corporation for corporate
goods is no breach of privilege, for to sue a corporation is to sue
a thing invisible, and therefore it cannot be sued, but the goods
only of a corporation are that that is sued.

It is affirmed that the judges were desired by the Lords to
give their opinion in this case, whether in the courts of Westminster Hall they could hear and determine the same; the judges
all gave their judgments that the courts in Westminster Hall
had power to try and determine the cause as far as concerned the
taking of Skinner's goods and assaulting his person, and therefore it was not proper for the Lords to judge and determine it;
but for taking from him the island which he saith he bought of
the King of Jambey, they had no power to meddle with it, nor
that any court of England ought to meddle with it, because it is
in a foreign jurisdiction and where the King of England hath no
jurisdiction or interest, and so no court, nor the Parliament of
England, have power to determine it, and if the courts and
Parliament have not a power in such cases, the House of Lords
cannot create such a power.

The King's royal power goeth along with his subjects and
their persons and goods into all foreign parts, and they may have
relief against one another by bringing their actions and laying
them within the limits and places and courts of England or the
King's dominions for personal estate and goods only, but not
for any real estate of land, because that lies in another kingdom
where the King of England hath no jurisdiction, and there cannot

[1] Maynard was also the author of the famous speech printed in Grey
(p. 445) and widely distributed in manuscript. This speech has not been
precisely dated, and may have been given at any stage in the controversy. Jambey or Jambi, a district in Sumatra.

be two kings or kingly jurisdictions in one and the same kingdom, and therefore the Lords cannot be judges in this case.

If the Lords say they judged in this case as in a case of equity, it may be answered, they may not in this case judge and make it a case of equity, for there can be no case of equity where there is no title of law.

It is a certain rule that a man cannot be punished for breaking the peace or striking his fellow English subject in a foreign prince's court or land, because the King of England's peace cannot be broken in the kingdom of another prince, where he hath no jurisdiction.

The Lords undoubtedly have gone too far, both in giving damages in case of the personal estate, which was properly to be determined and the person to be relieved in the courts of Westminster Hall, and also in respect of the real estate, the island, where the King of England had no dominion at all.

Mr. Prynne affirmed that the Lords had the only power to hear and determine this case of Skinner and the merchants, and not Westminster Hall, but he argued it so poorly and impertinently against reason that it was not worth taking notice of his discourse, and so it was judged almost by the whole House, although he said it had been anciently done, as appears by Parliament rolls.

Mr. Solicitor argued the case most excellently against this proceeding of the Lords, and said that if a cause be originally tried by the Lords it is then barred of all appeal.

If it be answered that the Lords do it to give a relief above, where the party can have no relief in any lower court, to this it may be replied, where no relief can be given in any of the lower courts, there can be no relief given by the Lords above, but such a case must be relieved by the legislative power of [the] land made by the three estates and the King.

There was a monastery in Yorkshire endowed by the King, and the endowment was to have a thrave[1] of corn of every parish within the monastery: this endowment was denied and the thrave of corn refused to be paid, and there was no relief to be had from any inferior court, nor from the Lords, therefore the

---

[1] A sheaf, a measure of twenty-four sheaves.

monastery appealed to the legislative power, and there it was ordered, where the law cannot determine a business the Lords cannot do it; but in all such cases the parties must have recourse to the legislative power, where only is the true power to relieve; for if the Lords shall take upon them this power, what will become of a commoner, if they may have power one week to convene them before their Bar, another week to hear their cause and a third week to pass sentence and judgments and to give damage without trial of a cause by a jury upon oath, and so leave the commoner without remedy?

It was moved that we should desire a conference with the Lords to debate the case, but it was answered by some that it was probable that the Lords will not consent to a conference, because it may and doth concern their jurisdiction and privilege, and therefore it will be requisite to consider of some other way to have this difference reconciled.

Although it may be questioned whether this judgment of the Lords and giving £5000 damage be a breach of privilege or not, yet it cannot be denied but the execution of this judgment must without all doubt be a breach of privilege, because some members of the House of Commons are of that Company and so must pay their proportion of it; especially this judgment being given against them, the Parliament sitting.

Sir Edward Thurland said that where the courts of Westminster have no power to determine a cause, there it is not proper for the Lords to take it into their judgment.

The Lords' House is as well bound and limited by Magna Charta as any other inferior court is in Westminster Hall.

The Lords in some cases have power to fine and to impose them upon men, and to imprison also where such fines are not paid; but they have no power to give damages, for damages ought not to be given in any case but where a verdict is given in the case by a verdict of twelve men upon their oaths, and therefore the Lords to give damage of £5000 in this case without any verdict upon oath is unlawful.

If a jury give unreasonable damages they may be attainted and so a remedy had against them, but if the Lords take upon them to hear and judge a cause and give unreasonable damages (as in this case), the commoner is left altogether without remedy.

Mr. Waller made a question whether the title of supreme judicature given to the Lords do properly belong to them or no; he thinks it doth not, for the supreme judicature is King, Lords and Commons, and [not] the Lords only.

After all this long debate the House thus resolved, that the Lords have proceeded irregularly in this judgment for Skinner against the East India Company of merchants; that it was against law, and deprived the subject of the right and benefit of the law, and was therefore illegal. And appointed Sir Robert Atkins, Sir Edward Thurland, Mr. Vaughan and others to draw up this sense of the House into form and to put it into decent words and to bring it in to the House this afternoon.

When the House met again at three of the clock in the afternoon after many smart debates and speeches[1] the House came to this resolution:

First, that the Lords' taking cognisance of and their proceeding upon the matter set forth as contained in the petition of Thomas Skinner, merchant, against the Governor and Company of merchants trading in the East Indies concerning the taking away the petitioner's ships and goods and assaulting his person, and their Lordships' over-ruling the plea of the said Governor and Company, the said cause coming before the House original upon the complaint of the said Skinner, being a common plea, is not agreeable to the law of the land, and tending to deprive the subject of his right ease and benefit due to him by the said laws.

Secondly, by that the Lords' taking cognisance of the right and title of the island in the petition mentioned, and giving damages thereupon against the said Governor and Company is not warranted by the laws of the kingdom.

Thirdly, that Skinner, in commencing and prosecuting a suit by petition in the House of Lords against the Company of merchants trading in the East Indies, whereof several of this House are parties concerned with the said Company in their interests and estates, and in procuring judgment therein with direction to be served upon the Governor, being a member of the House, and upon the deputy-governor of the said Company of merchants, is a breach of the privilege of the House.

[1] Add. MSS. 25116, f. 120, Howard's report.

It was resolved that the petition of the merchants trading to the East Indies and the two votes of this House now passed to regulate the jurisdiction of the Lords be delivered by a message at the Lords' Bar, with reasons enforcing the said votes.

This is referred to Mr. Vaughan, Mr. Swinsen and Sir Thomas Meers, Mr. Solicitor, Sir John Maynard and Sir Robert Howard.

The House being in a debate whether the Lords be desired to suspend [and vacate][1] their proceedings in this business, it was resolved that the further debate of this business be adjourned until Monday morning next, and then to be taken into debate the first business.

MAY 4TH. This day[2] the King sent a message to the House by Secretary Morice that in regard of the great business that the House had upon their hands and not as yet perfected he was pleased to let us sit a day or two longer.

Mr. Smith, a member of the House, complained that his privilege was violated by several persons that unjustly hindered him in his salt works, and one or more of them being sent for by the Serjeant to appear at the committee never as yet made their appearance; he therefore prays the House that they may be sent for into custody.

It came to a debate whether in this case these persons ought to be sent for into custody. It was resolved that if they were sent for to appear before the House by an order of the House, and that then if they did not appear, they ought to be sent for into custody, but if they were sent for to appear but at the committee, and that the committee did not sit that day nor any since, that then they ought not to be sent for into custody.

Then the House took up the debate of the jurisdiction of the Lords.

It was ordered that Sir Robert Carr be sent up to the Lords to desire a conference upon the petition of the East India Company.

[1] Add. MSS. 25116, f. 121, supplies the bracketed word.
[2] Grey omits 4 to 9 May. The records in the *Journals* of both Houses were crossed out by order of the King when the quarrel became so fierce. The erasures can, however, be easily supplied.

Mr. Vaughan informed the House that some of the committee had carried up precedents to the Lords and had discovered their debates to the Lords.

To this Mr. Prynne made a present reply by way of clearing himself, which did bring him to suspicion of guilt.

Sir Charles Harbord brought in a bill to cause a due payment to be made into the Exchequer of all moneys that are due to [the] King, and to force all receivers and others that have any of the King's moneys in their hands to bring it in by such a day upon a penalty. This bill engrossed, read and passed.

Colonel Birch was ordered to carry up the bill for the King's supply to the Lords, and also to move the Lords to expedite the bill against conventicles.

The House this day at twelve of the clock adjourned till two.

When the House met in the afternoon they fell upon Sir William Penn's answer to his impeachment which the Lords sent down to us.

The first article that was charged upon him was that he did conspire with divers others to break bulk and take divers goods out of the East India ships the *Golden Phoenix* and the *Slaughteny*, belonging to the Dutch, to the value of an hundred and fifteen thousand pounds, besides rubies and other jewels of great value.

To this article in his answer he pleads not guilty.

Secondly that he went on board in the ship of which Colonel Robert Werden was captain, whom he commanded to obey Sir William Barclay (whom he brought with him) in whatsoever he desired; and that Sir William Barclay did then carry away much goods, as silks and spices, and the said Sir William Penn did put divers seamen aboard the said ship to help Sir William Barclay to break bulk and carry away those goods.

To this article he denies that he gave any such order to Colonel Werden, nor that he put any men on board that ship to assist Sir William Barclay, but he doth not deny that he put some men aboard that ship, but did not give them any order to carry away any goods.

Colonel Sandys told the House that he did not think it

necessary to examine his answer at this time, but it did concern the House to make good their charge against him.

Thirdly, that Sir William Penn did take a considerable part of goods into his own possession and converted them to his own use, and sold them as his own goods.

To this article he saith that he had a share of goods, as other flag officers had, given to him, and that he sold them and converted them to his own use, being given to him by the King's warrant and privy seal. But he denies he took any other goods out of those ships but such as was delivered to him by warrant of Lord Sandwich and the King's privy seal.

But he is further charged that he had taken away those goods before he had the Lord Sandwich his warrant for them, or at least before he had the King's privy seal, for it is plain that after the bulk was broken and the goods embezzled they got the King's privy seal to justify that miscarriage.

Sir William Penn doth not make it appear that he had the Lord Sandwich his warrant in writing, but if he had it cannot justify him, for it is believed the Lord Sandwich is as deep and guilty in this miscarriage as he.

He denies that he used any means either directly or indirectly to gain either the Lord Sandwich his warrant or the privy seal, but that they were freely given to him to justify the taking of those goods that he had given him for his share as a gratuity for his service.

He also denies that he sold any more goods for his own use but what he formerly acknowledged, only he saith he sold some goods for Sir William Barclay and for Sir William's use, by his appointment.

To this Sir Fretchville Holles affirmed that goods which Sir William saith he sold for Sir William Barclay before he had the King's privy seal were not sold by Sir William Barclay's appointment, for Sir William Barclay declared that he would not meddle with any part of those goods nor sell any of them until they had got the King's privy seal and warrant for them.

This answer of Sir William Penn is ordered to be referred to the same committee that brought in the charge against him, to consider of the validity of it and to report it to the House.

After much opposition the House ordered Penn's impeachment to be read, which consisted of several articles, and ordered to be sent up to the Lords by Mr. Weld.

Then Mr. [Steward][1] reported the amendments of the London bill; the debate of it was adjourned till to-morrow.

Sir Robert Howard made his report from the Gentlemen of the Long Robe of the reasons that were to be given to the Lords at the conference concerning the East India merchants' petition.[2]

The reasons of the first vote were these:

First, that this action is not a plea of the Crown, but a trespass, and so relievable in the inferior courts of Westminster.

Secondly, by this proceeding of the Lords the subject is deprived of the liberty to be tried by a jury of twelve sworn men, also of the privilege of taking exception to any that are to be their triers. And also of any relief against extraordinary damages, which the law in any other courts doth relieve and moderate.

Thirdly, by their way of judgment the subject is deprived and barred of all appeal which may relieve him against the injustice of another court.

Also against this judgment of the Lords he cannot bring his writ of [error],[3] although there be just cause for it.

Fourthly, all actions ought to be proceeded to their trial by first beginning with original writs and process, and the Lords' original was Skinner's petition.

Fifthly, if the Lords may thus originally proceed to try actions of trespass they may by the same rule try titles of inheritance and men's real estates, and give damages in that as well as in this case of Skinner.

Sixthly, every such trial of the Lords is an absolute change of the course of the law.

---

[1] *C.J.* IX, 94. MS. omits Steward's name here.

[2] Milward is fuller than Add. MSS. 25116, f. 122.

[3] The MS. leaves blank the name of this writ. Probably a writ of error, or possibly of certiorari. Other accounts do not give this speech so fully and the blank cannot be supplied from them.

There are three more reasons, but I could not set them down; and it was ordered that no copies should be given of them.

The reasons of the second vote:

First, where the King hath no dominion, there the laws and Parliament of England have no jurisdiction.

Secondly, where the common law is not a remedy to anything there the House of Lords cannot create one.

These heads and reasons are to be enlarged upon at the conference if the Lords will admit of any, and in the meantime the House hath ordered that no copies shall be given of them to any member, but they are to be given back to Sir Robert Howard.

MAY 5TH. This day[1] the Earl of Sussex (who was Savile and had Howley House) brought in a bill which was read and did inform that he left his Dowager power to cut down woods in his several places and manors for the payment of £5000 for his daughter; he dying hath left a son under age: the bill prays that the heir may have power to sell so much land to pay the £5000, that so the woods may be preserved on the estate. This bill was passed and sent up by Sir Adam Brown.

Sir Charles Stanley's bill was read, which did inform the House that his elder brother had contracted a debt up[on] the estate, and to discharge this debt he by this bill did pray that he might be enabled to lease so much land for one and twenty years as would raise so much money as would pay this debt. This was mainly opposed by Mr. Seymour and Sir John Northcote, but justified by Sir John Birkenhead, Colonel Kirby and others, and was committed.

Mr. Vaughan moved that Sir Robert Carr should carry up to the Lords the desires of the House to desire a conference upon the petition of the East India merchants.

The Lords granted a conference; they met, and much time was spent in the debate, but it came to no resolution.[2]

The House fell upon the London bill and passed it, but I believe it will prove very unequal to many of the poorer sort in taking away their inheritance without a just recompense.

[1] C.J. IX, 94. MS. omits this date. Howley House was stormed by Newcastle 22 June 1643.

[2] Add. MSS. 25116, ff. 41–56, is interesting here.

MAY 6TH. This day Sir William Juxon's bill against Mr. Pory was read the last time. Mr. Pory was steward to the late Archbishop Juxon, and had the disposing of his money in his lifetime, and put out much of the Archbishop's money back upon bonds and mortgages, but always took the bonds and mortgages in his own name. The Archbishop when he died made Sir William Juxon his executor, and gave away many legacies and eleven thousand pounds to many charitable and pious uses. Sir William Juxon called Mr. Pory to account for the money and bonds and the mortgages, that so he might perform the Archbishop's will, but Mr. Pory would not be brought to an account, but constrained Sir William to commence a suit against him in the Chancery, where he got a decree against him, which Mr. Pory did not obey and submit to, but went and absented himself beyond the seas, and so hath left Sir William without remedy; who prays by this bill that an act may pass to make the decree effectual, and that he may be estated in the mortgages and bonds as effectually as if Mr. Pory had delivered them to him. The bill was passed.

Sir Thomas Gower moved in the vindication of Sir Gilbert Gerrard, whom Carr as it appeareth had aspersed for corrupting one Captain Aubrey by promising to get him his arrears and pay if he would waive his testimony against Lord Gerrard, and not be a witness for Carr in the difference between Lord Gerrard and Carr.

This charge against Sir Gilbert Gerrard is said to be very false, for Aubrey denies that ever Sir Gilbert spake any such word, or that there is any truth in the charge.

The House was not satisfied in the business at that time, and therefore ordered in Sir Gilbert Gerrard's vindication, that Captain Aubrey and both parties shall be sent for and examined, and that whosoever shall be found in fault shall suffer accordingly.

Mr. Whorwood moved to have his bill read in order to the overthrowing the decree which his wife had got for £300 per annum alimony. It was moved in her behalf that whereas she had by the Lord Cranbourn petitioned the House against her hard usage that she received from her husband in taking away the £300 a year for her alimony, that she might first be heard before this bill did pass or was read again. She was called in and did own the petition, and the business is referred to the next meeting of the Parliament.

The city bill engrossed was read, passed and ordered to be sent up to the Lords.

MAY 7TH. This day I went to Gray's Inn, where the two brothers Mr. Bigland sealed a bond to me of £500, and so it was ten of the clock before I came to the House.

After I came to the House a form of an impeachment was brought in against Mr. Brouncker; it was read by Sir Robert Brooke, and brought up to the table. Some exceptions were made to it in regard of some word (as "maliciously" and "treasonably"), which words some said were misplaced in the first article, and might better stand in the second and third articles; some other exceptions also were taken. In the end it was recommitted to certain members to put it into better form, which Mr. Vaughan, Sir Robert Atkins and others are to bring in to-morrow.

It was moved that Sir Robert Carr should have leave to bring in a bill for the building a church between Charing Cross and Pall Mall, and to make it a parish church distinct from St. Martin's.

It is said that Dr. Harding, the Dean of Rochester, and now parson of St. Martin's, will give way to it as a chapel-of-ease belonging to his parish, but not to be a distinct parish of itself.

It is ordered that Sir Robert Carr do bring in the bill.

It was moved by Mr. Buller to petition the King to give a longer time of adjournment than August. Some moved to adjourn until the Spring, others but until October; others to leave it to the King's own pleasure.[1]

Upon this debate Sir Robert Howard said that it was an unfit time to meet again in August, in regard of the nearness of the time, which would be very inconvenient to those members that dwell in the remote parts of the kingdom, which must of necessity spend a good part of this short time in coming and going;

[1] Add. MSS. 25116, ff. 57–8, on adjournment and the Lords, and Sloane 3956.

but the chief part of his speech was to inform the House and mind them that very many businesses were in their hands, and left in an unsettled condition, in regard that they had not time to perfect them. That we had only passed the bill of supply of money, that no bills were passed to redress the grievances of the people, which the subjects did and might justly expect. In particular the bill of accounts, and the several miscarriages of Mr. Brouncker and Sir John Harman, the sole obstructors of the Duke of York's prosecuting that notable victory that he had obtained against the Dutch. The impeaching of Sir William Penn for breaking bulk and embezzling the goods of the *Golden Phoenix* and the *Slaughteny*; the grievances of the collectors of the chimney bill. The Irish bill. The privileges of the Lords in the cause between Skinner and the East India merchants. And the bill concerning *Habeas Corpora*.

When he had ended his speech Mr. Coke said this gentleman hath forgotten one bill that is left unperfected, viz: the bill of conventicles. To which he might have added the impeachment against Pett, both which are favoured by him and his party.

Sir Job Charlton was to have made his report from the committee of privileges, but the report was put off until to-morrow.

I was sent for to Lambeth.

It was ordered that the cause of the Irish adventurers against the commissioners be taken again in hearing at the Bar the third Monday after the House met again.

It was put to the question whether the King should be sent to and desired to adjourn the Parliament further than August; it was carried in the negative.

Whilst this was in debate Sir Thomas Clifford and Sir William Coventry spake to the House and said that if the King should adjourn the House to a longer time than August he might run himself into a great inconvenience and extremity if any extraordinary occasion should be offered, by a difference with the French or any such-like important and unexpected thing should happen. In which case the King might be so bound up that he could not call the Parliament together, and so be forced either to call it irregularly or to dissolve it and call another, which would be a great inconvenience.

To which Mr. Hampden replied that he saw no inconvenience in dissolving this Parliament.

He was taken down to the orders of the House by Mr. Ford, who urged the Lord Clarendon's case, who was now banished after his impeachment, and one article of his impeachment against him was that he advised the King to dissolve this Parliament.

The Speaker desired the sense of the House in this case, viz: if the King do adjourn the House for a long time, whether in the interval the Mace should be carried before him.

It was resolved by Mr. Waller and others that this being but an adjournment the Mace must be carried before him in public, as to the church or any other public place of meeting, and that he may not plead at the Bar for his client as a counsel or at law; but if he went at any time *incognito* the Mace was not then to be carried.

MAY 8TH. This day Sir Job Charlton made his report from the committee of privileges of Sir George Probert's case, which seems to be this: Sir George during his attendance as a member of Parliament was put out of possession of some lands by one Andrew Nychols and two more, who entered the land and ousted him; this being a breach of privilege, they were sent for up into custody. The other two denied the fact, and no proof being made against them they were set at liberty; Nychols owned the fact: the House thereupon ordered him to be committed for breaking the privilege.

Sir George also made report of Lord Newburgh's case; it was like the other, he being interrupted in his possession by one Reynolds, a servant of a Peer and being a member of the House of Commons, this Reynolds and two more men were sent for up into custody. The debate grew upon it whether Reynolds, being a servant of a Peer, could be committed without breaking the privilege of Peers.

Mr. Vaughan said that he ought to be released by the House of Peers and not by the House of Commons.

Mr. Speaker said in this case the House of Commons may imprison a servant of a Peer, in point of breaking the privilege

of a member of the House of Commons, and when the House of
Peers do take notice of it they may require a conference, and
then determine the business.

In regard that the Parliament is now presently to adjourn,
and for some months, as it is probable, it was ordered that those
that are now in custody and have not been heard shall be set at
liberty upon bail, without paying fees, until they shall be heard.
And all others that are in custody upon breach of privilege, if
they will deliver possession or make restitution for what they
have indemnified or detained from a member of the House, they
shall be set at liberty upon bail until they be further heard.

Sir Richard Oakly moved to be relieved against one that had
served him with a *sub poena* out of the Chancery. It was
ordered that the business be referred to be read at the committee of privileges the first Saturday after our next meeting,
and in the meantime he that brought the *sub poena* to stay all
further proceedings against Sir Richard.

The bill that the Peers sent down to us for the trial of Peers
was debated whether it should be read the second time. It was
carried in the affirmative; I was one. Then it was put to the
question whether it should be read the third time, and the noes
carried it, of which I was one, and the bill was cast out.

The bill was this, that where any Peer was to be tried the
High Steward should send and summon all the Peers of the
nation to be at the trial, and that no Peer be tried by a less number
than 25 Peers, and every one to be of the full age of 21 years;
and if he do not send to all the Peers, yet every one may come
and give his voice in the case, and no cause shall be prejudiced
if the Steward fail in his summons.

Mr. Brouncker's impeachment,[1] consisting of three articles,
was sent up to the Lords by Sir Robert Brooke.

The Lords sent us down a message that they had agreed with
us in the business of the Forest of Dean for the preserving of
the timber there. And that they would sit this afternoon at three
of the clock, and desired us to sit likewise.

---

[1] On Brouncker, some notes amongst the Pepys papers, Rawl. A,
191, ff. 237 ff. are interesting. Grey has a similar note, dated 15 February
1667/8, p. 71. The Lords' message came down by Child and Brampston.

Mr. Waller said it was usual for the Lords to do so, but yet we may choose whether we will consent to sit or not; yet if they desire a conference then we are obliged to consent to it.

The House agreed that the Gentlemen of the Long Robe that managed the last conference shall again give their attendance if the Lords desire another conference.

It was moved by several members that the Gentlemen of the Long Robe do bring in writing as many of their reasons as they shall think material to make use of at the conference, that they may be entered in the Journal.

At three of the clock the Houses met, and the Lords sent to desire a conference.

The members employed to manage this conference were Sir Robert Howard, Sir John Maynard, Sir Robert Atkins, Sir Heneage Finch, Mr. Waller and some others.[1]

The conference held until eight of the clock, at what time our members returned to the House; candles being voted, those gentlemen made their report:

That the Lords asserted their power and precedents that they were the highest court of judicature, and that all inferior courts take their power from them.[2] That they had power to retain and try what causes they please, and to dismiss others as it shall seem meet to them to the inferior courts. That as almighty God did work by second causes and inferior means, so the Lords, being the supreme court of judicature, did for their own ease dismiss causes to the inferior courts.

As Jethro gave advice to Moses to try all the hard and difficult cases himself, and to refer the smaller matters to judges constituted by him, so they did not hear and determine all causes, but when any great matter came before them they tried it, and left the lesser causes to be tried by the judges, although they have the power to try all if they please.

Whereas we formerly objected against their proceedings with-[out] a jury of twelve sworn men, they made this reply: that it was as lawful for them to do so as it was for us to impeach any commoner of England, and to bring him to a trial before the

---

[1] Milward is fuller here than other accounts.
[2] Cf. Add. MSS. 25116, ff. 103–4.

Peers without a jury of twelve sworn men, and that impeachment to take its rise and beginning from themselves and not from any original process.

We continued these reports and debates upon it until four of the clock in the morning, and then the House passed these two votes.[1]

[1] Starkey speaks of the differences between the Houses (f. 97). Hasting MS. ii, 376, says the House sat till 5 a.m. and met at 9. Add. MSS. 36840, ff. 135–7, throws light on the two votes mentioned but not described here. On 8 May resolutions were passed that the Petition of Skinner was not scandalous, was no breach of the Lords' privilege. A third—that whosoever aided or abetted the execution of the Lords' sentence in the case shall be deemed a betrayer of the Rights and Liberties of the Commons of England—was rejected on the 8th, but passed on the 9th as the first resolution of that day. A fourth on the 8th sent a message to the Lords, asking them to forbear further proceedings, and set the prisoners at liberty. A second resolution on the 9th decided that the votes of the Lords delivered at the last conference be kept in the hands of the clerk of the House. Although Parliament was adjourned till 11 August, it did not actually meet again until 19 October 1669, when, on its first meeting, Milward was given leave to go into the country, probably to attend the funeral of his son John. This session ended 11 April. How much of it was attended by Milward is not known. His death is not mentioned in the *Journal* of the session which began on 24 October 1670.

APPENDIX I

Speeches

by SIR JOHN HOLLAND, Bart.

M.P. for Aldeburgh

SIR JOHN HOLLAND

The Bodleian Library contains many manuscripts in the hand-writing of Sir John Holland. Like John Milward and Sir Richard Temple, two of his fellow members, he seems to have been an indefatigable archivist and collector of documents about his own activities. His papers throw light on county history, on the history of the militia, on elections to Parliament and particularly on his own speeches in the House of Commons.[1] These speeches extend from 1640 to 1678 and seem hitherto to have escaped notice. A letter calendered in the Townshend papers, in the Historical Manuscript Commission reports, mentions some of the speeches in 1675 and the copies sent by Holland to Lord Townshend.[2]

Sir John Holland does not appear in the *Dictionary of National Biography*. The main outlines of his career are however easily traced. He was born on 6 October 1609, the son of Sir Thomas Holland, and was created a baronet on 15 June 1629.[3] He apparently stood for Norfolk in 1639/40[4] and sat for Castle Rising in that county in the Long Parliament.[5] There he spoke

[1] All Holland's papers seem to be in the Tanner collection.

[2] Townshend MS., p. 30.

[3] I have used the notes on Holland in the *Complete Baronetage*, Creations of Charles I.

[4] Some papers about this survive in his manuscripts, and his name appears in the *Returns* for 1640.

[5] In the Index to *D'Ewes' Diary* (ed. W. Notestein, 1926) he is once confused with Cornelius Holland, member for Windsor whose election was disputed (p. 121), but see *Returns*, pp. 485, 491, and although his name appears several times in the *Diary*, the copies of his speeches in Tanner do not seem to have been used by the editor here though his father's *Diary* appears in volume VI of *Commons Debates 1621* (1935).

not infrequently on the Parliamentary side, to which cause he gave help in money and time when war broke out, in spite of attempts to win him to the King's side. He is said to have been secluded in 1648, but a Sir John Holland appears in the list of passes granted 1652–8, so he may have made his peace with the Government by then.[1] He was a member of the Council of State in 1659/60 and was instrumental in hastening the restoration of the monarchy. He sat again for Castle Rising in the Convention of 1660 and appears to have wished to retire to his seat at Quidenham when that Parliament dissolved. The persuasions of his friends prevailing, he stood, this time for Aldeburgh in Suffolk, where the influence of his friend Henry Howard was strong enough to ensure his success although he did not find time to appear on election day there.[2] He does not seem to have made any effort to stand in 1679, although he lived to see the Revolution and died at a ripe old age in 1701/2.[3]

I have selected three speeches on excise, land tax, and hearth money which belong to the debates of 1666, and eight speeches belonging to the year 1667/8. The volume in the Tanner manuscripts from which they come contains many others given in the 'sixties and 'seventies, few of which are dated. A whole volume could easily be filled with Holland's parliamentary oratory, but the speeches selected here seemed most interesting in this period.

[1] H.M.C. 6th Report, pp. 446b, 462b. C.S.P.D. passim. H.M.C. 5th Report, p. 313, Holland to Whitelocke on an interview with Oliver. He was also in favour with the exiled King, Cal. Clarendon State Papers, III, pp. 141, 176.

[2] Tanner, 239, containing a number of letters collected by Holland about this election.

[3] There is a reference in the Townshend papers (p. 329) to a Sir John Holland's standing for the County in November 1701. If this indeed be the Sir John Holland of the earlier references he must have been extraordinarily vigorous in his ninety-second or ninety-third year.

Reference to Holland's position under James II may be found in Lothian MS. ff. 122, 132, and to his work on the Militia in the Gawdy MS. and his own papers in the Tanner collection in the Bodleian.

SPEECHES

(Tanner, 239)
> *Note at the top:*—"This to be placed before the former two speeches".

1666.

Mr. Speaker,

After the House had ascertained the sum of £180,000 to be given to his Majesty for the carrying on of the war, I doubt not that every man considered by what ways and means it was possible to raise so great a sum. I confess I did, and then there were but two ways in prospect to me, the one way by the way of a land rate to be levied by a monthly assessment, the other by way of an excise upon the consumption. But, Sir, then arose against both these ways such objections as I could not obviate, and filled me with distraction and fear. Hence was it that I made that motion in the beginning which have been so often mentioned that the committee be pleased to entertain all proposals, and to debate them but not to come to a resolution on them by a question before we had them all before us so as we might be at liberty to make choice of such of them as should best furnish the King with this sum and that with the greatest ease and contentment to the people, but I confess I found no relief until this proposition of the sale of the chimney money was made, which I do gladly embrace and did and do still believe that it is practicable and will furnish the King with ready money, and that upon the best and easiest terms without brokerage or much interest, for I conceive that the greatest part of this money will be advanced within less than six months for who can apprehend that every man who can but borrow so much money as the purchase of his chimney comes to, will not do it. To purchase a rent charge due to the King out of his lands, for so it is, and levyable by distraint and sale and for want of a distress liable to an Exchequer process and suit in that court with the King. That to prevent this will not give eight years purchase, aye for that which is well worth it, for so I would give for a rent charge whatsoever though there were given but a bare distress to secure the payment.

That there have been many days spent in it, I must acknowledge, but that it is no further advanced is not because it is not practicable, for that is acknowledged, that it may be made practicable even by those learned persons of the Long Robe to whose care it was recommended to bring in a bill for the settlement of it. And the practicableness thereof was excellently well opened last day.

But, Sir, the truth is the delay ariseth from another cause, and you will give me leave to speak plain English. Some gentlemen being desirous and abounding (as possibly I may in this of the sale of the hearth money) with an opinion of the best and safest way for the supplying the King will be by the way of a land rate, and others being of another opinion that the only way will be by a general excise. They have the more willingness to urge in opposition to the way of supply by the sale of the hearth money, although I do persuade myself it had been very much advanced before this time, but, Sir, to the end we may have all before us so as we may be better able to make a judgment of which ways are the more practicable that will speedy get supply to his Majesty and raise this sum with most certainty and with the least burthen to the people I do desire that you will be pleased to leave the chair by 9 of the clock to-morrow morning and that the house may be turned into a committee and there may enter into the debate, both of the excise and land rate. It will be equal to me which of them be first debated or whether you will debate them together, that you may by comparing make the clearer judgment which of them will be best to take, and if I shall find upon the debate that they or any of them are practicable and to be preferred before that of the hearth money, I do profess that I shall join to promote it, but I do desire that no question may be put upon the sale of the hearth money as is propounded but the same method you have hitherto held you will still hold, that if you see cause you may return to it.

Upon a proposal made that the £1,800,000 voted as a supply to be given the King should be raised by a general excise.

Mr. Speaker,

I could heartily wish that such a proposal could be made for the raising of this £1,800,000 voted as a present supply to his Majesty might be agreeable to all our senses for then we should be able to satisfy his Majesty's desires and expectations and the necessities of the navy. But Sir, as to this to raise it by a general excise is not of this nature. For there are such objections against it that I am not wise enough to obviate and I shall crave leave to state them shortly to you. I shall do it in as few words as I can.

In the first place I confess I checked at the name. The very name being ungrateful to the people of England; so ungrateful as no man durst name it upon occasion in Parliament, but this was what I soon overcame, considering that names ought not to prevail much with reasonable men if the things themselves were good and useful and changeable at pleasure. The monthly assessments were not at first very pleasing to us. We knew from whom these burdens had first their name, for whose sakes that called them so they were odious enough to the people. But those we could call by the name of a royal aid and additional supply to be raised by a monthly assessment. So might we call the excise too a royal aid to be raised by an imposition upon the consumption. But Sir, there are objections of more weight which sticks with me.

First, Sir, the excessive expense that his Majesty and the whole realm must be put to in the maintenance of such a number of officers and other persons that must necessarily be employed in the raising collecting and levying of this duty which will eat up a great part of what must be levied upon the people, who will soon become as so many vermin and caterpillars to devour us who will feed themselves with what should go into the mouths of the people and cloth themselves with what should go on to the people's backs, and who will enrich themselves at the cost of the whole kingdom.

Another thing that sticks with me is that when they are once vested in their offices, well fixed and find themselves warm in their places that through the countenance and encouragement that they must and will receive from those that do employ them whether the ministers of the King or farmers, they will become so insolent and oppressive in the execution of their several offices in the levying of this duty, that the spirits of the English nation will not bear it with patience so as we shall soon fall into disorders, distempers and tumults, which cannot but be very dangerous in this conjuncture, when we are engaged in a war abroad and have so many powerful enemies both abroad and at home, having so many discontented persons parties and factions amongst us, who will be industrious enough to foment them.

Another thing is this, Sir, the great expenses of time that must necessarily be spent in the settlement of this duty, especially since it is like to meet with such opposition here. How long will it be, Sir, before we agree upon what commodities we shall impose this duty and when that is done how long before we shall agree the proportion upon every particular.

How long before a preparation can be made of the several and necessary provisions in relation to the King, people and those that must collect it, so long Sir that it will be necessary for us to petition his Majesty that he will be pleased to obtain of his enemies a cessation of arms for therewith we shall lay open to their affronts at their pleasure this next spring.

For I do believe that a bill for the settlement and collection thereof (if all other objections were answered) would not be passed by earlier.

Another thing is this, Sir. That though we may quickly resolve to set up such an excise even with a breath by a hasty vote, yet if it be once up it will not be brought so safely down again. Whilst the war last it cannot.

And when the war is done, the necessities of the Crown will be so great that totally and finally we must not expect it. It is much easier being once up for to keep it, then it is to get it up. For these reasons I do desire you will be pleased to lay by the consideration of the raising of this sum by an excise.

Upon the proposal for raising the £1,800,000 by a land rate.

Mr. Speaker,

When we first took into consideration by what ways and means to raise this supply of £180,000 for carrying on the war there were then but two ways in proposal to do it, either by a land tax or a general excise. I did then I confess incline rather to have it done by the former than the latter.

First, in regard of the certainty by a land rate we know what we give the King, and his Majesty knows what it is that he receive from us which neither his Majesty nor we can do by the excise.

Next, in respect of that acquaintance we had with a land rate, we know the track thereof, and that it is neither chargeable to the King nor extreme troublesome to the people, it being assessed and collected by their neighbours, whereas the excise is a stranger to us, we are to seek our way through it and that with exceeding great charge both to the King and trouble to his people, it being to be collected by such a sort of people as must necessarily be employed in the collection of it, for these reasons and others I formerly gave you I incline to proceed to raise the supply by a land rate than by the excise.

But, Sir, upon second consideration, I found these objections against likewise a land rate that I can in no ways answer. As I formerly did against the excise so I crave leave now to do against a land rate, state the objections very shortly, and in the very stating of them they carry conviction with them, at least to meward.

The first, Sir, is the inequality of the distribution in the several counties where some county shall pay three times, nay may I not say six times as much as some other counties do. I am confident I may, Sir. An intolerable oppression and such as no man can expect can be borne with patience in such necessitous times as these are, and mine own county is of this number that are thus oppressed and give me leave to tell you, that there is not any person within the county that pays this duty that knows not this as well as we do and that with great discontentment, and if we that are of these counties that are thus oppressed should give our consent to draw a new unequal load upon them, we must no more look into our counties, but if we should we must look to receive a very ill welcome thither and I cannot but apprehend very ill consequences. Oppression continued and multiplied, if you should go this way, will distemper the best people in the world and make them to forget their duties, and I think it is no time now to go about to rectify the inequality of the rates upon the several counties we know, Sir, how much time it have formerly taken up very unprofitably so as there can be (now) no hope of that.

Another objection is what I have never heard answered—that our lands being already so much fallen in their value through the great scarcity of money the cheapness of all commodities and the present payment and burden that lieth upon them, if we should now charge our lands with the payment of this great sum they will fall in their value to little or nothing. And I beseech you consider what the consequences of that will be even the ruin of most of the nobility and gentry of England and what the consequence of that the shaking of the Government and the hazard of monarchy for we all know that the nobility and gentry are the necessary if not the only support of the crown, if they fall that must.

Another objection, which likewise I never yet heard answered and which is beyond all with me. That it will not do the work, that it will not be a sufficient foundation of credit for the raising of the present money for the setting forth of the fleet next spring, and I hope we are all equally sensible as we are equally concerned in that. For, Sir, this land tax must either be concurrent to what lieth now upon us, or it must be postponed [to] commence when these determine. To be concurrent we all agree that the nation cannot bear it, for certainly this was to destroy all. There would in that case be nothing paid I heartily pray that what lieth now upon the land may be brought up in time, but I do very much fear it by reason of the great scarcity now in the country which is much occasioned through the bringing of the money in specie out of the several counties and if there be not some speedy course taken to alter the course thereof we shall be so far from having money to pay the assessments that are already upon us that we shall not have wherewith to go to the weekly market to buy the family provisions, but I shall leave the consideration hereof to a more proper session.

If you shall postpone it, then will it give not credit for such funds as are necessary at present as was lately told you by an honourable person.

For there is none can furnish such a sum but the bankers, nor they upon so remote a security. For we all know that they cannot drive their trade but by a quick return. They drive it upon their credits with others, which is maintained only by a repayment upon very short warning, for that which brings money into them is when men can carry it to them, and with confidence expect their profits and their principal at very short warning, so as it is as ready for them as if it lay in their chest. But if they forsee what the Bankers must expect about twenty months as they must in this case before they can receive the first penny and near three years before the last will come in they that have money in their hands at present will call for it out and none will adventure their money with them, so as the bankers will not be able to furnish any considerable funds upon so remote a security. For all which reasons I do desire that you will lay by the further consideration of the land rate, and that you will return to that which I persuade myself will be so acceptable to the people, the sale of the hearth money, which will undoubtedly bring ready money and that in a short time and that with the least charge to the King and contentment to the people.

Upon a vote brought in by a report from the committee for thanks to be given the King amongst other things for the removing of the Earl of Clarendon.

[Either 14 or 16 October 1667.]

Mr. Speaker,

I rise not as an advocate for the Earl of Clarendon but only to discharge my duty here to you and more mine own conscience. This being my single design I hope I shall be heard with favour though I know the path I have to walk in is narrow and slippery.

You are now, Sir, enumerating those things which his Majesty have done in grace and honour to his people since the 25th of July last, and for these things to render unto his Majesty our humble and hearty thanks and this we do as the representative body and in the name of all the Commons of England. So as that which we are now to thank him for are for such things as we are convinced his Majesty have done in relation to his people.

Thus we are to thank him for his Majesty's favour in removing all Roman catholics from all places of trust and counsel, and this is in order to the better security of the religion and public peace of the kingdom.

Thus we thank him for quickening the execution of the Act forbidding the transportation of foreign cattle which is declared to be a common nuisance.

Thus we thank him likewise for recalling the Canary Patent which was an obstruction to trade, grievous to the merchant.

These things have been debated, transacted, transmitted to his Majesty from us and for which we can never enough multiply our thanks to his Majesty. But for this particular (brought in amongst the rest) of the removal of the Earl of Clarendon, I must say that I do not at all doubt but that his Majesty have done therein like himself. That which becomes a wise and just prince. But what the causes? These his Majesty have not been pleased to reveal to us, nor ought we to seek after them until his Majesty shall be pleased to give us leave. It being an undoubted prerogative of the King to remove his officers, his council, his servants as he makes them at his good will and pleasure. Possibly his Majesty may have removed him for some indignity offered towards his royal person. Possibly for the mal administration of justice, for giving corrupt and evil counsel for some oppression upon his people, but none of these things have yet appeared to us. And since his Majesty hath not been pleased to communicate the reasons thereof, nor that he have ever been complain of to us or by us, no, not so much to the best of my remembrance as to be named amongst us. It would be very unparliamentary I think for us to give thanks for his removal. It would be certainly the first precedent. It seems to me, even to amount to a prejudging of him, for we know not what, and that without any manner of hearing: which I would not do to him, nor to any man living.

But, Sir, I desire that you would proceed parliamentarily against him. Appoint a committee to draw up articles and to exhibit them against him, to which he may answer if he pleaseth, and if he shall be found guilty of half what the world is willing to lay to his charge (which is the fate of all them that are looked upon as the chief minister of state in time of miscarriages and misfortune) no person in the House shall have his hand lifted higher against him nor that shall fall heavier upon him. For I shall think myself obliged to duty to my King and country herein.

But, Sir, until this be done, I must crave pardon of these gentlemen who seem to be of another opinion. If I do not join with them in the vote as it is now brought in.

Upon the bringing in of the charges against the Earl of Clarendon.

6 November 1667. [Cf. Grey, 1, 20.]

Mr. Speaker,

An impeachment of the House of Commons in the name of all the Commons of England is not a light matter. It is not like a presentment of a grand jury at an assize, or quarter sessions to which I have heard it so often resembled. No, Sir, it is of that weight that no man though innocent is able to bear it. I have never yet heard of any person how great how supported soever that have been but thus impeached by the House, but it have so blasted him that he have withered for ever after. If this be so fell a judgment, certainly Sir, we ought in justice to be well advised to be thoroughly satisfied in our judgments and conference that the crime where with we charge any person be true, and this we can never be assured of without examination.

I remember, Sir, Sir Edward Coke in his jurisdiction of Courts under the Title of the High Court of Parliament tell us that if any lord of Parliament whether spiritual or temporal have committed any bribery extortion oppression or the like, that the House of Commons being the general inquisitors of the realm coming out of all the part thereof, may examine the same. And if they find by the vote of the House these charges to be true then they transmit the same to the Lords with the witnesses and proofs. So too, Sir, by the ancient way of proceeding before any transmission to the Lords, there ought to be judgement given of the truth of the charges by the vote of the House upon examination. And this, Sir, with great reason for if an accusation alone without examination and proof shall be enough for an impeachment I beseech you, Sir, consider who can then be safe? And if this hold in criminal case with stronger reason in capital where not only our liberty and estate but our life and posterity are concerned therein we cannot be too tender and considerate in all cases of blood. It hath always been a principle with me and I hope I shall ever make it the rule of my practice and actions, and I hope it is a rule which everyone of us finds in his own bosom: to do to all men in all things as we desire all men should by us. And then I appeal to every person present and do desire every one of us would lay his hand upon his heart and examine his own thoughts and then tell himself whether should he be so unhappy to be accused (as no man can assure himself he shall not) since every person here is at liberty to become an accuser; whether if upon an accusation without examination or any proof an impeachment should be carried up against him he would not think that he should be very severely dealt with, nay very unjustly. I confess I am in the number of those that should judge so. And this being my judgement in mine own case I cannot be of another opinion in any other's. We know Sir, with whom we begin here but know not who the next may be. I pray remember Sir, there [be] but one weight, one measure one rule one justice for all men.

As to that objection so much insisted upon that if you shall examine and so publish the evidence, the proofs and witnesses that you shall leave them open to a temptation to be taken off before they shall be examined before the Lords and so you shall fail in your proofs.

First Sir, I believe no person will dare give an evidence here and not make it good before the Lords, but if any shall be so unworthy, I think their evidence ought to have little credit to condemn any: but if they should, the fault would be theirs, not yours: your honour, your justice would still be clear having had evidence of impeachment.

On the other hand, Sir, if you should impeach without examination, and after having articled fall short in your proofs, would you not then suffer much more in your honour and justice?

We have heard of an impeachment carryed up to the Lords against an archbishop, which when the case came to hearing, the archbishop demurred, which demur was overruled and which demurrer acknowleged the truth of the crimes where with he was charged and so received judgement. But if he had pleaded you were told by a learned person, that was to manage the evidence against him that the House of Commons had not witnesses to prove one article against him. And this may fall out to be our case, if no examination of witnesses be taken but that we proceed to impeach upon an accusation only which would be to the dishonour of the House and that which would no ways become your justice.

As to that objection that possibly there may be some of the Peers that may be witnessed against him which we have no power to examine, nor will be examined by us. So as we cannot have their testimonies, and yet they will be examined later before the Lords, as to this, I answer, that if there be any gentlemen that will undertake to recite the article which is to be proved by the testimony of any of the Peers and that will undertake that such Peers will prove it, I shall not oppose the admission of that article.

But Sir, in most of these precedents which were enumerated by the learned person at the Bar, especially those of the later time, the proceeding was by examination and proof before the impeachment. Thus was it in the case of Mompesson, Mitchel, Bennet, and in the proceedings against the Viscount of St. Albans, 18 Jac: Thus was it in the case of the Earl of Middlesex in 21 Jac: Thus was it in the proceedings in the case of the Earl of Stafford 15 Car: I, for Sir, as I formerly told you,[1] Sir John Clotsworthy was not only the accuser but was a witness in many of these things which he charged him with and did take upon him to make good the charge by witness. And so did Sir Henry Vane by producing the minutes his father took at the council table of that advice the Earl gave to the King to dissolve the Parliament, for this was before the impeachment of him and this was in a case that was capital. And thus you have proceeded yourself in this Parliament against the Lord Mordaunt. In the case of the Duke of Buckingham 1 and 2 Car: I, it is very true Sir that he was impeached upon common fame. But the reason of that was in regard for his condition at that time he was impeached. Which was very far different from the condition of the Earl of Clarendon. For Sir the Duke was then very high in the King his Majesty's favour as high as ever favourite was. Whilst Sir the Earl of Clarendon lyeth low under the King's displeasure. The Duke was in possession of most of the great offices of the kingdom and had the disposal of most of those of which he was not possessed by which he had great dependents upon him, sat actually in the House of Lords, where he had great influence whilst the Earl is deserted, and declared by his Majesty no more to be employed in any public employment and this recorded in the Journal of the House of Peers where he sits not, nor having any influence. For nothing can be expected from him which was apprehended from the greatness of the Duke.

Yet, Sir, after I have said all this, if those gentlemen that brought in the heads of his charge will undertake to prove these heads, and express which of them they will prove, I have so great confidence of their prudence being assured they will understand the weight of such an undertaking by which the honour and justice of the house of Commons is borne upon their credit and for which they must answer: I shall not in that case oppose the present impeachment so desirous I am that the Lord Clarendon should be brought to answer so heavy a charge either of his vindication or condemnation, and that he may stand or fall according to his innocency or guilt.

Or if Sir, you shall be pleased to appoint a committee to take examinations of the witnesses under an obligation of secrecy that may report to you which of the articles they found to be sufficiently proved, if they shall report such to be sufficiently proved that will carry such weight with them that may deserve an impeachment, I shall not oppose it, but then Sir I shall desire that some of the long robe may be of that committee.

But Sir if these gentlemen will undertake no further than to say as

[1] Grey, 1, 22, 6 November, but Grey gives this *later* in same debate.

they have done what they do believe that the matter contained in these articles will be proved, as every man must be saved by his own faith, so I am not willing to condemn any man upon another's belief, much less to impeach any person of treason upon a blind and implicit faith.

Upon the justice of putting the question whether the Earl of Clarendon should be impeached of high treason.

11 November. [Cf. Grey, p. 35.]

Mr. Speaker,

I rise not out of any opinion that anything I can say after so long a debate can change any others opinion, I have no such vain opinion of myself. I rise only now in discharge of mine own conscience in so tender a case as this is, in a case of blood, one drop whereof I would not have lie at my door for all the world, for Sir when I have once given my vote for the impeachment of the Earl of Clarendon of high treason, I have done all that lieth in me to bring his head to the block and this I cannot do upon no stronger inducements (as we now call them) than we have yet had. For all the evidence that we having or yet had to prove that article of treason viz. the holding correspondency with the King's enemies and the discovery of his counsels to them, amounting only to this that two members of this House inform you that there is a person that will make it good, but who or what this person is we know not. Nay some of us desiring that those worthy members would but tell us whether this person be under the King's allegiance and obedience they have refused this from whence we have reason to believe he is not and possibly may be one that lyeth here under the character of a public minister to some foreign prince or state, [Marginal note—this more than suspected] whose master's interest it may be to remove and ruin the Earl of Clarendon who hath hitherto been looked upon abroad as the public minister of state. And when we have impeached the Earl of Clarendon of treason upon the presumption of this evidence and expect the proof, the person either shall be called home or if here still may refuse to give testimony and you have no coercion upon him. Wherefore it had been very fit and I think necessary that these gentlemen still be required to satisfy us, in that point before you put the question. For Sir, it is no new thing for foreign ministers to become accusers for their master's advantage. For thus did the Spanish ambassador in the time of King James, even of the prince then and Duke of Buckingham at their return in discontentment out of Spain. A story well known.

APPENDIX I

It might give some satisfaction if those gentlemen would deal frankly with us in this: the inducement would be of so much the greater force. But this not being done I can with the better and clearer satisfaction to mine own judgement and conscience give my negative to this question.

Upon the differences arising between the Houses touching the commitment of the Earl of Clarendon.

[2 or 5 December 1667.]

Mr. Speaker,

It had been much better the Earl of Clarendon had never been born than that he should become so fatal to his King and country as he must needs fall out to be if through the occasion of this unhappy business there should arise any breach between the Houses, as unavoidably there must do if you should be pleased to listen to that advice which have been given for us to remonstrate to his Majesty the obstructions we have met with in the Lords' House in our proceedings against the Earl of Clarendon.

I pray Sir, consider what is it that this hurt must necessarily produce. A remonstrance of the Lords' part for their vindication against the proceeding of the House of Commons, that they had made a breach upon their privileges by insisting upon that which wholely belonged to them in point of judicature, so as Sir there shall be one House remonstrating against another, the consequences whereof must be the dissolution of this Parliament, for to what end should we sit when a good intelligence cannot be restored between the Houses and cannot after such a breach.

Were his Majesty and the kingdom's affaires well settled our peace with our neighbours throughly confirmed, the stores well furnished and the kingdom sufficiently guarded, an end of this Parliament would be very acceptable to me for I confess I cannot bear the fatigue of this attendance. But Sir, to be dissolved by a necessity arising from discontentment divisions and remonstrating. This would be scandalous to the Parliament and give strong alarms abroad and have a strong influence at home and that in a dangerous conjuncture of time. In a time whilst the government is so distracted whilst the people are already so much divided and discontented, whilst the land is so impoverished and left naked and the seas so unguarded, the whilst our neighbours are both by sea and land so strongly and so powerfully armed, even our arbitrary and malicious neighbours: in so much that if we do not close in our counsels and unite certainly our very devising so great a division as this breach will make will now then invite France to close with Spain to break with us (as we know they can easily do) and declare against us and in the spring pour in all the forces they have raised which are numerous (and all those they shall and can raise) upon us which now we are able to withstand; I think every man by this time is able to judge.

We have heard and I think truely that the last winter at Paris it was under consultation whether the summer expedition should be for England or Flanders, but at length by the power and influence of General Turaine's counsel it was resolved for Flanders, but how great success soever the french had and how long progress so ever they made in that country last summer, yet it is said that the french king repented that engagement and reproached Monsieur Turaine for it. For after the unhappy business at Chatham and that he had heard how easily the Dutch had landed without fights, he believed England tho the more glorious yet the easier conquest. He have now greater encouragement by our divisions and distractions here and believe it Sir he will not lose a second opportunity that so much repented the loss of the first. So as Sir upon the matter we are here but doing still the french mans business as we have hitherto done in our wars with Holland.

I beseech you Sir let us look about us and so it will become the Lords too as well as us and the rather because they have more to lose by the privilege of the peerage.

But I pray Sir let it be your wisdom to save the nation which is now only to be done by moderate and healing counsels. Yet I am very far Sir from moving you utterly to abandon the privilege of the Commons for which you have so long contended and which was excellently well argued by those learned and able gentlemen which you entrusted in the management of the free conference the other day.

No Sir, I do desire that you will continue your claim by a salvo to the end that the case may not be brought in precedent. And in order to this I should humbly move you. And I crave your patience to hear me out that you would be pleased to lay by this debate for the present and that you would appoint a committee not to draw up the single article of treason but even all the articles against the Earl of Clarendon, and that you would transmit them to the Lords at a conference and that at the same time you will remonstrate to their lordships that right and dissatisfaction to messages last sent. That you did continue that claim, that in all cases where you shall in the name of all the Commons of England impeach any member of that House of treason in general that he ought to be sequestered and committed. But that we taking into our consideration the consequences both to the King and his people in the maintaining of a good intelligence between the Houses that we had thought fit to bring up our articles against the Earl of Clarendon, protesting still and saving of our own right.

Upon a petition delivered against Sir William Coventry.

[13 April 1668 (?), but see p. 197 above. A copy of the petition against Sir William Coventry is amongst Pepys's papers, Rawl. A. 195. f. 74. Another copy undated and with no mention of Coventry is listed, *C.S.P.D.* 1667 (?), p. 134.]

Mr. Speaker,

I must acknowledge that I have a respect for the honourable person that is concerned in this petition but if he were my brother as I have had cause to believe him to be my friend, yet if I could think him as corrupt as the promoters of this petition would willingly have you believe him to be, I would never appear in opposition of this petition or move against the petitioners. But Sir, whatsoever is suggested in this petition how severely so ever phrased and worded yet I cannot find how the least tincture of guilt can be fixed upon him. For as to the first charge upon which there seems to be the gravest weight, the sale of the offices of the fleet: it is no more than what he here some time since acknowledged with much frankness and ingenuity and with that reason that the House seemed to me to be so well satisfied as to give him a tacit approbation for there was not anyone person that took the least exception to him therein. He then told you, as I remember that he had done nothing therein but what he had the authority of the example of his predecessors in the same place of secretary who frequently had sold the like places in the fleet, yet all such as he had ever served the king his father were admitted freely into their places without paying one penny for them which were in number near 200. And that after he found the place was clamorous and that he had the war in prospect, he petitioned his Royal Highness and the King that his compensation for his service and support might arise some other way and he accepted a modest pension. And indeed Sir, if I have not been misinformed these inferior offices in the fleet have been disposed by the secretary of the admiral in all times.

Thus it was done in the time of the Earl of Nottingham, in the Duke of Buckingham's time and in the time of the Earl of Northumberland who were admirals successively and that without the least check either from the King, Council, or any Parliaments though there were some Parliaments which were searching parliaments and did punish corrupt officers too. And such was the parliament 21 Jac. and 3 Car. I in which parliament the Duke of Buckingham was questioned even in matters relating to the admiralty and some of his officers but not his secretary for the sale of these offices. Because the profits arising by the sale was left to them as a compensation for their services. And if it were no offence then, nor can it be one now. Nor was it forbidden ever by any law, no not by the statute 5 Edward VI which prohibited the sale of all offices relating to the administration of justice or to the receipt of the King's money or Revenue or surveying the King's land, or relating to the customs, or in keeping any of the King's towns, castles or fortresses. But no mention of the King's ships, which if the law makers had intended it the sale of these offices should have been forbidden they would not have omitted them. And where there is no prohibition, there can be no transgression.

As to the next charge touching tickets. I did observe ever when the commissioners of the navy were heard in their defense at the Bar. This gentleman was never so much as named, no not so much as the least reflection upon him, but Sir if he had been any way concerned herein, you know Sir, you have put the examination touching the tickets into another way. The inspection thereof is to be made by the Commissioners of accounts, and they are to report to you such miscarriages as they shall find.

And therefore I do desire you will lay by this petition.

Upon the reading of the Duke of Richmond's bill for ascertaining the duty of Allnage upon all new drapery and particularly upon the Norwich stuffs sent down by the Lords.

[20 April 1668.]

Mr. Speaker,

I cannot but acknowledge that I do know who is the promoter of this bill, a noble person that I have very great honour for and whom I would most willingly serve. Indeed I would but if I should prefer his grace's interest, before the interest of the city of Norwich and county of Norfolk, nay Sir (as I am well minded here by me) of the whole kingdom; for so it is, trade and manufacture are the precious interests and of every nation, it is these which makes a people rich and flourishing; I should at least in mine own opinion be unworthy to have the honour to sit any longer in the House, and therefore I must beg this lordship's pardon if I give this bill what opposition I can.

Sir, by the title of this bill it seems to take already for granted that the duty of Allnage upon the new draperies and Norwich stuff are due by law and that this bill is but ascertaining what the respective duties should be. Whereof clearly no such duty was ever due by law, and for this we have the opinion of all the judges of England upon a reference by King James to them upon a complaint made by the honourable weavers to his Majesty by petition against the proceeding of the officers of the allnager the Duke of Lenox. In the 2nd of that king's reign and reported by Sir Edward Coke.

I beseech you, Sir, consider what you do if you should join with the Lords in the passing of the bill, not what you have so often professed you would do. Make it your design and work to give all possible encouragement to trade and manufactures. No Sir, you will be very far from it for you shall bring a most intolerable burden and discouragement upon one of the best manufactures of the Kingdom. Such a manufacture as sets many thousand hands at work, which is a great relief to the poor, employs those wools which are not fit to make cloth and so of great advantage to the wool grower especially to those of the shortest staple. And so is one of the chiefest supports of one of the best trades we have, the Spanish trades. All the new draperies being very acceptable in all the king of Spain's dominions.

And is this Sir a time to put new taxes, new burdens, new officers, new searchers, new sealers, new seizers upon such a trade such a manufacture as this is? And that whilst there is a provision already made (or in the case of Norwich and Norfolk stuffs) not only by an ancient statute of the 7 Ed: the 4th but by another made in this Parliament, which have constituted twelve wardens and thirty assistants for the regulating of the trade of the worsted weavers of that county and city and have given them power to search the measures and seal such as are truely made and seize such as are faulty. And will you now by a law enable the allnager to do but only the same things whose officers we know look not so much after the sealing and seizing as vending (?) of the seals which may and have been bought by the pint pound or peck at the pleasure of the purchaser. Certainly Sir you will never do it. I have hoped and still do that it will be that you study and endeavour to ease trade and countenance all manufactures not to burden and discourage them. For any person's sake whatsoever. I pray Sir, remember that as you multiply officers you multiply vexations upon any trade or manufacture.

I beg leave to mind you that there was a bill brought into this House in a former session of this Parliament, I think in the 14th of the King, of this very nature and to the very purpose that this bill is and which took the commencement here as it ought, not with the Lords as this have done, and out of a respect to that noble person who is concerned in this bill it was twice read and committed. The committee was so well solicited that there was so diligent and full attendance given that no other business could well go on whilst that committee sat. I do not doubt but if you would be pleased to retain this bill and give it a second reading and commit it, it would be again so followed which would put an obstruction upon the public affairs of so much more advantage and contentment to the people and so necessary to be dispatched before we rise.

Upon the commitment of this bill several days were spent in hearing of counsel of both sides and the legality and illegality learnedly argued and after a long and learned debate by this numerous committee many of the long robe attending, this duty of allnage upon the new draperies passed in the negative clearly and that was the reason you had no report made of this bill, though voted at the committee to be referred but it seems it was thought more prudent to let it die with the session and to leave it banned in the prorogation to the end, I see now, that it might have its reformation in the Lords House, which is such an argument against the bill, if there were nothing else to be said against it that can never be answered, for Sir, it clearly chargeth the people which to commence in the Lords House is that which sticketh upon the most essential and most preciousest privilege of this House. The Lords in the passing of this bill you admit such a precedent as will rise up in judgement against you in the future as prejudice of this high privilege which when you have lost forever to the House of Commons you will never signify much after. And therefore as well for the indication of that ancient and undoubted privilege as for the other reasons given I desire that you will now even at the first reading throw out this bill.

This bill was presently thrown out by division of the House with above 100 votes difference.

[This was however on the second reading. C.J. 20 April 1668, IX, 84, 74–70 Newboro, Hawley, Fitzwilliams and Holland, 46–149 Talbot and Knatchbold, Richardson and Holland.]

Upon the King's desire of a supply after a peace made with the Netherlands.

[(February or March 1667/8.)
Possibly 26 February, see Grey, pp. 93–4.]

Mr. Speaker,

I am no promoter of the Dutch war for I always looked upon it as an engagement of such expense as the kingdom could not well bear and I think we have found it so by dear experience, for certainly there never was such levies made upon the people in so short a time, nay I think I may say almost in any time since the conquest as have been since the beginning of this war. In so much as the people have been so harassed and the kingdom so exhausted that now there is nothing left but poverty beggary and discontentment through the whole nation, this is clearly our condition. So as I profess Sir, by what ways and means how to supply the King, I am utterly to seek, and yet the King's condition seems to be such, his necessities so great so pressing that he must be supplied. We must supply him not only out of loyalty and duty but even out of prudence for our own sakes and for the sake of those which sent us hither for certainly if this be not done one of the principal and most precious ends of government will be lost, the protection of the people, for if the Crown be not supported the people cannot be protected.

We must supply him with relation to the affairs abroad that his Majesty may thereby be enabled to answer the just expectations of his confederates of the United Provinces according to the condition of their defensive league, to prevent the dangers threatened as well to us as them by the growing greatness of the French King. Sir, if the other league of mediation do not take effect but that either the French shall refuse or avoid it, let us not flatter ourselves to believe that his conquests in Flanders will satisfy his ambition. No Sir, he will but take that on his way. He seems to aim at greater things, so as it will become England as well as the Netherlands or Spain to join to give check to the progress of this aspiring prince. So as Sir there was a necessity for his Majesty to speed a conclusion of a defensive league with our neighbours of the United Provinces and certainly it was an act of very great prudence in his Majesty as it was likewise to make a league of mediation to prevent a war if it may be and these were those impressions which made once more you so early to give His Majesty our humble thanks for what he had done therein. And it hath been in all forms of his Majesty's proceeding the desire of this House as well in the days of his grandfather as of his royal father to draw into the nearest conjunction of alliance with the state of the United Provinces.

And now Sir, to carry on this league of defence and to secure us his Majesty is pleased to tell us that a considerable fleet must be set out this summer. More great ships must be built and some ports fortified which cannot be done without a supply, which how to raise I must still say Sir I am very much to seek. I can only say that it is not possible to be done as it hitherto hath else been done by a land rate. I shall give my reasons when that comes in question. In the meanwhile I shall crave leave to say that which way soever or what supply soever given, I hope there will be that care taken in these necessitous times that it may go entirely and with the best management to that end for which it is given and I do not doubt but his Majesty in his wisdom will be pleased to take the advice of his parliament therein.

[Some time after speech of 10 February 1667/8; not 19 December 1667 as catalogue says; probably 4, 11 March 1667/8, or 10 April 1668.]

Upon his Majesty's speech of some indulgence to be given to some of different judgement for the better union and composure of the hearts of his subjects.

Mr. Speaker,

You have now here a business of high and tender concernment wherein I do with some regret foresee that I shall differ in opinion with some very worthy persons whose judgements are of very great authority with me. But Sir, I find it very difficult to depart from my ancient principles of moderation which ariseth not only from my temper and complexion but even from my reason and judgement, I ever looking upon moderate ways and counsels as the wisest as being the safest to all established governments. His Majesty in his princely wisdom the better to settle a firm peace at home have thought fit even at this present to recommend to your serious consideration how to beget a union and composure in the hearts of his protestant subjects in matters of religion. Which appears to me as if it were a declaration of His Majesty's gracious intentions and earnest desires of some relaxation and indulgence to be given to some of the different judgement in matters of religion and God's worship. So as Sir, I conceive the question to which we are singly to debate is whether we shall agree to give any indulgence to such or no upon his Majesty's recommendation. And to this question I shall offer you my sense very shortly. I will not entertain you with long discourses or variety of arguments such a subject may well bear, I shall leave that to those who are more learned in this topic than I do or can pretend to be.

And in the first place I crave leave to say that how true how faithful and how obedient a son soever I am to our mother the church of England as she is now established in doctrine discipline and government in whose bosom and communion I hope and desire to live and die. Yet whilst I consider the present conjuncture of time and affairs the dangerous divisions in matters of religion and God's worship that are amongst us, the necessity of uniting as much as possible may be for our preservation in the enlargement of the foundation of our common interest, and whilst I consider the ill consequences that possibly may arise through the disappointment of his Majesty's expectations in what he tells us he conceives himself obliged at this present to recommend us, I cannot say Sir, whilst I consider these and the like matters but udge it very prudent to grant a relaxation of some things the law in force at present exacts and some indulgence to truely tender consciences but not to that latitude as to let in all persons of all opinions for that would amount to a general toleration. Which would soon let all loose and bring in all manner of confusion and ruin. In so much as the government could not stand unless it were supported and protected by a constant armed power which is a remedy with such a mischief as I hope I shall never live to see in England. And I believe no man can give me an instance where a toleration have been admitted under any form of government, but where there have been a standing army to defend it, and this it is Sir in Holland at this day. But Sir, I cannot but think it prudent in us to give some indulgence to those that are of sober principles and that agree with us clearly and intirely in fundamentals that will cheerfully submit to the government established and use the liturgy, that differ with us only in things that are indifferent in their own nature and which we so hold though possibly they do not and from thence scruple their conformity in the use of them. To give to such, such an indulgence as shall upon a sober and calm debate upon the next question touching the manner of measure of that indulgence as you shall think fit to give them be found to be such as may be allowed them without any the least hazard or prejudice to the government established in the church and to such an indulgence I shall willingly give my consent.

APPENDIX II

ADDITIONAL MANUSCRIPTS 35865, ff. 10–42

NOTES *attributed to* ARTHUR CAPEL

There are here two sets of notes on the debates of October and November 1667. The first and clearer is the copy of the second and rougher. I have however checked the first by the second and where they differ noted it below.

The notes, unlike other manuscript fragments of the period, seem to bear no relation to the *Proceedings* printed in 1701, nor do they depend on the *Journals*. They form an independent set of records of debates at the time and clarify certain confusions in the *Proceedings* and Grey.

The manuscript volume in the British Museum from which these are taken bears the bookplate of Phillip Hardwick, Baron, in the County of Gloucester.

ADD. MSS. 35865, ff. 10–42

f. 9. Articles against the Earl of Clarendon, late Lord Chancellor of England, together with the arguments Pro and Con in the House of Commons concerning his impeachment.

f. 10. Some passages in the House of Commons and Arguments Pro and Con of some members. Relating to the prosecution against the Earl of Clarendon together with the heads of the impeachment against him.

A committee being appointed to draw up several heads from the matter in the King's speech, presented these following votes which passed all in the affirmative.

Thanks for that your Majesty has been pleased to disband the late raised forces.

That your Majesty has dismissed the papists out of the Guards and the other your Majesty's military employment.

For the quickening the act for restraining Irish Cattle.

For causing the Canary Patent to be surrendered.

and more especially that your Majesty hath been pleased [to displace (f. 25)] the late Lord Chancellor and (to) remove him from public trusts employments and affairs of state.

To these votes the lords joined and both Houses going to the King, the King made this answer:

I thank you for your thanks. I do assure you I will never again trust the late Lord Chancellor in any place of public employment.

October 14 1667

The principal heads of arguments Pro and Con of some members touching that clause in the last vote relating to my Lord Chancellor Clarendon.

SERGT: MAYNARD. Pro

You condemn this great lord before you hear him. Although you take not from him by this vote life, limb nor estate yet you wound reputation. You bar yourselves of a liberty if an impeachment be brought against him and he prove not guilty to acquit him.

MR. MARVELL. Pro (f. 25)

The raising and destroying of favourites and creatures is the sport of kings not to be meddled with by us. Kings in the choice of their ministers move in a sphere distinct from us. It is said because the people rejoiced at his fall we must thank the King. The people also rejoiced at the restoration of the Duke of Buckingham the other day obnoxious. Shall we not thank the King for that too? It is said we hate him not. Would any man in this House be willing to have such a vote pass upon him?

We are to thank the King for the matter of his speech. This is not in particular any part of it and comes irregularly before us.

SIR THO: LITTLETON. Con

Were he not guilty yet ought he to be removed things having ill success through his hands. For though a general's conduct in the day of battle have been good, yet the success ill, for that reason alone its prudent to remove him.

MR. WALLER. Con

This great lord has committed acts of omission and acts of commission. Acts of omission the *dedimus potestatem*, acts of commission in passing the patent of the Canary Company in putting the Seal to it.

MR. VAUGHAN. Con

Were it no other than this good that we have in the remove of this great man, that now by some years' experience things have always gone worse and worse, by this change we may hope they will grow better.

SIR WM. COVENTRY

When the Kingdom was in such consternation I made it my request to the King that if I were any way so obnoxious to him or the nation he would remove me and so thought I did no man injury to let them be exposed to that which I offered myself. I think none fitting for his service that was not liking to him and his people, and those most proper that the nation most liked.

October 17th

[On ff. 3 and 4 of this MS. two fragments duplicate part of the entries below.]

WAR

That a committee be appointed to examine into the miscarriages of the late war.

That a committee be appointed for the sale of Dunkirk and whether any moneys were paid to any private hands for it.

October 19th

SIR WM. COVENTRY

reports his own carriage in the transaction of the whole war. The stopping sail when the Duke of York at ten at night, when the Duke had been victorious the whole day and the enemy in his power, he knows nothing of it. The division of the fleet was by an intelligencer that came from Toulon to the fleet informing Sir Edward Spragg and he informing the Prince that the French fleet were coming out. This being sent to the King and Duke they concluded upon advice of council to divide the fleet.

The business of Chatham Sir Edward Spragg had the whole care of, and sent the Duke word that all was well.

SIR THOS: CLIFFORD

says that Sir Edward Spragg recommended this frenchman to my Lord Arlington. And my Lord Arlington treats with him and advances money to him and he goes to Toulon and Marseilles, comes back to the fleet to Sir Edward Spragg and Sir Edward Spragg with that intelligence sends him to the Prince and the Prince writes it to the King.

Nota the man's name is not mentioned.

Many pressing that the committee should well enquire into the stopping of the sails and these relating to the Duke of York most, Mr. Brouncker rises up, says at Oxford he met with a common rumour that he was the man that made Captain Cock stop sail. He got Sir Wm Coventry to bring the said Captain to him and there asked him if he gave him any such orders. Cock replied no and, if he had obeyed him he ought to be hanged, but that only in discourse he might tell Lieutenant

Harman his opinion of such a thing, and that Harman did order the said Capt: Cock, Harman being his superior officer.

[Marginal]   Note Harman at this time at the West Indies.

MR. BROUNCKER.
If I used my reason to persuade him and he by executing of it made it his own he is to blame not I.
If I were such a fool as to give it and they such fools as to receive it, they ought to suffer for their foolishness not I.

Deposition taken at the committee to examine into the miscarriages of Chatham.

That when the General came down to Chatham he found no platform at the chain as was ordered. No man at work. No man in the yards. No powder, no bullets. Powder only in the *Monmouth* Frigate which was fain to be carried out for all other occasions at [Upnor] Castle.
When the General sent a company of foot over to strengthen it, there was a sentry at the door with a rusty musket, a gunner in the Castle and one boy, two barrels of ill powder, five guns mounted, but three carriages ready to break and thirty guns in all. That two boats took the *Royal Charles*. That when they first came down upon the Monday there were some twenty five boats but the day the Dutch came in not two to be found.

Commissioners of the Navy, Lord Brouncker, Sir Thos. Harvey, Mr Pepys and Mr Pett their defence before the House in the business of Chatham.

They showed that from the 3rd of December 1666 down to that time, that Commissioner Pett had by the Duke's order the charge of Chatham and the Commissioner of the Ordinance that of Sheerness.
The Duke's letters to the Commissioners. Their reply thereupon to the Duke.
The Duke's orders upon that were also read, by which it appeared that Commissioner Pett had by order the care of Chatham and the River Medway, the securing the vessels in that River and securing the chain and the platform upon that chain. The Commissioners of the Ordinance the care of Sheerness for the making the platform for twelve guns, Sir Edward Spragg the care of guarding the River.

Note from the 25th of March to the time the Dutch came in the orders were given for the securing of Chatham and Sheerness.

SIR EDWARD SPRAGG
The King and Duke did verily believe that when I came down in June to defend the fort at Sheerness that it had been fortified. And had

the Commissioners of the Ordinance done that in three months that the prince did in ten days the ships had all been saved.

After that I had set out the fortifications the charge to see it done was by me delivered up to the Commissioners of the Ordinance.

COMMISSIONERS OF THE NAVY

After we had made report to the Duke what was fitting to be done at Sheerness, it became in charge to the Commissioners of the Ordinance not us.

The Commissioners of the Ordinance confessed that the platform of twelve guns was upon their charge.

That their order from the Duke to that purpose was verbal.
It appeared that this order to Captain Penn [f. 29v.] was verbal.

October 26th 1667

MR. SEYMOUR

moves and acquaints the House of the Earl of Clarendon's being guilty of several great crimes and enumerates them.

SIR THOMAS LITTLETON

seconds him, mentioning others and moves that the House would immediately send up to the Lords to have him secured in order to an impeachment to be brought up by the Commons against him.

SIR THOMAS OSBOURNE

thirds that mentioning more crimes.

MR. VAUGHAN

shows how it was regular so to move the Lords, and that an impeachment be drawn up against him.

THE HOUSE

seems to think it something irregular to confine and impeach a person (out of favour with his prince and so not in danger of obstructing these proceedings) before proof were made, so it was conveyed by vote that

A committee be appointed to look into the ancient precedents of the method of proceedings in this House in causes of impeachment in capital crimes.

October 29th 1667

MR. VAUGHAN

reports precedents.

And that none capital were to be found, where in the proceedings of the Commons in cases capital did appear until that of the Lord Strafford, and that of my Lord of Canterbury.

A debate arising (those precedents not much prevailing) whether they should refer the information given by the members of the House against my Lord Clarendon to a select committee who should privately take the evidence and so impeach him to the Lords and there have their witnesses sworn

Or upon common fame by information of the members of the House send up an impeachment to the Lords

Or, lastly, refer it to the committee of grievances to take the evidence of witnesses and so report the facts to the House.

Much was said against the first way, that a juncto committee was of ill consequence and the precedent of my Lord Strafford ill.

Against the second that it was accusing upon common fame, judging without proof or witnesses.

For the first was said, men at a private committee secretly would give evidence

For the second that there could be no better way to accuse than by common fame.

The last being passed as most according to the liberty of the subject at the committee of grievances where evidence might appear and the things said appearing by the arguments of the Long Robe to be doubtful of treason or not, might be if but misdemeanour, be referred like that of my Lord Mordaunt to the committee.

Against it was said, that if witnesses would not come they could not compel them, if they did come, you could not punish them if they did not speak, besides some might be of quality. They could not nor would not come before a committee of Commoners.

The whole debate at last produced this vote

That it be referred to the committee to reduce into heads the accusations against the Earl of Clarendon.

Note. As an argument for the close committee was used that we were in the manner of a grand Jury, which are sworn not to reveal the evidence for the King until Publication.

November 6 1667

Sir Thomas Littleton reports from the committee that had reduced the accusations into heads as follows [blank page in MS.]

Upon this arose a great debate and consisting of two different points

Whether these eighteen heads should be referred to a committee in order to receive what evidence could be brought to make good each head, that from them an impeachment might be drawn up.

Or accept of these heads in the House, some members to each of them averring that either themselves or other persons they knew should in due time make them good.

Against the commitment of it these arguments were used as followeth:—

To a committee no man can be compelled to come and the prudence that every man carries naturally about with him will not suffer him when he is not upon oath to say what he knows against so great a man. If any man does come you cannot compel him to speak. If he does speak you must be contented to take what he will say, and force him to no more.

Some witnesses might be peers and they would not come before a committee.

Suppose any [witnesses] did come they not being upon oath might when they came to the Lords' bar upon oath vary from what they did say and so the Commons at the Lords' bar would come to affirm that which by these witnesses they could not make good.

The time that would be between their witnessing before the Commons and the Lords was so great that the accused had time knowing what they affirmed to take them off. Whereas if it were upon oath they could not recant.

Upon an indictment the party accused knew nothing of the accusers till publication, the Grand Jury being ever sworn to keep the King's evidence secret.

The House of Commons is in the nature of an Inquest or Grand Jury, which is that [if] any of the Jury affirm the fact it is enough to find the bill, no more is done in the members of the House, part of the Grand Jury; two witnesses of the notoriety of the fact affirm the fact, (thereby there is found grounds enough to tell the Lords)[1] they have grounds to impeach him and desire he may be secured and then upon his impeachment he has his fair trial before his peers, this being but in the nature of an inquest.[2]

Michael De la Pole and Neville,[William] De la Pole cases were cited.

Great men are to be accused upon common fame for no particular man dare accuse them.

These witnesses are not to be known and the thing in the Commons' House to be carried on with all privacy imaginable because great men may hinder the prosecution by their great power, or otherwise may break the Parliament and no injustice is done them as long as they are brought to their trial by their peers.

SIR RICHARD TEMPLE
      said he did not believe there was one head there that would not be made good.

MR. SEYMOUR
      said that witnesses he could affirm were threatened.

[1] f. 33: This by the House is found grounds enough to tell the Lords.
[2] This paragraph has been rearranged.

SIR THOMAS LITTLETON

    said let it not be referred to a committee and it should not go to the Lords' House without some proof.

[f. 33 v. some new proofs.]

    For the commitment of it these things were said

    The laws of God and man tie us to common justice. Judge no man before he is heard.

    When we have carried the impeachment up to the Lords it never returns to us, therefore let us hear before we determine, it may touch blood.

    In the case of my Lord Mordaunt you heard witnesses. You are not sure that any of these are treason but only misdemeanours. Why not in this too?

    This Lord is not so great a man but the meanest subject may call him to an account. He is laid low. He is dead in law. Out of his Majesty's favour. No danger that he shall break the Parliament and witnesses or do anything to obstruct proceedings.

    There was no precedent where it was clearly proved in capital crimes that any were impeached but witnesses were heard before but in criminals and misdemeanours always with proofs, as that of the Lord Cranfield etc.

    If any member would stand up and say that of their knowledge they would evidence any one fact it ought to be taken for good evidence. And that was the case of Grand Juries. It is their own knowledge that makes it good evidence but if they have it from abroad they ought to bring their proofs. If we are a grand Inquest or Jury lets do like them. If we know the fact they are all to know it, if any one gentleman know the fact this Lord had committed let us all know of it too, which must be either by these gentlemen avowing of it upon their own knowledge which is good evidence as in cases of Grand Juries, or making it good by witnesses, and then every man will be as able as they to give their judgment.

MR. SWINFIELD [SWINSEN]

    observed that the whole days debate was carried on, each side enforcing their arguments but no endeavour made to answer each other.

    So the question in short was this, whether they should go up with an impeachment with information by witnesses or without information.

    Then the question being put if it should be referred to a committee or not, it was carried in the negative a 128 affirmative, and a 194 negative.

The House then ordered the heads by the Speaker to be read one by one some member standing up to each head affirming either on their own knowledge that they would in due time make it good, or declaring that they had persons that would make it good, or if they did any ways decline what they had already told the House then the House was to be acquainted therewith.

[f. 18 contains the eighteen articles with their witnesses, which I have abbreviated here:]

1. Howard and Vaughan: On standing army and Parliament.
2. Lord St. John: The King a Papist.
3. Mr. Seymour and Sir Thomas Osbourne: Canary Patent.
4, 5, 6. Sir Richard Temple: Imprisonment, sale of offices, customs.
7. Sir Robert Carr: Vintners.
8. Sir Thomas Littleton: Great estate.
9. Sir Thomas Osbourne and Sir Thomas Littleton: The plantations.
10, 11. Sir Charles Wheeler: St. Kitt's, etc. Correspondence with Cromwell.
12. Sir Thomas Osbourne and Sir Thomas Littleton: Dunkirk.
13. Sir Thomas Littleton: Dr. Crowther's patent.
14. Mr. Thomas: Arbitrary imprisonment, titles, etc.
15. Sir Edward Masters [This is proved by Littleton in *Proceedings*, p. 26; Milward gives no name]: Quo warrantoes.
16. [No name here]: Ireland.
17. Sir Thomas Littleton: Betraying the King to enemies.
18. Mr. Thomas, Sir Thomas Littleton, Sir Robert Howard: Miscarriages.

The question was if this or anything in it was treason or by the House ought to be declared treason.

25 Ed. 3, 1 Hen. 2 cap 10, 1 Philip and Mary, 1 Edward 6, cap. 12, 13 and 14 of Car. 2 were all read.

Now follow some arguments to the articles Pro and Con of several members.

SERJEANT CHARLTON   Pro

Let any man show me that since the statute of Ed. 3 the 25th cap. anything where a fact was not committed was treason. Nothing can be treason that is not felony by the Common Law.

The Common Law is nothing but the custom of England and that custom determined by the Judges who at times had made so many things treasons that the subject did not know what was treason and what not.

By petition therefore to the King and that once denied but the second time granted. This statute of the 25th of Edward the 3rd was made and this in all times since has been taken to be the standard of treason. Had an indictment before the Judges been brought against him and they in dispute of treason, or not, you had been the proper Judges of it.

MR. HOWARD. Pro

Before life be taken there ought to be a promulgation of the law by the Judges. Nothing has been declared. Treason hitherto but the 25th Ed. 3. The rest referred to Parliament.

SIR FRANCIS GOODRICK. Pro

No person questioned for life since the statute of the 25th of Edward the 3rd but those things that are treason by the Common Law. That this is not treason by the Common Law is certain.

No person guilty of treason that was not capitally guilty at the Common Law.

Those cases that were not capital by the Common Law was [n]ever declared treason in the Parliament.

Whether at any time since taken away.

Nothing is treason that is not felony.

In emergent occasions councillors may give advice but not contrary to law and if other wise he is the highest criminal imaginable.

That seducing the King by Common Law was Treason.

Richard the 2 articles made with the King's consent treason.

SERJEANT MAYNARD. Pro

You cannot determine of anything in declaratory treason in this House but by bill.

The question being put if the Earl of Clarendon were upon the first article guilty of treason was carried in the negative.

Monday.

They resumed the debate of the rest of the articles of accusations against the Earl of Clarendon; they were all read to the sixteenth. No questions being put upon any but this debate upon this if it were treason or not went off without a question.

Nota the twelfth article was presumed to be treason but went off with a question.

Some arguments concerning the same 12th article.

MR. PRYNNE. Con

It is not annexed to the Crown. There was a bill to annex it to the Crown and it did not pass.

If it was annexed all that owe knight service were bound to attend and serve there and will any say that by the title the King holds it they were.

SIR EDWARD WALPOLE.

Tangier got by contract, may not the King sell it?

What power have princes in peace and war if not power to take and give in treaties?

Who dare act under their commission at the oath at this rate?

If the general be necessitated to free quarter is he guilty of Treason?

Advice is not treason.

The 17th head being read and Lord Vaughan adding these words "and discovered and betrayed his secret councils to his enemies" it was agreed on all hands that if this could be made out by good evidence, it was high treason.

LORD VAUGHAN
 said he had a person of quality would make it good.

SIR JOHN HOLLAND
 I desire to know if it be a foreigner, and that this be seconded [see Appendix I, p. 317].

 It was denied.

The words that my Lord Vaughan said when he offered these heads to the House coming from the person that told him he would make good that head, being desired once more by Mr. Laurence Hide to repeat those words:

 it was denied.

MR. PRYNNE.   Con
 Gondomar got Sir Walter Rawleigh's head off. I pray God this be not a foreigner's plot.

SIR FRA: GOODRICK.   Con
 The Common Law will have two witnesses.

SERJEANT SISE
 1st of Ed the 6 none under two witnesses to be admitted.

SIR EDWARD WALPOLE.   Con
 Will you go up to a trial to the Lords' bar, and there charge this Lord of high treason and misdemeanour upon these indictments and not know anything of the witnesses.

 It is [known] now that in my Lord of Strafford's case where they had a close committee where they received witnesses and took evidence and this upon evidence only of members standing up and reading each head saying that they have witnesses that in due time will prove it, does this become the gravity and justice of a parliament upon such indictments to proceed.

MR. WALLER.   Pro
 If this had come against my Lord Strafford I would have given my negative, and now I will give my affirmative.

R M D   22

The question being put if the member that gave this information to this head, if he received it from a foreigner or native. The question being put if the question should be put was carried in the negative.

The question being put if the Earl of Clarendon upon the article the 16th head being impeached of treason was carried in the affirmative.

161 affirmative.

88 negative.

That an impeachment of treason and other high crimes and misdemeanours be carried up to the bar of the House of Lords against the Earl of Clarendon.

Mr. Seymour carried up the charge in these words:—

[Then follow Seymour's speech, and on Friday 15th Lord Oxford's declaration to Vaughan and the vote of the Commons Saturday to leave it to a committee to draw up reasons against the Lords' decision. The next folios contain, besides the letter of Clarendon to the Lords, rough notes of the preceding pages; f. 42 the protest of those Lords who disagreed with the majority in not committing the Earl.]

INDEX

This is intended as a brief guide to the contents of Milward's *Diary*: names of members and their constituencies with a list of other persons mentioned will be found on pp. xliii–ci, a calendar for the period covered by the *Diary* is on pp. xxxi–xlii.